国际经济法(双语)(第二版)

温 融 主 编
袁振华 副主编

清华大学出版社
北京

内 容 简 介

本书共分八章，内容包括国际经济法概述、国际经济法的主体、国际货物买卖法律制度、国际知识产权与技术转让法、国际服务贸易法律制度、国际贸易管理法律制度、国际税法、世界贸易组织争端解决制度。

本书不仅适合高等院校法学专业本科生的基础性学习，还可作为高等院校商务英语、国际贸易、国际金融等专业的选修教材。同时，本书也可作为国际商务工作者、涉外法律实务者的自学教材。

图书在版编目(CIP)数据

国际经济法：双语：英文、汉文/温融主编. —2 版. —北京：清华大学出版社，2021.1 (2025.2重印)
ISBN 978-7-302-55972-6

Ⅰ．①国… Ⅱ．①温… Ⅲ．①国际经济法—教材—英、汉 Ⅳ．①D996

中国版本图书馆 CIP 数据核字(2020)第 120499 号

责任编辑：孟 攀
装帧设计：刘孝琼
责任校对：吴春华
责任印制：沈 露
出版发行：清华大学出版社
      网　　　址：https://www.tup.com.cn，https://www.wqxuetang.com
      地　　　址：北京清华大学学研大厦 A 座　　　邮　　编：100084
      社 总 机：010-83470000　　　邮　　购：010-62786544
      投稿与读者服务：010-62776969，c-service@tup.tsinghua.edu.cn
      质量反馈：010-62772015，zhiliang@tup.tsinghua.edu.cn
      课件下载：https://www.tup.com.cn，010-62791865
印 装 者：三河市铭诚印务有限公司
经　　　销：全国新华书店
开　　　本：185mm×260mm　　　印　张：21.5　　　字　数：520 千字
版　　　次：2013 年 8 月第 1 版　2021 年 1 月第 2 版　印　次：2025 年 2 月第 4 次印刷
定　　　价：65.00 元

产品编号：083549-01

前　言

党的十八大以来，我国开创了深化改革开放、推进"一带一路"建设和推动构建人类命运共同体的新的伟大实践。通过搭建开放合作的国际平台，我国开放型经济水平全面提升，与世界经济在更宽领域里实现更深融合，推动了全球经济治理体系朝着更加公正合理的方向发展。伟大实践的推进，对法学研究、法学教育和法治实践提出了新要求。尤其是国际经贸领域的法学研究、法学教育和法治实践，必须有新担当、新作为、新气象。

传播国际经贸法律知识，培养既具有扎实的法学专业知识，又具有娴熟外语语言技能的复合型、外向型、应用型法律人才，是国际经济法学教育的重要任务。近年来，我国高等院校纷纷实施国际经济法双语课程教学，开展双语课程建设。有的院校采取英文原版教材，以追求外语语言的准确、规范，但囿于学科设置、课程设计、作者所在国政治环境、经济发展状况、文化背景等方面的诸多不同，原版教材的体例安排与国内通行的教材知识体系存在较大差异，增加了学习难度。有的院校使用中文教材并将其英译，这固然与通行的知识架构相契合，但在译文语言方面无法做到如原版教材那样准确、地道，不当甚至错误的英语译文直接影响了学生运用英语理解、掌握国际经济法学理论和国际经济法律制度。

科学合理的国际经济法双语教材，应做到国内教学实际与法律英语语言的契合，以权威精准的英语语言为载体，让学生系统地学习、了解和掌握国际经济法基础理论与主要制度。为此，我们精心编写了本书，本书具有以下特点。

(1) 依照国内通行的国际经济法知识体系和主体内容要求安排体例，符合国际经济法教学实践和学生研习的需要。国外并无直接命名为国际经济法的本科专业教材，相关国际商法、WTO 组织法、国际私法等原版教材的体例结构与国际经济法课程存在较大差异，我们按照业已成熟的知识体系与内容要求编写教材，便于学生在英语语境中系统学习国际经济法基本理论与主要制度，同时也降低了教材使用难度。

(2) 挑选权威精准的英文法学文献并精心删节和概括，在选材上追求语言使用的地道、规范与国际经济法知识的概括性。为更好地满足教学需求，精选英文法学文献作为素材，以保证法律英语语言的权威、规范，同时进行精心概括和删节，既考虑到国际经济法课程的特点，又努力满足国际经济法基本制度、理论和实务课程的需要，实现理论、制度概况介绍与制度探讨的平衡。

(3) 精心组织英文素材的编译，保证了英文素材译文的高质量。国际经济法课程双语教材质量的关键在于对英文素材精准的汉语编译，本书编者均有英语和法学专业双重学历背景，有的还长期从事国际贸易、国际投资等领域的法律实务，经认真翻译和多轮严格校译，保证了英文素材译文的高质量，使学生能够运用英语学习国际经济法理论知识，同时也能够知晓相关法律概念和原理的英语表达方式。

(4) 为使学生从整体上把握各部分理论知识，在每章章前明确了学习目标，使学生能够有的放矢地阅读与学习；在每章章后编写了综合练习，供学生回顾和检测本章所学知识。

　　本书由温融副教授和袁振华副教授以《国际经济法(双语)》第一版为基础共同修订完成。《国际经济法(双语)》第一版各章具体编写分工为：第一章(陈冠伶)、第二章(衡爱民)、第三章(程璐)、第四章(温融)、第五章(袁振华)和第六章(张昕宇)。本次修订版的不同之处在于：增加了两个章节，即第七章"国际税法"(温融)和第八章"世界贸易组织争端解决制度"(袁振华)，由此丰富了原教材的知识体系。另外，对原教材中的不妥之处进行了修正，提升了读者的学习和阅读体验。

　　本书的编写出版获得了四川外国语大学教材建设基金资助，在此表示衷心感谢。

　　本书的编写汲取了众多国内外同行报告、论文、专著和教材的精华，在此谨向这些专家和作者表示感谢。刘丹、余娅、邹馥麟、白世琴等同学参与了本书校对工作，付出了辛勤劳动。

　　在编著本书的过程中，编者受学识水平所限，疏漏和错误在所难免，敬请大家批评指正。

编　者

目 录

第一章　国际经济法概述

学习目标

了解国际经济法的调整范围。

把握国际经济法的基本特征。

明确国际经济法的渊源。

把握国际经济法的基本原则。

Chapter 1　Introduction to International Economic Law (IEL)

Learning Objectives

To understand the coverage of IEL.

To master the features of IEL.

To master the legal sources of IEL.

To master the basic principles of IEL.

第一节　国际经济法的概念、调整范围与特征

一、国际经济法的概念

学界关于国际经济法的定义有广义的和狭义的两种观点。广义说认为，国际经济法的范围不仅包括纵向的与管理相关的规则，这主要是指存在于一国国内经济管理法律体系中和国际公法规范的总和；同时，还包括调整私人(自然人或者法人)横向经济流转关系中的法律，这些是指国内商法以及国际商法部分的法律规范。

按照狭义说的观点，其范围仅仅包含调整私人(自然人或者法人)横向经济流转关系中的法律，即指国内商法以及国际商法部分的法律规范。大多数国际经济法的学者和教科书支持狭义说，例如著名的国际法学者约翰 H.杰克逊。

在中国，关于国际经济法的界定，以陈安教授为代表的大多数法学学者持广义的观点。

1.1　Definition, Coverage and Features of IEL

1.1.1　Definition of IEL

The researchers hold that there are narrow and broad definitions of IEL. Under the broad definition, the scope of IEL shall not only include the vertical regulation-related rules, which mainly exist in the legal system of a country's domestic economic management and public international law norms, but also the horizontal rules regulating transaction-specific activities conducted by private entities (natural persons or legal persons), which refer mainly to the domestic commercial law with foreign elements and international commercial laws.

Under the narrow definition, the scope of IEL shall only include the horizontal rules regulating transaction-specific activities conducted by private entities (natural persons or legal persons). Most international scholars and textbooks, e.g. Professor John H. Jackson, a widely respected scholar in the academic community of international law, have adopted a narrow definition of the IEL in their papers and textbooks.

In China, with regard to the theory of international economic law, mainstream scholars and textbooks, e.g. Professor AN CHEN, a widely respected scholar in Chinese IEL community, adopt the broad definition of IEL.

二、国际经济法的调整范围

中国国际经济法通说认为，国际经济法的调整范围包含以下三个方面。

(1) 私法主体进行国际经济活动产生的法律关系。

(2) 国际经济规制行为产生的法律关系。

(3) 国家或国际组织因国际经济合作和全球治理而产生的法律关系。

本书作者认为，尽管不同国家或地区的自然人、法人或者其他经济组织因国际经济活动而产生的权利和义务关系可以在广义上定义为国际经济法律关系，但是，该类权利和义务关系纳入国际商法的调整范围更为合适。

国际经济法仅包含后者，也就是说，只包含因国际经济规制而产生的法律关系，或者更准确地说，包含两个方面的内容。

(1) 国家或者地区(国际经济组织)之间因国际经济活动而产生的权利和义务关系。

(2) 国家或者地区(国际经济组织)之间因经济规制或全球治理而产生的权利和义务关系。

前者属于国际公法的范畴，而后者属于对外国人的跨国经济活动进行规制的国内法范畴。

1.1.2　Coverage of IEL

Mainstream opinions of the Chinese academic community for IEL cover the following three components.

(1) Legal relationships arising from international economic activities by subjects of private law.

(2) Legal relationships arising from international economic regulatory activities.

(3) Legal relationships formed among states or international organizations regarding international cooperation and global governance in the economic area.

The author, however, always believes that, although the relationships in terms of rights and obligations between natural persons or legal persons and other economic entities of different states (regions) in relation to their international economic activities can be placed under IEL in the broad sense, it is more appropriate to incorporate them into the international business law in consideration of the nature of such relationship.

In the author's opinion, IEL covers the latter, i.e., legal relationship arising from international economic regulations, which can be further classified into two aspects.

(1) Relationships in terms of economic rights and obligations among states or regions (international economic organizations) regarding international economic activities.

(2) Relationships in terms of economic rights and obligations among states or regions (international economic organizations) regarding economic administration or regulation and global governance.

The former falls under the public international law while the latter falls under domestic regulations on transnational economic activities conducted by foreign persons.

具体而言,国际经济法的调整范围包括以下几方面。

1. 国际贸易管理法律关系

国际贸易管理法律关系主要包括国家、地区政府或者国际经济组织在国际货物贸易、服务贸易和技术贸易过程中产生的权利和义务关系,以及国家、地区政府(监管者)与其他国家或地区自然人、法人(被监管者)之间因国际货物贸易、服务贸易和技术贸易监管而产生的权利和义务关系。

2. 国际投资监管法律关系

国际投资监管法律关系不仅包含国家或地区政府和国际经济组织在国际投资中产生的权利和义务关系,还包括一个国家或地区政府与其他国家或地区的自然人、法人在投资保护和监管过程中产生的权利和义务关系。

3. 国际货币和金融监管法律关系

国际货币和金融监管法律关系不仅包含国家或地区和全球经济组织在跨境金融活动监管中进行国际合作产生的权利和义务关系,还包括国家或地区政府和其他国家或地区的自然人、法人在跨境金融服务过程中产生的监管关系。

Specifically, IEL covers the following:

1. The Legal Relationship of International Trade Regulation

The legal relationship of international trade regulation mainly covers rights and obligations between states or regional governments and international economic organizations arising out of the regulation on international trade in goods, services and technologies, and the relationship between government of one state or region (the regulator) and nationals of other states or regions (the regulated persons) arising out of the regulation of international trade in goods, services and technologies.

2. The Legal Relationship of International Investment Regulation

The legal relationship arising out of international investment regulation covers not only the relationship of rights and obligations between states or regional governments and international economic organizations regarding international investments, but also the relationship of rights and obligations between the government of one state or region and nationals of other states or regions in areas of investment protection and regulation.

3. The Legal Relationship of International Monetary and Financial Regulation

The legal relationship of international monetary and financial regulation covers not only the relationship of rights and obligations between states or regions and global economic organizations arising out of international cooperation in regulating cross-border financial activities, but also regulatory relationship between government of one state or region and nations of other states or regions in areas of cross-border financial services.

4. 国际税收法律关系

国际税收法律关系不仅包含国家或地区政府在国际税收分配中的权利和义务关系，还包括一个国家或地区政府在对其他国家或地区的自然人、法人进行税收征收或监管过程中产生的权利和义务关系。

5. 其他国际事务法律关系

除此之外，由于对生态环境的日益恶化和全球气候变化的担忧，包括对汽油、煤炭等不可再生资源濒临枯竭的担忧；发展中国家对建立公正、合理的国际经济新秩序的渴求；以及随着科学技术的发展，地区贸易安排和自由贸易协定的日益增加，国际环境保护、国际能源合作与分配、国际经济发展与援助、知识产权国际保护、区域经济融合领域的国际组织之间的法律关系也逐渐成为国际经济法的重要内容。

4. The Legal Relationship of International Taxation

The legal relationship of international taxation covers both the relationship of international tax revenue distribution between states or regional governments and the relationship of rights and obligations between the government of one state or region and nationals of other states or regions arising out of tax imposition and administration.

5. The Legal Relationship of Other International Affairs

In addition, because of the growing concern for the deterioration of ecological environment and global climate change, including the fear that the non-renewable resources such as oil and coal are on the verge of depletion; the quest of developing countries for a new international economic order of justice and rationality; with the development of science and technology, and with an increasing amount of Regional Trade Agreements(RTAs) and Free Trade Agreements (FTAs), the legal relationships among international organizations regarding international environmental protection, international energy cooperation and allocation, international economic development and assistance, international protection of intellectual property rights, and regional economic integration are becoming increasingly important components of IEL.

三、国际经济法的特征

1. 独特的国际经济法主体

国际经济法的主体不仅包括自然人、法人，还包括国际经济组织，甚至国家。主权国家和国际经济组织成为国际经济法律关系的主体是国际经济法主体的一个非常显著的特征。

(1) 主权国家是国际经济法中的重要主体。

(2) 跨国公司也是国际经济法中的重要主体。

2. 国际经济法的内容

国际经济法涵盖国际投资、贸易和技术转让等领域中政府之间或者政府和国际组织之间的法律关系。除此之外，政府和自然人、法人之间因国际经济管理而产生的法律关系也是国际经济法的重要内容。后者不仅受国际公法规范的调整，而且受有关国家国内经济法律法规的调整。

1.1.3 Features of IEL

1. Unique Subjects of IEL

Subjects of IEL cover not only natural person, legal person, but international economic organizations, or states. The fact that sovereign states and international economic organizations become the subjects of the legal relationship of IEL is a remarkable feature in terms of subjects of IEL.

(1) Sovereign States are important subjects of IEL.

(2) Transnational corporations (TNCs) are important subjects of IEL.

2. The Content of IEL

Economic legal relationships among national governments or between national governments and international organizations in areas of international investment, trade, and technology transfer are all covered by IEL. In addition, international economic management relationships with government authority of one state as one party and an individual person or a legal entity as the other party are also governed by IEL. The latter is covered and regulated not only by the related norms of the public international law, but also by norms of domestic economic laws of the concerned countries.

在这一调整过程中，国际公法和国内法同时发挥各自的作用，互相渗透，互相影响。正因为如此，国际经济法的内容非常广泛，这也可以从下面的国际投资项目中得到印证。

假设某发达国家(甲国)的甲公司在一个发展中国家(乙国)投资某一项目。通过对国际或跨国投资行为或关系的自行考察，可以发现这些投资行为都要受到多种类型和各个层面的国际公法的调整和约束。

首先，根据国际公法上普遍接受的原理，任何独立的国家都具有司法主权。也就是说，一个国家在其领土范围内，可以根据其国内法律、政策对所有人、物和所有事项进行司法管辖，除非享有外交特权或者根据国际法可以豁免的情况。因此，甲公司在乙国的投资行为自然将受到作为东道国乙国制定的在其领域内关于外来投资的法律和政策的保护、监管和约束。直接适用的法律包括乙国的外商投资法、外汇管制法、涉外税法等。

In the process of addressing and regulating such international economic legal relationship, the public international law and domestic law tend to play their roles simultaneously, influence and supplement each other. Because of that, IEL is comprehensive in content, which is reflected in the following assumed international investment project.

Assume Company A from Country A, a developed country, invests a plant in Country B, a developing country. Careful analysis of such international or transnational investment activities or relations finds that they are subject to constraint and governance by public laws of multiple types and layers.

First, according to the basic principle widely accepted under the public international law, all the independent countries will enjoy territorial jurisdiction. That is to say, the country has the right to exercise full jurisdiction over all people, objects and events within its territory in accordance with its domestic laws and policies, except for diplomatic privileges and exemptions under international law. Therefore, investment activities of Company A conducted within the territory of Country B shall naturally be subject to protection, regulation and constraint by laws and regulations of Country B, which have been drafted by Country B, as a host country, to address foreign investments within its territory. Directly applicable laws include foreign investment laws, foreign exchange regulation laws, and tax laws with foreign elements of Country B.

其次，发达国家为了保护本国国民的海外投资的安全，通常都会和吸引外资的发展中国家订立双边条约和协定，对各自在对方国家的投资予以保护。同时，发达国家政府设立的保险公司(比如美国设立的海外私人投资公司)通常会和从事海外投资的公司订立海外投资保险协议，对海外投资的政治风险等进行投保。一旦保险合同约定的意外事件发生，投资者将获得赔偿，随后保险公司作为债权人将对东道国行使代位求偿权。为了防止东道国拒绝支付赔偿金，发达国家通常会在和发展中国家订立投资保护协议时，在协议中约定东道国同意海外投资保险公司享有代位求偿权。假设甲乙两国已经订立双边投资保护条约或协定，甲国的海外投资保险体系也非常健全，那么在乙国进行投资的甲公司将不但受到乙国国内法的保护，同时还可以受到甲国国内法的保护。甲公司的投资行为不仅受到两国国内法的保护，同时，还受到双边条约和协定的保护。

Second, in order to ensure the safety of overseas investment made by their own nationals, many developed countries tend to respectively conclude bilateral treaties or agreements with the developing countries that absorb foreign investments on the mutual protection of investments made by nationals of the other party. At the same time, investment insurers established by governments of the developed countries (such as the Overseas Private Investment Corporation, or OPIC, set up by US Government) usually conclude insurance contracts with their own investors that invest overseas to insure political risks related to such overseas investment. Upon occurrence of risk incidents covered by such insurance, these insurers will pay claims as stipulated in the contract and then replace the insured's legal status as the creditor and exercise their subrogation rights to claim from the host country government. To prevent the host country government from refusing to pay claims afterward, the developed countries will incorporate special provisions into their bilateral treaties or agreements with the host countries about mutual protection of investment by their respective nationals to constrain the host country governments, i.e., stipulating that the host country governments agree that the foreign investment insurers enjoy the rights of subrogation. Assuming that Countries A and B have concluded a bilateral investment protection treaty or agreement and that the above-mentioned overseas investment insurance system is popular in Country A, then, Company A's investment in Country B will enjoy not only protection under the domestic laws of Country B but also protection, regulation and constraint under the domestic laws of Country A (especially those on overseas investment insurance). Such investment is addressed not only by domestic law of Countries A and B but also by their bilateral treaties and agreements.

3. 国际经济法的另一个特色：边界模糊

上述代位求偿权，本来是甲国国内合同法和保险法规定的一项权利，即是甲国国内私法的权利，但现在通过上述的双边投资条约或类似协定而"国际化"了。

国际投资是国际商事交易中最常见的现象，从中我们可以发现在调整国际经济关系的过程中，国际法、国内法、公法、私法已经在互相渗透与融合。

第二节 国际经济法的渊源

一般认为，国际经济法的渊源不仅限于调整私法领域的法律规制，比如国际货物买卖法、公司法、票据法和海商法，也包括很多公共领域的制度规定。因此，国际经济法的渊源不仅包括国际经济条约，也包括国际惯例、关于管制外部经济活动的国内立法、重要的国际组织的决议、学说等。

---

3. Vague Boundary as One of the Features of IEL

For the above-mentioned right of subrogation, it is originally a right based on Country A's domestic contract law and insurance law, i.e., a right under domestic private law of Country A, but is "internationalized" via special provisions in the above-mentioned bilateral investment treaties (BITs) or other agreements of a similar function.

International investment is one of the most common phenomena in international business transactions, from which we can witness the mutual penetration, integration and supplementation of international law, domestic law, "public law" and "private law" in the process addressing international economic relations.

1.2　Legal Sources of IEL

Mainstream Chinese scholars hold that the IEL not only covers private law norms such as law on international sale of goods, company law, law on commercial papers and maritime, but also many public norms. Legal sources of IEL not only include various international economic treaties, but also cover conventions, domestic legislations on regulation of external economic activities, resolutions of important international organizations, theories, etc.

一、国际经济条约(国际惯例)

国际经济条约是国际经济法重要的法律渊源之一，是指国家(地区)之间为了确定相互经济的权利和义务关系而达成的具有法律约束力的书面协议。根据条约主体的多少，国际经济条约可以分为双边条约和多边条约，或者是国际性条约和区域性条约。根据它们的范围，可以分为综合协定和关于特别事项的经济条约。

二、国内立法

国内立法机关制定的调整和管理具有涉外因素的规范性文件是国际经济法的一项重要法律渊源。

首先，因为很多领域缺乏统一适用的国际法规范，国内对涉外经济领域的立法构成了国际经济规则中不可或缺的一部分。尽管它是由国内立法机关制定，但国内立法对于国际经济活动以及监管本身都具有重要的法律影响。它一方面适用于外来自然人和法人及其财产，另一方面，也适用于本国在境外的自然人、法人和财产。在许多法律领域没有统一的国际实体法，缺乏国内立法的监管将不可能维持法律秩序，甚至导致不必要的混乱，并且使法律的可预测性大大降低，从而对国际商事交易的发展和繁荣造成不利影响。

1.2.1 International Economic Treaties (Conventions)

International economic treaties, an important source of IEL, are legally binding written agreements between states (regions) for the determination of their mutual economic rights and obligations. According to the number of contracting parties, international economic treaties can be classified into bilateral and multilateral treaties, or into global treaties and regional agreements. In view of their scope, there are comprehensive international economic treaties and special international economic treaties.

1.2.2 Domestic Legislations

Domestic legislations of states for regulation and control of foreign-related economic relations are an important legal source of IEL for the following reasons.

Firstly, because of the lack of uniform international law in many areas, domestic legislations on regulation of foreign-related economic activities constitute an integral part of international economic rules. Although these domestic laws are enacted by national legislatures, they have important legal impacts on the regulation of international economic activities or regulatory relations thereof, as they apply to not only foreign natural and legal persons and their assets but overseas native natural or legal persons and their assets. In many legal areas without uniform international substantive law, the absence of regulation by such domestic legislations will make it impossible to maintain the right legal order or even lead to unnecessary chaos and greatly reduce legal predictability, thereby adversely impacting development and prosperity of international business transactions.

其次，尽管在许多国际经济领域存在着统一的国际实体法律，但是这些法律是不能直接调整特定的商事交易关系或跨境经济调控关系的，因此可能只有通过缔约国适用相应的国内立法才能得以实施。此种情行下，调整涉外经济活动相关的国内立法仍然是执行上述国际法的一个重要的国际法渊源。与统一的国际法一样，这些国内法是必不可少的多边经济法律框架的组成部分。最典型的例子是世界贸易组织(WTO)多边货物贸易协定和相应的国内立法。

通过关税与贸易总协定缔约各方近半个世纪的努力，世界贸易组织规则已日臻完善。即便如此，如果这些规则得不到成员方的贯彻实施，都不过是流于形式。当执行世界贸易组织规则的时候，成员方采取的是间接而非直接的适用。由于世界贸易组织不再适用"祖父条款"，成员之间的立法必须与世界贸易组织协定以及它的附件同时生效。因此，关税与贸易总协定演进到世界贸易组织的过渡期间，各成员方必须颁布新法律或修订现有的国内法律以使之适应新的世界贸易组织规则。

三、重要国际组织的决议

中国国际法学界的学者们的主流意见认为重要的国际组织的决议，特别是联合国大会的特别决议，也是国际经济法的法律渊源之一。

Secondly, despite the existence of unified substantive public international laws in many areas of international economic relations, these laws are not directly applicable to specific business transaction relations or cross-border economic regulation relations, and therefore may only get implemented via corresponding domestic laws of the contracting countries. Under this situation, the domestic legislation that regulates foreign-related economic activities remains an important legal origin for implementation of the above international laws. Together with the unified international laws, such domestic laws are indispensable components of the multilateral economic legal framework. The most typical example in this regard is the WTO Multilateral Agreements on Trade in Goods and the corresponding domestic legislations.

Through the effort of GATT Contracting Parties for nearly half a century, WTO rules have already evolved into a ripe system. Even so, if not implemented by competent authorities of members, these rules would remain to work only upon paper. When implementing WTO rules, the competent authorities of WTO members resort to indirect rather than direct application. Since WTO no longer uses grandfather clauses, legislations of members must come into effect simultaneously with the WTO Agreement and its covered agreements. Therefore, after entry into force of the WTO Agreement, members immediately enacted their new domestic laws or revised their existing laws to implement such WTO rules.

1.2.3 Resolutions of Important International Organizations

Mainstream Chinese scholars of international law hold that resolutions of important international organizations, especially special resolutions of the UN General Assembly, are also one of the legal sources of IEL.

这些学者认为，联合国大会做出的旨在宣示国际法的原则和准则的特别决议，应当具有法律效力，其他的决议在国际实践中也逐步被认可，成为具有法律效力的准则。在国际经济事务中，联合国大会自 20 世纪 60 年代以来通过了一系列重要决议，比如 1962 年的《关于自然资源之永久主权宣言》、1974 年的《建立国际经济新秩序宣言》和《各国经济权利和义务宪章》。联合国的许多成员国都投票赞成这些决议和宣言，这些决议和宣言都体现了国际经济法的重要原则和准则。对这些成员国来说，投赞成票本身就表明他们承认这些决议的法律效力。至少表明他们承认那些投赞成票的决议，这些决议应当具有法律效力。

应当说明的是，许多学者，包括作者在内，对上述意见持保留意见。除了那些针对联合国内部事务的决议外，不论是根据《联合国宪章》的规定，还是根据"约束力"的定义，联合国大会做出的决议都仅为"建议"。即使一些决议或者宣言体现了未来国际实践发展中国际经济法的原则和准则，也不能认为这些决议或者宣言本身就具有法律约束力，毕竟要成为具有法律约束力的国际法准则，还必须经过相应的法律程序。一些决议成为国际实践中的国际法准则本身并不意味着所有的这些决议都从一开始就具有法律约束力，而是事后经过特定的程序才赋予其法律约束力。这也从另一个层面表明，不具有法律约束力的决议和具有法律约束力的国际法准则之间还有不小的距离。

According to these scholars, some special resolutions of the UN General Assembly that aim at announcing principles and norms of international law should have legal effects and some other resolutions are gradually accepted in international practices and become legally binding norms. In terms of international economic affairs, the UN General Assembly has adopted a series of important resolutions since the 1960s, e.g. the 1962 *Declaration on Permanent Sovereignty over Natural Resources,* the 1974 *Declaration on the Establishment of a New International Economic Order* and *the Charter of Economic Rights and Duties of States.* Many UN member countries voted for these resolutions and declarations that reflected or indicated the important principles and rules of IEL. For these member countries, the voting itself exhibits their recognition of the legal effect of these resolutions. At least for those they voted in favor of the resolutions, the resolutions shall be legally binding.

It should be pointed out that many scholars including the author have reservations about the viewpoint above. Expect for some resolutions on internal UN affairs, resolutions of the UN General Assembly are all suggestions about whether according to provisions of the UN Charter or according to general meaning of "binding force". Even if some resolutions or declarations reflect or indicate the principles and rules of IEL in the process of formation with development of international practices, we cannot say that such resolutions are legally binding as they need to undergo certain legal procedure to become legally binding international legal norms. The fact that some resolutions are accepted as norms of international law in international practices do not indicate that these resolutions are legally binding from the very beginning, because certain procedures or actions should be followed to recognize their legal effects. This illustrates from another aspect that there is still a way to go between such unbinding resolutions and binding international laws.

四、国际经济法的学说

一些最权威的学者们的学说也被认为是立法的重要依据。原因是，这样的学说本身对于国际法的适用产生了深远的影响。很大一部分法律规则都是先由法学家们在他们的著作中总结和提出的，然后在不同国家的法律实践中得以广泛的认同。国际经济法也不例外，例如著名的阿根廷法学学者和外交官卡尔沃先生所阐释的学说被广泛用于拉美国家解决他们和外来投资者的争端，因此也演进成为国际经济法的一条重要渊源。

再举一个例子，在"乌拉圭回合"之后，为了修改世界贸易组织的基本体系使其更好地适应不断发展的全球贸易体系，前世界贸易组织总干事素帕猜组织了以彼得·萨瑟兰和约翰 H.杰克逊为首的著名的学者、专家们撰写了《萨瑟兰报告》。这份报告认真地研究了世界贸易组织的局限性和面临的挑战，并提出了长期的应对措施。而后来通行的国际经济法的原则正是来源于此。这份报告正是国际经济法的学说作为国际经济法的渊源在国际实践中得到执行的典型案例，它对未来的世界贸易组织规则产生了深远的重要影响。

1.2.4 Theories of IEL

Theories of the most authoritative scholars may also be regarded as important means for determination of rules of law. The reason is that such theories exert great impacts on application of international law. Quite a number of new legal rules tend to be summarized or established by outstanding scholars in their works and later on acknowledged in legal practices of different states. IEL is no exception. For instance, theories elaborated by Mr. Calvo, the famous Argentine legal scholar and diplomat, had impacted greatly on Latin American countries in handling disputes between these countries and foreign investors, hence had become an important source of IEL.

For another instance, after the Uruguay Round, in order to reform some fundamental systems of the WTO to better meet requirements of the developing global trade system, the former WTO Director General Supachai engaged outstanding scholars of the international law led by Mr. Peter Sutherland and John H. Jackson to write *The Sutherland Report*. The report carried out thorough analysis of institutional deficiencies and challenges confronting the WTO, and put forward some long-term countermeasures, some of which shed valuable insights on the establishment of new principles of IEL. This report, a typical example where theories of IEL authorities are implemented in international practices as a source of IEL, may as well exert certain impacts on future WTO rules.

第三节　国际经济法的基本原则

一、国家经济主权原则

国家经济主权原则是国际公法的最基本的原则。国家主权原则是指主权国家对于其领域内的所有人、物和各项事务享有专属管辖权，除依据国际法享有豁免权的除外。这条原则长期以来得到了广泛的认同。国家主权原则包括了政治主权原则，即是指所有的国家都独立地享有主权，且各国主权平等。国家经济主权原则即是表现为一国对其领土内所有经济事务享有排他的管辖权。除此之外，国家主权原则还包括社会主权、文化主权等，即国家对其社会和文化事务享有上述权力。

因此，所谓的国家经济主权原则是指一国对其境内资源享有永久主权，有权对其自然资源及其经济事务独立自主地进行控制和管理。

《各国经济权利与义务宪章》第 1 条和第 2 条规定："各个国家都有充分的永久主权，自由行使，包括占有、使用和处置境内所有财富、自然资源和经济活动的权力。"

1.3　Basic Principles of IEL

1.3.1　The Principle of Economic Sovereignty of States

The principle of economic sovereignty of states has long been one of the accepted basic principles of the public international law. A definition of national sovereignty is that a sovereign state enjoys exclusive jurisdiction over all people, objects and events within its territory except for those entitled to exemption under international law. This is an internationally acknowledged concept and has won consensus for a long time. National sovereignty includes not only political sovereignty whereby all states are independent of and equal to each other and economic sovereignty that is defined as independent management of all economic affairs within the territory, but also social and cultural sovereignty that dominate the social and cultural affairs within the territory of a state.

Therefore, the so-called principle of economic sovereignty of states refers to the permanent power of the state to control and dispose natural resources of the country and manage all its economic affairs at home and abroad with independence and autonomy.

Articles 1 and 2 of *the Charter of Economic Rights and Duties of States* provide that: "Every State has and shall freely exercise full permanent sovereignty, including possession, use and disposal, over all its wealth, natural resources and economic activities."

二、平等互利原则

《建立国际经济新秩序宣言》强调国际经济新秩序应建立在彼此公平对待的基础上，国际社会一切成员应当根据公平原则，开展最广泛的合作，借以消除经济差距，达到共同繁荣。

所谓的平等原则即是指所有国家在法律上一律平等，有权充分切实地参与决策过程，这种平等既不光是指实质平等，还包括形式平等。互利则意味着共谋利益，而不是牺牲一方利益来满足另一方利益。将平等和互利合并提出，这是国际经济法的一项新原则，意味着二者互为基础以及共同适用。一方面，互利是平等的基础，没有互利就没有平等。只有在互利的基础之上，最终才能实现平等。另一方面，只有真正的平等，才能导向最终的双赢局面。

1.3.2　The Principle of Equality and Mutual Benefit

The Declaration on the Establishment of a New International Economic Order points out that a new international economic order should be established on the basis of mutual equality treatment and that all members of the international community should conduct the most extensive cooperation on the principle of equality so as to eliminate economic gaps and achieve common prosperity.

The so-called equality means that all states, as equal members of the international community, enjoy equitable and fair treatments, i.e., equitable treatments in both form and substance. Mutual benefit means taking care of other parties' interests. Integration of equality and mutual benefit into one has become a new principle of IEL, which indicates that equality and mutual benefit are unified in implications and mutually based. On the one hand, mutual benefit is the foundation for equality. Without mutual benefit, there is no equality. Only on the basis of mutual benefit can they achieve equitable results. On the other hand, only genuine equality may lead to mutual benefit finally.

1. 普惠制待遇是适用平等互利原则的结果

普惠制是指发展中国家出口到发达国家的成品和半成品(包括一些初级产品)享受非歧视的优惠关税待遇原则，它包括三个方面的内容：(1)普遍优惠待遇，所有发达国家都对源于发展中国家的成品和半成品提供普遍的优惠关税待遇；(2)非歧视原则，即所有发展中国家均享受优惠关税待遇，不受例外和歧视的限制；(3)单边性，即发达国家应向发展中国家提供特殊单边的关税优惠，并没有权利要求发展中国家提供相应的优惠政策。

2. 特殊和差别待遇是多边贸易体制中平等互利原则的体现

如果发达国家修改《1994 年关税与贸易总协定》中的个别条款，使得平等互利原则向前迈出一小步而加入到他们自己的国内贸易法体系中，世界贸易组织之下的特殊和差别待遇可被认为是平等互利原则体现在多边贸易法律体系中更为实质的结果，它是世界贸易组织框架范围内法律进程的里程碑。

特殊和差别待遇意味着在多边贸易体系中，世界贸易组织的发展中国家成员方有权偏离最惠国待遇原则，享受特殊和优惠的待遇政策，以此区别于其他世界贸易组织成员方。

---

1. Generalized System of Preferences (GSP) Is One of the Outcomes of Applying the Principle of Equality and Mutual Benefit in Trade

The Generalized System of Preferences (GSP) is the system of general, non-discriminative preferential tariff treatments that developed countries provide for finished goods and half-finished goods(including some primary products) that developing countries export. The three principles of GSP are: (1)General principle, i.e., all developed countries provide export finished goods originating from developing countries with general preferential tariff treatments; (2)Non-discrimination principle, i.e., all developing countries are entitled to preferential tariff treatments under GSP without exception, and without discrimination; and, (3)Non-reciprocity principle. That is, developed countries should unilaterally provide developing countries with special tariff concessions without seeking reciprocity from developing countries.

2. Special and Differential Treatment Is the More Substantial Outcome of Implementing the Principle of Equality and Mutual Benefit in the Multilateral Trade System

If developed countries revised individual clauses of the 1994 GATT and enabled the GSP to make one small step forward in incorporating the principle of equality and mutual benefit in national trade law systems, the Special and Differential Treatment (S&DT) for developing countries under the WTO is a more substantial outcome of the further recognition of the principle of equality and mutual benefit by the multilateral trading legal system, symbolizing holistic establishment of the legitimate status of the principle in the network of the WTO and its Covered Agreements.

The implication of S&DT is that within the multilateral trading system, developing country members of the WTO are entitled to deviate from the MFN principle and enjoy special and more preferential treatments, which should be different from those accessible to other WTO members.

三、国际合作以谋发展原则

《各国经济权利和义务宪章》规定："为了共同发展而开展国际合作是所有国家的共同的目标和责任。每个国家应通力合作，积极扩大援助发展中国家，加速其经济和社会的发展，并为其提供有利的外部条件和协助条件，严格尊重他国国家主权平等和自由。"

当前世界经济全球化和相互依存日益加深，没有一个国家能够在国家社会经济发展的同时寻求充分的"独立"，除非它们完全与其他国家或地区隔绝。《建立国际经济新秩序宣言》指出：发达国家的利益同发展中国家的利益不能再相互隔开，发达国家的繁荣和发展中国家的成长与发展是紧密相连的。整个国际大家庭的繁荣取决于它的组成部分的繁荣。

因此，各国的发展，特别是发展中国家的发展，不仅是国内问题也是国际问题，要求国际社会所有国家进行有效的合作。

1.3.3　The Principle of International Cooperation for Development

The Charter of Economic Rights and Duties of States explicitly provides that "International cooperation for development is the shared goal and common duty of all States. Every State should cooperate with the efforts to support developing countries, accelerating the development of its economy and society, and providing the external conditions and assistance in better condition for them, with strict respect for the sovereign equality of States and free of any conditions derogating from their sovereignty."

In the current world of accelerating economic globalization and growing inter-dependence of states, no state is able to seek its national social-economic development with full "independence" or in full isolation from other states and regions. *The Declaration on the Establishment of a New International Economic Order* points out "that the interests of developed countries and those of developing countries can no longer be isolated from each other, that there is a close relationship between the prosperity of developed countries and the growth and development of developing countries, and that the prosperity of the international community as a whole depends upon the prosperity of its constituent parts."

As such, development of states, especially development of developing countries, is both a domestic and international issue, and requires effective cooperation of all countries in the world.

1. 真诚和开放的南北合作是国际合作的核心

对于历史上的敌对阵营来说，建立互信是不容易的，把这些历史的冲突转化成以未来为导向的全球合作则更难。然而，解决人类面临的许多全球问题需要真诚合作，人类的和平与发展也需要彼此相互接纳和消除仇恨，以此求同存异。

总之，双方阵营必须长期共同努力，以实现互利共赢的共同愿望，在诚实、真诚和相互信任的基础上，通过交流、合作，最终实现全球共同发展。

2. 有效的南南合作是国际合作的助推器

应该指出的是，当我们说南北合作已成为国际合作的核心组成部分的时候，我们并不否认其他阵营之间的合作的重要性，特别是，发展中国家之间的南南合作是国际合作的前提和动力，是国际经济合作的根本保证和重要组成部分。因为没有了南南合作，南北合作的南方阵营就失去了基础，南北合作将被损坏。

---

1. Sincere and Open South-North Cooperation Is the Core Component of International Cooperation

It is not easy for the two historically hostile camps to establish mutual trust, and even harder to turn such historical conflicts into the future-oriented global cooperation. However, solution to many global issues that confront humankind requires sincere cooperation of the two camps while human peace and development also calls for mutual acceptance and accommodation of each other on the basis of dissolving hatred, seeking commonalities and preserving differences.

In a word, countries of the two camps must exert long-term concerted efforts to realize the shared wishes for mutual benefit and win-win outcome on the basis of honesty, sincerity and mutual trust and through exchanges and cooperation and ultimately realize great harmony of the world.

2. Effective South-South Cooperation Is a Driver of International Cooperation

It should be pointed out that when we say South-North cooperation has become the central component of international cooperation in the current world, we do not deny the importance of cooperation between other camps. In particular, South-South cooperation among developing countries is the prerequisite and driving force of such international cooperation, and South-South cooperation is the fundamental guarantee and central component for substantial effect of international economic cooperation, because without South-South cooperation, the South camp thus loses foundation, South-North cooperation will be damaged.

　　《建立国际经济新秩序宣言》强调，全世界的发展中国家必须通过单独或集体行动加强经济、贸易、金融和技术的相互合作。它进一步指出，集体范围的自力更生和扩大发展中国家的相互交流合作，将进一步提高他们在新的国际经济秩序中扮演的角色。实际上，宣言将南南合作作为建立国际经济新秩序一个重要原则。

　　发展中国家之间的南南合作是一种新型的经济合作关系，它的特点是相互支持和帮助，取长补短，互利互惠，共同发展。20 世纪 70 年代以来，南南合作在一系列重大国际会议上成为一个重要议题，吸引了发展中国家越来越多的关注。发展和加强新的南南合作关系已成为发展中国家开展国际经济活动的一个关键因素。

　　3. 不同的国际经济合作组织建立和完善公平而有效的争端解决机制是国际经济合作成功的关键

　　无论是发达国家和发展中国家之间，还是发展中国家之间，国际经济合作是一个长期的历史过程，充满了曲折与艰辛。在这个过程中，冲突、纠纷和矛盾是不可避免的。为了防止争端和利益冲突的升级，在各种国际经济合作组织中，必须建立公平而有效的争端解决机制。在这方面，世界贸易组织争端解决机构(DSB)就是一个很好的例子。

The Declaration on the Establishment of a New International Economic Order emphasizes that developing countries worldwide must enhance their mutual cooperation in the areas of economy, trade, finance and technology through separate or collective actions. It further points out that collective self-reliance and expanding mutual cooperation of developing countries will further enhance their roles in the new international economic order. Actually, the Declaration lists enhancing such cooperation as one of the important principles for establishing a new international economic order.

South-South cooperation between developing countries is a new type of economic cooperation relationship that features mutual help and support, mutual learning to offset deficiencies, mutual benefit and reciprocity and common development. Since the 1970s, South-South cooperation has attracted increasing attention from developing countries who regarded such cooperation as an important issue at a series of important international conferences. Development and enhancement of such new cooperation relationship has become a key component of international economic activities conducted by developing countries.

3. Establishment and Improvement of Fair and Effective Dispute Settlement Mechanism within Various International Economic Cooperation Organizations Is the Key to Successful International Economic Cooperation

Whether between developed and developing countries or between developing countries, international economic cooperation is a long historical process full of complications and hardships. Conflicts, disputes and contradictions are inevitable in this process. To prevent intensification and escalation of disputes and conflict of interests, fair and effective mechanism for dispute settlement must be established within various international economic cooperation organizations. In this regard, the WTO Dispute Settlement Body(DSB) is a good example.

就世界贸易组织相关问题，尽管存在许多学术争议。有一种观点被大多数学者所接受，即世界贸易组织的成功运作体现在它建立起了有效的争端解决机构。世界贸易组织的争端解决机构成立以来的几十年里，专家组和上诉机构以争端解决机构的名义出具了成百上千的报告。这些报告理论深入，在多数报告中，大国败诉。

一些学者甚至称此争端解决机制为世界贸易组织"王冠上的宝石"，世界贸易组织争端解决机制是最权威和最重要的纠纷解决机制，在所有现有的国际多边司法程序中，它可能是最令人印象深刻的。

四、义务必须履行原则

从法律角度来看，义务可分为约定义务和法定义务(责任)。约定义务来自于合同，而法定义务是法定的，比如某些特定的主体(例如，医生、警察和政府官员)必须依法履行的职责。如果合同义务履行是合同参与方自愿一致的结果，那么应当遵循意思自治的原则，而缔约各方担心受到法律制裁，就不得不自觉履行法定义务。然而，虽然合同的约束力来自缔约各方自己的意志，但合同的履行有法律的保证，即在缔约方违反合同的情形下，法律也将提供救济。

Despite many academic controversies about relevant WTO issues, there is one view accepted by most scholars, i.e., the most important insight regarding successful operation of the WTO is that it sets up an effective WTO DSB. Hundreds and thousands of panel and Appellate Body reports have been produced in the name of the WTO DSB during the decades since its establishment. The reasonings of these reports are very much in-depth. And there are many reports in which the major powers lost their cases.

Some scholars even call this system "the jewel of the crown" of the WTO, the WTO DSB is the most authoritative and most important dispute settlement mechanism of all existing international multilateral judicial systems, and may well be the most impressive one ever witnessed by this world.

1.3.4 The Principle that Obligations Must Be Performed

From the legal perspective, obligations can be classified into contractual and statutory obligations (duties). Contractual obligations are obligations that arise from contracts while statutory obligations (duties) are statutory duties that certain specific subjects (e.g. doctors, policemen and civil servants) must perform according to law. If contractual obligations to be performed are the results of their own will of the contracting parties and thereby observed self-consciously, the concerned parties have to abide by statutory obligations (duties) for fear of legal sanctions. However, although the binding force of contractual obligations comes from the contracting parties' respect to their own will, their implementation is equally assured by legal enforceability, i.e., in the case of breach of contract by the contracting party/parties, the law will also provide relief.

"义务必须履行原则"是一条古老的习惯国际法原则。1974 年联合国大会通过的《各国经济权利与义务宪章》确立的国际经济关系基本原则中，也要求各国真诚地履行各种国际义务。这实际上是重申和强调"义务必须履行"的基本原则。

就国际经济法而言，两国之间的条约必须遵守；主权国家作为合同一方(比如特许权合同的一方)必须遵守合同。然而，除了条约义务(责任)，国际经济法的主体也必须遵守和履行法定义务(职责)。法定义务(职责)可能来自国内法或国际法规定。总之，有效的履行约定或法定的义务，都是国际经济法的主体从事跨境活动或交易不可推卸的责任。

1. 条约必须遵守

毫无疑问，"条约必须遵守原则"来自于"有约必守"这条古老的原则。这也是一条著名的拉丁语法律谚语。它最初的意思是"约定必须遵守"。

根据这一原则，双方之间的协议一旦达成，必须严格遵守和忠实执行。国家之间的条约被看成是国家之间的合同，一旦条约缔结，各国必须同样遵守，无正当理由，不得违反，除非发生不可抗力。

The principle that "obligations must be performed" can be regarded as one of the basic principles of customary international law. *The Charter of Economic Rights and Duties of States* adopted by the UN General Assembly in 1974 lists "sincere performance of various international (economic) duties by States" as one of the basic standards for addressing international economic relations, which is in fact the reiteration of and emphasis on "obligations must be performed", the basic principle of customary international law.

In terms of IEL, treaties between two countries must be kept; contracts (such as concession contracts) with one party being a sovereign-state must also be observed. However, in addition to treaty obligations, subjects of IEL must also abide by and perform statutory obligations (duties).Statutory obligations (duties) may come from provisions of domestic law or international law. In summary, valid obligations, whether contractual or statutory, are both obligations that subjects engaged in cross-border activities or transactions, which each state may not shift.

1. Treaties Must Be Honored

There is no doubt that "treaties must be honored" comes from "Pacta Sunt Servanda". It is a famous legal proverb in Latin, and a legal principle with a long history. Its original meaning is that "agreements must be kept".

According to this principle, the two parties, once the agreement between them is concluded, must strictly abide by and faithfully perform the agreement. As treaties are contracts between states in nature, once treaties are concluded between two or more states, the states must equally abide by them and no party may violate the treaties without due causes, except when force majeure arises.

"条约必须遵守"原则在习惯国际法领域居于首要地位，后来在《维也纳条约法公约》中成为一个基本原则。该公约 1969 年通过，1980 年生效。其序言强调，"条约必须遵守的规则是一个普遍公认的"国际法的基本原则。《公约》第 26 条进一步规定，"每一个条约生效，都对双方有约束力，必须由它们真诚地履行。"

联合国大会 1974 年通过的《各国经济权利与义务宪章》将"真诚履行国际(经济)义务"作为一个基本的标准来处理国际经济关系，这在本质上强调了"义务必须履行"原则。国际经济义务最先来自国际经济条约。因此，上述原则可能被理解为另外一种"条约必须遵守"的表达方式。

2. 依法缔结的生效合同必须被遵守

在横向的国际经济贸易或纵向的国际经济监管关系中，包括国家在内的法律主体不可避免地会签订很多合同，将这些合同作为改善其经济状况的必要法律工具和加强经济活动可预测性的重要手段。

"Treaties must be honored" was an important principle of customary international law in the first place and later on became a basic principle reiterated explicitly by *the Vienna Convention on Law of Treaties. The Vienna Convention on Law of Treaties*, which was opened for signature in 1969 and entered into force in 1980, emphasizes in its preface that "the pacta sunt servanda rule is a universally recognized" basic principle of international law. Article 26 of the Convention further describes the contents of the principle, i.e., "Every treaty in force is binding upon the parties to it and must be performed by them in good faith."

The Charter of Economic Rights and Duties of States adopted by the UN General Assembly in 1974 lists "sincere performance of international (economic) duties by States" as one of basic standards for addressing international economic relations, which in essence emphasizes the principle that "obligations must be performed". International economic obligations first of all come from international economic treaties. Therefore, the above principle may be interpreted as an alternative expression of "treaties must be honored".

2. Legitimately Concluded Contracts in Force Must Be Honored

In horizontal international economic exchanges or vertical regulatory relations, legal subjects including state will inevitably conclude many contracts which are indispensable legal tools for the parties to improve their economic situations and also important means for the parties to enhance predictability of economic activities.

一方当事人应被允许就另一方当事人的违约行为得到公平的法律救济的权利，否则法律的执行和可预测性将流于形式。因此，一国国内的涉外经济立法和国际条约都明确规定，一旦签订的经济合同生效，不管合同的主体一方是自然人或法人或者是国家，当事人应当诚实履行合同。除非合同各方同意修改合同或合同必须根据法律加以修订，任何人在没有合法授权的情况下无权变更合同内容，更不用说违约行为。

纵观国内立法，世界著名的 1804 年《拿破仑法典》就已包含上述的法定原则，即"依法成立的合同对当事人具有同等效力"。几百年来，这个条款已经成为一条口口相传的法谚。

国际法如《联合国国际货物销售合同公约》必须被遵守。因为同样的原因，根据相关国内法订立的特许权协议(包括有关 BOT 项目合同)，也应被遵守。在国有化或基于公共政策目的而实行征收时，国家也应向外国投资者提供合理赔偿。

然而，"合同必须遵守"也不是绝对的，这一原则有下述两项限制性规则。

(1) 合同，必须是依法订立和有效的。

(2) 情势变更、合同落空或不可抗力，可以成为解除合同义务的合法理由。

Should one party be allowed to breach the contract randomly without providing fair legal reliefs to the abiding party, the expectation to enhance predictability of economic activities by contract conclusion would come to nothing. As such, internal foreign-related economic legislations and international treaties both explicitly provide that once an economic contract is validly concluded between natural persons and legal persons or between natural persons or legal persons and a state, the parties shall perform the contract in good faith. Unless all parties to the contract agree to revise the contract or the contract must be revised according to law, no party has the right to alter any content of the contract without due authorization, let alone breach the contract.

From the perspective of domestic law, the world famous *Code Napoleon of* 1804 contains straightforward legal provisions on the above principle, i.e., "A contract established according to law shall have the same binding force as that imposed on the parties by law". This provision has become a legal proverb on everyone's lips for hundreds of years.

International law, such as *the UN Convention on Contracts for International Sale of Goods (CISG)*, should be abided by. For the same reason, Concession Agreements (including relevant contracts for BOT projects) concluded according to relevant domestic laws shall also be abided by. Where nationalization or expropriation is practiced for the purpose of public policy, the state shall provide foreign investors with rational compensation thereof.

However, the principle that "contracts must be honored" is not absolute, either. This principle is constrained by the following two rules.

(1) A contract that must be kept shall be legally concluded and validated.

(2) A fundamental change of circumstances, frustration of contract or force majeure constitutes legitimate reasons for eliminating contractual obligations.

综 合 练 习

1. 国际经济法的特征是什么？
2. 国际经济法的渊源是什么？
3. 国际经济法的基本原则是什么？

Comprehensive Exercises

1. What are the features of IEL?
2. What are the legal sources of IEL?
3. What are the basic principles of IEL?

第二章 国际经济法的主体

学习目标

掌握国际经济法主体的概念、国际经济法主体的范围。

掌握跨国公司的概念、特征。

了解跨国公司的法律地位，以及对跨国公司的国际管制。

了解世界上主要国际经济组织以及其作为国际经济法主体的资格要求。

Chapter 2　Subjects of International Economic Law(IEL)

Learning Objectives

To master the concept and scope of the subjects of IEL.

To master the concept, characteristics of transnational corporations.

To understand the legal status of transnational corporations and the international regulation over transnational corporations.

To understand the major international economic organizations in the world and their qualification requirements as the subjects of IEL.

第一节　国际经济法的主体概述

国际经济法的主体是指在国际经济关系中能行使权利和承担义务的法律人格者，它包括自然人、法人、国家和国际组织。

一、自然人

自然人作为国际经济法主体，首先必须具有一般的法律能力，包括权利能力和行为能力。自然人的权利能力指其享有权利和承担义务的资格。自然人的权利能力同其自身不可分离，始于出生，终于死亡。自然人的行为能力指其通过自己的行为实际取得权利和承担义务的资格。各国法律都根据个人不同的智力、年龄等因素，把自然人分为有行为能力人、无行为能力人和限制行为能力人。作为国际经济法主体的自然人，首先必须是有完全行为能力的人。

2.1　An Overview of the Subjects of IEL

The subjects of IEL are defined as the legal personalities who can exercise rights and undertake obligations in international economic relations, which include natural person, legal person, state and international organizations.

2.1.1　Natural Person

As the subject of IEL, first of all, natural persons must have the general legal capacity, including the right capacity and behavior capacity. The right capacity of the natural person refers to the qualification of his/her rights and obligations. The right capacity of the natural person, beginning from birth and ending at death, is inseparable from himself/herself. The capacity to act of the natural person refers to the qualification of actually exercising rights and undertaking obligations by his/her own acts. Laws of various countries vary the natural person as a person with complete capacity to act, a person without capacity to act or a person with limited capacity to act according to mental capacity, age or other factors. As the subject of IEL, the natural person must be a person with complete capacity to act firstly.

作为国际经济法主体的自然人不仅应具有一般权利能力，而且应该具有能从事国际经济交往的权利能力或资格。自然人的权利能力和行为能力一般是依其属人法确定的，许多国家的国际私法规范均对此有明确规定。但对于特殊权利能力，根据国际私法，则须视不同的法律关系，依所在地法或契约准据法确定。对于行为能力，不少国家为了保护内国交易安全，对属人法的适用给予一定的限制，而以行为地法作为确定自然人行为能力的准据法。

二、自然人的身份与地位

自然人的能力一般是由其属人法确定的，因此要确定其能力与地位就必须确定其国籍。国籍是指一个人作为某一国家的成员的一种法律上的身份。

一个自然人是否具有某一国家的国籍，原则上应依该国法律规定。各国一般均规定自然人可因出生和入籍两种方式取得国籍。但由于各国对这方面的具体规定不同，往往造成一个人同时具有双重国籍或多重国籍，即国籍的积极冲突；或无一国籍，即国籍的消极冲突的情况。

As the subject of IEL, natural persons should not only have the general right capacity, but also the right capacity or the qualification to engage in international economic exchanges. The right capacity and capacity to act of natural persons are generally determined by the personal law, and in many countries the norms of the international private law have specific provisions. But for the special right capacity, according to the international private law, it should be determined by the proper local law or applicable law of contracts considering different legal relationship. For capacity to act, many countries make certain restrictions to application of the personal law in order to protect the security of domestic transactions, but use lex loci actus as applicable law for determining the capacity to act of the natural person.

2.1.2 The Identity and Status of Natural Person

The civil capacity of the natural person is generally determined by the personal law, thus the nationality of the natural person should be determined in order to determine his/her capacity and status. Nationality refers to a legal identity of a person as a member of a country.

Whether a natural person has nationality of a country should be judged by the laws of the country. Generally various countries make provisions that a natural person can obtain the nationality by two ways, birth and naturalization. But due to the different specific regulations, it often results in a person with dual or multiple nationalities, that is the positive conflict of nationality; or without a nationality, that is negative conflict of nationality.

为消除和防止国籍冲突，很多国家在国内立法上和国际条约中作出努力。对于国籍的积极冲突，若自然人所具有的多重国籍中有一个是内国国籍时，通常是内国国籍优先；若其所具有的多重国籍都是外国国籍时，大多以与其有最密切联系的国家的法律为其本国法。对于国籍的消极冲突，一般主张以其人的住所所在地国国籍为准；不能确定住所时，以居所地国籍为准。

任何自然人，如果不具有某国国籍，就是该国的外国人。外国人在内国享有何种权利，即外国人在内国的法律地位，是完全依据内国的法律及有关的条约来决定的。每个主权国家都有权根据本国的情况，通过国内立法或缔结的条约给予外国人以国民待遇，或者最惠国待遇、优惠待遇、不歧视待遇。各国一般在民事权利方面给予外国人以国民待遇。但在经济领域，有些国家对外国人的权利予以限制。有些国家考虑到外国人间经济实力相差悬殊，不给外国投资者以国民待遇，而是给予最惠国待遇、不歧视待遇等，有的国家为了吸引外资，还给予外国投资者以优惠待遇。

In order to eliminate and prevent the conflict of nationalities, many countries make efforts in the domestic legislation and international treaties. For positive conflict of nationality, usually the natural person's own nationality is of priority if he/she has multiple nationalities and one is his/her own nationality. If the multiple nationalities are foreign nationalities, his/her own law is most closely connected with himself/herself. For the negative conflict of nationality, generally the nationality is advocated to be the country of residence; if the residence cannot be determined, the nationality is determined by the place where he/she lives.

Any natural person is a country's foreigner if he/she does not have a nationality of the country. What rights foreigners enjoy, namely the legal status of foreigners, is entirely decided by the country's laws and the relevant treaties. Every sovereign state according to its own circumstances has the right to give foreigners national treatment, most-favored-nation treatment, preferential treatment, or without discrimination treatment, through domestic legislation or treaties. Generally every country gives foreigners national treatment in civil rights. But in economic field some countries restrict the rights of foreigners. Some countries, considering the disparity of foreign economic strength, don't give foreign investors national treatment, but most-favored-nation treatment or without discrimination treatment. Some countries also give preferential treatment to foreign investors in order to attract foreign investment.

三、法人

1. 法人作为国际经济法主体的资格

法人是指依法定程序设立，有一定的组织机构和独立的财产，能以自己的名义享有权利和承担义务的社会组织。

法人能否成为特定国际经济法律关系的主体，取决于其权利能力的范围。例如，根据1983年中国与罗马尼亚两国政府《关于相互促进和保护投资协定》第2条的规定，能在对方境内作为国际投资法律关系主体的法人，必须是按照其本国法律有权同外国进行经济合作的经济组织。在实行对外贸易垄断制的国家，只有那些经过国家审查批准，取得对外贸易经营权的企业，方可从事进出口业务，才能成为国际贸易法律关系的主体。还必须注意的是，法人权利能力中的权利和义务是统一的。在国际经济交往中，法人不仅应有缔约能力，还应有履约能力，如法人不具备履约所需的资金、技术、人员等，就不具备承担相应义务的能力。凡不具备缔约能力和履约能力的假公司、纸上公司均不是国际经济法的合格主体。

2.1.3　Legal Person

1. The Qualification of Legal Person as the Subject of IEL

A legal person refers to the social organization which is set up in accordance with legal procedures, has the certain organization and independent property, and can exercise rights and undertake obligations on behalf of itself.

Whether a legal person can be the subject of international economic legal relation depends on the range of its capacity. For example, according to the second article of *the Agreement on Reciprocal Promotion and Protection of Investment* formulated by China and Romania government in 1983, the legal person who can be the subject of international investment legal relations in other party's territory must be the economic organization having legal rights with foreign economic cooperation according to its own law. In the country implementing state monopoly in foreign trade business, only those enterprises, with the national examination and approval, obtaining the right to operate foreign trade and engaging in import and export business, can be the subject of the international trade legal relation. What's more, the rights and obligations of the legal person's right capacity are unified. In the international economic exchanges, the legal person should not only have the contracting capacity, but also the performance ability, if not having funds, technology, personnel etc. necessary for performance, then it doesn't have the ability to undertake corresponding obligations. The fake company and paper company, who do not have the contracting capacity and performance ability, are not the qualified body of IEL.

法人的权利能力和行为能力一般依其属人法确定。法人的属人法不仅决定法人是否存在、是否具有一般权利能力，而且还决定法人的内部关系、特殊权利能力、行为能力等问题。

2. 法人的国籍与地位

法人的属人法指法人国籍所属国的法律。要确定法人的能力和地位，就必须确定法人的国籍。

确定法人国籍的标准通常有如下几种。

(1) 成立地说，即法人具有登记地(或批准地)国的国籍，因为法人是依据该国的法律创设的。

(2) 住所地说，即法人的住所在哪一个国家，就具有哪国国籍。但对于何处为法人的住所，又有两种不同的看法。一种认为，法人住所是指管理中心地，因为这里是法人的董事会作出重要决定和实行中央控制的地方，也是它完成许多重要行为的地方。另一种意见认为，法人住所是指营业中心地或开发中心地，因为法人的中心往往不在董事会或股东会开会的地方，而是在它进行活动的地方，并在活动中心地实现其目的。但由于营业中心地可以同时分散在几个不同的国家，因而这种主张实际上很少采用。

Generally, the right capacity of the legal person and its capacity to act are determined by its personal law. The legal person's personal law not only determines the existence of the legal person and its general right capacity, but also decides the legal person's internal relations, special right capacity and its capacity to act, etc.

2. The Nationality and Status of Legal Person

The legal person's personal law refers to the law of its country. To determine the legal person's capacity and status, its nationality must be determined.

The standards of determining the nationality of the legal person are usually classified into the following categories.

(1) Theory of establishment. The legal person has the nationality of the country where it is registered (or approved), because the legal person is created in accordance with the laws of such a country.

(2) Theory of domicile. The legal person's residence lies in one country so it has the nationality of this country. But what is a legal residence? There are two kinds of different views. One thought is, the legal residence refers to the management center, because this is the place where the legal person's board of directors makes important decisions, implements central control and finishes many important behaviors. The other thought is, the legal person's domicile refers to the business center or development center, because the legal person's center often lies in where it performs activities but not where board of directors and shareholders conduct a meeting, and achieve its purpose in this activity center. But as the business center can be dispersed in several different countries, in fact this claim is rarely used.

（3）控制说，或称成员国籍说、资本控制说，即法人的资本控制在哪一国国民手中，就具有哪一国的国籍，因为法人只不过是覆盖在其成员身上的一层面纱，法人的国籍应依其成员国籍来确定。

（4）复合标准说，即把法人的住所地和法人的成立地结合起来确定法人国籍。一国究竟采取什么标准确定法人的国籍，要考虑到保护本国及本国公民的权益，同时在平等互利的基础上，保护外国人的合法权益，以利于国际经济技术的合作与交流。

任何法人，如果不具有某国的国籍，在该国就是外国法人。外国法人通常必须通过内国的承认才能在内国作为一个法人而存在，才能被认为具有独立的法律人格。一个外国法人在内国被承认为法人后，虽具有法人的一般权利能力，但外国法人在内国的权利能力和行为能力及其范围还要受内国法的支配。除条约另有规定外，每个国家都有权自由规定外国法人在内国享有权利和进行活动的范围。例如，每个国家都有权禁止或限制外国法人在国防、军事工业以及支配国家经济命脉的部门投资，限制外国法人经营内国公用事业、金融、保险等企业。一般来说，外国法人被承认后，可以在其章程范围内享有内国的同类法人所能享有的权利。各国可以根据本国的国情给予外国法人以国民待遇、最惠国待遇、优惠待遇等。

---

(3) Theory of controlling, or theory of members' nationality, theory of capital controlling. The legal person's capital is controlled by one country's national so it has the nationality of this country, because the legal person is just like a veil covered on its members, the legal person's nationality should be determined in accordance with its members' nationality.

(4) Theory of composite standard. We should combine the legal person's domicile and the place established in order to determine the legal person's nationality. Some factors shall be taken into consideration for one country when choosing the criteria for determining the nationality of the legal person. It should consider the protection of national and its citizens' rights, at the same time, on the basis of equality and mutual benefit, and should protect the legitimate rights and interests of foreigners, in order to benefit international economic and technological cooperation and exchanges.

Any legal person is a foreign legal person in the country if it does not have the nationality. The foreign legal person usually must be admitted by the national law, then can exist and be considered to have independent legal personality. After being recognized as the legal person by a country, the foreign legal person obtains the legal person's general right capacity, but its right capacity and capacity to act are also restricted by the law. Unless otherwise stipulated in the treaty, each country has right to freely regulate the scope of the foreign legal person's rights or activities the foreign legal person may take. For example, each country has right to prohibit or limit foreign legal persons' investment in national defence, military industry and the department of controlling national economy, and limit the foreign legal person engaging in public utilities, finance, insurance and other businesses. Generally speaking, after being recognized, the foreign legal person can enjoy the same right as the national in the range of its associated articles. Countries can give a foreign legal person national treatment, most-favored-nation treatment, preferential treatment etc. according to the national condition.

四、国家

1. 国家作为国际经济法主体的资格

国家作为主权者，具有独立参加国际关系的能力和直接承担国际法权利和义务的能力。因此，国家有权同其他国家或国际组织签订国际经济条约或协定，以调整国家、国际组织之间的经济关系；国家有权参加各国际组织的经济活动，在国际法院进行诉讼，以维护自己的主权和利益；国家对其全部财富、自然资源和经济活动享有永久主权，并可自由行使此项主权。

同时，国家还可以以特殊民事法律关系主体的身份直接参加国际经济贸易活动，可以与另一国家的国民(包括自然人和法人)缔结各种经济合同。例如，国家可以同外国私人投资者签订特许协议，以开发本国自然资源或发展公用事业；国家可以同外国或外国人签订各种外贸合同，直接在国际市场上采购商品等。但在国际经济贸易活动中，应严格区分以国家名义签订的经济合同和以具有独立法人资格的国有企业名义签订的经济合同，因为后者应由该国有企业依法在其所支配的财产或资金的范围内承担责任，而不应以国库财产来承担责任。

2.1.4 State

1. The Qualification of States as the Subjects of IEL

A state, as a sovereignty, has the ability of independently participating in international relations and directly assuming rights and obligations of international law. Therefore, the state has the right to sign international economic treaties or agreements with other states or international organizations in order to adjust the economic relationships between states and international organizations. The state has the right to participate in the economic activities of international organizations, proceeding in the international court in order to safeguard its sovereignty and interests. The state has permanent sovereignty of all its wealth, natural resources and economic activities, and has freedom to exercise the sovereignty.

At the same time, the state also can directly participate in the international economic and trade activities as the main body of the special civil legal relationship and can sign all kinds of economic contracts with other citizens (including natural persons and legal persons). For example, states may sign concession agreement with foreign private investors to exploit its natural resources or develop public utilities; states can sign all kinds of international trade contracts and directly purchase in foreign trade market etc. But in activities of international economic and trade, we should strictly distinguish economic contract signed in the name of the state from the one signed in the name of the state's enterprise of independent legal personality, because for the latter the enterprise should be responsible by its property or within the scope of funds in accordance with the law, but not the state's property.

国家以民事主体参与国际经贸活动时，其地位具有特殊性。一方面，国家若作为合同一方当事人，应与另一方私人当事人处于平等的地位；另一方面，国家同时还具有另一种身份，即主权者身份，国家及其财产享有豁免权。

2. 国家及其财产豁免问题

国家豁免一般指一个国家不受另一个国家管辖。其主要内容如下。

(1) 管辖豁免，指未经一国同意，不得在他国法院对其起诉或以其财产作为诉讼标的。

(2) 执行豁免，指未经一国同意，不得对其财产加以扣押或执行。

国家及其财产豁免的法律根据是主权原则，各主权国家都是平等的，平等者之间无管辖权，因此，任何一个主权国家都不受他国司法管辖。

As the civil subject in international trade and economic activities, the state's status is special. On the one hand, if as a party to the contract, the state should be equal to the other party; on the other hand, the state also has another identity, namely the sovereign status. The state and its property have immunity.

2. The Issue of Immunity of State and Its Property

State immunity generally refers to a state free from another state's jurisdiction. Its main contents are:

(1) Immunity from jurisdiction refers that without consent of a state, a foreign court shall not exercise its jurisdiction over the state nor take its property as the object of litigation.

(2) Immunity from execution refers that without consent of a state, the state's property shall not be distressed or executed by other states.

The law of immunity of state and its property is based on the principle of sovereignty, for sovereign states are equal, then there isn't jurisdiction between equal sides, therefore, any sovereign state is not subject to others' jurisdiction.

西方国家从 19 世纪初起，通过其司法实践和国内立法，逐渐系统地形成了相互给予管辖豁免的惯例。许多著名国际法学者也充分肯定这一原则。但后来由于国家参与通常属于私人经营范围的事业逐渐增多，欧洲大陆有些国家开始实行限制，只对国家的主权行为(或公法行为、统治权行为)给予豁免，而对国家的非主权行为(或私法行为、事务管理权行为)则拒绝给予豁免。其理由是，国家从事属于私人经营的商业活动，与个人和法人的私法地位并无不同，即使属于主权行为，若对国家的私法行为给予司法豁免，就会使国家同与之发生经济关系的私法主体处于不平等地位，不足以保护私人的利益。

因此，国际上就存在着绝对豁免和限制豁免两种理论与实践。所谓绝对豁免，是指不论国家从事的是公法上的行为还是私法上的行为，除非该国放弃豁免，都给予豁免。英美原来是采取这种立场。苏联和某些东欧国家一贯主张绝对豁免。所谓限制豁免是只对外国公法行为给予豁免，对私法行为则不予豁免。许多西方发达国家，如奥地利、比利时、德国、卢森堡、荷兰、瑞士等，均采取这一立场，英国、美国后来也逐渐转向限制豁免。美国 1976 年颁布的《外国主权豁免法》规定，外国如有下列情况之一，不享有豁免：①放弃豁免；②在美国从事商业活动；③没收在美国的财产；④涉及在美国的不动产；⑤在美国发生侵权行为等。

From the beginning of nineteenth century, through their domestic judicial practices and legislation systems, the western countries gradually formed convention to give each other jurisdictional immunities. Many famous international law scholars also fully affirm the principle. But later as a result that business gradually increased, which was usually in line of private business while state joined, some European states began to impose restrictions, and only granted immunity to the state's sovereign act (public law behavior, dominance behavior), while refused to grant immunity to the non-sovereign act (or private behavior, transaction management rights behavior). The reason was that, when the state was engaged in private business activity, there was no difference between personal and legal status in the private law as it fell into sovereign act. If the national private behavior was given judicial immunity, it would make the state and the private parties have economic relations with the state in unequal status, and wouldn't protect the personal interests enough.

Therefore, internationally there exist two kinds of theories and practices, absolute immunity and restrictive immunity. The so-called absolute immunity means that regardless of the state engaging in the behavior of public or private law, immunity should be given unless it waives. The UK and the United States took this position before. The former Soviet Union and some Eastern European countries have consistently advocated absolute immunity. The so-called restrictive immunity means that it only gives immunity to the behavior in foreign public law but not private law. Many western developed countries, such as Austria, Belgium, Germany, Holland, Switzerland, agree this principle, later the United States and UK gradually turn to the restrictive immunity. *The Foreign Sovereign Immunities Act (FSIA)* of 1976 by the United States regulates, if there is any of the following circumstances, then the foreign states are not entitled to immunity: (a)waiving immunity; (b)engaging in a commercial activity in the United States; (c)expropriating property in the United States; (d)real property involved in the United States; (e)committing a tort in the United States and so on.

我国在理论上和实践上均坚持国家及其财产豁免是一项国际法原则，坚持以国家名义从事的一切活动都享有豁免权，注意将国家与国有企业的活动与财产区别开来，主张具有独立法人资格的国有企业不享有豁免权，并赞成通过国际条约消除各国在国家及其财产豁免问题的分歧。

3. 国家行为原则

国家行为原则是指主权国家在其领域内所为的行为，外国法院无权审查其行为的合法性效力。国家行为原则与国家豁免原则相辅相成，构成主权国家应有的权力与尊严。但两者的意义与效用又不同，国家豁免是一国是否服从外国法院管辖，而国家行为是在国家服从外国法院管辖问题上的一种积极抗辩，否认外国法院对一国政府在其境内行为的合法性的审查权。

In theory and practice, our country insists that immunity of the state and its property is a principle of international law, adheres that all the activities in the name of the country have immunity, pays attention to the difference between the state and the state-owned enterprises' activities and property, persists the state-owned enterprises with independent legal personality do not enjoy immunity, and supports to eliminate the disagreements on immunity of states and their properties by international treaties.

3. The Doctrine of State's Action

The doctrine of state's action means that foreign courts may not review the legitimacy effect of the behavior of a sovereign country conducting in its territory. The doctrine of state's action and the doctrine of state immunity together constitute sovereign state's rights and dignity. But their meaning and utility are different, state immunity is whether a state agrees to foreign court's jurisdiction, while state action doctrine means an affirmative defense when a state agrees to foreign court's jurisdiction, and denies the legitimacy review right of foreign court on the government in its territory.

第二节　跨　国　公　司

跨国公司是国际经济关系的重要参加者，在国际经济中有着举足轻重的影响和作用，是国际经济法的重要主体。跨国公司作为一种经济组织，在法律性质上与一般商业组织没有什么不同，但由于其本身的特点，产生了一些特殊的法律问题，这里对其予以专节介绍。

一、跨国公司的概念与特征

跨国公司又称多国公司、多国企业、国际企业、全球公司等，指由分设在两个或两个以上国家的实体组成的企业，其业务是通过一个或多个决策中心，根据一定的决策体制进行经营，因而具有一贯的政策和共同的战略。跨国公司具有如下特征。

2.2　Transnational Corporation

A transnational corporation is an important participant in international economic relations, having great influence and playing a decisive role in international economy, and is the important subject of IEL. As a kind of economic organization, the transnational corporation has no difference with the general business organizations in legal nature, but due to its own characteristics, it also produces some special legal issues and it is to be specifically introduced here.

2.2.1　Concept and Characteristics of Transnational Corporation

A transnational corporation, known as a multinational corporation, a multinational company, an international company, a global corporation, refers to the enterprise, consisted by two or more than two national entities, operating through one or more decision-making centers according to a certain decision system, thus adhering to a consistent policy and common strategy. The transnational corporation has the following characteristics.

1. 跨国性

跨国公司的实体虽分布于多国，在多国从事投资经营活动，但一般仍以一国为基地，受一国大企业的控制、管理和指挥。跨国公司在国外经营可采取子公司、参与公司、分公司等多种形式，但母公司或总公司通过所有权或其他手段对这些实体行使决定性的控制。因此，某国的跨国公司是指其母公司或总公司位于某国，而在其他国家设有各种实体从事跨国经营活动的公司集团。

2. 战略的全球性和管理的集中性

跨国公司制定战略时，不再是从某个分公司、某个地区着眼，而是从整个公司的利益出发，以全世界市场为角逐目标，从全球范围考虑公司的生产、销售、发展的政策和策略，以取得最大限度和长远的高额利润。跨国公司的全球战略，是由母公司制定的。母公司的决策中心对整个公司集团的各实体拥有高度集中的管理权。

1. The Multinational Characteristic

Although the entities of the transnational corporation are distributed and engaged in investment business activities in many countries, they are still based on one country and under the control, management and command of a big company in such a country. The transnational corporation operates abroad by adopting a variety of forms, such as subsidiary, participating company, branch, but a parent company or general company controls these entities decisively through ownership or other means. Therefore, one country's transnational corporation refers to a group of companies with parent company or general company located in such a country, while various entities of which are engaging in international business in other countries.

2. Global Strategy and Centralized Management

When the transnational corporation formulates strategic, it no longer focuses on one branch and one region, but on the entire company's interests and takes the world market for competition goal, considering global company production, sale, development policy and strategy, in order to obtain the maximum and long-term profits. The transnational corporation's global strategy is set by its parent company. The parent company's decision-making center has a high concentrating power of management on the entire entities of the company group.

3. 跨国公司内部的相互联系性

跨国公司是由它分布在各国的实体所组成的企业，其内部各实体之间，特别是母公司和子公司之间存在着密切的关系，从而使母公司或公司内的某些实体，能与其他实体分享知识、资源和分担责任。因此，有人认为，跨国公司的主要法律形式，是根据各国法律制度成立的多个公司的聚集体，但受母公司的集中控制，因而构成一个单一经济体，也就是说，跨国公司内部各实体间在法律上往往是相互独立的实体，而在经济上又是在母公司控制下所形成的一个整体。从跨国公司具有共同的商业目的、集中控制和内部一体化的活动等方面看，可以说，跨国公司具有企业的特征，是一个经济实体，但它并不是一个法律实体。

---

3. The Characteristic of Internal Interrelation of the Entities of a Transnational Corporation

The transnational corporation is an enterprise formed by its various entities distributed in many countries, in which a close relationship exists among various entities, especially between parent company and subsidiaries, so that some certain entities of parent company or company can share knowledge and resources with other entities and undertake responsibility. Therefore, some people think that the legal form of the transnational corporation is accumulation of many companies from each national legal system, but in the control of the parent company, thus constitutes a single economic entity, that is to say, the transnational corporation's interior entities are mutually independent in law, while it is an entity under the control of the parent company in economy. From the aspects of transnational corporation's common business purpose, central control and internal integration of activity, transnational corporation has the feature of enterprise, then it is an economic entity but not a legal entity.

二、跨国公司的法律地位

在国内法上，跨国公司诸实体没有特殊地位。它们与所在国的商业组织具有的地位相同。跨国公司的母公司或总公司在其母国，与母国的其他商业公司一样，是根据母国的法律成立的，其法律能力也是由母国的法律决定的。跨国公司在东道国的实体，或是根据东道国法律成立而由母公司控制的子公司，与东道国其他公司处于相同地位；或是作为分公司在东道国登记注册，其地位仍属外国公司。无论跨国公司在东道国的这些实体是内国公司还是外国公司，它们与其他商业公司在法律地位上没有差别。但是，在法律上，子公司与分公司具有不同的法律地位。

2.2.2 The Legal Status of Transnational Corporations

In domestic law, the entities of the transnational corporations have no special status. They have the same status as that of the country's commercial organizations. The transnational corporation's parent company or corporation in their home country, like other business companies, is established according to the law of the home country, and its legal capacity is also decided by the law of the home country. The entities of the transnational corporation in the host country, or the subsidiaries established according to the laws of the host country and under the control of the parent company, are in the same position as that of other companies of the host country; or as a branch in the host registration, its status is still a foreign company. However, these entities of the transnational corporation in the host country, regardless of domestic companies or foreign ones, aren't different from other business companies in legal status. However, subsidiaries and branches have different legal status in law.

1. 子公司

子公司通常是指由母公司持有全部或多数股份的企业，或者通过合约、契约等形式对公司实际行使决定性控制权的企业。但是，由于跨国公司行使控制的手段已经不限于所有权，还有各种各样的合同与安排，因而子公司的概念也发生了某些变化。根据某些欧洲国家，如德国、意大利、丹麦、瑞士的法律，由于持股或协议而处于另一公司决定性影响下的公司，是该另一公司的子公司。因此，一国公司在他国举办的受其控制的合营企业、独资公司均可纳入其子公司的范围。

国外的子公司是依东道国法律设立的。它们可以根据东道国法律的规定，采取有限责任公司、股份有限公司等形式。无论采取哪种形式，都必须遵守东道国规定的程序和条件。

同时，这些子公司具有独立的法律人格，相对于其母公司，它们是独立的法律实体。子公司根据东道国法律的规定，能独立以自己的名义享有权利能力和行为能力，行使权利和承担义务，能独立进行诉讼，并能独立承担民事责任。它们同其他法人组织一样，是国内法民事法律关系的主体。

---

1. Subsidiary

A subsidiary usually refers to the enterprise that the parent company owns all or a majority of company shares, or takes decisive control over enterprises by contract and covenant or other forms. However, because the controlling means of the transnational corporation has already not been limited to the ownership, but various contracts and arrangements, thus the concept of the subsidiary has changed. According to the laws of some European countries, such as Germany, Italy, Denmark and Swiss, due to ownership or agreement, a company under the decisive influence of another company is a subsidiary of such a company. Therefore, a joint venture and a wholly-owned enterprise under the control of a company and established in other country can be incorporated into the scope of the subsidiary.

A foreign subsidiary is established by the law of the host country. They can take the form of the company with limited liability and the company limited by shares etc. according to the law of the host country. No matter taking whatever form, they must comply with the prescribed procedures and conditions of the host country.

At the same time, these subsidiaries have an independent legal personality relative to their parent companies, and they are separate legal entities. According to the provisions of the host law, the subsidiaries can independently enjoy legal capacity in their own names, exercise their rights and undertake their obligations, conduct an independent action, and independently assume civil liability. They are the main subjects of domestic laws' civil legal relationship as the same as other legal person organizations.

2. 分公司

跨国公司还可以通过在东道国设立分公司的方式进行投资经营活动。国外分公司是总公司在国外设立的办事机构、经营机构。分公司没有独立的法律地位，不具有独立的法律人格，只不过是总公司的增设部分，具有总公司的国籍。总公司对分公司的行为直接负责任。

3. 母公司

与子公司的概念相对应，凡是在子公司中享有全部或多数股权，或通过合同等其他手段在国内活动的就是母公司。它们没有直接承担国际权利和义务的能力。它们只有当国际法成为国内法时才能享有该国际法上规定的某种权利并承担某种义务。这样，既然跨国公司缺少作为国际法主体的法律能力，也就不可能是国际法主体。

---

2. Branch

The transnational corporation can also make investing and operating activities through establishing branches in the host country. Foreign branches are offices and operating organizations set by the parent company in foreign countries. The branch has no independent legal status and legal personality, but just is the extension of the parent company and has the parent company's nationality. The parent company is directly responsible for the acts of branch.

3. Parent Company

In contrast to the concept of subsidiary, the parent company refers to the company that holds all or most equities of subsidiaries, or carries out domestic activities by contract and other means. It has no capacity of directly undertaking international rights and obligations. Only when the international law is used as domestic law, it can exercise certain rights and undertake certain obligations under the international law. Thus, since the transnational corporation lacks legal capacity as a subject of international law, it is impossible to be the subject of international law.

　　然而，跨国公司虽不是国际法主体，但这并不妨碍国际法对它们的活动进行规范。实际上在国际上早已存在许多规定个人和公司的行为的国际法规则，而且随着国际经济的发展，国际交往的增多，这类规则会越来越多。但这并不意味着个人和公司就是国际法主体。因为，第一，这些规则一般并不赋予个人或公司权利；第二，即便当条约明确规定个人和公司应承担某些权利和义务时，实际上也是缔约当事国承担的一种义务，即必须通过国内法给予个人或公司以某种权利和义务，国家是这种权利义务的直接承担者，而个人和公司只是间接承担者。

However, although the transnational corporation is not a subject of international law, this does not hinder the international law to regulate its activity. Actually in the world there already exist many provisions of international laws regulating personal and corporate behavior, while with the development of world economy and increase of international communication, there will be more and more such rules. But this does not mean that individuals and companies are subjects of international law. The reasons are that, firstly, these rules generally do not give the rights to individuals or companies; secondly, even when the treaty specifies that individuals and companies should undertake certain rights and obligations, in fact they are the obligations that contracting parties should assume. That is to say, certain rights and obligations shall be given to individuals or companies by domestic law. States are the direct undertakers of rights and obligations, while individuals and companies are indirect undertakers.

三、跨国公司母公司对其子公司的债务责任

1. 问题的提出

如前所述，位于不同国家的跨国公司母公司和子公司，一般在法律上相互独立，但在经济上却又相互联系。这样，在关于跨国公司的责任问题上，就会出现一些奇怪的现象，即其法律责任与它们的经济联系相分离。尽管母公司管理和控制着各子公司，并根据其全球战略指示子公司为了整个集团的利益进行活动，把子公司作为推行其商业政策的工具，有时甚至无视或损害某个子公司的利益。但是，根据法人的有限责任原则，只能由各该子公司对其产生的债务责任负责，母公司对子公司的债务，即使是由自己的指示或行为造成的，也不负任何责任。显然，这会给子公司里的少数股东和债权人，甚至子公司所在国的利益带来严重的损害。因此，必须考虑母公司对其子公司的债务责任问题。

2.2.3 The Debt Liability of Transnational Corporation's Parent Company to Subsidiary

1. The Problem Put Forward

As mentioned above, the transnational corporation's parent company and subsidiary in different states are legally independent of each other in general, but interconnected in economy. So, on the responsibility of the transnational corporations, there will be some strange phenomena, namely, their legal responsibilities separated from their economic contacts. Although parent company administrates and controls all subsidiaries, and indicates the subsidiaries to make activities for the entire group's interests according to its global strategy, makes the subsidiaries as tools to handle its business policy, sometimes even ignores or damages the interests of a certain subsidiary. However, according to the legal person's limited liability principle, only the subsidiary can be responsible for the liability caused by itself, the parent company does not bear any responsibility for the subsidiary's debt, even caused by its own instructions or actions. Obviously, this will bring serious damage to the subsidiary's minor shareholders and creditors, even the interests of the subsidiary's state. Therefore, we must consider the debt liability problem that the parent company brings to the subsidiary.

在实践中，印度的博帕尔毒气泄漏惨案就提出了这样的问题。1984 年 12 月 3 日，印度中央邦首府博帕尔市的美资联合碳化物印度有限公司(美国联合碳化物公司的印度子公司)所属的工厂贮存的甲基异氰酸盐的金属罐泄漏，致使当地居民 2000 多人丧生，严重受害者达 3 万~4 万人，其余受害受伤者达 52 万人。该案发生后，某些受害者的代理人和印度政府向纽约联邦法院就美国公司的赔偿提起了诉讼，但是被驳回。印度政府于 1986 年 9 月向印度法院提出诉讼。

原告认为这一毒气惨案的发生，美国联合碳化物公司负有不可推卸的责任。因为博帕尔工厂是由美国联合碳化物公司设计的，工厂的贮气设备设计太差，又没有安装它在美国的同类工厂安装的应急预警计算机系统；同时，这家公司没有就这种剧毒气体的危险性对住在工厂附近的居民发出过警告，住在附近的居民根本不知道这家工厂到底生产什么产品。甲基异氰酸盐这种剧毒气体只能少量贮存，有的西方国家早已停止生产和贮存这种剧毒气体，但美国联合碳化物公司仍然不顾当地公司有关负责人的警告而决定在博帕尔工厂大量贮存。显然，美国母公司对这一惨案的发生负有直接责任。

In practice, the India Bhopal poison gas leakage accident put forward such a problem. On December 3, 1984, in Bhopal, Indian Madhya Pradesh, metal tank owned by the U.S.-funded Union Carbide (India) Limited Company (The India subsidiary of Union Carbide Limited Company), leaked methyl isocyanate, causing more than 2000 local residents' death, serious victims up to 30000 ~ 40000, other injured victims up to 520000. After the case occurred, some victims' agent and the Indian government sued this U.S. company for compensation to the federal court in New York, but the suit was dismissed, then the Indian government filed a complaint against the U.S. company with the India court in September, 1986.

Plaintiff held that the Union Carbide Limited Company (hereinafter called "Union Carbide") should be responsible for this poison gas leakage tragedy. Because the Bhopal factory was designed by the Union Carbide, the equipment design of the factory gas storage was too poor, and no early emergency warning computer system, which was usually installed in similar factory in the USA, was installed in the Bhopal plant. At the same time, the company did not warn the residents living near the factory about the hazard of this kind of poison gas, and the residents nearby even didn't know exactly what products this factory produced. The highly poison gas, methyl isocyanate, can only be stored a small amount. Some western countries have already stopped production and storage of this highly poison gas, but the Union Carbide still made large storage in Bhopal factory regardless of the warning of the local company's head. Obviously, the parent company in the U.S. should be directly responsible for this tragedy.

可见，母公司的责任问题，是客观实际向人们提出的应予解决的课题。就揭开法人面纱而言，除美国外，其他国家，如欧洲大陆国家，很少有这样的案例，法院对此一般持慎重态度。而且对于哪些情况属于有限责任的例外，怎样认定，没有确定的准则和权威的解释，各国判例之间，甚至一国内的判例之间，也不一致，没有固定的模式。德国公司集团法中关于母公司对子公司的直接责任仅限于国内，不适用于跨国公司。因此，有必要寻找一个能为国际社会所接受的解决跨国公司责任的解决办法。

2. 母公司责任的根据

就跨国公司来说，应在什么情况下，在什么程度上，让母公司对其子公司的债务承担责任？这种责任的根据是什么？我们认为，母公司对子公司的责任应该与子公司所享有的自主性的程度相联系，视子公司自主性被剥夺的程度来让母公司负部分或全部责任。具体来说有以下几个方面。

It is thus clear that the parent company's responsibility is objectively and actually presenting people the problem to be solved. For piercing the corporation's veil, besides in the United States, in other countries there are seldom such cases, such as in the continental European countries, and the courts generally adopt cautious attitude. And on what condition falling within the exception of limited liability and how to identify, there is no determining criteria and authoritative interpretation for the courts, all cases even in a domestic precedent are not the same, and also no fixed patterns are available. In German company law the direct liability of the parent company to the subsidiary is limited to the domestic corporations, not applicable to the transnational corporations. Therefore, it is necessary to find a solution on transnational corporations' responsibility, which can be accepted by international community.

2. The Basis of Parent Company's Liability

As to the transnational corporation, under what circumstances and to what extent, should it let the parent company undertake obligation of the subsidiary's debts? What is this responsibility based on? We think that the responsibility of the parent company to the subsidiary has relation with the autonomy degree of the subsidiary, and according to the degree of deprivation of the subsidiary's autonomy, then decide the parent company should undertake all or part of liability. Specifically as follows:

(1) 在子公司具有足够的或必要的自主性，是一个独立自主的自治体，能独立作出决定从事各种民事活动，独立对外承担民事责任时，有限责任的原则应占有优势，母公司对子公司的债务不负责任。这时，衡量的标准可以法人应具备的条件为依据，如当该子公司具有其经营活动所必要的资产，有自己的经营管理机构，并根据自己的意思独立进行活动并承担责任时，可以认为子公司具有自主性，应独立承担责任。

(2) 当子公司在某些事项上的自主性由于母公司的干涉和支配，如母公司的错误决策或不当指示，而被剥夺，并对子公司或其债权人造成损害时，母公司应对由此造成的特定损害承担责任。德国公司法对事实公司集团的责任态度，在这方面具有可取性。在这种情况下，子公司并没有全部丧失自主性，而是在某些事项上丧失了自主性，因此，母公司并不对子公司的全部债务负责任，而只就由于其干涉控制所造成的特定损害负责任。

---

(1) When the subsidiary has sufficient or necessary independence, is an autonomous body, can make independent decisions in various civil activities, and can independently undertake civil liability, the principle of limited liability should take advantage, and the parent company shouldn't be responsible for the subsidiary's debts. At this time, the measuring standard is based on the conditions the legal person should have. For example, when the subsidiary has necessary assets needed by its business activities, and its own management mechanism, takes independent activities according to its own ideas, and undertakes responsibility, we can think that the subsidiary has autonomy and should undertake responsibility independently.

(2) When the subsidiary's autonomy in some certain matters is deprived because of the parent company's interference and control, such as the parent company's wrong decision or improper instructions, and it causes some damage to the affiliate or its creditors, the parent company should be responsible for the specific damage. The responsible attitude of German company law on De Facto Corporation group is desirable in this matter. In this case, the subsidiary does not lose its independence completely but only in some certain matters, therefore, the parent company should not be responsible for the subsidiary's whole debts but some specific damage caused by its interference and control.

在这种情况下追究母公司的法律根据，可依具体情况而定，如由于母公司的干涉造成合同不能履行而导致损害发生时，可依据合同法的有关规定追究责任；由于母公司的过错，而发生了侵权行为时，可依据侵权行为法的有关规定，将母公司作为侵权行为人来追究责任；如果有关法律没有明文规定，还可以采用代理说，即在某些事项或交易中，母公司利用其子公司作为代理人，来推行自己的政策，谋取自己的利益，从而应对自己的这种干涉控制造成的损害或债务承担责任。

Under this condition, the legal basis for investigating the parent company for responsibility shall be subject to the specific circumstances. For example, the contract is unable to be fulfilled owing to the parent company's interference and thus causes some damages. The parent company shall undertake liability according to contract law; if violations occur owing to the parent company's fault, the parent company should be blamed as tort-feasor according to the relevant provisions of tort law; in absence of law stipulations, the theory of agency can also be adopted, that is to say, in some events or transactions, the parent company makes its subsidiary as agent carry out its own policy, seek their own interests, in order to cope with the damage or liability caused by their such interference and control.

(3) 当子公司由于母公司的控制而基本或完全失去自主性时，应让母公司对子公司的债务直接负责任，因为这时子公司已失去独立性，实际上与母公司的分支机构的地位差不多。在这种情况下应注意掌握两点：一是如何确定控制的标准；二是确定控制的程度。一般说来，仅有控制还不够，这种控制还须达到完全或基本上剥夺了子公司的自主性的程度时才能让母公司对子公司债务负责任，对子公司的控制并不等于完全剥夺了其自主性。实际上跨国公司母子公司间始终存在着控制与受控制的关系，在存在控制关系的同时，子公司也能具有一定的自主性，因此，仅依据控制而让母公司对子公司的债务全面负责的观点遭到了非议。当然，如何衡量实际控制的程度是个复杂而困难的问题，目前在国际实践上也没有一个统一的检验标准。只有对具体情况进行具体分析，根据有关因素，例如资产混合，统一管理的程度，组织是否分立等，综合加以考察。

---

(3) When the subsidiary faces the loss of autonomy generally or completely due to the control of the parent company, the parent company should be responsible for the subsidiary's debt directly, because at this time the subsidiary has lost its independence, and in fact it nearly faces the same position as the parent company's branch. In this case, we should grasp two points: one is how to determine the standard of control, and the other one is to determine the degree of control. Generally speaking, only control is not enough. Only when this control reaches to the degree of depriving the subsidiary's autonomy completely or nearly, can the parent company be responsible for the subsidiary's debt. The control on the subsidiary doesn't mean completely depriving its autonomy. In fact, there is always a controlling and controlled relationship between the transnational parent company and subsidiary, in the presence of control relations. The subsidiary can also have some certain autonomy, therefore, the view has been criticized that the parent company should be responsible for the subsidiary's debt only from the fact of controlling. Of course, how to measure the actual degree of control is a complex and difficult problem. At present there isn't a unified inspection standard in international practice. We can only make some concrete analysis for concrete conditions and comprehensive investigations according to relevant factors, such as asset mixing, degree of unified management, whether the organization split or not.

四、对跨国公司的国际管制

1. 跨国公司与有关国家的矛盾和冲突

由于跨国公司具有强大的经济实力，且根据其全球战略在世界范围里追逐高额利润，这就会在跨国公司与东道国间、跨国公司与母国间、东道国与母国间产生种种矛盾和冲突。

跨国公司对东道国的经济发展既有积极作用，又有消极影响。这种消极影响表现在多个方面。例如，跨国公司可能采取各种手段，无视或违反东道国的法律，逃避东道国的管辖；控制和掠夺东道国的自然资源；跨国公司的"全球战略"可能与东道国的发展方向不一致；它们可能采取转移定价的手段逃避东道国的税收，逃避东道国的外汇管制措施；还可能采取各种限制性商业惯例，限制竞争，垄断市场，牟取暴利；它们产生的大量的国际资金流动可能会给东道国的国际收支带来重大影响；它们还可能利用东道国环境法不健全的空子，开设有严重污染和公害的工厂，给东道国的环境和人民生命财产带来重大损害等。在上述各方面，跨国公司的利益可能与东道国的主权和利益发生矛盾和冲突。因此，东道国必须通过各种法律手段，对跨国公司的活动进行管制。一般来说，由于跨国公司具有不同于一般单个商业公司的特殊性，东道国对跨国公司活动进行法律管制的任务也更加艰巨、复杂。

2.2.4 International Control on Transnational Corporations

1. Contradictions and Conflicts Between Transnational Corporation and the Related Countries

Because the transnational corporation has strong economic power, and is in pursuit of huge profits according its global strategy, this leads to various contradictions and conflicts between the transnational corporation and the host country, the transnational corporation and the home country, the host country and the home country.

The transnational corporation has not only positive but also negative effect on the development of the host country's economy. This negative impact has performance in many aspects. For example, transnational corporations may adopt various means, ignoring or violating the laws of the host country, to evade the host's jurisdiction; they may control and plunder the natural resources of the host country; the global strategy of the transnational corporation may be not consistent with the host country's development direction; they may adopt the means of transferring pricing to evade the host country's tax and exchange controls; also they may take various restrictive business practices to restrict competition and monopoly market, so as to get huge profits; their large international capital flow is likely to exert great influence on the host country's international balance of payments; they may also use the defects of the host's imperfect environment law and set up the factory with serious pollution and public nuisance, thus bring gross damage to the host country's environment and people's life and property. From the above aspects, the interests of transnational corporations may have contradictions and conflicts with the sovereignty and interests of the host country. Therefore, the host country must control the activities of transnational corporations through various legal means. In general, because the transnational corporation has particularity different from the general single business company, the task of the host country's legal control over the activities of transnational corporations is more difficult and complex.

跨国公司不仅与东道国存在着矛盾与冲突，而且与其母国也存在着矛盾与冲突。例如，跨国公司资本的大量输出，可能会减少母国国内的就业机会，减少母国商品的出口，导致技术外流、国内投资减少，影响母国的国际收支。跨国公司还可能利用避税港，通过转移定价的方式逃避母国的税收等。因此，母国对跨国公司的这些活动也会采取法律措施予以管制。

跨国公司母国与东道国对跨国公司活动的反应，可能转过来成为这些国家间紧张关系的祸端。例如，东道国实行财产国有化，母国行使外交保护，母国法律的域外适用以及税收管辖权的行使等，造成了东道国与母国间的种种严重冲突，从而给国际关系也带来影响。

2. 管辖冲突及其解决

跨国公司是国内法的产物，是国内法人，必须受国家管辖和管制。同时，由于跨国公司从事跨国投资经营活动，又会导致有关国家间的管辖冲突。

Transnational corporations have contradictions and conflicts not only with the host countries but also with their home countries. For example, large output of the transnational corporation's capital may reduce domestic jobs opportunities as well as domestic goods' exports, lead technology outflow, reduce domestic investment, and have influence on the balance of the home country's international payments. Transnational corporations may also use tax avoidance port to evade the home country's tax through transferring pricing. Therefore, the home country will also take legal measures to control the transnational corporation's activities.

The responses of the home country and the host country to the transnational corporation's activity, may in turn become the scourge of tight relationship between these countries. For example, when the host country executes property nationalization, the home country may exercise diplomatic protection, the extraterritorial application of laws and tax jurisdiction, which causes a variety of serious conflicts between the host and the home countries, also brings influence on international relations.

2. Jurisdictional Conflict and Its Solution

The transnational corporation, being established and running under the domestic law, is a domestic legal person, which must be subject to national jurisdiction and control. At the same time, because the transnational corporation is engaged in transnational investment and business operations, it will lead to the jurisdictional conflicts between the countries concerned.

1) 管辖冲突产生的原因

根据国际法，国家行使管辖权的依据主要有领域原则和国籍原则。跨国公司设在东道国的实体无论采取何种形式，均须服从东道国的领域管辖。但是，由于跨国公司又是其母国的实体，母国在某种情况下会对位于东道国的实体行使管辖权，从而可能导致管辖冲突。

但是，从国际实践上看，管辖的严重冲突主要源于有关国家将其经济法规域外适用。其域外管辖依据主要有两个。

(1) 效果原则。它是指当公司在国外的行为对国内产生"效果"(影响)时，就对其行使管辖权。效果原则是美国法院在 1948 年的"美国铝公司案"中提出的。在该案中，法国、瑞士、英国和加拿大的铝生产商在美国之外签订了一个国际卡特尔协议，分配铝的生产限额，影响到美国的商业。美国铝公司并未直接参与该卡特尔协议(只有其加拿大的子公司涉及该协议)，但美国依据效果原则对美国铝公司等提起诉讼。美国法院在该案中认为，在美国之外订立的合同或行为如对美国商业有重大效果(影响)，美国法院就对该行为享有管辖权。这一原则后来又被立法所确认。现在欧共体的有关国家也均接受并采纳这一原则。

---

1) The Reason of Jurisdictional Conflict

According to the international law, national jurisdiction is mainly based on the principles of field and nationality. No matter what form the entity uses, and the entity refers to the transnational corporation located in the host country, it shall be subject to the jurisdiction of the host domain. However, because the transnational corporation is the entity of the home country, in some cases the home country will exercise jurisdiction on the entity located in the host country, which may lead to the jurisdictional conflict.

However, from international practice, the serious conflicts of jurisdiction are originated from the economic laws' extraterritorial application by the countries concerned. The extraterritorial jurisdiction is mainly based on two principles.

(1) The principle of effect. It refers that when the company's foreign behavior has effect on the domestic, it should be exercised jurisdiction. The principle of effect is presented by the United States court in 1948 during the case of the Aluminum Company of the United States. In this case, aluminium producers of France, Switzerland, the UK and Canada signed an international cartel agreement outside the United States, distributing aluminum production quota, and affected the United States business. The Aluminum Company of the United States was not directly involved in the cartel agreement(only its Canadian affiliate has relation to the agreement), but the United States filed a lawsuit according to the principle of effect against the Aluminum Company of the United States. In this case the United States court thought that if contracts signed outside the United States or actions outside have significant effect on its business, the United States court has jurisdiction on this behavior. Later this principle was confirmed by the legislation. Now EC countries concerned have accepted and adopted this principle.

(2) 单一实体原则。根据这种理论，当跨国公司的母公司完全控制了其子公司，母子公司作为一个实体行动时，可无视它们各自具有的独立的法律人格，将其作为一个实体来进行管辖。例如，在"商业溶剂公司案"和"大陆制罐公司案"中，欧共体就是依据单一实体理论，把外国母公司及其位于欧共体内的子公司看作一个单一实体，对外国母公司行使管辖。

2) 解决管辖冲突的原则和方法

国家的管辖权是国家主权的重要内容之一，国家主权是平等的，因此，平等互利原则应是解决管辖冲突的出发点和目的。解决管辖冲突应采取如下原则和方法。

(1) 属地管辖权优先的原则。若根据国家管辖权原则，两国对同一经济实体或行为均有管辖权时，为解决管辖冲突，应确定领域管辖权或属地管辖权优先的原则。因为属地管辖权是一国主权的重要属性。跨国公司进入东道国之后，也就自动地置于该国的领域管辖之下，当其母国和东道国的利益发生冲突时，后者必须优先，这是一个原则，也是平等互利原则的一个必然结果。

(2) The principle of single entity. According to this theory, when the transnational corporation's parent company has fully controlled its subsidiary and takes action as an entity, we may ignore the respective independent legal personalities of parent company and its subsidiary and regard them as an entity to exercise jurisdiction. For example, in the "Case of Commercial Solvents Corporation." and the "Case of Continental Can Company", based on the theory of single entity, the European Community regarded the foreign parent company and its subsidiaries located in the European Community as a single entity, then exercised jurisdiction on the foreign parent company.

2) Principles and Methods for Resolving Jurisdictional Conflicts

National jurisdiction is one of the important contents of national sovereignty, and national sovereignty is equal, therefore, the principle of equality and mutual benefit should be the starting point and purpose to resolve the jurisdictional conflict. To resolve the jurisdictional conflict, the following principles and methods should be adopted.

(1) The principle of territorial jurisdiction's priority. If according to the principle of national jurisdiction, two states all have jurisdiction on the same economic entity or behavior, in order to resolve the conflict of jurisdiction, the principle of the area juris diction's or territorial jurisdiction's priority should be determined. Because the territorial jurisdiction is the important attribute of one state's sovereignty. After the transnational corporation enters the host country, it is automatically placed under its area jurisdiction, when its home country's and the host country's interests come into conflict, the latter must be in priority, it is a rule and also an inevitable result of the principle of equality and mutual benefit.

（2）域外管辖权的行使应有合理的依据。虽然目前国际法上尚不存在关于跨国公司管辖权问题的具体规则，但是一国在确定和行使域外管辖权时必须有合理的依据，不得滥用或过度行使管辖权，从而侵犯他国的主权。例如，前述效果原则就一直受到国际社会的批评。这一原则虽说是以客观领土原则为基础推导而来的，但是把它等同于国际社会普遍接受的领域原则是牵强附会的，因而也未被国际法和国际社会所接受。对于跨国公司实体的管辖来说，如海外子公司由于母公司的全面控制而完全失去自主性时，将母子公司看作一个单一实体进行管辖，可以说是一种可以接受的根据。

但值得注意的是，管辖权的行使是否合理，不是根据一国的标准来判断，而应根据国际法的平等互利原则来加以判断和权衡，应充分尊重别国的主权和利益。

（3）通过双边或多边途径协调。有关国家可以通过协议，在平等互利的基础上进行国际合作，规定事先通知和协商的程序来减缓冲突或采取措施避免冲突。例如，美国与联邦德国、澳大利亚、加拿大、欧共体等签订的关于反托拉斯相互合作的协议，对于解决管辖冲突就具有重要意义。可以说，这种在平等互利的基础上通过协议来解决管辖冲突的做法代表了未来的发展趋势。

---

(2) The exercise of the extraterritorial jurisdiction should have reasonable basis. Although in current international law there does not yet exist specific rules on the transnational corporation's jurisdiction, a country must have a rational basis while identifying and exercising extraterritorial jurisdiction, and shall not abuse or excessively exercise jurisdiction to infringe upon the sovereignty of other states. For example, the above principle of effects has been criticized by international community. Although this principle may be derived from objective territorial principle, it is not right to make it equivalent to the internationally accepted territorial principle, and thus this principle is not accepted by international law and international community. For the transnational corporation's jurisdiction, regarding the subsidiary and parent company as a single entity to exercise jurisdiction can be accepted as an acceptable basis when the subsidiary overseas completely loses autonomy because of the parent company's comprehensive control.

But it should be noted that, whether the exercise of jurisdiction is reasonable or not is not judged according to one state's standards, but judged and balanced in accordance with the principle of international laws' equality and mutual benefit, and any state should fully respect other states' sovereignty and interests.

(3) Cooperation through bilateral or multilateral approaches. The states concerned may take international cooperation by agreement on the basis of equality and mutual benefit, and regulate prior notification and consultation procedures to mitigate conflicts or take measures to avoid conflicts. For example, the agreement on antitrust mutual cooperation signed by the United States and the Federal Republic of Germany, Australia, Canada, EC, is of great significance to resolve the jurisdictional conflicts. It is certain that in practice such action to resolve the jurisdictional conflicts by agreement on the basis of equality and mutual benefit, represents the development trend of the future.

3.《联合国跨国公司行为守则》(草案)

由于跨国公司的组织和经营具有跨国性和全球性等特点，对于跨国公司的不当行为，单靠单个国家的法律管制是不可能有效的。鉴于在管理跨国公司的行为方面的困难，作为其主要东道国的广大发展中国家都希望制定一部统一的国际立法，以管理和控制跨国公司的行为，加强对跨国公司的活动的有效管制。与此同时，作为跨国公司母国的一些国家出于保护本国公司的投资安全和利益的考虑，也希望制定一套国际规范，确立关于跨国公司的公平和公正的待遇标准，以营造一种世界性的有利于外国直接投资的国际环境。正是在这种情况下，制定关于跨国公司行为守则的方案被提上了国际社会的议事日程。

1972 年，经过联合国经社理事会的一致同意，决定研究跨国公司对世界发展和国际关系的影响。1974 年 12 月经社理事会通过决议，决定成立跨国公司专门委员会，该委员会于 1982 年完成了《联合国跨国公司行为守则》(以下简称《守则》)草案的拟订工作，《守则》草案主要包括六大部分：①序言；②定义和适用范围；③跨国公司的活动与行为；④跨国公司的待遇；⑤政府间合作；⑥守则的实施。依其序言的规定，《守则》的目标在于尽量促使跨国公司对经济发展和增长作出贡献，尽量减少跨国公司活动的消极影响。

---

3. United Nations Code of Conduct on Transnational Corporations(Draft)

Because of the transnational and global characteristics of transnational corporations' organization and business, for their improper behavior, it is not likely to be effective just by the regulation of only one state's law. In view of the difficulties of management of transnational corporations' behavior, as their main host countries, many developing countries hope to formulate a unified international legislation to manage and control transnational corporations' behavior, in order to strengthen the effective jurisdiction on transnational corporations' activities. At the same time, some countries, as transnational corporations' home countries, in view of the protection of their domestic companies' security and interests, also hope to establish a set of international standards on transnational corporations' fair and equitable treatment standards, in order to build a worldwide international environment conducive to foreign direct investment. Under such condition, the scheme of conducting a code of conduct for transnational corporations has been put on the schedule of international community.

In 1972, the United Nations Council agreed to decide to study the transnational corporation's influence on the world development and international relations. In December 1974, the Agency Council agreed to set up a transnational corporation specialized committee. In 1982, the Committee completed *the United Nations Code of Conduct on Transnational Corporations*. The draft of the Code mainly includes six parts: (a)preface; (b)definitions and scope of application; (c)the activities and actions of transnational corporations; (d)the treatment of transnational corporations; (e)the cooperation between governments; (f)the implementation of the Code. According to its preface's provisions, the goal of the Code is to urge transnational corporations to make a contribution to economic development and growth and minimize the negative effects of transnational corporations' activities as far as possible.

1）跨国公司的活动

关于跨国公司活动的规范是《守则》草案的核心部分。这一部分的规定基本上是成功的。它从"一般性和政治性问题"，"经济、财务和社会问题"以及"资料公开"三个方面对跨国公司的权利和义务作了系统的规定，大体上确立起有关跨国公司各项活动和行为之准则的基本框架。

《守则》草案关于经济、财务和社会问题的规定主要涉及对投资的所有权和控制权、国际收支和金融财务、转移定价、税收、竞争和限制性商业惯例、技术转让、消费者保护、环境保护等问题，并大体上达成了一致。此外，草案关于资料公开方面的规定，现已全部达成了一致。

这一部分也有一些尚未解决的关键性问题，如关于国家的永久主权、关于跨国公司不应干涉东道国的内部事务等。对此，各国还存在着较大分歧。

1) The Activities of Transnational Corporations

The regulation on the activities of transnational corporation is the core part of the Code. The provisions of this part are basically successful. It made a systematic regulation of the transnational corporation's rights and obligations from three aspects, "the general and political problems", "the economic, financial and social problems" and "information disclosure", and it generally established a framework of standards on the transnational corporation's activities and behavior.

The draft of the Code's regulations on economic, financial and social issues is mainly related to the investment's ownership and controlling rights, balance of payments and financing, transferring pricing, taxation, competition and restrictive business practices, transferring technology, consumers' protection, environmental protection and other issues, and has reached an agreement in generally. In addition, now in the draft, all the regulations of information disclosure have been agreed.

This section also has some key issues unsolved, such as the state's permanent sovereignty and the transnational corporation should not interfere in the internal affairs of the host country. There are still great differences between countries.

2) 跨国公司的待遇

这一部分主要论及所在国对跨国公司的一般待遇、国有化、补偿、管辖权和争端解决。其中心思想是确立判断东道国对跨国公司待遇的适当和合法的标准。《守则》草案承认各国有权管制跨国公司的进入和设立企业；有权对其领域内的跨国公司财产实行征用或国有化，并支付补偿；跨国公司的实体受所在国管辖。与此同时，跨国公司应享有公正平等的待遇。

由于跨国公司的待遇问题在国际经济关系中是最有争议的问题，试图通过《守则》对其规定出一个普遍认同的国际标准无疑存在许多困难。从制定《守则》的谈判来看，在这一部分仍有许多问题悬而未决，其中，最关键的问题涉及国际法或国际义务问题。

3) 政府间合作和守则的实施

《守则》草案强调了政府间合作在实现其目标中的重要性，并为这种合作及其在国家层面和国际层面上的实施规定了一个框架。此外，《守则》草案还建立了定期审查守则的程序。上述这些规定一并构成了支配守则的实施途径。

---

2) The Treatment of Transnational Corporations

This part mainly deals with general treatment, nationalization, compensation, jurisdiction and dispute resolution of the host country to the transnational corporation. The central idea is to decide the appropriate and legal standard of the treatment of the host country to the transnational corporation. The draft of the Code admits that each country has the right to control the transnational corporation entering and setting up enterprise and the right to implement expropriation on the transnational corporation's property in its field or nationalization and pay compensation. The entity of the transnational corporation is under the jurisdiction of its host country. At the same time, the transnational corporation should enjoy equal treatment.

Because the treatment of the transnational corporation is the most controversial issue in international economic relations, no doubt there are many difficulties in regulating generally accepted international standards just according to the Code. According to the negotiation of the Code's formulation, in this part there are still many problems to be solved, in which the most crucial issue is related to international law or international obligations.

3) The Cooperation between Governments and the Implementation of the Code

The draft of the Code also emphasizes the importance of the collaboration between governments in achieving its objectives, and regulates a framework for such cooperation and its implementation at national and international level. In addition, the draft of the Code also establishes a regular program to review the Code. All the above provisions together constitute the ways of dominating the Code's implementation.

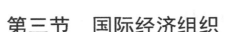

第三节 国际经济组织

一、国际经济组织作为国际经济法主体的资格

从广义来说，国际经济组织可分为政府间组织和非政府间组织两大类。这两类组织虽都是一种超出国界的跨国机构，但两者在国际法上的法律地位显然是不同的。这里所说的是狭义上的国际组织，即政府间的国际经济组织。

国际经济组织的主要特征如下所述。

(1) 国际经济组织的主要参加者是国家。

(2) 国际经济组织是国家间基于主权平等原则设立的机构，不是凌驾于国家之上的组织。

(3) 国际经济组织是以国家间的正式协议为基础的，这种协议在性质上属于国家间的多边条约。

2.3 International Economic Organizations

2.3.1 The Qualification of International Economic Organizations as the Subjects of IEL

In a broad sense, international economic organizations can be divided into two categories, intergovernmental and non-governmental organizations. These two types are multinational institutions beyond the boundaries, but in international law, they are obviously different in position. Here is an international organization in the narrow sense, namely the intergovernmental international economic organization.

The main characteristics of the international economic organization are as follows.

(1) The main participants of the international economic organization are states.

(2) The international economic organization is an institution established by countries based on the principle of sovereign equality, not an organization to override the country.

(3) The international economic organization is based on a formal agreement in the nature of the multilateral treaty between states.

1. 国际经济组织的法律人格

国际经济组织必须具有一定的法律人格，才能作为国际经济法的主体行使权利和承担义务，在其职能范围内开展活动。一个国际经济组织是否具有法律人格，取决于各成员国建立该组织的基本文件的规定。

一般来说，一些重要国际经济组织，为了实现其宗旨，均被赋予其法律人格，使其能在法定范围内行使权利并履行义务。与主权国家具有的法律人格不同，国际经济组织的法律人格取决于国家的授权，其权利能力和行为能力的范围取决于其特定的宗旨与职能，取决于其基本文件的规定。

具有法律人格的国际经济组织，在其基本文件规定的范围内不受任何国家权力管辖，具有在国际法和国内法上的符合其宗旨和职能的法律能力。其基本的法律能力包括缔约能力、取得和处置财产的能力、进行法律诉讼的能力。

(1) 缔约能力。国际经济组织为了执行其职能有权同有关国家缔结条约，同时也有权在成员国内同有关自然人和法人订立契约等。

(2) 取得和处置财产的能力。国际经济组织要执行其职能，从事活动，必然要具有和涉及相应的财产，因此，取得和处置财产(包括动产和不动产)是其法律能力的重要内容之一。

---

1. The Legal Personality of International Economic Organizations

International economic organizations must have legal personality to exercise rights and undertake obligations as the subject of international economic law, and carry out activities within their functions' scope. Whether an international economic organization has legal personality or not, depends on the regulation of the organization's basic documents that each member country uses to establish this organization.

In general, in order to achieve their purposes some important international economic organizations are given legal personality, so that they can exercise their rights and perform their duties in the statutory scope. Different from a sovereign state's legal personality, the international economic organization's legal personality depends on the state's authorization. Its range of power and capacity depends on its specific purpose, function, and the basic documents.

In the range of basic documents, the international economic organization with legal personality is not subject to the jurisdiction of any states' authority, and has legal capacity due to its purpose and function in international and domestic law. The basic legal abilities include contracting, acquiring and disposing property, and ability of legal proceedings.

(1) Contracting capacity. In order to perform its function, the international economic organization has the right to sign a treaty with the countries concerned, and also has the right to conclude a contract with the relevant natural persons and legal persons of its member states.

(2) The capacity of acquisition and disposition of the property. The international economic organization must have corresponding property in order to perform its function and take part in activities, therefore, to acquire and dispose the property (including movable and immovable property) is one of the important contents of its legal capacity.

（3）进行法律诉讼的能力。国际经济组织既有在国际法庭诉讼的能力，同时也有在成员国内进行诉讼的能力，以使其可以通过诉讼维护其权利。

必须注意的是，国际经济组织如果要在非成员国进行活动，其法律人格和法律能力必须得到非成员国的承认。因为国际经济组织赖以建立的基本文件的性质是一种多边条约，它只对成员国具有拘束力，成员国参加或批准该基本文件就表明它承认了该国际经济组织具有法律人格。但国际经济组织的基本文件对非成员国没有约束力，非成员国无义务授予该国际经济组织以某种法律能力。

2. 国际经济组织的特权与豁免

国际经济组织享有一定的特权和豁免。这种特权与豁免也来自于成员国的授权。成员之所以赋予某国际经济组织以特权与豁免在法理解释上有两种主张，一为职能必要说，二为代表性说。前者认为国际经济组织享有特权与豁免是为了使其能更好地履行其职能，实现其基本文件规定的宗旨和任务；后者认为国际经济组织在其规定的范围内代表了成员的愿望和利益，应以国家集合体的身份享有一定的外交特权与豁免。

---

(3) Ability of legal proceedings. The international economic organization has the ability of legal proceedings both in international court and in the member countries, so that it can protect its rights and interests through lawsuit.

It should be noted that if the international economic organization takes part in activities in non-member countries, its legal personality and capacity must be admitted by the non-member countries. Because the nature of the basic documents that the international economic organization is based on is a multilateral treaty, and it has binding effect only on the members, the members' participating or approval of the basic documents means that they admit the international economic organization's legal personality. But the international economic organization's basic documents have no binding effect on the non-member countries, and the non-member countries have no obligation to authorize the international economic organization legal capacity.

2. The Privileges and Immunities of International Economic Organizations

The international economic organization has certain privileges and immunities, which are also from the authority of the member countries. In legal interpretation, there are two kinds of views for the reason why the member countries give the international economic organization privileges and immunities. One is the theory of the functions necessary and the other is the theory of representative. The former is that the international economic organization should have privileges and immunities in order to perform its functions much better and to achieve the purposes and tasks regulated by its basic documents; the latter is that the international economic organization represents the member countries' aspiration and interests in the specified range, so it should have some certain diplomatic privileges and immunities as the body of the National Assembly.

国际经济组织所享受的特权与豁免因其性质和职能而异。国际经济组织的特权与豁免通常限于执行职能所必要的范围。一般来说，其具体内容通常包括财产和资产免受搜查、征用、没收或其他形式的扣押，档案不受侵犯等。但由于各国际经济组织的职能不同，其特权与豁免的范围也有宽有窄。例如，世界银行集团与国际货币基金组织的特权与豁免就不完全相同。国际货币基金组织的财产或资产享受任何形式司法程序的豁免，只有当它已作为原告表示放弃司法豁免时，才能对它进行诉讼。而世界银行集团的资产，可以在诉讼一方经法院判决后予以扣押或执行。国际经济组织的工作人员的特权与豁免则限于独立执行任务的范围。

二、主要的国际经济组织

国际经济组织根据其宗旨、职能、成员构成等因素可分成以下几类。

(1) 普遍性国际经济组织，指那些成员资格对世界各国开放，调整国际经济重要事务的组织，如国际货币基金组织、世界银行集团、世界贸易组织等。

The international economic organization has different privileges and immunities due to its character and function. The international economic organization's privileges and immunities are usually limited to the range of necessary performing functions. In general, the specific contents usually include property and asset's immunity from searching, requisition, confiscating or other form of seizure, and files' immunity from infringement, etc. But because of the difference of each international economic organization's function, the ranges of the privileges and immunities also have difference. For example, the privileges and immunities of World Bank Group and International Monetary Fund are not completely the same. The property or asset of International Monetary Fund has immunity from any legal process, only when it gives up judicial immunity as plaintiff, the proceedings for it can be conducted. While World Bank Group's assets can be seized or executed after the proceedings' party has been sentenced by the court. The privileges and immunities for the staff of the international economic organization are limited to the range of performing tasks independently.

2.3.2　The Major International Economic Organizations

The international economic organizations can be divided into several categories according to the purposes, functions, members and other factors.

(1) Universal international economic organizations, referring to the organizations whose membership open to the world and restructuring the important international economic affairs, such as International Monetary Fund, World Bank Group, World Trade Organization.

（2）区域性国际经济组织，指那些由同一区域若干国家组成的国际经济组织，例如欧洲联盟、北美自由贸易区、安第斯条约组织等。

（3）专业性国际经济组织，这主要是指初级产品出口国和国际商品组织。初级产品出口国包括石油输出国组织、铜矿出口国政府联合委员会、天然橡胶生产国联盟、香蕉输出国联盟等；国际商品组织是指某种商品的出口国与消费国就该商品的购销和稳定价格等问题缔结的政府间多边贸易协定以及据此建立的国际组织。

普遍性国际经济组织涉及国际货币、金融、贸易等重要领域，且成员众多，在调整国际经济关系中发挥着十分重要的作用。下面对世界贸易组织加以简介。

世界贸易组织是根据 1994 年 4 月 15 日在摩洛哥马拉喀什签订的《世界贸易组织协定》成立的，是关税与贸易总协定(简称为"关贸总协定")乌拉圭回合谈判取得的重大成果之一。世界贸易组织(简称为"世贸组织")是《1947 年关贸总协定》的继续和发展。关贸总协定虽然可以说是一个事实上的国际组织，但它毕竟不是一个正式制度化的组织，而世贸组织则是一个在关贸总协定基础上发展而成的正式国际组织。

除该协定或其他多边贸易协定另有规定外，世界贸易组织应受《1947 年关贸总协定》缔约方大会及总协定框架内各机构所有规定、程序和习惯做法的指导。

---

(2) Regional international economic organizations, referring to the international economic organizations consisted by some nations from the same region, such as European Union, North American Free Trade Area, Andean Pact Organization, etc.

(3) Professional international economic organizations, mainly referring to the countries of primary products export and international commodity organizations. The former includes the Organizations of Petroleum Exporting Countries, Copper Exports Country and Government Council, Natural Rubber Producers Union, Union of Banana. The latter refers to international organizations according to the multilateral trade agreements, which are concluded between the governments on the buying and selling of goods and the commodity's stable price.

Universal international economic organizations involve international monetary, financial, trade and other important areas, have many members, and play a very important role in the adjustment of international economic relations. In the following part, the World Trade Organization will be briefly introduced.

World Trade Organization is set up based on *Agreement of World Trade Organization* signed on April 15, 1994 in Morocco, and is one of the significant results achieved by the negotiations of GATT's Uruguay Round. World Trade Organization (WTO) is the continuation and development of *GATT(1947)*. GATT can be said to be a *de facto* international organization, but not a formal organization, while WTO is a formal international organization on the basis of the development of GATT.

In addition to the agreement or other multilateral trade agreement providing otherwise, WTO is under the guidance of *GATT(1947)* Contracting Party Congress and the rules, procedures and practices inside the GATT frame bodies.

世界贸易组织的职能，概括说来，是为世界贸易组织协定和若干单项贸易协议的执行、管理、运作提供方便和共同机构的框架，为各成员方的多边贸易关系谈判提供场所，对《关于争端解决的规则和程序的谅解》进行管理等。

世界贸易组织的主要机构有部长级会议、总理事会、秘书处等。

(1) 部长级会议。由各成员的部长级代表组成，是世界贸易组织的最高权力机构，每两年至少召开一次会议，它有权对各多边贸易协定所涉及的一切问题按法定程序作出决定并在其职能范围内采取行动。

(2) 总理事会。由所有成员各派常驻代表组成，是部长会议休会期间代行其职权的执行机关，执行《世界贸易组织协定》赋予的各项职能，如履行贸易政策、审查及解决争端等职责。总理事会下设几个分理事会：货物贸易理事会、服务贸易理事会、与贸易有关的知识产权理事会，负责监督执行有关多边贸易协定、《服务贸易总协议》以及《与贸易有关的知识产权协定》。

(3) 秘书处。它是一个以部长会议任命的一位总干事为其最高负责人的日常工作机关。总干事任期4年，是世界贸易组织的行政首长。

Generally speaking, World Trade Organization is to provide convenience and common institutional framework for the WTO agreements and several individual trade agreements' implementation, management and operation, to provide a place for the multilateral trade negotiations of their members, and to manage the procedures of *Understanding on Rules and Procedures Governing the Settlement of Disputes*.

The main bodies of World Trade Organization are Ministerial Conference, the General Council, the Secretariat, and etc.

(1) Ministerial Conference. It is made up of the members' ministerial representatives, has the highest authority of WTO, and at least has one meeting every two years. It has the right to make decisions on the multilateral trade agreements involving the related issues in accordance with legal procedures and take actions within the scope of its functions.

(2) The General Council. It is made up of all member parties' representatives, which is the organ in place of Ministerial Conference's executive functions and powers during its rest, and performs every function given by *Agreement of World Trade Organization*, such as performing trade policy, reviewing and resolving disputes and other duties. The General Council also has several branch councils: Council for Trade in Goods, Council for Trade in Services, Council for Trade-Related Aspects of Intellectual Property Rights, and they are responsible for overseeing the implementation of the multilateral trade agreements, *the General Agreement on Trade in Services* and *Agreement on Trade-Related Aspects of Intellectual Property*.

(3) The Secretariat. It is responsible for routine work organ with a general director appointed by ministers. The general director works for a term of 4 years, who is the chief administrative officer of WTO.

在决策程序和表决制度方面，世界贸易组织继续沿用 1947 年的关税与贸易总协定所适用的协商一致的决策程序。若未能协商一致，则采取投票方式。各成员均有一票投票权。除基本文件另有规定外，部长级会议与总理事会的决议应以多数票通过。对于某些特定事项，如对有关协定的解释、撤销有关协定施加给某成员的义务，其决定须经成员的四分之三多数票通过。

世界贸易组织的成员分为创始成员和纳入成员两类。创始成员是指在《世界贸易组织协定》生效之前已是《1947 年关税与贸易总协定》的缔约成员，并已表示接受《世界贸易组织协定》及其他各协定及文件者。纳入成员则指其他任何国家和地区按照法定条件及程序进行申请，并经部长级会议三分之二以上多数票同意吸收的成员。

综 合 练 习

1. 自然人作为国际经济法主体的资格是什么？
2. 法人作为国际经济法主体资格应如何确认？
3. 跨国公司的法律地位是什么？
4. 跨国公司母公司对子公司债务责任的学说根据是什么？

In the process of decision-making and the voting system, WTO continues using the consensus decision-making process applied by General Agreement on Tariffs and Trade (GATT)in 1947. If consensus is not reached, then it is decided by voting. Each member is entitled to one vote. In addition to the basic document specified otherwise, the decision of the Ministerial Conference and the General Council shall be made by majority votes. For some specific issues, such as the interpretation of agreements, the revoking of a member's obligations required by the agreement, its decision must be approved by a three-fourths majority of the members' votes.

Members of WTO are divided into two kinds, original members and acceding members. Original members refer to those that have got *GATT(1947)* membership and have accepted the WTO Agreement and all other agreements and documents before the *Agreement of World Trade Organization* took into force. Acceding members refer to the members that any other countries and regions that make an application in accordance with statutory conditions and procedures, and are agreed by the above two-thirds majority votes of the Ministerial Conference.

Comprehensive Exercises

1. What's the qualification of the natural person as the subject of IEL?
2. How can we identify the legal person's qualification as the subject of IEL?
3. What's the legal status of transnational corporations?
4. What's the theory basis of the debt liability of transnational corporation's parent company to subsidiary?

第三章 国际货物买卖法律制度

学习目标

掌握国际货物买卖合同的内涵。

掌握提单、海运单、国际多式联运的概念。

掌握《联合国国际货物销售合同公约》和《国际贸易术语解释通则》等法律文件，理解国际货物买卖法律体系的特征。

Chapter 3 Legal System on the International Sale of Goods

Learning Objectives

To grasp the connotation of contracts for the international sale of goods.

To grasp the concept of bill of lading, sea waybill, international multimodal transport.

To understand the characteristics of the legal system on the international sale of goods through *the United Nations Convention on Contracts for the International Sale of Goods (CISG)* and *the International Rules for the Interpretation of Trade Terms (INCOTERMS)* etc.

第一节　国际货物买卖

一、国际货物买卖的国际商业惯例

1. 国际货物买卖惯例概述

国际货物贸易也许可以离开国际条约，但却很难离开国际货物买卖惯例。各种民间组织制定的许多标准规则和共同条件是提高国际货物贸易效率，减少国际货物贸易纠纷的最有力工具。这些标准规则和共同条件带有任意性，由当事人自主选择适用，其中最著名的包括：《国际贸易术语解释通则》(以下简称《通则》)、《1932 年华沙——牛津规则》和《美国 1941 年对外贸易定义》。

3.1　The International Sale of Goods

3.1.1　International Commercial Practices in the International Sale of Goods

1. An Overview of Commercial Practices in the International Sale of Goods

International sale of goods may go without conventions, but it can hardly go without commercial practices in the international sale of goods. Nongovernmental organizations in different characters map out standard rules and general conditions to promote trade efficiency and to decrease trade disputes. Those standard rules and general conditions have optional nature, and are based on the self-determined option of the parties. The most famous commercial practices include *International Commercial Terms of International Chamber of Commerce (INCOTERMS)*, *Warsaw-Oxford Rules 1932* and *Revised American Foreign Trade Definitions 1941*.

《1932 年华沙——牛津规则》和《美国 1941 年对外贸易定义》均为 CIF 术语(成本、保险加运费)提供了标准化的解释，而交货条款在美洲的国际货物买卖中的运用极为广泛。然而，在实践中得到最广泛使用的则是《国际贸易术语解释通则》。《通则》由国际商会首次发布于 1936 年，其界定了成本、风险，以及国际贸易中买方和卖方的义务。而且，国际商会每隔一段时间就会以发布新版《通则》的形式对旧版本的《通则》进行修改和补充。这些修改和补充使得《通则》中的术语具有适应国际货物贸易中的技术和实践的发展变化的能力。历经 1953 年、1967 年、1976 年、1980 年、1990 年和 2000 年的修订，目前最新版的《通则》是《通则 2010》。

使用术语的目的在于使国际货物买卖合同的解释更加便利并且得到全球范围内的一致认可。当然，为精确理解这些世界范围内广泛使用的术语，人们最频繁使用的参考文献就是《通则》。《通则》最显著的意义就在于为合同双方提供了一套对双方意义完全一致，能够被世界各国司法机构作出一致解释的标准术语。《通则》并不是国内法或国际法的组成部分，但只要国际贸易双方在贸易合同中明确指定了适用某个版本的《通则》，这一版本的《通则》就对买卖双方具有约束力。

Warsaw-Oxford Rules 1932 and *Revised American Foreign Trade Definitions 1941* respectively provide standard interpretation for CIF (cost, insurance, freight) and delivery terms which are widely used in America. However, it is *INCOTERMS* that have been most widely used in international trade. *INCOTERMS* were first published by the International Chamber of Commerce (ICC) in 1936, which defined the costs, risks, and obligations of buyers and sellers in international transactions. Furthermore, the ICC has periodically introduced new trade terms and revised existing terms to accommodate new technological and practical changes in the international sale of goods. The amendments and additions were made in 1953, 1967, 1976, 1980, 1990, 2000 and presently the latest version of *INCOTERMS* was published in 2010.

Trade terms, primarily used to interpret contracts for the international sale of goods in a more convenient way, have been recognized by the markets all over the world. Of course, as to the precise understanding of those widely used trade terms, the most frequently used reference is *INCOTERMS*. The most remarkable significance of *INCOTERMS* is to provide a set of standardized terms which mean exactly the same to both parties to a contract and which will be interpreted in exactly the same way by courts in every country. *INCOTERMS* are not part of national or international laws, but they can be binding on buyers or sellers provided the sale contract specifies that a particular *INCOTERMS* will apply.

若必须适用特定贸易地的习俗或交易双方在此前的交易中确立起来的交易惯例，则交易双方应在贸易合同中表明遵守这些习俗和惯例，并确定双方的有关权利和义务。这些贸易合同中的特殊约定可以更改任何《通则》载明的术语解释规则。

2. 《2010 国际贸易术语解释通则》

2010 年 9 月 27 日，国际商会正式推出《通则 2010》，新版本于 2011 年 1 月 1 日正式生效。《通则 2010》旨在防止贸易合同理解差异造成的争议，帮助国际贸易双方划分权利和义务、成本和交货时的风险转移界限。同时，依据《通则 2000》或其他版本的通则订立的合同并不会在 2011 年以后受到影响。国际贸易双方既可以使用国际商会推荐的《通则 2010》，也可以使用《通则 2000》或者交易双方更加熟悉的任何其他版本的《通则》。因此，在国际贸易合同中明确所适用的《通则》版本至关重要。

需要强调的是，《通则》的适用范围限于国际货物贸易双方的权利与义务(且仅限于有形物，而不包括无形物，比如绘图软件)。

If it is necessary to refer to the customs of a particular trade place or to the practices which the parties themselves may have established in their previous dealings, it is desirable that sellers and buyers clarify the customs and practices to comply with, and determine rights and obligations in their sale contract. Such special provisions in a sales contract would change anything that is set forth as a rule for interpreting the various *INCOTERMS*.

2. *INCOTERMS 2010*

Launched on September 27, 2010, *INCOTERMS 2010* came into effect on January 1, 2011. *INCOTERMS 2010* rules help buyers and sellers avoid the dispute from misunderstandings by clarifying the rights and obligations, costs and risks involved in the delivery of goods in international sale contract. At the same time, all contracts made under *INCOTERMS 2000* or any other version of *INCOTERMS* remain valid even after 2011. Parties to a contract for the sale of goods can agree to choose any version of *INCOTERMS*. Either the 2010 version recommended by the ICC, or *INCOTERMS 2000*, or any other version that the traders may be more familiar with. As a result, it is important to clearly specify the chosen version.

It should be noted that the scope of *INCOTERMS* is limited to matters relating to the rights and obligations of the parties to the contract of sale with respect to the delivery of goods sold (in the sense of "tangibles", not including "intangibles" such as plot software).

《通则》在传统意义被用于存在跨境运输的国际销售合同中，此种交易需要将货物进行跨越国境的运输，但《通则》在实践中也不时出现在纯粹的国内货物贸易合同中。时至今日，在世界许多地区，如欧盟这样的商贸集团已经使得不同国家间的过关手续变得不那么重要。因此，《通则 2010》通过副标题正式认可该通则既可以适用于国内的也可以适用于国际的销售合同。而且，《通则 2010》在某些条款明确规定，只有在适当的情形下，才存在遵守进/出口手续义务。

　　《通则 2010》在前言中提到，《通则》的术语设置考虑了不断增加的免税贸易区，在商务中不断增多的电子沟通，以及被更加重视的货物运输中的安全和联合运输等问题。《通则 2010》更新并加强了交货规则，将规则总量从 13 条减少到了 11 条(见表 3-1)，并且使得所有规则的表述更加简洁、明确。《通则 2010》也是第一个供买卖双方公平适用的国际贸易术语解释版本。

　　INCOTERMS rules have traditionally been used in international sales contracts where goods pass across national borders, but in practice *INCOTERMS* are at times also incorporated into contracts for the sale of goods within purely domestic markets. Nowadays, in various areas of the world, however, trade blocs, like the European Union, have made border measures between different countries less significant. Consequently, the subtitle of *INCOTERMS 2010* rules formally recognizes that they are available for application to both international and domestic sale contracts. Furthermore, *INCOTERMS 2010* rules clearly state some places that the obligation to comply with export/import formalities exists only where applicable.

　　According to the foreword of *INCOTERMS 2010*, the rules take account of the continued spread of customs-free zones, the increased use of electronic communications in business transactions, heightened concerns about security in the movement of goods and consolidation in transport practices. *INCOTERMS 2010* updates and consolidates the delivery rules, reducing the total number of rules from 13 to 11(as shown in Table 3-1), and offers a simpler and clearer presentation of all the rules. *INCOTERMS 2010* is also the first version of *INCOTERMS* rules to make all references to buyers and sellers evenhanded.

表 3-1　《通则 2010》贸易术语简表

简　写	全　称	采用运输方式
EXW	工厂交货	任何运输方式
FCA	货交承运人	
CPT	运费付至	
CIP	运费和保险费付至	
DAT *	终点站交货	
DAP *	目的地交货	
DDP	完税后交货	
FAS	船边交货	海上及内陆水运方式
FOB	船上交货	
CFR	成本加运费	
CIF	成本、保险费加运费	

注：DAT 和 DAP 是新增加的术语。

Table 3-1　Rules of *INCOTERMS 2010*

Abbreviation	Full name	Modes of transport
EXW	Ex Works	Any mode of transport
FCA	Free Carrier	
CPT	Carriage Paid to	
CIP	Carriage and Insurance Paid to	
DAT *	Delivered at Terminal	
DAD *	Delivered at Place	
DDP	Delivered Duty Paid	
FAS	Free alongside Ship	Sea and inland waterway modes of transport
FOB	Free on Board	
CFR	Cost and Freight	
CIF	Cost , Insurance and Freight	

Note: Two new *INCOTERMS* rules —— DAT and DAP.

3. 《通则 2010》术语

《通则 2010》中的十一种术语如下。

1) 工厂交货(EXW)

"工厂交货(指定地点)"是指当卖方在其所在地或其他指定的地点(如工场、工厂、仓库等)将货物交给买方处置时，即完成交货。卖方无须将货物装上任何运输工具，在需要办理出口清关手续时，卖方亦不必为货物办理出口清关手续。

双方都应该尽可能明确地指定货物交付地点，因为此时(交付前的)费用与风险由卖方承担。买方必须承担在双方约定的地点或在指定地受领货物的全部费用和风险。

EXW 是卖方承担责任最小的术语。它应遵守以下使用规则：卖方没有义务为买方装载货物，即使在实际中由卖方装载货物可能更方便。若由卖方装载货物，相关风险和费用亦由买方承担。如果卖方在装载货物中处于优势地位，则使用由卖方承担装载费用与风险的 FCA 术语通常更合适。买方使用 EXW 术语与卖方进行交易时应知晓，卖方仅在买方要求(更符合合术语特质)办理出口手续时负有协助的义务：(但是)卖方并无义务办理出口清关手续。因此，如果买方不能直接或间接地办理出口清关手续，建议买方不要使用 EXW 术语。

---

3. *INCOTERMS 2010* Rules

INCOTERMS 2010 consists of eleven trade terms, which including:

1) Ex Works (EXW)

"Ex Works" means that the seller delivers when it places the goods at the disposal of the buyer at the seller's premises or at another named place (i.e., works, factory, warehouse, etc.). The seller does not need to load the goods on any collecting vehicle, nor does it need to clear the goods for export, where such clearance is applicable.

The parties are well advised to specify as clearly as possible the point within the named place of delivery, as the costs and risks to that point are for the account of the seller. The buyer bears all costs and risks involved in taking the goods from the agreed point, if any, at the named place of delivery.

EXW represents the minimum obligation for the seller. The rule should be used with care as: The seller has no obligation to the buyer to load the goods, even though in practice the seller may be in a better position to do so. If the seller does load the goods, it does so at the buyer's risk and expense. In cases where the seller is in a better position to load the goods, FCA, which obliges the seller to do so at its own risk and expense, is usually more appropriate. A buyer who buys from a seller on an EXW basis for export needs to be aware that the seller has an obligation to provide only such assistance as the buyer may require to effect that export: the seller is not bound to organize the export clearance. Buyers are therefore well advised not to use EXW if they cannot directly or indirectly obtain export clearance.

买方承担向卖方提供关于货物出口之信息的有限义务。但是，卖方可能需要这些信息用于诸如纳税、报关等目的。

2) 货交承运人(FCA)

这一术语可以适用于任何一种选定的运输方式，也可以适用于多种运输方式联合使用的情况。

"货交承运人"是指卖方于其所在地或其他指定地点将货物交付给承运人或买方指定人。买卖双方尽可能清楚地明确说明指定交货的具体地点，风险将在此地点转移至买方。若买卖双方意图在卖方所在地交付货物，则应当确定该所在地的地址，即指定交货地点。另一方面，若买卖双方意图在其他地点交付货物，则应当明确确定一个不同的具体交货地点。

"货交承运人"要求卖方在需要时办理出口清关手续。但是，卖方没有办理进口清关手续的义务，也无须缴纳任何进口关税或者办理其他进口海关手续。

3) 运费付至(CPT)

这一术语适用于所选择的任何一种运输方式，也适用于多种运输方式联合使用的情况。

The buyer has limited obligations to provide to the seller any information regarding the export of the goods. However, the seller may need this information for, e.g. taxation or reporting purposes.

2) Free Carrier (FCA)

This rule may be used irrespective of the mode of transport selected and may also be used where more than one mode of transport is employed.

FCA means that the seller delivers the goods to the carrier or another person nominated by the buyer at the seller's premises or another named place. The parties are well advised to specify as clearly as possible the point within the named place of delivery, as the risk passes to the buyer at that point. If the parties intend to deliver the goods at the seller's premises, they should identify the address of those premises as the named place of delivery. If, on the other hand, the parties intend the goods to be delivered at another place, they must identify a different specific place of delivery.

FCA requires the seller to clear the goods for export, where applicable. However, the seller has no obligation to clear the goods for import, pay any import duty or carry out any import customs formalities.

3) Carriage Paid to (CPT)

This rule may be used irrespective of the mode of transport selected and may also be used where more than one mode of transport is employed.

"运费付至"指卖方在指定交货地向承运人或由其(卖方)指定的其他人交货，并且其(卖方)须与承运人订立运输合同，载明并实际承担将货物运送至指定目的地所产生的必要费用。

在 CPT, CIP, CFR, 或 CIF 适用的情形下，卖方的交货义务在于将货物交付承运人，而非货物到达指定目的地时，即告完全履行。

此术语有两个关键点，因为风险和成本在不同的地方发生转移。买卖双方应在买卖合同中尽可能准确地确定两个地点：风险转移至买方的交货地点；卖方须订立运输合同中载明的指定目的地。如果使用多个承运人将货物运至指定目的地，且买卖双方并未对具体交货地点有所约定，则合同默认风险自货物由买方交给第一承运人时转移，卖方对这一交货地点的选取具有排除买方控制的绝对选择权。如果双方希望风险的转移推迟至稍后的地点(例如：某海港或机场)，那么它们需要在买卖合同中明确约定这一点。由于将货物运至指定目的地的费用由卖方承担，因而双方应尽可能准确地确定目的地中的具体地点，且卖方须在运输合同中载明这一具体的交货地点。卖方基于其运输合同，在指定目的地卸货时，如果产生了相关费用，卖方无权向买方索要，除非双方有其他约定。

"运费付至"要求卖方在需要时办理出口清关手续。但是，卖方没有办理进口清关手续的义务，也无须缴纳任何进口关税或者办理其他进口海关手续。

CPT means that the seller delivers the goods to the carrier or another person nominated by the seller at an agreed place and that the seller must contract for and pay the costs of carriage necessary to bring the goods to the named place of destination.

When CPT, CIP, CFR or CIF are used, the seller fulfills its obligation to deliver when it hands the goods over to the carrier and not when the goods reach the place of destination.

CPT has two critical points, because risk passes and costs are transferred at different places. The parties are well advised to identify as precisely as possible in the contract both the place of delivery, where the risk passes to the buyer, and the named place of destination to which the seller must contract for the carriage. If several carriers are used for the carriage to the agreed destination and the parties do not agree on a specific point of delivery, the default position is that risk passes when the goods have been delivered to the first carrier at a point entirely of the seller's choosing and over which the buyer has no control. Should the parties wish the risk to pass at a later stage (e.g. at an ocean port or airport), they need to specify this in their sale contract. The parties are also well advised to identify as precisely as possible the point within the agreed place of destination, as the costs to that point are for the account of the seller. The seller is advised to procure contracts of carriage that match this choice precisely. If the seller incurs costs under its contract of carriage related to unloading at the named place of destination, the seller is not entitled to recover such costs from the buyer unless otherwise agreed between the parties.

CPT requires the seller to clear the goods for export, where applicable. However, the seller has no obligation to clear the goods for import, pay any import duty or carry out any import customs formalities.

4) 运费和保险费付至(CIP)

这一术语可适用于任何一种选定的运输方式，也可以适用于多种运输方式联合使用的情况。

"运费和保险费付至"含义是在约定的地方(如果双方约定了这样的地点)卖方向承运人或是卖方指定的另一个人发货，卖方必须签订运输合同并支付将货物运至目的地的运费。

卖方还必须订立保险合同以防买方货物在运输途中灭失或损坏的风险。买方应注意到CIP(运费和保险费付至指定目的地)术语只要求卖方投保最低限度的保险险别。

由于风险和费用转移的地点不同，本规则有两个关键的地点。买卖双方最好在合同中尽可能精确地确认这两个交货地点：风险转移至买方的交货地，以及卖方必须订立运输合同将货物运达的指定目的地。若将货物运输至约定目的地用到若干承运人而买卖双方未就具体交货点达成一致，则默认为风险自货物于某一交货点被交付至第一承运人时转移；而这一交付地点完全由卖方决定，不由买方控制；如果买卖双方希望风险在之后的某一阶段转移，则它们需要在其买卖合同中明确规定。卖方最好签订与此次交易精确匹配的运输合同。

CIP 术语要求卖方在需要时办理货物出口清关手续。但是，卖方没义务办理货物进口清关手续，支付任何进口关税或者履行任何进口报关手续。

---

4) Carriage and Insurance Paid to (CIP)

This rule may be used irrespective of the mode of transport selected and may also be used where more than one mode of transport is employed.

CIP means that the seller delivers the goods to the carrier or another person nominated by the seller at an agreed place (if any such place is agreed between the parties) and that the seller must contract for and pay the costs of carriage necessary to bring the goods to the named place of destination.

The seller also contracts for insurance cover against the buyer's risk of loss of or damage to the goods during the carriage. The buyer should note that under CIP the seller is required to obtain insurance only on minimum cover.

CIP has two critical points, because risk passes and costs are transferred at different places. The parties are well advised to identify as precisely as possible in the contract both the place of delivery, where the risk passes to the buyer, and the named place of destination to which the seller must contract for carriage. If several carriers are used for the carriage to the agreed destination and the parties do not agree on a specific point of delivery, the default position is that risk passes when the goods have been delivered to the first carrier at a point entirely of the seller's choosing and over which the buyer has no control. Should the parties wish the risk to pass at a later stage, they need to specify this in their sale contract. The seller is advised to procure contracts of carriage that match this choice precisely.

CIP requires the seller to clear the goods for export, where applicable. However, the seller has no obligation to clear the goods for import, pay any import duty or carry out any import customs formalities.

5) 终点站交货(DAT)

这一术语适用于任何一种选定的运输方式，也适用于多种运输方式联合使用的情况。

"终点站交货"是指卖方在指定的目的港或目的地的指定的终点站卸货后将货物交给买方处置，即完成交货。"终点站"包括任何地方，无论约定或者不约定，包括码头、仓库、集装箱堆场，或公路、铁路及空运货站。在《通则 2010》中，这是唯一一个需要卖方承担卸货费用的术语。"终点站交货"被认为是被删除的"目的港码头交货"术语的扩展应用。

货物运至终点站以及在终点站卸货期间的风险均由卖方承担。买卖双方最好尽量明确地指定终点站，如果可能，在约定的目的港或目的地的终点站内明确指定一个特定地点，因为(货物)到达这一地点之前的风险是由卖方承担。建议卖方签订一份与这种选择准确契合的运输合同。此外，若双方希望卖方承担从终点站到另一地点的运输及管理货物所产生的风险和费用，那么此时应该使用 DAP(目的地交货)或 DDP(完税后交货)术语。

在必要的情况下，DAT 术语要求卖方在需要时办理货物出口清关手续。但是，卖方没有义务办理货物进口清关手续，支付任何进口税或办理任何进口报关手续。

---

5) Delivered at Terminal (DAT)

This rule may be used irrespective of the mode of transport selected and may also be used where more than one mode of transport is employed.

DAT means that the seller delivers when the goods, once unloaded from the arriving means of transport, are placed at the disposal of the buyer at a named terminal at the named port or place of destination. "Terminal" includes any place, whether covered or not, such as a quay, warehouse, container yard or road, rail or air cargo terminal. This is the only rule in *INCOTERMS 2010* that tasks the sellers with the cost of unloading. DAT is considered to be expansion of "DEQ" which has been eliminated.

The seller bears all risks involved in bringing the goods to and unloading them at the terminal at the named port or place of destination. The parties are well advised to specify as clearly as possible the terminal and, if possible, a specific point within the terminal at the agreed port or place of destination, as the risks to that point are for the account of the seller. The seller is advised to procure a contract of carriage that matches this choice precisely. Moreover, if the parties intend the seller to bear the risks and costs involved in transporting and handling the goods from the terminal to another place, then the DAP or DDP should be used.

DAT requires the seller to clear the goods for export, where applicable. However, the seller has no obligation to clear the goods for import, pay any import duty or carry out any import customs formalities.

6) 目的地交货(DAP)

这一术语适用于任何一种指定的运输方式，同时在多种运输方式联合使用的情形下也能适用。

"目的地交货"的意思是：卖方在指定的交货地点，将仍处于交货的运输工具上尚未卸下的货物交给买方处置，即完成交货。"目的地交货"是《通则 2010》新添加的术语，取代了边境交货、目的港船上交货和未完税交货三个术语。

卖方须承担货物运至指定目的地的一切风险。双方应尽可能明确地指定交货目的地，因为(货物)到达这一地点之前的风险是由卖方承担。建议卖方签订精确匹配这种选择的运输合同。如果卖方基于运输合同，在目的地卸货时，产生了费用，那么除非双方另有约定，卖方无权向买方追讨该笔费用。

DAP 术语要求卖方在需要时办理货物的出口清关手续，但卖方没有义务办理货物的进口清关手续，支付任何进口税或者办理任何进口海关手续。如果双方希望卖方办理货物的进口清关手续，支付任何进口税和办理任何进口海关手续，则应使用 DDP 术语。

7) 完税后交货(DDP)

这一术语可以适用于任何一种选定的运输方式，也可以适用于多种运输方式联合使用的情况。

---

6) Delivered at Place (DAP)

This rule may be used irrespective of the mode of transport selected and may also be used where more than one mode of transport is employed.

DAP means that the seller delivers when the goods are placed at the disposal of the buyer on the arriving means of transport ready for unloading at the named place of destination. DAP is a new added rule in *INCOTERMS 2010*, it replaces DAF, DES & DDU, which were eliminated.

The seller bears all risks involved in bringing the goods to the named place. The parties are well advised to specify as clearly as possible the point within the agreed place of destination, as the risks to that point are for the account of the seller. The seller is advised to procure contracts of carriage that match this choice precisely. If the seller incurs costs under its contract of carriage related to unloading at the place of destination, the seller is not entitled to recover such costs from the buyer unless otherwise agreed between the parties.

DAP requires the seller to clear the goods for export, when necessary. However, the seller has no obligation to clear the goods for import, pay any import duty or carry out any import customs formalities. If the parties wish the seller to clear the goods for import, pay any import duty and carry out any import customs formalities, the DDP should be used.

7) Delivered Duty Paid (DDP)

This rule may be used irrespective of the mode of transport selected and may also be used where more than one mode of transport is employed.

"完税后交货"是指卖方在指定的目的地，办理完进口清关手续，将在交货运输工具上准备卸下的货物交与买方处置，即完成交货。卖方承担将货物运至指定目的地的一切风险和费用，并有义务办理出口清关手续与进口清关手续，支付进出口货物的任何关税以及办理一切海关手续。

在 DDP 术语下卖方承担最大责任。因为到达指定地点过程中的费用和风险都由卖方承担，双方最好尽可能明确地指定目的地的具体地点。建议卖方签订的运输合同应精确地符合选择的地点。如果卖方基于运输合同，在目的地卸货时，产生了费用，则卖方无权向买方追讨此费用，双方另有约定的除外。

如果卖方不能直接或间接地办理进口清关手续，不建议双方使用 DDP 术语。如果双方希望买方承担办理进口清关手续的所有风险和费用，应使用 DAP 术语。

任何增值税或其他进口时需要支付的税项由卖方承担，合同另有约定的除外。

8) 船边交货(FAS)

这一术语仅适用于海运和内陆水运方式。"船边交货"是指卖方在指定装运港将货物交到买方指定的船边(例如码头上或驳船上)，即完成交货。货物到达指定船边之后，货物灭失或损坏的风险发生转移，并且由买方承担所有费用。

DDP means that the seller delivers the goods when the goods are placed at the disposal of the buyer, cleared for import on the arriving means of transport ready for unloading at the named place of destination. The seller bears all the risks and costs involved in bringing the goods to the place of destination and has an obligation to clear the goods not only for export but also for import, to pay any duty for both export and import and to carry out all customs formalities.

DDP represents the maximum obligation for the seller. The parties are well advised to specify as clearly as possible the point within the agreed place of destination, as the costs and risks to that point are for the account of the seller. The seller is advised to procure contracts of carriage that match this choice precisely. If the seller incurs costs under its contract of carriage related to unloading at the place of destination, the seller is not entitled to recover such costs from the buyer unless otherwise agreed between the parties.

The parties are well advised not to use DDP if the seller is unable directly or indirectly to obtain import clearance. If the parties wish the buyer to bear all risks and costs of import clearance, the DAP should be used.

Any VAT or other taxes payable upon import are for the seller's account unless expressly agreed otherwise in the sale contract.

8) Free alongside Ship (FAS)

This rule applies only to sea and inland waterway modes of transport, which means that the seller delivers when the goods are placed alongside the vessel (e.g. on a quay or a barge) nominated by the buyer at the named port of shipment. The risk of loss of or damage to the goods passes when the goods are alongside the ship, and the buyer bears all costs from that moment onwards.

买卖双方应当尽可能清楚地明确指定出在指定装运港的装货地点，因为货物到这一地点之前的费用与风险由卖方承担，并且根据港口交付惯例，这些费用及相关的手续费可能会发生变化。卖方在船边交付货物或者获得已经交付装运的货物。这里所谓的"获得"迎合了链式销售，在商品贸易中十分普遍。当货物通过集装箱运输时，卖方通常在终点站将货物交给承运人，而不是在船边。在这种情况下，"船边交货"术语不适用，而应当使用"货交承运人"术语。

"船边交货"要求卖方在需要时办理货物出口清关手续。但是，卖方没有任何义务办理货物进口清关，支付任何进口税或者办理任何进口海关手续。

9) 船上交货(FOB)

这一术语只适用于海运或内陆水运方式。

"船上交货"是指卖方在指定的装运港，将货物交至买方指定的船只上，或者指设法获取已经这样交付装运的货物。一旦货物装船，货物灭失或损坏造成的所有风险发生转移，由买方承担所有费用。卖方被要求将货物交至船只上或者获得已经这样交付装运的货物。

"船上交货"术语要求卖方在需要时办理货物出口清关手续。但卖方无义务办理货物进口清关手续，缴纳进口关税或是办理任何进口海关手续。

The parties are well advised to specify as clearly as possible the loading point at the named port of shipment, as the costs and risks to that point are for the account of the seller and these costs and associated handling charges may vary according to the practice of the port. The seller is required either to deliver the goods alongside the ship or to procure goods already so delivered for shipment. The reference to "procure" here caters for multiple sales down a chain ('string sales'), particularly common in the commodity trades. Where the goods are in containers, it is typical for the seller to hand the goods over to the carrier at a terminal and not alongside the vessel. In such a situation, the FAS would be inappropriate, and the FCA should be used.

FAS requires the seller to clear the goods for export, where applicable. However, the seller has no obligation to clear the goods for import, pay any import duty or carry out any import customs formalities.

9) Free on Board (FOB)

This rule applies only to sea and inland waterway modes of transport.

FOB means that the seller delivers the goods on board the vessel nominated by the buyer at the named port of shipment or procures the goods already so delivered for shipment. The risk of loss of or damage to the goods passes when the goods are on board the vessel, and the buyer bears all costs from that moment onwards. The seller is required either to deliver the goods on board the vessel or to procure goods already so delivered for shipment.

FOB requires the seller to clear the goods for export, where applicable. However, the seller has no obligation to clear the goods for import, pay any import duty or carry out any import customs formalities.

10) 成本加运费(CFR)

这一术语只适用于海路及内陆水运方式。

"成本加运费"是指卖方在装运港交付货物于船舶之上或获得已如此交付装运的货物，而货物的损毁或灭失的风险从货物装至船舶之上起转移，卖方应当签订运输合同并支付必要的成本加运费以使货物运送至指定的目的港。

本术语有两个关键点，因为风险转移地点和运输成本的转移地点是不同的。尽管合同中通常会指定一个目的港，而不一定指定装运港，即风险转移给买方的地方。如果装运港关乎买方的特殊利益，建议双方就此在合同中尽可能精确地加以确认。双方对于目的港内的具体地点也尽可能准确地确认，因为以此地点之前产生的费用由卖方承担。卖方应订立与目的港选择精确相符的运输合同。如果卖方根据运输合同，在目的港的指定地点卸货时，产生了费用，那么除非双方另有约定，否则卖方无权从买方追讨这些费用。卖方被要求将货物交至船只上或者获得已经这样交付装运至目的地的货物。

"成本加运费"对于货物在装到船舶之上前就已经交给承运人的情形可能不适用，例如通常在终点站交付的集装箱货物。在这种情况下，宜使用 CPT 术语。

---

10) Cost and Freight (CFR)

This rule applies only to sea and inland waterway modes of transport.

CFR means that the seller delivers the goods on board the vessel or procures the goods already so delivered for shipment. The risk of loss of or damage to the goods passes when the goods are on board the vessel. The seller must contract for and pay the costs and freight necessary to bring the goods to the named port of destination.

CFR has two critical points, because risk passes and costs are transferred at different places. While the contract will always specify a destination port, it might not specify the port of shipment, which is where risk passes to the buyer. If the shipment port is of particular interest to the buyer, the parties are well advised to identify it as precisely as possible in the contract. The parties are well advised to identify as precisely as possible the point at the agreed port of destination, as the costs to that point are for the account of the seller. The seller is advised to procure contracts of carriage that match this choice precisely. If the seller incurs costs under its contract of carriage related to unloading at the specified point at the port of destination, the seller is not entitled to recover such costs from the buyer unless otherwise agreed between the parties. The seller is required either to deliver the goods on board the vessel or to procure goods already so delivered for shipment to the destination.

CFR may not be appropriate where goods are handed over to the carrier before they are on board the vessel, for example goods in containers, which are typically delivered at a terminal. In such circumstances, the CPT should be used.

"成本加运费"术语要求卖方在需要时办理出口清关手续。但是，卖方无义务为货物办理进口清关手续，支付进口关税或者办理进口海关手续。

11）成本、保险费加运费(CIF)

这一术语仅适用于海运和内陆水运方式。

"成本、保险费加运费"指卖方将货物装上船或获取已经这样交付装运的货物。货物灭失或损坏的风险在货物于装运港装船时转移给买方。卖方须自行订立运输合同，支付将货物装运至指定目的港所需的运费和费用。

卖方须订立保险合同以防买方货物在运输途中灭失或损坏的风险。买方须知晓在 CIF 术语下卖方有义务投保的险别仅是最低保险险别。如买方希望得到更为充分的保险保障，则需与卖方明确地达成协议或者自行做出额外的保险安排。

与上述 CPT、CIP 和 CFR 术语一样，CIF 也具有两个关键点，即风险转移和费用的转移地点不同。

卖方必须将货物送至船上或者获取已经这样交付的货物并运送到目的地。除此之外，卖方必须签订一个运输合同或者获得这样的合同。这里的"获得"适合链式销售的情况，尤其在商品贸易中很普遍。

CFR requires the seller to clear the goods for export, where applicable. However, the seller has no obligation to clear the goods for import, pay any import duty or carry out any import customs formalities.

11) Cost, Insurance and Freight (CIF)

This rule applies only to sea and inland waterway modes of transport.

CIF means that the seller delivers the goods on board the vessel or procures the goods already so delivered for shipment. The risk of loss of or damage to the goods passes when the goods are on board the vessel. The seller must contract for and pay the costs and freight necessary to bring the goods to the named port of destination.

The seller also contracts for insurance cover against the buyer's risk of loss of or damage to the goods during the carriage. The buyer should note that under CIF the seller is required to obtain insurance only on minimum cover. Should the buyer wish to have more insurance protection, it will need either to agree as much expressly with the seller or to make its own extra insurance arrangements.

As mentioned above in CPT, CIP and CFR, CIF also has two critical points, because risk passes and costs are transferred at different places.

The seller is required either to deliver the goods on board the vessel or to procure goods already so delivered for shipment to the destination. In addition the seller is required either to make a contract of carriage or to procure such a contract. The reference to "procure" here caters for multiple sales down a chain (string sales), particularly common in the commodity trade.

"成本、保险费加运费"术语并不适用于货物在装上船以前就转交给承运人的情况，例如通常在终点站交货的集装箱货物。在这样的情况下，应当使用"运费和保险费付至"术语。

"成本、保险费加运费"术语要求卖方在必要的情况下办理货物出口清关手续。但是，卖方没有义务办理货物进口清关手续，缴纳任何进口关税或办理进口海关手续。

二、《联合国国际货物销售合同公约》

1. 《联合国国际货物销售合同公约》概述

《联合国国际货物销售合同公约》(以下简称《公约》)的目的在于，为国际货物销售活动提供现代化的、统一的、公平的制度支持。因此，《公约》在增加贸易确定性和减少贸易成本方面为促进国际货物贸易作出了突出贡献。

CIF may not be appropriate where goods are handed over to the carrier before they are on board the vessel, for example goods in containers, which are typically delivered at a terminal. In such circumstances, the CIP should be used.

CIF requires the seller to clear the goods for export, where applicable. However, the seller has no obligation to clear the goods for import, pay any import duty or carry out any import customs formalities.

3.1.2　*United Nations Convention on Contracts for the International Sale of Goods*

1. Introduction to *the CISG*

The purpose of *the United Nations Convention on Contracts for the International Sale of Goods (CISG)* is to provide a modern, uniform and fair regime for the international sale of goods. Thus, *the CISG* contributes significantly to increasing certainty in commercial exchanges and decreasing transaction costs.

　　早在 1930 年，罗马国际统一私法协会就开始筹备一部关于国际货物销售的统一法规范。这一工作一度被第二次世界大战中断了很长时间。直到 1964 年，统一法草案终于在罗马国际统一私法协会海牙会议上被提交。1964 年的海牙会议正式通过了《国际货物销售统一法公约》(ULIS)和《国际货物销售合同成立统一法公约》(ULF)。但这两个公约刚刚正式通过，就遭到了广泛的批评。批评者认为，由于公约最积极的筹备者来自西欧，公约的条款主要反映了西欧地区的法律传统和贸易实践。

　　因此，这两个公约并没有像人们最初预期的那样获得世界各国的广泛接受。1969 年，联合国国际贸易法委员会组建了专门的工作小组，研究这两个公约，并确定使公约能够得到不同法律制度及社会、经济体制国家的广泛认可的修改方法。联合国国际贸易法委员会的研究成果融合了两项公约的主旨，形成了《联合国国际货物销售合同公约》。《公约》在 1980 年 4 月 11 日召开的维也纳外交会议上获得正式通过。《公约》于 1980 年 8 月签署于维也纳，自 1988 年 1 月 1 日起生效。截至 2012 年 2 月 24 日，联合国国际贸易法委员会统计，已有 78 个国家和地区批准或加入了《公约》。这些国家包括：澳大利亚、加拿大、中国、法国、德国、日本等。至此，加入《公约》并受《公约》约束的国家和地区发生的贸易额已经超过全球贸易额的四分之三。

　　Preparation of a uniform law for the international sale of goods began in 1930 at the International Institute for the Unification of Private Law (UNIDROIT) in Rome. After a long interruption in the work as a result of the Second World War, the long-waited draft was submitted to a diplomatic conference in Hague in 1964, which adopted two conventions: *The Uniform Law on the International Sale of Goods (ULIS)* and *The Uniform Law on the Formation of Contracts for the International Sale of Goods (ULF)*. Almost immediately upon the adoption of the two conventions, there was wide-spread criticism of their provisions as reflecting primarily the legal traditions and trade realities of continental Western Europe, which was the region that had most actively contributed to their preparation.

　　As a result, the acceptance of the two conventions is not as people wished. One of the tasks undertaken by UNCITRAL on its organization in 1969 was to form a working group to study the two conventions to ascertain which modifications might render them capable of wider acceptance by countries of different legal, social and economic systems. The result of this study was the adoption by Vienna Diplomatic Conference on April 11, 1980 of *the United Nations Convention on Contracts for the International Sale of Goods*, which combines the subject matter of the two prior conventions. *CISG*, signed in August, 1980 in Vienna and entered into force on January 1, 1988. As of February 24, 2012, UNCITRAL reports that 78 States have adopted *the CISG*. The main contracting countries of *the CISG* are as follows: Australia, Canada, China, France, Germany, Japan and so on. Thus *the CISG* is the uniform international sales law of countries that account for over three-quarters of all world trade.

该《公约》共 101 条，分为四个部分：第一部分为"适用范围和总则"；第二部分为"合同的订立"；第三部分为"货物销售合同中的买卖双方的权利和义务"；第四部分为"最后条款"，包括《公约》于何时在何等条件下生效，《公约》允许的保留与声明，对《公约》范围内的事项具有相同或非常近似的法律规则的两个或两个以上的缔约国的《公约》适用。

2. 《公约》适用范围

《公约》适用范围的限制包括以下四个方面。

(1) 仅适用于国际贸易。

(2) 仅适用于商业目的的货物贸易。

(3) 不适用于销售合同当中的某些问题。

(4) 合同双方可以减损或排除《公约》的适用。

The CISG has 101 articles, which is divided into four parts: Part I deals with the scope of application of the Convention and the general provisions; Part II contains the rules governing the formation of contracts for the international sale of goods; Part III contains the substantive rules for the sale contract (obligations and rights of the parties); Part IV contains the final clauses of the Convention concerning such matters as how and when it comes into force, the reservations and declarations that are permitted and the application of the Convention to international sale where both States concerned have the same or similar law on the subject.

2. Scope of *the CISG*

The scope of *the CISG* is limited in the following four aspects.

(1) It governs only sales of international goods.

(2) It applies only to the commercial sale of goods.

(3) It does not apply to certain questions often encountered in sale contracts.

(4) The parties are free to derogate from its provisions, or exclude the application of *the CISG*.

按照《公约》第一部分的规定，《公约》适用于以下情况。

(1) 缔约国中营业地分处不同国家的当事人之间的货物买卖。如果当事人有一个以上的营业地，则以与合同及合同的履行关系最密切的营业地为其营业地。

(2) 营业地分处不同国家的当事人之间的货物买卖，由国际私法规则导致适用某一缔约国法律。根据《公约》第 1 条第 1 款第 2 项的规定，《公约》不但可以适用于只有一方是《公约》缔约国的情况，还可以适用于货物贸易合同双方均不是《公约》缔约国的情况。中国对于《公约》第 1 条第 1 款第 2 项的规定作出了保留。因此，国际货物贸易中的中国一方，仅仅在最典型的情况下，即交易对方的营业地所在国也批准了《公约》的情形下，才受《公约》约束。

According to Part I of *the CISG*, *the CISG* applies to the following aspects.

(1) The parties to the contract have their places of business in different Contracting States. Where a party has more than one place of business, the relevant place of business is the one most closely connected to the sale transaction.

(2) When the rules of the private international law lead to the application of the law of a Contracting State. Under Article 1(1) (b), *the CISG* could apply where only one party has its place of business in a Contracting State and, conceivably, where neither party has its place of business in a Contracting State. China has made a reservation excluding the application of Article 1(1) (b) so that, in the typical transaction, *the CISG* will only apply to a Chinese party where both contracting parties have their relevant places of business in States that have ratified *the CISG*.

《公约》适用于商业目的的货物买卖，但存在两项例外。

首先，《公约》明确排除了消费性交易的适用，除非卖方在订立合同前的任何时候或订立合同时不知道而且没有理由知道这些货物是用于这种用途的。需要注意的是，《公约》排除的是消费性交易，而不是消费品本身。《公约》还使用排除法，列举了不适用《公约》的货物买卖的情况。

(1) 由拍卖方式进行的销售。

(2) 根据法律执行或其他依法进行的销售。

(3) 股票、公债、投资证券、流通票据或货币的销售。

(4) 船舶、船只、气垫船或飞机的销售。

(5) 电力的销售。

其次，《公约》排除以下合同的适用：买方保证供应货物制造或生产所需的大部分重要原材料的订购合同，供应货物一方的绝大部分义务在于提供劳力或其他服务的合同。(《公约》第 3 条)《公约》并没有对"大部分""绝大部分"等词汇予以界定。因此，当提供劳力或其他服务在合同总额中占有相当比例的时候，或者重要的货物生产原材料是由买方供应的时候，即使存在《公约》第 3 条的限定性规定，合同双方仍应当在合同中明确载明"适用《公约》"的内容，以免"适用《公约》"的意图无法实现。

The CISG applies to a commercial sale of goods with two exceptions.

First, the CISG expressly excludes coverage of consumer sale, unless the seller, at any time before or at the conclusion of the contract, neither knew nor ought to have known that the goods were bought for any such use. What deserves notice is that the exclusion is against consumer sale; not against consumer goods itself. The CISG also excludes sale:

(1) By auction;

(2) On execution or otherwise by authority of law;

(3) Of stocks, shares, investment securities, negotiable instruments or money;

(4) Of ships, vessels, hovercraft or aircraft;

(5) Of electricity.

Second, the CISG excludes sale in which labor or other services constitute a preponderant part, and manufacturing contracts where the buyer supplies a substantial portion of the materials(Article 3 of the CISG). The CISG does not define the words "preponderant" or "substantial". Where labor or other services constitute a significant portion of a contract or where important materials are supplied by the buyer and the parties desire to have the contract governed by the CISG, it would therefore be prudent to specifically state in the contract that the CISG shall apply, notwithstanding the restrictive adjectives of Article 3.

　　《公约》不适用于销售合同中的某些问题。与《美国统一商法典》不同，《公约》并没有涉及信用证、改善货物安全利益及其他商务事项，即使这些问题也可能与货物销售有关。单就买卖合同而言，《公约》仅适用合同的订立和买卖双方的权利和义务，而不涉及：①合同的效力，或其任何条款的效力或惯例的效力；②合同对销售货物所有权的影响；③货物对人身造成的伤亡或损害的产品责任问题。

　　由于这些限制，有时就《公约》不适用的问题需要援引其他法律来解决。此外，《公约》刻意回避了一些在国内法中使用的具有国内法意义的法律术语。这么做的目的在于，对于《公约》涉及的事实定性，应当适用《公约》的架构体系来进行，而不应落入任何国内法的框架体系之中。

　　最后，《公约》的适用范围可能因合同意思自治原则而受到进一步限制或者突破前面提到的限制。《公约》明确规定，双方当事人可以不适用本公约，或在一定条件下减损本公约的任何规定或改变其效力。在遵守有关可能适用的国内法的前提下，贸易双方的法律顾问可以在本来应适用《公约》的贸易合同中加入某些条款，以修改或排除《公约》中的不同规定。

　　如前所述，中国已经批准加入《公约》。从中国的国内法中，可以发现《公约》在涉及中国当事方的案件中的适用情况。

　　The CISG does not address certain questions that arise frequently in the contract of sale. Unlike *the U. S. Uniform Commercial Code*, *the CISG* does not contain provisions on letters of credit, methods of perfecting security interests in goods and other commercial subjects, many of which can also be relevant to sale of goods. A further limitation upon the scope of *the CISG* is that, although it governs the formation of the sale contract and rights and obligations of the buyer and the seller, it excludes (a)certain questions relating to the validity of the contract or of any of its provisions or of any usage; (b)the effect of the contract on the property in the goods sold; (c)claims for death or personal injury caused by the goods.

　　Because of these limitations, there will be occasions when it is necessary to resort to a gap-filling law. In addition, *the CISG* deliberately seeks to avoid the use of legal code words, many of which have established meanings under the domestic law. The general intent is respond to that fact pattern within the framework of *the CISG*, not the framework of any domestic body of law.

　　Finally, the scope of *the CISG* is limited or expanded by *the CISG*'s recognition of the principle of freedom of contract. *The CISG* specifically provides that parties are free to exclude the application of *the CISG* or (under certain condition) derogate from or vary the effect of any of its provisions. Subject to domestic validity laws that may remain applicable, counsel preparing contracts to which *the CISG* applies therefore have the latitude to include clauses in their contracts modifying or eliminating various provisions that *the CISG* would otherwise mandate.

　　As mentioned above, *the CISG* is applicable in China. With the materials of China's laws, we can find how *the CISG* applies in cases related P.R.C.

首先，作为缔约国，中国有权对《公约》作出保留。中国政府在加入《公约》时作出了两项保留，对于《公约》第 1 条第 1 款第 2 项和第 11 条规定的义务予以保留。因此，我国当事人在缔结国际货物销售合同时，应采用书面形式。由于国际货物销售合同的本质是合同双方的一致意思表示，随着中国的经济发展和立法变迁，中国国内法关于国际货物销售合同的形式要求已经从过去的强制性书面形式要求转变为买卖双方意思表示一致。但是，即使这一保留与中国现行《合同法》对于国际货物销售合同形式的规定存在不一致，中国对于《公约》第 11 条的保留仍然有效。中国当事人在缔结国际货物销售合同时仍应考虑中国的这一保留。

其次，根据《公约》第 1 条第 1 款之规定："本公约适用于营业地在不同国家的当事人之间所订立的货物销售合同。"在有关判例中，买卖双方营业地所在国均为《公约》缔约国，但买卖双方的贸易合同中并未就法律适用问题作出约定。就这种情况，根据"法[2000]51 号"《最高人民法院关于审理和执行涉外民商事案件应当注意的几个问题的通知》："除《中华人民共和国合同法》第 126 条第 2 款规定的三类合同必须适用中国法律外，均应依照有关规定或者当事人约定，准确选用准据法；对我国参加的国际公约，除我国声明保留的条款外，应予优先适用，同时可以参照国际惯例。"因此，《公约》应适用于该类情形。

First, as a contracting state, China has rights to make reservations about *the CISG*. Chinese government made reservations, under the Article 1 (1) (b) and Article 11, for which China reserved not to bear the obligations. Thus, the contract of international sale of goods entered by Chinese party should be in written form. Because the nature of contract for the international sale of goods is the uniform expressions of the will of both parties, with the development of Chinese economy and changes in her legal systems, the specification of a contract for the international sale of goods has also been changed from a compulsory written form to the one which respects the will of both parties. However, the reservation of Article 11 of *the CISG* still exists, which is not in compliance with the format of contract for international sale of goods as stipulated in the present Contract Law. Howbeit the Chinese parties concluding a contract for the international sale of goods should consider the reservation.

Second, according to Article 1(1) of *the CISG*, "*the CISG* applies to contracts of sale of goods between parties whose places of business are in different States." In the foregoing case, the countries of the buyer and the seller are Contracting States of *the CISG*, and the two parties failed to stipulate the applicable law in the contract. According to the Notice on Several Issues Regarding Trial and Enforcement of Civil and Commercial Cases Involving Foreign Interest issued by the Supreme Court (Law No. [2000] 51), which stipulates that: "Except otherwise as stipulated in Article 126(2) of Contract Law of the P.R.C. or agreed by the parties, the applicable law shall be decided properly; international conventions to which China is a Contracting State have priority except the provisions on which China has made reservations, and international usages shall be considered." Thus, *the CISG* shall apply to this case.

3. 要约与承诺

为了使《公约》的第二部分"合同的订立"能够在广泛的缔约国中得以适用，《公约》借鉴了在英美法系以及大陆法系均得以确立的传统法律概念：要约与承诺。

1) 要约

向一个或一个以上特定的人提出的订立合同的建议，如果十分确定并且表明要约人在得到接受时承受约束的意旨，即构成要约。一个建议如果写明货物并且明示或暗示地规定数量和价格或规定如何确定数量和价格，即为十分确定。并非向一个或一个以上特定的人提出的建议，仅应视为要约邀请，除非提出建议的人明确地表示相反的意向。

要约于送达被要约人时生效。一项要约，即使是不可撤销的，如果撤回通知于要约送达被要约人之前或同时，送达被要约人，则得予撤回。在未订立合同之前，如果撤销通知于被要约人发出接受通知之前送达被要约人，则要约得予撤销。但有下列情况之时，要约不得撤销：①要约写明接受要约的期限或以其他方式表示要约是不可撤销的；②被要约人有理由信赖该项要约是不可撤销的，而且被要约人已本着对该项要约的信赖行事。一项要约，即使是不可撤销的，于拒绝通知送达要约人时终止。

3. Offer and Acceptance

To be in conformity with the standard approach throughout the contracting states, the formation rules of *the CISG* (Part II) are founded on the traditional notions admitted by both the Anglo-American law system and the civil law system, that is "offer" and "acceptance".

1) Offer

A proposal for concluding a contract addressed to one or more specific persons constitutes an offer if it is sufficiently definite and indicates the intention of the offeror to be bound in case of acceptance. A proposal is sufficiently definite if it indicates the goods and expressly or implicitly fixes or makes provision for determining the quantity and the price. A proposal other than one addressed to one or more specific persons is to be considered merely as an invitation to make offers, unless the contrary intention is clearly indicated by the person making the proposal.

An offer becomes effective when it reaches the offeree. An offer, even if it is irrevocable, may be withdrawn if the withdrawal reaches the offeree before or at the same time as the offer. Until a contract is concluded, an offer may be revoked if the revocation reaches the offeree before he/she has dispatched an acceptance. However, an offer cannot be revoked: (a)if it indicates, whether by stating a fixed time for acceptance or otherwise, that it is irrevocable; (b)if it was reasonable for the offeree to rely on the offer as being irrevocable and the offeree has acted in reliance on the offer. An offer, even if it is irrevocable, is terminated when a rejection reaches the offeror.

2) 承诺

被要约人声明或作出其他行为表示同意一项要约，即是承诺，缄默或不行动本身不等于承诺。

承诺于表示同意的通知送达要约人时生效。如果表示同意的通知在要约人所规定的时间内，或者未规定时间，在一段合理的时间内，未曾送达要约人，承诺就成为无效，但须适当地考虑到交易的情况，包括要约人所使用的通信方法的迅度。对口头要约必须立即承诺，特殊情况不在此限。但是，如果根据该项要约或依照当事人之间确立的习惯做法和惯例，被要约人可以做出某种行为，例如与发运货物或支付价款有关的行为，来表示同意，而无须向要约人发出通知，则承诺于该项行为做出时生效，但该项行为必须在《公约》所规定的承诺期间内做出。

对要约表示承诺但载有添加、限制或其他更改的答复，即为拒绝该项要约，并构成还价。但是，对要约表示承诺但载有的添加或不同条件的答复，如所载的添加或不同条件在实质上并不变更该项要约的条件，除要约人在不过分迟延的期间内以口头或书面通知反对这些差异外，仍构成承诺。如果要约人不做出这种反对，合同的条件就以该项要约的条件以及承诺通知内所载的更改为准。有关货物价格、付款、货物质量和数量、交货地点和时间、一方当事人对另一方当事人的赔偿责任范围，或解决争端等的添加或不同条件，均视为在实质上变更要约的条件。

---

2) Acceptance

A statement made by or other conduct of the offeree indicating assent to an offer is an acceptance. Silence or inactivity does not in itself amount to acceptance.

An acceptance of an offer becomes effective at the moment when the indication of assent reaches the offeror. An acceptance is not effective if the indication of assent does not reach the offeror within the time he/she has fixed or, if no time is fixed, within a reasonable time, due account being taken of the circumstances of the transaction, including the rapidity of the means of communication employed by the offeror. An oral offer must be accepted immediately unless the circumstances indicate otherwise. However, if, by virtue of the offer or as a result of practices which the parties have established between themselves or of usage, the offeree may indicate assent by performing an act, such as one relating to the dispatch of the goods or payment of the price, without notice to the offeror. If the act is performed within the period of time for acceptance laid down in *the CISG*, it is effective immediately as an acceptance.

A reply to an offer which purports to be an acceptance but contains additions, limitations or other modifications is a rejection of the offer and constitutes a counter-offer. However, a reply to an offer which purports to be an acceptance but contains additional or different terms which do not materially alter the terms of the offer constitutes an acceptance, unless the offeror, without undue delay, objects orally to the discrepancy or dispatches a notice to that effect. If he/she does not so object, the terms of the contract are the terms of the offer with the modifications contained in the acceptance. Additional or different terms relating, among other things, to the price, payment, quality and quantity of the goods, place and time of delivery, extent of one party's liability to the other or the settlement of disputes are considered to alter the terms of the offer materially.

要约人在电报或信件内规定的承诺期间，从电报交发时刻或信上载明的发信日期起算，如信上未载明发信日期，则从信封上所载日期起算。要约人以电话、电传或其他快速通信方法规定的承诺期间，从要约送达被要约人时起算。在计算承诺期间时，承诺期间内的正式假日或非营业日应计算在内。但是，如果承诺通知在承诺期间的最后1天未能送到要约人地址，是因为那天在要约人营业地是正式假日或非营业日，则承诺期间应顺延至下一个营业日。

逾期承诺仍有承诺的效力，如果要约人毫不迟延地用口头或书面将此种意见通知被要约人。如果载有逾期承诺的信件或其他书面文件表明，它在传递正常的情况下是能及时送达要约人的，则该项逾期承诺具有承诺的效力，除非要约人毫不迟延地用口头或书面方式通知被要约人：他认为他的要约已经失效。如果撤回通知于承诺生效之前或同时，送达要约人，则承诺得予撤回。

按照《公约》规定，一项要约的承诺生效时，合同即订立。

A period of time for acceptance fixed by the offeror in a telegram or a letter begins to run from the moment the telegram is handed in for dispatch or from the date shown on the letter or, if no such date is shown, from the date shown on the envelope. A period of time for acceptance fixed by the offeror by telephone, telex or other means of instantaneous communication, begins to run from the moment that the offer reaches the offeree. Official holidays or non-business days occurring during the period for acceptance are included in calculating the period. However, if a notice of acceptance cannot be delivered at the address of the offeror on the last day of the period because that day falls on an official holiday or a non-business day at the place of business of the offeror, the period is extended until the first business day which follows.

A late acceptance is nevertheless effective as an acceptance if without delay the offeror orally informs the offeree or dispatches a notice to that effect. If a letter or other writing containing a late acceptance shows that it has been sent in such circumstances that if its transmission had been normal it would have reached the offeror in due time, the late acceptance is effective as an acceptance unless, without delay, the offeror orally informs the offeree that he/she considers his/her offer as having lapsed or dispatches a notice to that effect. An acceptance may be withdrawn if the withdrawal reaches the offeror before or at the same time as the acceptance would have become effective.

A contract is concluded at the moment when an acceptance of an offer becomes effective in accordance with the provisions of *the CISG*.

4. 卖方的义务

统一不同国家对于买方及卖方的义务内容的法律规定是《公约》的主要目的之一，因此，"卖方和买方的义务"在《公约》中占据了重要篇幅。

根据《联合国国际货物销售合同公约》的规定，卖方应承担以下四项义务：提交货物、交付单据、品质担保、所有权担保。

1) 提交货物

提交货物与单据是国际货物买卖中卖方的一项主要义务，包括卖方应在合同指定的时间和地点移交货物和单据。如果合同中对交货时间、地点未作规定，则应按照《公约》的规定办理。

(1) 交货地点。

如果卖方没有义务要在任何其他特定地点交付货物，他的交货义务如下：(a)如果销售合同涉及货物的运输，卖方应把货物移交给第一承运人，以运交给买方；(b)在不属于上款规定的情况下，如果合同指的是特定货物或从特定存货中提取的或尚待制造或生产的未经特定化的货物，而双方当事人在订立合同时已知道这些货物是在某一特定地点，或将在某一特定地点制造或生产，卖方应在该地点把货物交给买方处置；(c)在其他情况下，卖方应在他订立合同时的营业地把货物交给买方处置。

---

4. Obligations of the Seller

One of the principal purposes of *the CISG* is to unify the different content of different countries' law on the obligations of the seller and buyer, thus that content becomes the main part of *the CISG*.

The CISG specifies that the seller mainly bears the following obligations: delivery of goods, delivery of documents; quality warranty; warranty of title.

1) Delivery of Goods

One of the general obligations of the seller is to deliver the goods, which means the seller hands over the goods to the buyer in the particular place and at the particular time as required by the contract. But, if the delivery time and place cannot be specified in the contract, the seller should fulfill the delivery as *the CISG* specifies.

(1) Place of delivery.

If the seller is not bound to deliver the goods at any other particular place, his/her obligation to deliver consists: (a)if the contract of sale involves carriage of the goods—in handing the goods over to the first carrier for transmission to the buyer; (b)in cases not within the preceding subparagraph, if the contract relates to specific goods, or unidentified goods to be drawn from a specific stock or to be manufactured or produced, and at the time of the conclusion of the contract the parties knew that the goods were at, or were to be manufactured or produced at, a particular place—in placing the goods at the buyer's disposal at that place; (c)in other cases—in placing the goods at the buyer's disposal at the place where the seller had his/her place of business at the time of the conclusion of the contract.

(2) 交货时间。

如果合同规定有日期，或从合同可以确定日期，卖方应在该日期交货。但在国际货物贸易中，常见的做法是将交货时间限定在一段时间以内。这就使卖方在备货和组织运输时具有一定的灵活性。如果合同规定有一段交货时间，或从合同可以确定一段时间，除非情况表明应由买方选定一个日期外，卖方可以在该段时间内任何时候交货。在其他情况下，卖方应在订立合同后一段合理时间内交货。合理时间的界定取决于在案件情形下，可以接受的商业行为应如何界定。

2) 交付单据

在国际货物买卖中，有两种交货方式：一种是实际交货，即卖方把货物连同代表货物所有权的单据一起交到买方手中，完成货物所有权与占有权的同时转移；另一种方式是象征性交货，即卖方只把代表货物所有权的证书(提单)交到买方手中，完成货物所有权的转移即为完成交货义务。无论是实际交货还是象征性交货，货运单据都是完成交货的重要文书。货运单据是买方可以提货、报关、转售或向运输公司、保险公司索赔的必备文书。

---

(2) Date of delivery.

If the date for delivery is fixed by or determinable from the contract, the seller must deliver on that date. In international goods trade it is common for the date of delivery to be fixed in terms of a period of time. This is generally to allow the seller some flexibility in preparing the goods for shipment and in providing for the necessary transportation. If a period of time is fixed by or determinable from the contract, at any time within that period the seller may deliver the goods, unless circumstances indicate that the buyer is to choose a date. In all other cases the seller must deliver the goods within a reasonable time after the conclusion of the contract. What is a reasonable time depends on what constitutes acceptable commercial conduct in the circumstances of the case.

2) Delivery of Documents

In the international sale of goods, there are two ways of delivery: (a)Physical delivery. It requires the seller delivers the goods with all the documents representing the title to the goods so as to transfer the ownership and possession of the goods at the same time; (b)Symbolic delivery. The seller just has to deliver the documents to the buyer. Completion of the transfer of ownership of the goods completes delivery obligations. Shipping documents play a very important role not only in physical delivery but also in symbolic delivery. Shipping documents are the indispensable profiles for the buyer to pick up the goods, go through the customs formalities, resell the goods and to the carrier or the insurance company to claim compensation.

《公约》第 34 条规定，如果卖方有义务移交与货物有关的单据，他必须按照合同所规定的时间、地点和方式移交这些单据。如果卖方在那个时间以前已移交这些单据，它可以在那个时间到达前纠正单据中任何不符合合同规定的情形，而且此项权利的行使不得使买方遭受不合理的不便或承担不合理的开支。但是，买方保留《公约》所规定的要求损害赔偿的任何权利。

　　因此，依据《公约》，卖方交付单据义务包括：①卖方应保证单据的完整性和符合合同及《公约》的规定。单据完整性是指，卖方应该向买方提交所有与货物有关的单据，以确保买方能够获得货物所有权并占有货物。这些单据包括：提单、保险单、发票、商检证明、进出口许可证、临时签证、货物原产地证明书。②应按合同约定的时间、地点和方式交付单据。

　　3）品质担保

　　依据《公约》，国际货物贸易中的卖方具有四重货物担保义务：货物质量、数量、规格符合贸易合同中的约定，并按照合同所规定的方式装箱或包装。

Article 34 of the sale contract stipulates that if the seller is bound to hand over documents relating to the goods, he/she must hand them over at the time and place and in the form required by the contract. If the seller has handed over documents before that time, he/she may, up to that time, cure any lack of conformity in the documents, and the exercise of this right does not cause the buyer unreasonable inconvenience or unreasonable expense. However, the buyer retains any right to claim damages as provided for in this *CISG*.

So, according to *the CISG*, the obligation of the seller to hand over the documents including: (a)The seller should guarantee the document's wholeness and conformity to the specifications of the contract and *CISG*. The wholeness，means the seller ought to hand over all the documents relating to the goods and ensure that the buyer is able to properly acquire the ownership and possess the goods. These documents often include bill of lading, insurance bill, receipt, commodity inspection certificate, import and export license, temporary visa, certificate of origin. (b)If the seller is to hand over documents relating to the goods, he/she must hand them over at the time and place and in the form required by the contract.

3) Quality Warranty

Under *the CISG*, a seller has a fourfold obligation to deliver goods of quantity, quality and description required by the contract, contained or packaged in the manner as required by the contract.

除双方当事人另有协议外，货物除非符合以下规定，否则即为与合同不符：①货物适用于同一规格货物通常使用的目的；②货物适用于订立合同时曾明示或默示地通知卖方的任何特定目的，除非情况表明买方并不依赖卖方的技能和判断力，或者这种依赖对他是不合理的；③货物的质量与卖方向买方提供的货物样品或样式相同；④货物按照同类货物通用的方式装箱或包装，如果没有此种通用方式，则按照足以保全和保护货物的方式装箱或包装。

如果买方在订立合同时知道或者不可能不知道货物不符合合同，卖方就无须按上述①项至④项承担货物不符合合同的责任。

卖方应按照合同和《公约》的规定，对风险移转到买方时所存在的任何不符合合同的情形，承担责任，即使这种不符合合同的情形在该时间后才开始明显。卖方对在前述时间后发生的任何不符合合同的情形，也应负有责任，如果这种不符合合同的情形是由于卖方违反他的某项义务所致，包括违反关于在一段时间内货物将继续适用于其通常使用的目的或某种特定目的，或将保持某种特定质量或性质的任何保证。

Except where otherwise agreed, the goods do not conform with the contract unless: (a) they are fit for the purposes for which goods of the same description would ordinarily be used; (b) they are fit for any particular purpose expressly or impliedly made known to the seller at the time of the conclusion of the contract, except where the circumstances show that the buyer did not rely, or that it was unreasonable for him/her to rely, on the seller's skill and judgment; (c) they possess the qualities of goods which the seller has held out to the buyer as a sample or model; (d) they are contained or packaged in the manner usual for such goods or, where there is no such manner, in a manner adequate to preserve and protect the goods.

The seller is not liable under (a) to (d) of the above paragraph before for any nonconformity of the goods if at the time of the conclusion of the contract the buyer knew or could not have been unaware of such nonconformity.

The seller is liable in accordance with the contract and this *CISG* for any lack of conformity which exists at the time when the risk passes to the buyer, even though the lack of conformity becomes apparent only after that time. The seller is also liable for any lack of conformity which occurs after the time just mentioned above and which is due to a breach of any of his/her obligations, including a breach of any guarantee that for a period of time the goods will remain fit for their ordinary purpose or for some particular purpose or will retain specified qualities or characteristics.

如果卖方在交货日期前交付货物，他可以在那个日期到达前，交付任何缺漏部分或补足所交付货物的不足数量，或交付用以替换所交付的不符合合同规定的货物，或对所交付货物中任何不符合合同规定的情形做出补救，而且此项权利的行使不得使买方遭受不合理的不便或承担不合理的开支。但是，买方保留本《公约》所规定的要求损害赔偿的任何权利。

4) 所有权担保

所有权担保，是指卖方所提交的货物必须是第三者不能提出任何权利或要求的货物。《公约》中虽然没有明确提到"所有权"或"担保"，但《公约》中确实存在所有权担保的规定。

《公约》第 41 条规定："卖方所交付的货物，必须是第三方不能提出任何权利或要求的货物，除非买方同意在这种权利或要求的条件下，收取货物。但是，如果这种权利或要求是以工业产权或其他知识产权为基础的，卖方的义务应依照第 42 条的规定。"这意味着卖方违反所有权担保义务的情形不但包括第三方对合同货物具有某种权利的情形，还包括任何第三方提出与合同货物有关的诉讼的情形。当然，这并不代表卖方必须对买方所遭受的不必要的第三方诉讼承担责任，但卖方必须承担使买方确信这些诉讼于法无据的责任。

If the seller has delivered goods before the date for delivery, he/she may, up to that date, deliver any missing part or make up any deficiency in the quantity of the goods delivered, or deliver goods in replacement of any non-conforming goods delivered or remedy any lack of conformity in the goods delivered, provided that the exercise of this right does not cause the buyer unreasonable inconvenience or unreasonable expense. However, the buyer retains any right to claim damages as provided for in *the CISG*.

4) Warranty of Title

The seller is also obligated to deliver goods that are free from any right or claim of third parties. *The CISG* has a warranty of title even though *the CISG* does not use the words "warranty" or "title".

Article 41 provides that "The seller must deliver goods which are free from any right or claim of a third party, *unless the buyer agreed to take the goods subject to that right or claim.* However, if such a right or claim based on industrial or other intellectual property, the seller's obligation is governed by Article 42." This means that the seller has breached his/her obligation not only if the third party's claim is valid, the third party has a right in or to the goods; but also if a third party makes a claim in respect of the goods. Of course, it does not mean that the seller is liable for breach of his/her contract with the buyer while a third person makes a frivolous claim in respect of the goods. However, it is the seller who must carry the burden of demonstrating to the satisfaction of the buyer that the claim is frivolous.

第三者根据工业产权或知识产权提出要求时，根据《公约》第42条规定：

"(1)卖方所交付的货物，必须是第三方不能根据工业产权或其他知识产权主张任何权利或要求的货物，但以卖方在订立合同时已知道或不可能不知道的权利或要求为限，而且这种权利或要求根据以下国家的法律规定是以工业产权或其他知识产权为基础的。

① 如果双方当事人在订立合同时预期货物将在某一国境内转售或做其他使用，则根据货物将在其境内转售或做其他使用的国家的法律。

② 在任何其他情况下，根据买方营业地所在国家的法律。

(2) 卖方在上(1)款中的义务不适用于以下情况。

① 买方在订立合同时已知道或不可能不知道此项权利或要求。

② 此项权利或要求的发生，是由于卖方要遵照买方所提供的技术图样、图案、程式或其他规格。"

5. 买方的义务

根据《联合国国际货物销售合同公约》的规定，买方的主要义务为支付价款与收取货物，买方不履行合同或《公约》规定的义务，则卖方可依法得到救济。

While claim is based on industrial property or other intellectual property, the Article 42 holds that：

"(1) The seller must deliver goods which are free from any right or claim of a third party based on industrial or intellectual property, of which at the time of the conclusion of the contract the seller knew or could not have been unaware, provided that that right or claim is based on industrial or intellectual property.

(a) Under the law of the State where the goods will be resold or otherwise used if it was contemplated by the parties at the time of the conclusion of the contract that the goods would be resold or otherwise used in that State.

(b) In any other case under the law of the State where the buyer has his/her place of business.

(2) The obligation of the seller under paragraph (1) of this article does not extend to cases where：

(a) at the time of the conclusion of the contract the buyer knew or could not have been unaware of the right or claim.

(b) the right or claim results from the seller's compliance with technical drawings, designs, formulae or other such specifications furnished by the buyer."

5. Obligations of the Buyer

According to *the CISG*, the principal obligations of the buyer are to pay the price for the goods and to take delivery of them. If the buyer fails to perform any of his/her obligations under the contract or *the CISG*, the seller may get redress.

1）支付价款

《公约》第54条至59条对买方支付价款的义务作了细致的规定，包括支付价款的义务以及为支付价款而完成一系列事先准备步骤。这些步骤包括：开立信用证或银行保函；向政府有关部门或银行进行合同登记备案；获得必要的外汇或获取用汇许可。

（1）价格计算。

如果合同已有效订立，但没有明示或暗示地规定价格或规定如何确定价格，在没有任何相反表示的情况下，双方当事人应视为已默示地引用订立合同时此种货物在有关贸易的类似情况下销售的通常价格。若价格是按货物的重量规定的，如有疑问，应按净重确定。

（2）付款地点。

在国际货物贸易中，在合同中明确约定付款地点具有重要意义，但未作此种约定的情况也时有发生。这时，《公约》为买卖双方提供了替代解决方法。《公约》第57条规定，如果买方没有义务在任何其他特定地点支付价款，他必须在以下地点向卖方支付价款。

① 卖方营业地。

---

1) Paying the Price

Articles 54 to 59 provide a number of the details involved in the obligation of the buyer to pay the price. It includes as part of the buyer's obligation to pay the price and obligation to take a number of preliminary actions in order to make possible the payment of the price. These actions may include applying for a letter of credit or a bank guarantee of payment, registering the contract with a government office or with a bank, procuring the necessary foreign exchange or applying for official authorization to remit the currency abroad.

(1) Calculation of the price.

Where a contract has been validly concluded but does not expressly or implicitly fix or make provision for determining the price, the parties are considered, in the absence of any indication to the contrary, to have impliedly made reference to the price generally charged at the time of the conclusion of the contract for such goods sold under comparable circumstances in the trade concerned. If the price is fixed according to the weight of the goods, in case of doubt, it is to be determined by the net weight.

(2) Place of payment.

It is important that the place of payment should be clearly established when the contract is for the international sale of goods, but sometimes it can't be found in the contractual language. *The CISG* offers some supplements for the parties under this circumstance. Article 57 provides if the buyer is not bound to pay the price at any other particular place, he/she must pay it to the seller as follows.

(a) At the seller's place of business.

② 在凭货物或凭单据付款时，则为提交货物或单据的地点。卖方必须承担因其营业地在订立合同后发生变动而增加的与支付有关的费用。

(3) 付款时间。

① 如果买方没有义务在任何其他特定时间内支付价款，他必须于卖方按照合同和《公约》规定将货物或控制货物处置权的单据交给买方处置时支付价款。卖方可以将支付价款作为移交货物或单据的条件。

② 如果合同涉及货物的运输，卖方可以在支付价款后方可把货物或控制货物处置权的单据移交给买方作为发运货物的条件。

③ 买方在未有机会检验货物前，无义务支付价款，除非这种机会与双方当事人议定的交货或支付程序相抵触。

买方必须按合同和《公约》规定的日期，或按合同和《公约》可以确定的日期支付价款，而无须卖方提出任何要求或办理任何手续。

2) 收取货物

根据《公约》的规定，买方收取货物的义务包括两方面：①采取一切理应采取的行动以期卖方能提交货物；②接收货物。

(b) If the payment is to be made against the delivery of the goods or of documents, at the place where the delivery takes place. The seller must bear any increase in the expenses incidental to payment which is caused by a change in his/her place of business subsequent to the conclusion of the contract.

(3) Time of payment.

(a) If the buyer is not bound to pay the price at any other specific time, he/she must pay it when the seller places either the goods or documents controlling their disposition at the buyer's disposal in accordance with the contract and *the CISG*. The seller may make such payment a condition for handing over the goods or documents.

(b) If the contract involves carriage of the goods, the seller may dispatch the goods on terms whereby the goods, or documents controlling their disposition, will not be handed over to the buyer except against payment of the price.

(c) The buyer is not bound to pay the price until he/she has had an opportunity to examine the goods, unless the procedures for delivery or payment agreed upon by the parties are inconsistent with his/her having such an opportunity.

The buyer must pay the price on the date fixed by or determinable from the contract and *the CISG* without the need for any request or compliance with any formality on the part of the seller.

2) Taking Delivery

According to *the CISG*, the buyer's obligation to take delivery consists: (a) in doing all the acts which could reasonably be expected of him/her in order to enable the seller to make delivery; and (b) in taking over the goods.

6. 违反合同的补救方法

1) 卖方违约的补救方法

卖方未能履行合同或《公约》所规定的卖方义务，买方可以要求卖方实际履行、减价，也可以宣告合同无效，要求卖方进行损害赔偿。

(1) 实际履行。

实际履行是法院作出的要求当事一方采取一定行为的指令，该行为通常是合同中载明的行为，比如交货。《公约》第 46 条第 1 款规定："买方可以要求卖方履行义务，除非买方已采取与此要求相抵触的某种补救办法。"如果货物不符合合同，买方只有在此种不符合合同情形构成根本违反合同时，才可以要求交付替代货物，而且关于替代货物的要求，必须与依照第 39 条发出的通知同时提出，或者在该项通知发出后一段合理的时间内提出。在其他情形下，如果货物不符合合同，买方可以要求卖方通过修理对不符合合同之处进行补救，除非他考虑了所有情况之后，认为这样做是不合理的。

6. Remedies for Breach of Contract

1) Remedies for the Seller's Breach of Contract

If the seller fails to perform any of his/her obligations under the contract or *the CISG*, the buyer may require specific performance, reduction of price, avoidance of contract and damages.

(1) Specific performance.

Specific performance is an order of a court which requires a party to perform a specific act, usually what is stated in a contract, e.g. delivery of goods. Article 46(1) provides that "The buyer may require performance by the seller of his/her obligations unless the buyer has resorted to a remedy which is inconsistent with this requirement." The buyer may require delivery of substitute goods only if the lack of conformity constitutes a fundamental breach of contract and a request for substitute goods is made either in conjunction with notice given under Article 39 or within a reasonable time thereafter. Otherwise, if the goods do not conform with the contract, the buyer may require the seller to remedy the lack of conformity by repair, unless this is unreasonable having regard to all the circumstances.

(2) 减少价金。

如果货物不符合合同，不论价款是否已付，买方都可以减低价款，减价按实际交付的货物在交货时的价值与符合合同的货物在当时的价值两者之间的比例计算。但是，如果卖方按照《公约》第 37 条或第 48 条的规定对任何不履行义务做出了补救，或者买方拒绝接受卖方按照该两条规定履行义务，则买方不得减低价款。

(3) 宣告合同无效。

根据《公约》第 51 条第 2 款之规定，买方只有在卖方完全不交付货物或不按照合同规定交付货物构成根本违反合同时，才可以宣告整个合同无效。所谓根本违反合同，是指一方当事人违反合同的结果，使另一方蒙受损失，实际上剥夺了他根据合同规定有权期待得到的东西，除非违反合同一方并不预知而且一个同等资格、通情达理的人处于相同情况中也没有理由预知会发生这种结果。

宣告合同无效的声明，必须向另一方当事人发出通知，方始有效。

---

(2) Reduction of price.

If the goods do not conform with the contract whether or not the price has already been paid, the buyer can reduce the price in the same proportion as the value that the goods actually delivered had at the time of the delivery bears to the value that conforming goods would have had at that time. However, if the seller remedies any failure to perform his obligations in accordance with Article 37 or Article 48 of *the CISG* or if the buyer refuses to accept performance by the seller in accordance with those articles, the buyer may not reduce the price.

(3) Avoidance of contract.

According to Article 51(2) of *the CISG*, the buyer may declare the contract avoided in its entirety only if the seller fails to make delivery completely or in conformity with the contract amounts to a fundamental breach of the contract. A breach of contract committed by one of the parties is fundamental if it results in such detriment to the other party as substantially to deprive him/her of what he/she is entitled to expect under the contract, unless the party in breach did not foresee and a reasonable person of the same kind in the same circumstances would not have foreseen such a result.

A declaration of avoidance of the contract is effective only if made by notice to the other party.

值得注意的是，当卖方交付的货物中有部分符合合同时，买方应接受符合规定的部分；只有当卖方完全不交货或不按合同规定交货构成根本违反合同时，才能宣告整个合同无效。当卖方交货数量大于合同规定数量时，买方有权选择，全部接受或拒绝多交部分。

(4) 损害赔偿。

《公约》第 74 条规定："一方当事人违反合同应负的损害赔偿额，应与另一方当事人因他违反合同而遭受的包括利润在内的损失额相等。这种损害赔偿不得超过违反合同一方在订立合同时，依照他当时已知道或理应知道的事实和情况，对违反合同预料到或理应预料到的可能损失。"

2) 买方违约的补救方法

买方违反合同或《公约》的情况发生时，卖方可选择以下救济方法。

(1) 实际履行。

卖方可要求买方支付价款、收取货物或履行其他义务。除非卖方已采取了与此项要求相抵触的救济方法。

It shall be noted that, if the seller delivers only a part of the goods or if only a part of the goods delivered is in conformity with the contract, the buyer should accept the part of goods conformed to the contract. The buyer can declare the contract avoided in its entirety only if the failure to the seller to make delivery completely or in conformity with the contract amounts to a fundamental breach of the contract. If the seller delivers a quantity of goods greater than that provided for in the contract, the buyer may take delivery or refuse to take delivery of the excess quantity.

(4) Damages.

According to Article 74 of *the CISG*: "Damages for breach of contract by one party consist of a sum equal to the loss, including loss of profit, suffered by the other party as a consequence of the breach. Such damages may not exceed the loss which the party in breach foresaw or ought to have foreseen at the time of the conclusion of the contract, in the light of the facts and matters of which he/she then knew or ought to have known, as a possible consequence of the breach of contract."

2) Remedies for the Buyer's Breach of Contract

If the buyer fails to perform any of his/her obligations under the contract or *the CISG*, the seller may choose the following ways of remedy.

(1) Specific Performance.

The seller may require the buyer to pay the price, take delivery or perform his/her other obligations, unless the seller has resorted to a remedy which is inconsistent with this requirement.

(2) 宣告合同无效。

在下列情况发生时，卖方可以宣告合同无效。①买方不履行其在合同或《公约》中规定的任何义务构成根本违反合同；②买方不在卖方给予的额外履约时间内履行支付价款或收取货物的义务，或买方声明他将不在所规定的时间内这样做。但是，如果买方已支付价款，卖方就丧失了宣告合同无效的权利，除非对于买方迟延履行义务，他在知道买方履行义务前这样做；或者对于买方迟延履行义务以外的任何违反合同的情形，他在已知道或理应知道这种违反合同的情形后的一段合理时间内这样做；或他在卖方给予的任何额外时间满期后，或在买方声明他将不在这一额外时间内履行义务后的一段合理时间内这样做。

(3) 损害赔偿。

无论是买方还是卖方，作为合同一方当事人因违反合同应支付的损害赔偿额，应与另一方当事人因他违反合同而遭受的包括利润在内的损失额相等。声称另一方违反合同的一方，必须按情况采取合理措施，减轻由于该另一方违反合同而引起的损失，包括利润方面的损失。卖方可能享有的要求损害赔偿的任何权利，不因他行使采取其他补救办法的权利而丧失。

---

(2) Avoidance of contract.

The seller may declare the contract avoided:(a)If the failure by the buyer to perform any of his/her obligations under the contract or *the CISG* amounts to a fundamental breach of contract; (b)If the buyer does not, within the additional period of time fixed by the seller, perform his/her obligation to pay the price or take delivery of the goods, or if he/she declares that he/she will not do so within the period so fixed. However, in cases where the buyer has paid the price, the seller loses the right to declare the contract avoided unless he/she does so: (a)in respect of late performance by the buyer, before the seller has become aware that performance has been rendered; or (b)in respect of any breach other than late performance by the buyer, within a reasonable time: (i)after the seller knew or ought to have known of the breach; or (ii) after the expiration of any additional period of time fixed by the seller, or after the buyer has declared that he/she will not perform his/her obligations within such an additional period.

(3) Damages.

Regardless of the seller or the buyer, damages for breach of contract by one party consist of a sum equal to the loss, including loss of profit, suffered by the other party as a consequence of the breach. A party who relies on a breach of contract must take such measures as are reasonable in the circumstances to mitigate the loss, including loss of profit, resulting from the breach. The seller is not deprived of any right he/she may have to claim damages by exercising his/her right to other remedies.

7. 货物所有权与风险的转移

1) 货物所有权转移

在国际货物买卖中，货物所有权从何时起从卖方转移到买方，是一个十分重要的问题。在许多国际贸易争议中，通常只有先确定了货物的财产权归属问题，才能进而解决双方的具体权利和义务问题。由于各国法律对所有权转移适用不同的原则和规定，因此，《公约》对货物所有权何时转移以及合同对所有权可能产生的影响等问题均未涉及，而由解决争议的法院或仲裁庭依照《公约》的一般原则(即国际惯例)或依照冲突法规定适用的国内法律来解决。

(1) 国际贸易惯例的规定。

在国际贸易惯例中，只有 1932 年《华沙——牛津规则》明确规定了货物所有权转移的时间。

按照该规则第 20 条第 2 款的规定，卖方依据法律对所售货物所享有的留置权、保留权或中止交货权，不受本规则的影响。在依据《华沙——牛津规则》订立的合同中，货物所有权的转移时间是在卖方将有关单据交由买方掌握的时间。

---

7. Ownership of Goods and Transfer of Risk

1) Transfer of Ownership of Goods

In the international sale of goods, it is important when the ownership of goods transfers from the seller to the buyer. In many international trade disputes, the resolution usually answers the question of title first, then can tell the right and obligation of the parties. While different countries have different principles and stipulations about the transfer of ownership of goods, *the CISG* does not pay attention to that area. It depends on the courts or the tribunals hearing the cases to solve the problem through the principles of *the CISG* (that is the international trade practices) and the domestic laws applicable according to rules of the conflict law.

(1) Regulations of international trade practices.

According to the international trade practices, *Warsaw—Oxford Rules* of 1932 shows when the ownership of goods shall be transferred expressly.

The rule 20(2) shows: Nothing contained in *Warsaw—Oxford Rules* shall affect any right of lien or retention or stoppage in transit to which the seller may be entitled by law, in respect of the goods contracted to be sold. Subject to the provisions of the rule 20 (2) the time of the passing of the property in the goods shall be the moment when the seller delivers the documents into the possession of the buyer.

(2) 我国的有关规定。

根据我国《民法通则》第 72 条第 2 款之规定，按照合同或其他合法方式取得财产的，财产所有权从财产交付时起转移，法律另有规定或者当事人另有约定的除外。

2) 风险转移

在国际货物买卖中，货物遭受高温、水浸、火灾、沾污、盗窃或查封等非正常情况下发生的破损、串味或灭失等损失难以避免。货物在风险移转到买方承担后发生灭失或损坏，买方支付价款的义务并不因此解除，除非这种灭失或损坏是由于卖方的作为或不作为所造成。划分风险的目的就是为了分清买卖双方的法律责任。

(1) 风险分担原则。

《公约》对于买卖双方风险的划分采用的主要原则是以交货时间确定风险。《公约》第 69 条规定，从买方接收货物时起，风险转移由买方承担。但是这一原则的适用有一个前提，即风险的转移是在卖方无违约行为的情况下。假若卖方发生违约行为，则不适用该原则。

---

(2) Regulations of P.R.C.

Article 72(2) of *General Principles of the Civil Law of the P.R.C.*, provides: Property ownership shall not be obtained in violation of the law. Unless the law stipulates otherwise or the parties concerned have agreed on other arrangements, the ownership of property obtained by contract or by other lawful means shall be transferred simultaneously with the property itself.

2) Transfer of Risk

It is unavoidable that the goods of international sale suffer from heating, leakage, fire, contamination, thieves or seizure caused losses of dilapidation, odor or no-delivery. Loss of or damage to the goods after the risk has passed to the buyer does not discharge him/her from his/her obligation to pay the price, unless the loss or damage is due to an act or omission of the seller. The purpose of risk share is to establish bounds of legal liability of the sellers and the buyers.

(1) Risk sharing principle.

The CISG agrees in principle that the time of delivery of goods is the time of passing of risk. Under the Article 69 of *the CISG*, the risk passes to the buyer when he/she takes over the goods. However, the application of the principle assumes that no contract violation of the seller happened, or the principle of risk transfer is not applicable.

(2) 风险转移时间。

如果销售合同涉及货物的运输，但卖方没有义务在某一特定地点交付货物，自货物按照销售合同交付给第一承运人以转交给买方时起，风险就转移到由买方承担。如果卖方有义务在某一特定地点把货物交付给承运人，在货物于该地点交付给承运人以前，风险不转移到买方。卖方受权保留控制货物处置权的单据，并不影响风险的转移。但是，在货物以"货物上加标记、装运单据、向买方发出通知或其他"方式清楚地注明有关合同以前，风险不转移给买方。

对于在运输途中销售的货物，从订立合同时起，风险就转移而由买方承担。但是，如果情况表明有此需要，从货物交付给签发载有运输合同单据的承运人时起，风险就由买方承担。尽管如此，如果卖方在订立合同时已知道或理应知道货物已经灭失或损坏，而他又不将这一事实告知买方，则这种灭失或损坏应由卖方负责。

---

(2) Time of transfer of risk.

If the contract of sale involves carriage of the goods and the seller is not bound to hand them over at a particular place, the risk passes to the buyer when the goods are handed over to the first carrier for transmission to the buyer in accordance with the contract of sale. If the seller is bound to hand the goods over to a carrier at a particular place, the risk does not pass to the buyer until the goods are handed over to the carrier at that place. The fact that the seller is authorized to retain documents controlling the disposition of the goods does not affect the passage of the risk. Nevertheless, the risk does not pass to the buyer until the goods are clearly identified to the contract, whether by markings on the goods, by shipping documents, by notice given to the buyer or otherwise.

The risk in respect of the goods sold in transit passes to the buyer from the time of the conclusion of the contract. However, if the circumstances so indicate, the risk is assumed by the buyer from the time the goods were handed over to the carrier who issued the documents embodying the contract of carriage. Nevertheless, if at the time of the conclusion of the contract of sale the seller knew or ought to have known that the goods had been lost or damaged and did not disclose this to the buyer, the loss or damage is at the risk of the seller.

在不涉及货物运输的情况下，从买方接收货物时起，或如果买方不在适当时间内这样做，则从货物交给他处置但他不收取货物从而违反合同时起，风险转移由买方承担。但是，如果买方有义务在卖方营业地以外的某一地点接收货物，当交货时间已到而买方知道货物已在该地点交给他处置时，风险才始移转。如果合同指的是当时未加识别的货物，则这些货物在未清楚划归合同项下以前，不得视为已交给买方处置。

第二节　国际货物运输与保险

一、国际海上货物运输

国际货物运输以海上货物运输为主，目前国际上 70％的货物使用海上运输方式。海上货物运输主要有两种形式：一是提单运输，也称班轮运输；二是租船运输。前者主要适用于散杂货物的运输，后者主要用于大宗货物的运输。

In the absence of cargo transport, the risk passes to the buyer when he/she takes over the goods. If he/she does not do so in due time, from the time when the goods are placed at his/her disposal, he/she commits a breach of contract by failing to take delivery. However, if the buyer is bound to take over the goods at a place other than a place of business of the seller, the risk passes when delivery is due and the buyer is aware of the fact that the goods are placed at his/her disposal at that place. If the contract relates to goods not then identified, the goods are considered not to be placed at the disposal of the buyer until they are clearly identified to the contract.

3.2　International Transportation and Insurance of Cargo

3.2.1　International Carriage of Goods by Sea

International transport of goods mainly relies on marine transport. Around 70% of the goods in international transaction transport by sea, mainly through liner service and tramp service. The liner service is used for less-than-container goods, while the tramp service is suitable for goods in large quantity.

1. 班轮运输

1) 提单的含义与功能

提单是一种用以证明海上运输合同和货物已由承运人接管或装船，以及承运人保证凭以交付货物的单据。从上述定义中可以看出，提单具有以下作用。

(1) 提单是运输合同的凭证。在班轮运输中，当托运人与承运人之间已事先就货物运输订有货运协议，提单就是运输合同的凭证。如果事先没有货运协议，则提单就是双方订立的运输合同。当托运人通过背书将提单转让给第三人，提单就是承运人与第三人之间的运输合同。

(2) 提单是接收货物的收据。提单是在承运人收到所交运的货物后，向托运人签发的证明承运人按提单上所列内容收到了货物。提单在托运人与承运人之间起到收据的作用，直到货物所有权被转移到第三方(收货人)手中。此后，提单成为第三方与承运人之间的运输合同。依据提单，第三方获得与托运人相一致的法律上的权利、义务和责任。当货物承运人将货物交付海上货物承运人运输时，货物承运人又会反过来从海上货物承运人那里收到一张承运人提单或海运单，货物承运人将以此为依据，证明其将货物交付给了海上货物承运人。

---

1. Liner Service

1) Definition and Function of Bill of Lading

Bill of lading is a document issued by a carrier to a shipper, listing and acknowledging receipt of goods for transport and specifying terms of delivery. As defined above, a bill of lading has three functions.

(1) Bill of lading is the evidence of a contract of carriage. During liner service, the contract of carriage is the underlying agreement between the carrier and the customer to transport his/her goods. The bill of lading is the evidence of this. If there is no contract of carriage by sea between the carrier and the customer, the bill of lading is directly used as the contract of carriage. On the condition that the shipper has endorsed the bill of lading to the third party, the bill of lading can be used as a contract of carriage between the carrier and the third party.

(2) Bill of lading is the evidence of receipt of cargo. The bill of lading is a receipt by the carrier that the goods are in his/her custody. The bill of lading acts as a receipt between the shipper and the carrier until such time as title has been passed to a third party (the consignee). Then it becomes an independent contract between the carrier and the third party. The third party assumes the rights, responsibilities and obligations identical to those of the shipper. Remember that when the carrier delivers the goods to the ocean carrier for shipment, he/she will in turn receive a carrier bill of lading or a sea waybill which will act as his/her receipt that the cargo is in the custody of the carrier.

（3）提单是货物所有权的凭证。因此，提单项下的货物的财产权利可以背书的方式予以转让。承运人收到货物并签发提单之后，负有在目的地只向合法持有经连续背书的正本提单的人交付货物的义务。

2) 班轮运输的当事人

班轮运输的当事人包含承运人和托运人，其权利义务应在提单中明确加以规定。下面根据《海牙规则》的规定，将其主要内容分述如下。

（1）承运人的责任。

《海牙规则》第3条规定了承运人必须履行的最低限度责任。

① 提供适航船舶。承运人在开航前与开航时必须谨慎处理，以使船舶具有适航性，并适当地配备船员、装备船舶和供应船舶，使货舱、冷藏舱和该船其他载货处所能适宜和安全地收受、运送和保管货物。

② 管理货物的基本义务。承运人应适当和谨慎地装载、操作、积载、运送、保管、照料和卸载所承运的货物。该义务尤其强调承运人在装船时的责任。

这两项义务是强制性的，在提单中解除或降低承运人这两项义务的任何条款均属无效。

(3) Bill of lading is the document of title of cargo. The legal right to the goods covered by the bill of lading can therefore pass from one party to another by means of endorsements. The carrier will only release the goods at destination to a rightful holder of a duly endorsed original bill of lading.

2) The Parties of Liner Service

The parties of liner service include the carrier and the shipper, the boundary of the liability of both parties shall be stated clearly in the bill of lading. *The Hague Rules* shows the boundary mainly as follow.

(1) Liability of the carrier.

Article 3 of *the Hague Rules* stipulates the carriers minimum obligations.

(a) Ship seaworthy. Before and at the beginning of the voyage, the carrier shall be bound to exercise due diligence to make the ship seaworthy; properly man, equip and supply the ship; make the holds, refrigerating and cool chambers, and all other parts of the ship in which goods are carried, fit and safe for their reception, carriage and preservation.

(b) Basic obligations to manage goods. The carrier shall properly and carefully load, handle, stow, carry, keep, care for, and discharge the goods carried. The obligation of loading is especially stressed.

Those obligations mentioned above are compulsory. Any item in the bill of lading aimed to exclude or derogate those obligations is invalid.

(2) 承运人的责任豁免。

《海牙规则》以不完全过失责任来确定承运人的责任。对于对下述原因引起的灭失或损坏，承运人不承担责任：①船长、船员、引水员或承运人的雇佣人员，在驾驶船舶或管理船舶中的行为、疏忽或不履行义务；②火灾，但由于承运人的实际过失或私谋所引起的除外；③海上或其他可航水域的灾难、危险和意外事故；④天灾；⑤战争行为；⑥公敌行为；⑦君主、当权者或人民的扣留或管制，或依法扣押；⑧检疫限制；⑨托运人或货主及其代理人或代表的行为或不行为；⑩任何原因所引起的局部或全面罢工、关厂停止或限制工作；⑪暴动和骚乱；⑫救助或企图救助海上人命或财产；⑬由于货物的固有缺点、质量或缺陷引起的体积或重量亏损，或任何其他灭失或损坏；⑭包装不充分；⑮标志不清或不当；⑯虽恪尽职责亦不能发现的潜在缺点；⑰非由于承运人的实际过失或私谋，或者承运人的代理人，或雇佣人员的过失或疏忽所引起的其他任何原因；但是要求引用这条免责利益的人应负责举证，证明有关的灭失或损坏既非由于承运人的实际过失或私谋，亦非承运人的代理人或雇佣人员的过失或疏忽所造成；⑱为救助或企图救助海上人命或财产而发生的绕航，或任何合理绕航，都不能作为破坏或违反《海牙规则》或运输合同的行为；承运人对由此而引起的任何灭失或损坏，都不负责。

(2) Exemption of the liability of the carrier.

Under *the Hague Rules*, imperfect liability for the negligence principle is regarded as the fundamental principle undertaken by the carrier of carriage contract. The carrier shall not be responsible for loss or damage arising or resulting from: (a)Act, neglect, or default of the master, mariner, pilot, or the servants of the carrier in the navigation or in the management of the ship; (b)Fire, unless caused by the actual fault or privity of the carrier; (c)Perils, dangers and accidents of the sea or other navigable waters; (d)Act of God; (e)Act of war; (f)Act of public enemies; (g)Arrest or restraint of princes, rulers or people, or seizure under legal process; (h) Quarantine restrictions; (i)Act or omission of the shipper or owner of the goods, his/her agent or representative; (j)Strikes or lockouts or stoppage or restraint of labour from whatever cause, whether partial or general; (k)Riots and civil commotions; (l)Saving or attempting to save life or property at sea; (m)Wastage in bulk or weight or any other loss or damage arising from inherent defect, quality or vice of the goods; (n)Insufficiency of packing; (o)Indistinct or improper marks; (p)Latent defects not discoverable by due diligence; (q)Any other cause arising without the actual fault or privity of the carrier, or without the actual fault or neglect of the agents or servants of the carrier, but the burden of proof shall be on the person claiming the benefit of this exception to show that neither the actual fault or privity of the carrier nor the fault or neglect of the agents or servants of the carrier contributed to the loss or damage; (r)Any deviation in saving or attempting to save life or property at sea or any reasonable deviation shall not be deemed to be an infringement or breach of the Hague Rules or of the contract of carriage, and the carrier shall not be liable for any loss or damage resulting therefrom.

承运人或是船舶方，在任何情况下对货物或与货物有关的灭失或损坏，每件或每计费单位超过一百英镑或与其等值的其他货币的部分，都不负责；但托运人于装货前已就该项货物的性质和价值提出声明，并已在提单中注明的，不在此限。经承运人、船长或承运人的代理人与托运人双方协议，可规定不同于本款规定的另一最高限额，但该最高限额不得低于上述数额。如托运人在提单中，故意谎报货物性质或价值，则在任何情况下，承运人或是船舶方，对货物或与货物有关的灭失或损害，都不负责。

(3) 承运人的责任期间和诉讼时效。

按照《海牙规则》第 1 条的规定，"货物运输"是从货物装上船起，至卸下船止的整个期间。因此，承运人的责任期间实行"钩到钩原则"。

从货物交付日或应交付日起，托运人或收货人应就货物的灭失或损坏情况在一年内提起诉讼，否则免除承运人依照《海牙规则》应当承担的一切责任。

The carrier shall in any event not be or become liable for any loss or damage to or in connexion with goods in an amount exceeding 100 pounds sterling per package or unit, or the equivalent of that sum in other currency unless the nature and value of such goods have been declared by the shipper before shipment and inserted in the bill of lading. By agreement between the carrier, master or agent of the carrier and the shipper another maximum amount than that mentioned in this paragraph may be fixed, provided that such maximum shall not be less than the figure above named. The carrier shall not be responsible in any event for loss or damage to, or in connexion with, the goods if the nature or value thereof has been knowingly misstated by the shipper in the bill of lading.

(3) Period of liability and limitation of action of the carrier.

Based on *the Hague Rules* Article 1, "Carriage of goods" covers the period from the time when the goods are loaded on to the time they are discharged from the ship. Therefore, the period of liability of the carrier keeps to "hook to hook principle".

In any event, the carrier shall be discharged from all liability in respect of loss or damage under *the Hague Rules* unless the suit is brought by the shipper or consignee within one year after delivery of the goods or the date when the goods should have been delivered.

(4) 托运人责任。

根据《海牙规则》第 3 条的规定，托运人的责任有两项，即保证和通知。首先托运人应被视为已在装船时向承运人保证，由他提供的标志、件数、数量和重量均正确无误；并应赔偿给承运人由于这些项目不正确所引起或导致的一切灭失、损坏和费用。承运人的这种赔偿权利，并不减轻其根据运输合同对托运人以外的任何人所承担的责任和义务。其次，托运人托运危险物品，应通知承运人。

3) 关于班轮运输的三个国际公约

国际上规范班轮运输的国际公约主要有三个，即 1924 年《统一提单的若干法律规则的国际公约》(以下简称《海牙规则》)、1968 年《修改统一提单的若干法律规则的国际公约的议定书》(以下简称《维斯比规则》)和 1978 年《联合国海上货物运输公约》(以下简称《汉堡规则》)。

(4) Liability of the shipper.

According to Article 3 of *the Hague Rules*, the shipper undertakes two obligations, that is guarantee and notice. Firstly, The shipper shall be deemed to have guaranteed to the carrier the accuracy at the time of shipment of the marks, number, quantity and weight, as furnished by him/her, and the shipper shall indemnify the carrier against all loss, damage and expenses arising or resulting from inaccuracies in such particulars. The right of the carrier to such indemnity shall in no way limit his/her responsibility and liability under the contract of carriage to any person other than the shipper. Secondly, if the shipper consigned dangerous cargo, the shipper shall notice the carrier.

3) Three International Conventions on Liner Service

There are mainly three international conventions that govern the liner service. They are *the International Convention for the Unification of Certain Rules of Law Relating to Bill of Lading 1924 (the Hague Rules)*, *Protocol to Amend the International Convention for the Unification of Certain Rules of Law Relating to Bills of Lading 1968 (the Visby Rules)*, and *the United Nations Convention of the Carriage of Goods by Sea 1978 (the Hamburg Rules)*.

(1)《海牙规则》。

《海牙规则》共有 16 条，是国际海上运输法律体系中最重要的国际条约。一直以来，船货双方对于船方能否对其应当承担的货物运输途中的灭失、损坏责任进行随意限制存在矛盾，《海牙规则》被认为是协调承运人与托运人及海上货物运输保险公司之间这一由来已久的承运人责任限制问题的产物。1921 年，国际法海事委员会在荷兰海牙制定了《海牙规则》，将班轮运输中的承运人和海上货物承运人的基本权利、义务、责任标准化。1924 年 8 月 25 日，《海牙规则》由 26 个国家在布鲁塞尔签订，1931 年 6 月 2 日生效。《海牙规则》在全球范围内适用于大约 90%的国家，包括许多欧美国家。在《海牙规则》经过一定修订以后，美国于 1936 年以美国《海上货物运输法》的形式对《海牙规则》的内容予以承认。我国于 1981 年承认该公约，1993 年的《中华人民共和国海商法》吸纳了《海牙规则》中关于承运人责任和豁免的规定。

(2)《维斯比规则》。

《维斯比规则》也被称为"1968 年布鲁塞尔议定书"，其于 1968 年 2 月 23 日在布鲁塞尔外交会议上通过，并于 1977 年 6 月生效。需要注意的是，《维斯比规则》不应该被认为是一项独立的国际条约，任何批准加入《维斯比规则》的国家均为《海牙规则》("海牙-维斯比规则")的缔约方。目前已有英国、法国、丹麦、挪威、新加坡、瑞典等 29 个国家和地区参加了《维斯比规则》。

---

(1) *The Hague Rules.*

With 16 articles, *the Hague Rules* is the most important international convention in the area of international carriage of goods by sea. These rules were the result of widespread dissatisfaction among shippers and their insurers with arbitrary restrictions imposed by carriers to limit their liability in case of loss of, or damage to cargo. In 1921, in Hague, Netherlands, Comité Maritime International instituted *the Hague Rules*, which established standard basic rights, obligations and responsibilities of the shipper and ocean-carrier for goods covered under a bill of lading. Then, on August 25, 1924, 26 countries signed the convention in Brussels. *The Hague Rules* went into effect on June 2, 1931. These rules are followed by some 90% of nations, including many Euro-American countries. After some changes, the US adopted them in 1936 as *Carriage Of Goods By Sea Act (COGSA)*. China accepted the convention in 1981. *The Maritime Code of The People's Republic of China*(1993) absorbed the rules of responsibilities and exemptions of the carrier of the Hague Rules.

(2) *The Visby Rules.*

The Visby Rules is also called the 1968 Brussels Protocol, which adopted on Brussels diplomatic conference February 23, 1968. The rules came into effect in Jun. 1977. It should be noticed that *the Visby Rules* should not be considered as a separate convention. Thus, the result of ratification of or accession to *the Visby Rules* by a nation is that the nation consents to be bound by *the Hague-Visby Rules*. For the present, 29 countries such as Britain, France, Denmark, Norway, Singapore, Sweden and so on have become parties of the convention.

由于《海牙规则》的实施并没有终止船货双方关于承运人责任限制的争论，相反，许多托运人认为《海牙规则》给予承运人的责任限制保护过多，《海牙规则》于 1968 年被《维斯比规则》修改。修改后的《海牙-维斯比规则》增强了对托运人利益的保护。《维斯比规则》对《海牙规则》的最后修改完成于 1979 年。这些修改主要内容如下。

① 提单的证据力。《维斯比规则》第一条明确规定提单对于提单的善意受让人是最终证据。

② 责任限制。《海牙规则》关于责任限制的规定比较简单，《维斯比规则》在内容上做了较大的扩充和修改。

③ 承运人的雇佣人或代理人的责任限制。依《维斯比规则》的规定，对承运人提起的货损索赔诉讼，无论是以合同为依据，还是以侵权行为为依据，均可以适用责任限制的规定。如果这种诉讼是对承运人的雇佣人员或代理人(而该雇佣人员或代理人不是独立的缔约人)提出的，则该雇佣人员或代理人适用按照该规则承运人可援引的各项答辩和责任限制。

(3) 《汉堡规则》。

《汉堡规则》是与《海牙-维斯比规则》相区别的另外一套规制国际海上运输的规则。《汉堡规则》于 1978 年 3 月 31 日在汉堡通过。

The implementation of *the Hague Rules* did not terminate the debate between the shipper and the carrier on limitation on responsibility of the carrier. Ever since *the Hague Rules* came into force, many shippers continuously complained *the Hague Rules* about its excessive limitations to the carriers' liability. Thus, *the Hague Rules* was amended by *the Visby Rules*. After the amendment, the Rules became known as *the Hague-Visby Rules*, which increased the protection of the interests of the shipper. A final amendment was made in the Protocol in 1979. The main contents of those amendments include:

(a) The evidential weight of the bill of lading: the article one of *the Visby Rules* stipulates that proof to the contrary of the bill of lading shall not be admissible when the bill of lading has been transferred to a third party acting in good faith.

(b) Liability limitations: *the Visby Rules* has much more complicated and detailed rules on liability limitation than *the Hague Rules*.

(c) Liability limitations to a servant or agent of the carrier: based on *the Visby Rules*, the defences and limitations of liability provided for in *the Visby Rules* shall apply in any action against the carrier in respect of loss or damage to goods covered by a contract of carriage whether the action be founded in contract or in tort. If such an action is brought against a servant or agent of the carrier (such servant or agent not being an independent contractor), such servant or agent shall be entitled to avail himself/herself of the defences and limitations of liability which the carrier is entitled to invoke under *the Visby Rules*.

(3) *The Hamburg Rules.*

Different from *the Hague-Visby Rules, the Hamburg Rules* is another set of rules governing the international shipment of goods, resulting from the convention adopted in Hamburg on March 31, 1978.

根据《汉堡规则》第 31 条之规定，加入《汉堡规则》的国家必须退出《海牙规则》；若须推迟退出《海牙-维斯比规则》，最迟在《汉堡规则》生效后五年内，《汉堡规则》的批准国必须退出《海牙-维斯比规则》。《汉堡规则》意图建立一套国际统一适用的远洋船舶货物运输规则，其产生发展的动力主要来自于希望在远洋船舶货物运输领域获得更公平的参与机会，获得更好的托运人利益保护的发展中国家。

按规定，《汉堡规则》须自第二十份批准书交存之日起满一年后的次月第一日方能生效，《汉堡规则》在其通过后的第十五个年头，即 1992 年 11 月 1 日，才得以生效。虽然《汉堡规则》只有约 26 个缔约国，而《海牙规则》及《海牙-维斯比规则》却在世界上大多数从事海运的国家有效，《汉堡规则》对于扩大承运人责任的努力仍然值得关注。

① 《汉堡规则》将《海牙规则》中承运人的不完全过失责任制改为承运人的推定过失责任制，取消了"过失免责条款"。

② 《海牙规则》没有规定延迟交货的责任，《汉堡规则》规定承运人应对延迟交货负责。

③ 《汉堡规则》规定，承运人对货物的责任期间包括在装货港，在运输途中以及在卸货港，货物在承运人掌管的全部期间。

Pursuant to Article 31 of *the Hamburg Rules*, entry into force of *the Hamburg Rules* coupled to denunciation of *the Hague Rules*. Ratifying states should denounce the conventions governing *the Hague-Visby Rules* in the latest five years after entry into force of *the Hamburg Rules*. *The Hamburg Rules* was an attempt to form a uniform legal base for the transportation of goods on oceangoing ships. A driving force behind *the Hamburg Rules* was the attempt of developing countries' to level the playing field and get more interests protection for the shippers.

According to the stipulation, *the Hamburg Rules* doesn't enter into force until the first day of the month following the expiration of one year from the date of deposit of the twentieth instrument of ratification, it took more than 14 years to wait for the effective date of the Rules before November 1, 1992. Though *the Hamburg Rules* is in force in about twenty-six countries, while *the Hague Rules* or *the Hague-Visby Rules* are presently in force in most of the world's shipping nations, we should notice the nice try to extend the liabilities of the carrier.

(a) *The Hamburg Rules* changes the imperfect liability for negligence principle established by *the Hague Rules* into the presumption liability for negligence principle, and annulled the neglect escape clause.

(b) Based on *the Hamburg Rules*, the carrier shall be liable for the delay of delivery, while *the Hague Rules* does not have such rules.

(c) The responsibility of the carrier for the goods under *the Hamburg Rules* covers the period during which the carrier is in charge of the goods at the port of loading, during the carriage and at the port of discharge.

④　《汉堡规则》第一次在一定范围内承认了保函的效力，其第 17 条规定，托运人为了换取清洁提单可向承运人出具保函，保函只在托运人与承运人之间有效。

⑤　《汉堡规则》对实际承运人的概念加以了界定。

2．租船运输

与班轮运输承运人是公用运输业者相对应，租船运输承运人是合约承运人。班轮运输遵照固定的线路、费率，而理想的租船运输则可以将任何货物运输到任何地方，其运费费率由市场供求量决定。一般来说，租船运输合同在船主与租船者之间签订。

租船者要么接管船舶一段特定的时间(定期租船)，要么接管船舶从事一段特定的航程(航次租船)，因此，租船运输可以分为定期租船运输和航次租船运输。定期租船运输的一类又被叫作光船运输。

1) 航次租船运输

航次租船运输，是指航次出租人向承租人提供船舶或者船舶的部分舱位，装运约定的货物，从一港运至另一港，船长、船员、燃料、补给均由船主提供的运输方式。

(d) To some degree, *the Hamburg Rules* admits the effect of letter of guarantee issued by the shipper to the carrier. According to the Article 17 of the Rules, the shipper may trade letter of guarantee for clean bill of lading; the letter of guarantee is effective only between the shipper and the carrier.

(e) *The Hamburg Rules* clearly defined "actual carrier".

2. Tramp Service

The tramp ship carrier is a contractual carrier. Unlike a liner, often called a common carrier, which has a fixed schedule and a published tariff, the ideal tramp can carry anything to anywhere, and freight rates are influenced by supply and demand. To generate business, a contract to lease the vessel known as a charter party is drawn up between the ship owner and the charterer.

The charterer takes over the vessel for either a certain amount of time (a time charter) or for a certain point-to-point voyage (a voyage charter), giving rise to these two main types of charters: voyage charter and time charter. There is a subtype of time charter called the demise or bareboat charter.

1) Voyage Charter

In a voyage charter, the charterer hires the vessel for a single voyage, and the vessel's owner provides the master, crew, bunkers and supplies.

按照我国《海商法》第 93 条的规定，航次租船合同的主要内容包括：出租人和承租人的名称、船名、船籍、载货重量、容积、货名、装货港和目的港、受载期限、装卸期限、运费、滞期费、速遣费以及其他有关事项。

根据《海商法》第 94 条的规定，出租人的责任与班轮运输中承运人的责任相同。另一方面，承租人责任主要有：①提供约定的货物；②将租用的船舶转租第三人；③解除租船合同。

根据《海商法》第 95 条的规定，对按照航次租船合同运输的货物签发的提单，提单持有人不是承租人的，承运人与该提单持有人之间的权利、义务关系适用提单的约定。但是，提单中载明适用航次租船合同条款的，适用该航次租船合同的条款。

2) 定期租船运输

定期租船运输是指船舶的租期是固定的，船舶出租人向承租人提供约定的由出租人配备船员的船舶，由出租人管理船舶，承租人给出货运指令，或者将船舶以航次租船或定期租船的形式转租的运输方式。

定期租船合同的内容，主要包括出租人和承租人的名称、船名、船籍、船级、吨位、容积、船速、燃料消耗、航区、用途、租船期间、交船和还船的时间和地点以及条件、租金及其支付，以及其他有关事项。

According to Article 93 of *the Maritime Code* of the P.R.C.: A voyage charter party shall mainly contain the name of the shipowner, name of the charterer, name and nationality of the ship, its bale or grain capacity, description of the goods to be loaded, port of loading, port of destination, laydays, time for loading and discharge, payment of freight, demurrage, dispatch and other relevant matters.

According to Article 94 of *the Maritime Code* of the P.R.C.: Rules about the liability of the carrier in liner service shall apply to the shipowner under the voyage charter party. Besides, the obligations of the charterer includes: (a)providing the intended goods, (b)subletting the ship, (c)cancelling the charter party.

Based on Article 95 of *the Maritime Code* of the P.R.C.: Where the holder of the bill of lading is not the charterer in the case of a bill of lading issued under a voyage charter, the rights and obligations of the carrier and the holder of the bill of lading shall be governed by the clauses of the bill of lading. However, if the clauses of the voyage charter party are incorporated into the bill of lading, the relevant clauses of the voyage charter party shall apply.

2) Time Charter

In a time charter, the vessel is hired for a specific amount of time. The owner still manages the vessel but the charterer gives orders for the employment of the vessel, and may subcharter the vessel on a time charter or voyage charter basis.

A time charter party mainly contains the name of the shipowner, the name of the charterer, the name, nationality, class, tonnage, capacity, speed and fuel consumption of the ship, the navigation area, the agreed service, the contractual period, the time, place and conditions of delivery and redelivery of the ship, the hire and the way of its payment and other relevant matters.

（1）出租人应当履行以下义务。

① 出租人交付船舶时，应当做到谨慎处理，使船舶适航。交付的船舶应当适合于约定的用途，否则，承租人有权解除合同，并有权要求赔偿因此遭受的损失。

② 出租人应在约定的时间交付船舶，否则，承租人有权解除合同，出租人将船舶延误情况和船舶预期抵达交船港的日期通知承租人的，承租人应当自接到通知时起 48 小时内，将解除合同或者继续租用船舶的决定通知出租人。

（2）承租人责任如下。

① 承租人应当保证船舶在约定航区内的安全港口或者地点之间从事约定的海上运输。

② 承租人应当保证船舶用于运输约定的合法的货物。

③ 承租人可以将租用的船舶转租，但是应当将转租的情况及时通知出租人。租用的船舶转租后，原租船合同约定的权利和义务不受影响。

④ 在合同期间，船舶进行海难救助的，承租人有权获得扣除救助费用、损失赔偿、船员应得部分以及其他费用后的救助款项的一半。

(1) The shipowner shall carry out the following obligations.

(a) At the time of delivery, the shipowner shall exercise due diligence to make the ship seaworthy. The ship delivered shall be fit for the intended service. Otherwise, the charterer may cancel the contract and seek redress related to the charter party.

(b) The shipowner shall deliver the ship within the time agreed upon in the charter party, or the charterer is entitled to cancel the charter party. However, if the shipowner has notified the charterer of the anticipated delay in delivery and has given an estimated time of arrival of the ship at the port of delivery, the charterer shall notify the shipowner, within 48 hours of the receipt of such notice from the shipowner, of his/her decision whether to cancel the charter party or not.

(2) The charterer shall assume the following obligations.

(a) To guarantee that the ship shall be employed in the agreed maritime transport between the safe ports or places within the navigation area agreed upon.

(b) To guarantee that the ship shall be employed to carry the lawful merchandise agreed.

(c) To sublet the ship under charter, but he/she shall notify the shipowner of the sublet in time. The rights and obligations agreed upon in the head charter shall not be affected by the sub-charter.

(d) Should the ship be engaged in salvage operations during the charter period, the charterer shall be entitled to half of the amount of the payment for salvage operations after deducting therefrom the salvage expenses, compensation for damage, the portion due to crew members and other relevant costs.

⑤ 承租人应当按照合同约定支付租金。承租人未按照合同约定支付租金的，出租人有权解除合同，并有权要求赔偿因此遭受的损失。承租人未向出租人支付租金或者合同约定的其他款项的，出租人对船上属于承租人的货物和财产以及转租船舶的收入有留置权。

⑥ 还船。承租人向出租人交还船舶时，该船舶当具有与出租人交船时相同的良好状态，但是船舶本身的自然磨损除外。船舶未能保持与交船时相同的良好状态的，承租人应当负责修复或者给予赔偿。

3) 光船租船运输

光船租船运输是定期租船运输的一种。在光船运输中，船舶承租人负责配置全体船员以及船舶维护，承租人有权在承租期间占有、使用和营运船舶。

按照我国《海商法》第 145 条的规定，光船租赁合同的内容，主要包括出租人和承租人的名称、船名、船籍、船级、吨位、容积、航区、用途、租船期间、交船和还船的时间和地点以及条件、船舶检验、船舶的保养维修、租金及其支付、船舶保险、合同解除的时间和条件，以及其他有关事项。

(e) To pay the hire as agreed upon in the charter. Where the charterer fails to pay the hire as agreed upon, the shipowner shall be entitled to cancel the charter party and claim any losses resulting therefrom. In case the charterer fails to pay the hire or other sums of money as agreed upon in the charter, the shipowner shall have a lien on the charterer's goods, other property on board and earnings from the sub-charter.

(f) When redelivering the ship to the shipowner, the ship shall be in the same good order and condition as it was at the time of delivery, fair wear and tear excepted. Where, upon redelivery, the ship fails to remain in the same good order and condition as it was at the time of delivery, the charterer shall be responsible for rehabilitation or for compensation.

3) Bareboat Charter

A bareboat charter is a kind of time charter in which the charterer takes responsibility for the crew allocation and maintenance of the ship during the time of the charter, while the charterer has the right to occupy, use and operate the ship.

Article 145 of *the Maritime Code* of the P.R.C. stipulates: A bareboat charter party mainly contains the name of the shipowner and the name of the charterer; the name, nationality, class, tonnage and capacity of the ship; navigation area, the employment of the ship and the charter period; the time, place and condition of delivery and redelivery; the survey, maintenance and repair of the ship; the hire and its payment; the insurance of the ship; the time and condition for the termination of the charter and other relevant matters.

出租人应当在合同约定的港口或者地点，按照合同约定的时间，向承租人交付船舶以及船舶证书。交船时，出租人应当做到谨慎处理，使船舶适航。交付的船舶应当适于合同约定的用途。否则，承租人有权解除合同，并有权要求赔偿因此遭受的损失。

　　光船租赁期间，承租人负责船舶的保养、维修。在光船租赁期间，承租人应当按照合同约定的船舶价值，以出租人同意的保险方式为船舶进行保险，并负担保险费用。在光船租赁期间，因承租人对船舶占有、使用和营运的原因使出租人的利益受到影响或者遭受损失的，承租人应当负责消除影响或者赔偿损失。

　　因船舶所有权争议或者出租人所负的债务致使船舶被扣押的，出租人应当保证承租人的利益不受影响；致使承租人遭受损失的，出租人应当负赔偿责任。在光船租赁期间，未经出租人书面同意，承租人不得转让合同的权利和义务或者以光船租赁的方式将船舶进行转租。承租人应当按照合同约定支付租金。承租人未按照合同约定的时间支付租金连续超过 7 日的，出租人有权解除合同，并有权要求赔偿因此遭受的损失。船舶发生灭失或者失踪的，租金应当自船舶灭失或者得知其最后消息之日起停止支付，预付租金应当按照比例退还。

The shipowner shall deliver the ship and its certificates to the charterer at the port or place and time as stipulated in the charter party. At the time of delivery, the shipowner shall exercise due diligence to make the ship seaworthy. The ship delivered shall be fit for the agreed service. Where the shipowner acts against the obligations above, the charterer shall be entitled to cancel the charter party and claim any losses resulting therefrom.

The charterer shall be responsible for the maintenance and repair of the ship during the bareboat charter period. During the bareboat charter period, the ship shall be insured, at the value agreed upon in the charter and in the way consented to by the shipowner, by the charterer at his/her expense. During the bareboat charter period, if the charterer's possession, employment or operation of the ship has affected the interests of the shipowner or caused any losses thereto, the charterer shall be liable for eliminating the harmful effect or compensating for the losses.

Should the ship be arrested due to any disputes over its ownership or debts owed by the shipowner, the shipowner shall guarantee that the interest of the charterer is not affected. The shipowner shall be liable for compensation for any losses suffered by the charterer thereby. During the bareboat charter period, the charterer shall not assign the rights and obligations stipulated in the charter party or sublet the ship under bareboat charter without the shipowner's consent in writing. The charterer shall pay the hire as stipulated in the charter party. In default of payment by the charterer for seven consecutive days or more after the time as agreed in the charter party for such payment, the shipowner is entitled to cancel the charter party without prejudice to any claim for the loss arising from the charterer's default. Should the ship be lost or missing, payment of hire shall cease from the day when the ship was lost or last heard of. Any hire charge paid in advance shall be refunded in proportion.

二、国际航空货物运输

国际航空货物运输的国际法渊源主要包括：《蒙特利尔公约》和华沙公约体系。由于《蒙特利尔公约》主要是将华沙公约体系予以整理，华沙公约体系仍是目前最重要的国际货物航空运输法渊源。

1. 华沙公约体系

目前，华沙公约体系主要包含以下国际法文件。

(1)《关于统一国际航空运输某些规则的公约》(以下简称《华沙公约 1929》)规定了以航空运输承运人为一方和以旅客和货物托运人与收货人为另一方的权利义务关系，为调整国际航空旅客、行李和货物运输法律关系创立了基本制度，是国际航空运输的一项最重要的公约。《华沙公约 1929》于 1933 年 2 月 13 日正式生效。我国已于 1958 年正式加入该公约。

(2)《修订 1929 年 10 月 12 日在华沙签订的〈统一国际航空运输若干规则公约〉的议定书》(以下简称《海牙议定书 1955》)。该议定书在 1955 年 9 月 28 日于海牙制定，自 1963 年 8 月 1 日起生效，目前已有将近 100 个国家成为会员国。《海牙议定书 1955》就责任限制、运输单证的项目、航行过失免责及索赔期限等事项，对《华沙公约 1929》作了修改，是《华沙公约 1929》与时俱进的产物。我国于 1975 年加入该议定书。

3.2.2　International Carriage of Goods by Air

The law relating to the international carriage of goods by air can be found in two separate sources: *Montreal Convention* and Warsaw Convention System. While the Montreal Convention is largely a tidying-up of fragmentation of law founding the Warsaw Convention System, the Warsaw Convention System still occupies the most important position of the law of international carriage of goods by air.

1. Warsaw Convention System

Warsaw Convention System consists of the following legal instruments.

(1) *Convention for the Unification of Certain Rules Relating to International Carriage by Air (Warsaw Convention 1929)* is an international convention which regulates liability for international carriage of persons, luggage or goods performed by aircraft. The Convention came into effect on February 13th, 1933. Our country formally participated in the Convention in 1958.

(2) *Protocol to Amend the Convention for the Unification of Certain Rules Relating to International Carriage by Air (Hague Protocol 1955)*, signed at Warsaw on October 12, 1929, done at Hague on September 28, 1955. The protocol went into effect on August 1, 1963, so far having almost 100 member countries. The protocol amended *the Warsaw Convention 1929* in liability limitation, items of the documents, exemption of neglect and time limit for claim damages and so on. The protocol is the creature of the times. The P.R.C. acceded to the protocol in 1975.

（3）《统一非订约承运人所从事国际航空运输若干规则以补充〈华沙公约〉的公约》（以下简称为《瓜达拉哈拉公约 1961》），订立于 1961 年 9 月 18 日，1964 年 5 月 1 日生效。我国未加入该公约。

2. 国际航空货物运输合同

下面以《华沙公约 1929》和《海牙议定书 1955》为例，阐述国际航空货物运输合同的有关规定。

1）航空货运单

根据《华沙公约 1929》的规定，承运人有权要求托运人填写航空货运单。货运单一式三份，在托运人交货时交付给托运人。货运单是双方订立合同，承运人收到货物及货运条件的初步证据。

航空货运单的主要内容包括：①货运单的填写时间地点（《海牙议定书 1955》删除了这一要求。）；②起运地、目的地；③约定的经停地点；④托运人，承运人或第一承运人及必要时收货人的名称、地址；⑤货物的基本情况；⑥运费金额、支付时间、地点、付费人；⑦货运单份数及随附单证；⑧货运期限及航线；⑨注明该货运单受《华沙公约 1929》或《海牙议定书 1955》约束。

（3）*Convention Supplementary to the Warsaw Convention for the Unification of Certain Rules Relating to International Carriage by Air Performed by a Person Other Than the Contracting Carrier (Guadalajara Convention 1961)*, signed in Guadalajara, on September 18, 1961, went into effect on May 1, 1964. The P.R.C. has not signed the protocol yet.

2. Contract of International Carriage of Goods by Air

The following contents about the contract of international carriage of goods by air mainly in accordance with *the Warsaw Convention 1929* and *the Hague Protocol 1955*.

1) Air Consignment Note

As *the Warsaw Convention 1929* stipulated, the air consignment note shall be made out by the consignor in three original parts and be handed over with the goods. The air consignment note is *prima facie* evidence of the conclusion of the contract, of the receipt of the goods and of the conditions of carriage.

The air consignment note shall contain the following particulars: (a)the place and date of its execution (has been deleted by *the Hague Protocol 1955*); (b)the place of departure and of destination; (c)the agreed stopping places; (d)the names and addresses of the consignor, the carrier, the first carrier, or the consignee, if the case so requires; (e)the general information of the goods; (f)the freight, if it has been agreed upon, the date and place of payment, and the person who is to pay it; (g)the number of parts of the air consignment note, and the documents handed to the carrier to accompany the air consignment note; (h)the time fixed for the completion of the carriage and a brief note of the route to be followed; (i)a statement that the carriage is subject to the rules relating to liability established by *the Warsaw Convention 1929* or *the Hague Protocol 1955*.

2) 航空承运人的责任

《华沙公约 1929》规定，承运人对于任何已登记的行李或货物因毁灭、遗失或损坏而产生的损失应负责任，只要造成这种损失的事故是发生在航空运输期间。所谓"航空运输期间"，即承运人保管货物的整个时间内。该期间包括货物在航空站内、航空器上或航空站外降落的任何地点。在运输已登记的行李和货物时，承运人对行李或货物的责任以每公斤 250 法郎为限，除非托运人在交运时，曾特别声明行李或货物运到后的价值，并缴付必要的附加费。

《华沙公约 1929》对承运人的免责规定有三个方面。

第一，承运人如果能证明自己及其代理人或雇佣人员为了避免损失的发生，已经采取了一切必要的措施，或者证明自己及其代理人或雇佣人员不可能采取这种防范措施时，承运人对货物的损失可不承担责任。

第二，承运人如果能证明损失的发生是由于受害人的过失所引起或促成时，法院可以根据具体情况免除承运人的全部或部分责任。

第三，承运人如果能证明损失的发生是由于驾驶上、航空器的操作上或领航上的过失所引起，并能证明他及其代理人已经在其他一切方面采取了一切必要措施以避免损失，对该项损失可以免除责任。

---

2) Liability of Air Carrier

According to *the Warsaw Convention 1929*, the carrier is liable for damage sustained in the event of the destruction or loss of, or of damage to, any registered luggage or any goods, if the occurrence which caused the damage so sustained took place during the carriage by air. "The carriage by air" means the period during which the luggage or goods are in the charge of the carrier, whether in an aerodrome or on board an aircraft, or, in the case of a landing outside an aerodrome, in any place whatsoever. In the carriage of registered luggage and goods, the liability of the carrier is limited to a sum of 250 francs per kilogram, unless the consignor has made, at the time when the package was handed over to the carrier, a special declaration of the value at delivery and has paid a supplementary sum if the case so requires.

The Warsaw Convention 1929 stipulates that the carrier shall be exempt from liabilities in the following three conditions.

Firstly, the carrier is not liable if he/she proves that he/she and his/her agents have taken all necessary measures to avoid the damage or that it was impossible for him/her or them to take such measures.

Secondly, if the carrier proves that the damage was caused by or contributed to the negligence of the injured person the Court may, in accordance with the provisions of its own law, exonerate the carrier wholly or partly from his/her liability.

Thirdly, the carrier is not liable if he/she proves that the damage was occasioned by negligent pilotage or negligence in the handling of the aircraft or in navigation and that, in all other respects, he/she and his/her agents have taken all necessary measures to avoid the damage.

《海牙议定书 1955》对承运人责任限制作了补充规定：如果损失的发生是由于承运人的有意的违法行为，或由于承运人的过失，而根据受理法院的法律，这种过失被认为等于有意的违法行为，承运人就无权引用《华沙公约 1929》关于免除或限制承运人责任的规定。同样，如果上述情况造成的损失是承运人的任何代理人在执行他的职务范围内所造成的，承运人也无权引用这种规定。

　　3）索赔程序

　　《华沙公约 1929》规定，对货物享有权利的人应该在货物收到后 7 天内向承运人提出异议；如果货物发生延期交货，收货人应在货物交由其支配之日起 14 天内提出异议。任何异议应该在规定期限内写在运输凭证上或另以书面方式提出。除非承运人方面有欺诈行为，如果在规定期限内没有提出异议，就不能起诉承运人。

　　诉讼应该在航空器到达目的地之日起，或应该到达之日起，或从运输停止之日起两年内提出；诉讼期限的计算方式根据受理法院的法律规定为准。有关赔偿的诉讼，应该按原告的意愿，在一个缔约国的领土内，向承运人住所地法院、承运人管理处的所在地法院、签订合同机构所在地法院或目的地法院提出。

The Hague Protocol 1955 gives supplementary stipulations on the limitation of the liabilities of the carrier: the carrier shall not be entitled to avail himself/herself of the provisions of *the Warsaw Convention 1929* which exclude or limit his/her liability, if the damage is caused by his/her wilful misconduct or by such default on his/her part as is considered to be equivalent to wilful misconduct. Similarly, the carrier shall not be entitled to avail himself/herself of the said provisions, if the damage is caused as aforesaid by any agent of the carrier acting within the scope of his/her employment.

3) Claims Procedures

The Warsaw Convention 1929 stipulates that in the case of goods damage, the person entitled to delivery must complain to the carrier, at the latest, within seven days from the date of receipt. In the case of delay the complaint must be made at the latest within fourteen days from the date on which the luggage or goods have been placed at his/her disposal. Every complaint must be made in writing upon the document of carriage or by separate notice in writing despatched within the times aforesaid. Failing complaint within the times aforesaid, no action shall lie against the carrier, save in the case of fraud on his/her part.

The right to damages shall be extinguished if an action is not brought within two years, reckoned from the date of arrival at the destination, or from the date on which the aircraft ought to have arrived, or from the date on which the carriage stopped. The method of calculating the period of limitation shall be determined by the law of the Court seised of the case. An action for damages must be brought, at the option of the plaintiff, in the territory of one of the Contracting Parties, either before the Court having jurisdiction where the carrier is ordinarily resident, or has his/her principal place of business, or has an establishment by which the contract has been made or before the Court having jurisdiction at the place of destination.

《海牙议定书 1955》规定，收货人在发现货物损坏后，应立即向承运人提出异议，或最迟应在收到货物后 14 天内提出；发生迟延交货时，最迟应在货物交付收货人自由处置之日起 21 天内提出异议。

三、国际铁路货物运输

1. 国际铁路货物运输公约

调整国际铁路货物运输的公约目前有两个：《国际货约》与《国际货协》。

《国际货约》全称《关于铁路货物运输的国际公约》，是最早的关于国际铁路运输的国际公约。该公约于 1890 年在伯尔尼签字，1893 年生效；1980 年修改后的新版公约于 1985 年 5 月生效。公约成员国主要为欧洲国家。《国际货协》全称《国际铁路货物联运协定》。1951 年在华沙订立。我国于 1953 年加入。

It is laid down in *the Hague Protocol 1955* that in the case of goods damage, the person entitled to delivery must complain to the carrier, at the latest, within fourteen days from the date of receipt. In the case of delay the complaint must be made at the latest within twenty-one days from the date on which the luggage or goods have been placed at his/her disposal.

3.2.3 International Carriage of Goods by Rail

1. Conventions on International Carriage of Goods by Rail

The law concerning international carriage of goods by rail is to be found in *the Convention Concerning International Carriage of Goods by Rail (COTIF/CIM)* and *the Agreement on International Railroad through Transport of Goods(CMIC)*.

The COTIF/CIM was the first convention about the international carriage of goods by rail contract, which signed in 1890, Bern, then came into effect in 1893; after the amendment in 1980, the revised *COTIF/CIM* came into force in May 1985. The contracting parties of *the CIM* are mainly European countries. *The CMIC* was signed in 1951, Warsaw, then came into effect in 1951. The P.R.C. signed *the CMIC* in 1953.

2.《国际货约》的主要内容

1) 托运单

托运单由托运人和实际承运人签发。托运单必须签名，或者以其他适当的方法和工具加盖印记。每票货物应单独填写一张运单。同一张运单只能办理一车货物，承运人与托运人之间的任何相反约定无效。

在通过欧盟管辖的关税区时，每一票货物都必须附随一张含有所有《国际货约》所要求的必要信息的托运单。

各个国际运输协会均能提供实用的标准形式的托运单。使用这些标准文本即可达到区域经济一体化组织所组建的有权管理关税立法的国际政府间组织的有关要求。此外，托运单的正本及副本均可以电子电文的形式存在，只要这些电文可以翻译成清晰可读的文字。特别是考虑到电文形式的托运单的证明力问题，用于翻译和记录电文的规程必须具有与书面表达等效的功能。

国际铁路运输合同是承运人承担将货物运至指定目的地并将货物交给收货方的有偿契约。国际铁路运输合同必须与形式统一的托运单相印证，但没有托运单，遗失托运单，或托运单的形式不够规范，并不会影响国际铁路货物运输合同的效力，运输合同仍由《国际货约》规制。

---

2. The Main Contents of *COTIF/CIM*

1) Consignment Note

The consignment note will be signed by the consignor and by the transport provider. Signature can be substituted by a stamp, printing by an accounting machine or any other appropriate medium. A consignment note must be created for each consignment. Saving contrary agreement between the consignor and the transport provider, one consignment note can only cover the cargo in a single wagon.

In the case of carriage provided in the customs territory of the European Community, each consignment must be accompanied by a consignment note which contains all the necessary information required by *the COTIF/CIM*.

The international associations of transport providers will establish the standard forms for consignment notes, in accordance with any intergovernmental organization of regional economic integration that has authority over its own customs legislation. In addition, the consignment note, including its duplicate copy, can be created by electronic recording of the data, which can be transformed into readable written signs. The procedures used for recording and processing the data must be functionally equivalent, especially as regards the strength of evidence of the consignment note represented by this data.

The transport contract is an onerous contract by which the transport provider undertakes to convey the goods to the place of destination and to deliver them to the consignee. The transport contract must be supported by a consignment note adhering to a uniform model. However, the absence, irregularity or loss of the consignment note will not affect the existence or validity of the contract, which remains subject to *COTIF/CIM*.

2) 承运人的责任

承运人应依货物运输合同的规定将货物安全地运至目的地。无论采取何种铁路运输方式，承运人对于接运货物至交付货物期间发生的货物的全部或部分灭失和货物发生损坏造成的损失负责；即使这些损坏或灭失造成的损失已经超过运输期限，承运人也仍应负责。

但是，在损失范围内，承运人应免除责任，如运输期限的超过或货物的灭失或损坏是由于索赔人的任何错误行为和疏忽，由于索赔人的指示而非承运人的错误行为或疏忽，或货物固有的缺陷(腐烂、自然缩水等)，或由于承运人不可避免的情况以及此种情况的不能阻止的后果所造成。承运人对下列一种或几种情况下固有的特殊危险所引起的货物灭失或损坏免责。

(1) 按适用的条件或按与发货人的协议条款和运单所载条款，当使用敞车运输时。

(2) 基于货物自身特性，如无包装或包装不良，货物将易于损耗或损坏，当货物未包装或当货物未妥善包装时。

(3) 按适用的条件或按与托运人协议条款和运单所载条款，当托运人装车或由收货人卸车时。

(4) 具有破碎、生锈、腐烂、变质或损耗，特别是使货物全部或部分灭失与损坏的某类货物的性质时。

---

2) Liability of the Transport Provider

The transport provider shall deliver the goods safely to the contractual destination. The transport provider will be responsible for damages resulting from total or partial loss, or from damage to the goods occurring from the moment it takes charge of the goods up to their delivery, as well as for damages resulting from exceeding the delivery periods, whatever the rail infrastructure used.

However, the transport provider will be exempt from this liability insofar as the loss, damage or exceeded delivery period resulting from a mistake by the claimant, an order from the claimant ensuing from a mistake by the transport provider, a defect in the goods themselves (internal deterioration, natural shrinkage, etc.), or circumstances beyond the transport provider's control with unavoidable consequences. The transport provider will be exempt from this responsibility insofar as the loss or damage resulting from particular risks inherent in one or more of the following.

(1) Carriage provided in an open freight wagon by reason of the general transport conditions, or because this has been expressly agreed and attested to in the consignment note.

(2) Absence of, or defects in, packaging for goods that, by their nature, are exposed to loss or damage when they are not packaged or are badly packaged.

(3) When the consignor loads or the consignee unloads the delivered goods by reason of the general transport conditions, or because this has been expressly agreed and attested to in the consignment note.

(4) The nature of certain goods that are inherently exposed to total or partial loss or damage, especially in cases of breakage, rust, spontaneous internal deterioration, dehydration and loss.

（5）对包裹或编号的记载不合常规、不正确或不完全时。

（6）活动物运输。

（7）按照此公约适用的条件，或按照与托运人订立的协议和运单所载条款，必须配备押运人的货物运输，如系由押运人负责防止的任何危险而造成的灭失或损坏时。

如按照《国际货约》的规定，铁路承运人负责有关货物的全部或部分灭失的赔偿时，该项赔偿应计算如下：按照商品交易所的价格；如没有此种价格，则按照当时市场价格；如两种价格都没有，则按照正常价值。计算应以货物承运地当时同类、同质货物为基础。短缺货物毛重每公斤的赔偿不得超过 17 国际记账单位。此外，关于灭失货物运输所产生的运费、关税和其他费用应退回。

3）索赔与时效

向承运人提出的有关运输合同的索赔应以书面形式提出。索赔可由有权向承运人提起索赔的人提出。如发货人提出索赔，他应提交运单副本。如未提交运单副本，只有经收货人允许，或他证明收货人已拒绝提货时，发货人方可提出索赔。当收货人提出索赔时，如运单已交给他，他应提交运单。在索赔处理时，铁路承运人可要求提交运单、运单副本或交货付款凭证的原件，以便在这些文件上注明处理事宜。

---

(5) Description of the packages or their numbering, whether irregular, inexact or incomplete.

(6) Transport of live animals.

(7) Transport that, by reason of applicable provisions or of agreements between the consignor and the carrier indicated in the consignment note, must be carried out with an accompanying passenger, if the loss or damage is the result of a risk that the accompanying passenger has the purpose of avoiding.

In the event of total or partial loss of the goods the carrier must pay compensation calculated according to the commodity exchange quotation or, if there is no such quotation, according to the current market price, or if there is neither such quotation nor such price, according to the normal value of goods of the same kind and quality at the time and place at which the goods were accepted for carriage. Compensation shall not exceed 17 units of account per kilogram of gross mass short. In addition, the railway shall refund carriage charges, customs duties and other amounts incurred in connection with carriage of the lost goods.

3) Claims and Limitation

Claims pertaining to the transport contract should be made in writing to the transport provider against which legal action may be taken. The right to make a claim lies with persons who have the right to file a lawsuit against the transport provider. To make the claim the consignor must present the duplicate copy of the consignment note. Failing this, it must present authorisation from the consignee or provide proof that the consignee has rejected the goods. In order to make the claim, the consignee must present the consignment note if it has already been delivered. On settling the claim, the transport provider can require presentation of the original and duplicate copy of the consignment note or of the reimbursement form, in order to record the settlement in them.

追索按照运输合同已付金额的诉讼，只能由该项金额的支付人提起。关于退还已付货款的诉讼，只能由发货人提起。

因运输合同引起的对铁路承运人的其他诉讼，可由下列各方提起：在收货人持有运单，或接受货物，或行使要求铁路承运人交付运单和货物，或行使修改合同的权利之前，由发货人提起；之后，则由收货人提起，但是收货人诉讼权应自收货人指示货物交付于到站国家非运单指定的其他人持有运单，或接受货物，或行使要求铁路承运人交付运单和货物的权利起消灭。

运输合同引起的诉讼的时效期限为一年。但是，在下列情况下，时效期限为两年。

(1) 对收回铁路承运人向收货人收取的现款交货之金额的诉讼。

(2) 对收回由铁路承运人售出货物之净收入的诉讼。

(3) 对故意的错误行为或者明知很可能造成损失仍然放任为之的过失行为所造成的灭失或损坏的诉讼。

(4) 在对转运情形的推定适用的情形下，对由转运前运输合同之一引起的诉讼。

Legal action for the recovery of a sum paid pursuant to the transport contract can only be taken by the person who has made the payment. Legal action regarding reimbursements can only be taken by the consignor.

The other legal action based on the transport contract can be taken by: The consignor, up to the moment when the consignee has held the consignment note, accepted the goods, or exercised the rights to request the transport provider to deliver the consignment note and the goods, or to modify the transport contract. The consignee, from the moment when the consignee has held the consignment note, exercised the rights to request the transport provider to deliver the consignment note and the goods, or to modify the transport contract. The right of the consignee to take legal action will extinguish from the moment when the person designated by the consignee holds the consignment note, accepts the goods or exercises his/her rights to request the transport provider to deliver the consignment note and the goods.

Legal action arising from the freight transport contract will have a limitation period of a year. However, the limitation period will be two years in the following case of legal action.

(1) In settlement of the reimbursement charged to the consignee by the transport provider.

(2) In settlement of the result of a sale handled by the transport provider.

(3) For damage resulting from an act or omission with intent to cause such damage, or from negligence with awareness that such damage would be the probable result.

(4) Based on one of the freight transport contracts prior to the reissue, in circumstance to which the "presumption of damages in the case of reissue" applies.

四、国际货物多式联运

国际货物多式联运是承运人以一份运输合约，通过两种以上运输方式将货物从一个国家运至另一个国家的运输。

尽管运输全程涉及铁路、海上、陆上等多种运输方式，从法律意义上讲，承运人对整个运输过程负责。运输合同中的承运人不一定要从事各种形式的运输业务，在实践中，这些承运人一般也不从事多种多样的运输；实际运输活动通常由"实际承运人"完成。对国际货物多式联运的整个运输过程负责的承运人被称为联运经营人。

目前尚未生效，也可能不会生效的《联合国国际货物多式联运公约》(以下简称《多式联运公约》，于1980年5月24日在日内瓦通过)的第1条第1款把"国际多式联运"界定为："按照多式联运合同，以至少两种不同的运输方式，由多式联运经营人将货物从一国境内接管货物的地点运至另一国境内指定交付货物的地点。"

3.2.4 International Multimodal Transport of Goods

International multimodal transport of goods(also known as international combined transport) is the transportation of goods under a single contract, but performed with at least two different means of transport to remove the goods from one country to another.

The carrier is liable (in a legal sense) for the entire carriage, even though it is performed by several different modes of transport, such as by rail, sea and road. The carrier does not have to possess all the means of transport, and in practice usually he/she does not; the carriage is often performed by sub-carriers (referred to in legal language as "actual carriers"). The carrier who is responsible for the entire carriage is referred to as a multimodal transport operator, or MTO.

Article 1(1) of *the United Nations Convention on International Multimodal Transport of Goods* (*Multimodal Transport Convention*, Geneva, May 24, 1980) which has not yet, and may never enter into force, defines multimodal transport as follows: "International multimodal transport means the carriage of goods by at least two different modes of transport on the basis of a multimodal transport contract from a place in one country at which the goods are taken in charge by the MTO to a place designated for delivery situated in a different country."

1.《多式联运公约》的适用范围

此公约适用于两国境内各地之间的所有多式联运合同，条件是：①多式联运合同规定的多式联运经营人接管货物的地点是在一个缔约国境内；②多式联运合同规定的多式联运经营人交付货物的地点是在一个缔约国境内。

2. 多式联运单据

多式联运单据是多式联运合同的证明，是多式联运经营人收到货物的收据及凭以交货的凭证。多式联运经营人接管货物时，应签发一项多式联运单据，该单据应依托运人的选择，为可转让单据或为不可转让单据。

多式联运单据应由多式联运经营人或经他授权的人签字。多式联运单据上的签字，如不违背签发多式联运单据所在国的法律，可以是手签、手签笔迹的复印、打透花字、盖章、符号或用任何机械或其他的形式。经托运人同意，可以用任何机械或其他能够保存《多式联运公约》所规定的多式联运单据应列明的事项的方式，签发不可转让的多式联运单据。在这种情况下，多式联运经营人在接管货物后，应交给托运人一份可以阅读的单据，载有用此种方式记录的所有事项，基于本公约之立法目的这份单据即被视为多式联运单据。

---

1. Scope of Application of *Multimodal Transport Convention*

The provisions of this Convention shall apply to all contracts of multimodal transport between places in two States, if the place for taking in charge of the goods by the MTO as provided for in the multimodal transport contract is located in a Contracting State, or if the place for delivery of the goods by the MTO as provided for in the multimodal transport contract is located in a Contracting State.

2. Multimodal Transport Document

The multimodal transport document is the evidence of the multimodal transport contract, the evidence of receipt of cargo and the evidence to take delivery. When the goods are taken in charge by the MTO, he/she shall issue a multimodal transport document which, at the option of the consignor, shall be in either negotiable or non-negotiable form.

The multimodal transport document shall be signed by the MTO or by a person authorized by him/her. The signature on the multimodal transport document may be in handwriting, printed in facsimile, perforated, stamped, in symbols, or made by any other mechanical or electronic means, if not inconsistent with the law of the country where the multimodal transport document is issued. If the consignor agrees, a non-negotiable multimodal transport document may be issued by making use of any mechanical or other means preserving a record of the particulars stated in the Convention to be contained in the multimodal transport document. In such a case the MTO, after having taken the goods in charge, shall deliver to the consignor a readable document containing all the particulars so recorded, and such a document shall be deemed to be a multimodal transport document for the purpose of the provisions of this Convention.

多式联运单据应记载货物基本情况、货物外表状况、托运人名称、接货地点和日期、交货地点、交货的日期或期间、单据可转让或不可转让的声明、多式联运单据的签发地点和日期、多式联运经营人的签字、运费、预期经过的路线和运输方式等内容。

如果已对本公约准允保留的事项作出保留，则除其保留的部分之外：多式联运单据应是该单据所载货物由多式联运经营人接管的初步证据；但当多式联运单据以可转让方式签发，而且转给当地信赖该单据所载明货物状况的包括收货人在内的善意第三方，该单据就成了最终证据。

3. 多式联运经营人的责任

《多式联运公约》规定的多式联运经营人的责任期间为从其接管货物之时起至交付货物时止的期间。具体来说如下。

The multimodal transport document shall contain the general conditions of the goods, the apparent condition of the goods, the name of the consignor, the place and date of taking in charge of the goods, the place of delivery, the date or the period of delivery, negotiable or non-negotiable statement, the place and date of issue of the document, the signature of the MTO, the freight, the intended journey route and modes of transport and so on.

Except for particulars in respect of which and to the extent to which a reservation permitted by the Convention has been entered, the multimodal transport document shall be *prima facie* evidence of taking in charge by the MTO of the goods as described therein; and the proof to the contrary by the MTO shall not be admissible if the multimodal transport document is issued in negotiable form and has been transferred to a third party, including a consignee, who has acted in good faith in reliance on the description of the goods therein.

3. Liability of Multimodal Transport Operator

The liability of the MTO for the goods under this Convention covers the period from the time he/she takes the goods in his/her charge to the time of his/her delivery.

自多式联运经营人从下列各方接管货物之时起：①发货人或其代表；②根据接管货物地点适用的法律或规章，货物必须交其运输的机构或其他的第三方。直到多式联运经营人以下列方式交付货物时为止：①将货物交给收货人；②如果收货人不提取货物，则按多式联运合同或交货地适用的法律或特定行业惯例，将货物置于收货人支配之下；③将货物交给根据交货地点适用的法律或规章必须向其交付的机构或其他第三方。

《多式联运公约》在赔偿责任上采用了完全推定责任原则。如果造成灭失、损坏或延迟交货的事故发生于货物由其掌管期间，多式联运经营人对于货物的灭失、损坏和延迟交付所引起的损失应负赔偿责任，除非多式联运经营人证明其本人、受雇人或代理人或《多式联运公约》第 15 条所指的任何其他人为避免事故的发生及其后果已采取一切合理的措施。

关于多式联运经营人的赔偿责任限制，《多式联运公约》规定的两种赔偿限额分别适用于下列两种情况。

(1) 如在国际多式联运中包括了海运或内河运输，多式联运经营人的赔偿责任限额为每件 920 特别提款权或货物毛重每公斤 2.75 特别提款权，以较高者为准。

The MTO is deemed to be in charge of the goods: (a)from the time he/she has taken over the goods from: (i) the consignor or a person acting on his/her behalf; or (ii) an authority or other third party to whom, pursuant to law or regulations applicable at the place of taking in charge, the goods must be handed over for transport; (b)until the time he/she has delivered the goods: (i)by handing over the goods to the consignee; (ii)in cases where the consignee does not receive the goods from the MTO, by placing them at the disposal of the consignee in accordance with the multimodal transport contract or with the law or with the usage of the particular trade applicable at the place of delivery; (iii)by handing over the goods to an authority or other third party to whom, pursuant to law or regulations applicable at the place of delivery, the goods must be handed over.

Multimodal Transport Convention adopts the principle of presumption of fault. The multimodal transport operator shall be liable for loss resulting from loss or damage to the goods, as well as from delay in delivery, if the occurrence which caused the loss, damage or delay in delivery took place, while the goods were in MTO's charge, unless the MTO proves that he/she, his/her servants or agents or any other person referred to in Article 15 of the Convention took all measures that could reasonably be required to avoid the occurrence and its consequences.

On the limitation of the liability, the Convention gives two kinds of limitations separately adpting to the following two different circumstances.

(1) If the international multimodal transport does include carriage of goods by sea or by inland waterways, the liability of MTO shall be limited to an amount not exceeding 920 SDRs per package or 2.75 SDRs per kilogram of gross weight of the goods lost or damaged, whichever is the higher.

（2）如在国际多式联运中未包括海运或内河运输，多式联运经营人的赔偿责任限额为货物毛重每公斤 8.33 特别提款权。

此外，因延迟交付造成损失的赔偿限额为延迟交付货物的应付运费的 2.5 倍，但不得超过多式联运合同规定的应付费用的总额。在确知发生货损的区段时，如该区段适用的公约或国家法律规定的赔偿责任限额高于《多式联运公约》的规定，则适用该区段适用的公约或国家强制法的规定。

4. 索赔与时效

对于货物一般性的灭失或损坏通知，收货人应在货物交给他的次一工作日提出，否则此种货物的交付即为多式联运经营人交付多式联运单据所载货物的初步证据。当货物的损坏不明显时，收货人应在货物交付后连续 6 日内提出索赔通知。对于延迟交付的货物，收货人应在货物交付后连续 60 日内提出索赔通知。

---

(2) If the international multimodal transport does not include carriage of goods by sea or by inland waterways, the liability of the multimodal transport operator shall be limited to an amount not exceeding 8.33 SDRs per kilogram of gross weight of the goods lost or damaged.

In addition, the liability of the MTO for loss resulting from delay in delivery shall be limited to an amount equivalent to two and a half times the freight payable for the goods delayed, but not exceeding the total freight payable under the multimodal transport contract. When the loss of or damage to the goods occurred during one particular of the multimodal transport, in respect of which an applicable international convention or mandatory national law provides a higher limitation of liability than the limitation that would follow *the United Nations Multimodal Transport Convention*, then the limitation of the multimodal transport operator's liability for such loss or damage shall be determined by reference to the provisions of such convention or mandatory national law.

4. Claims and Limitation

Unless notice of loss or damage, specifying the general nature of such loss or damage, is given in writing by the consignee to the multimodal transport operator not later than the working day after the day when the goods were handed over to the consignee, such handing over is *prima facie* evidence of the delivery by the multimodal transport operator of the goods as described in the multimodal transport document. Where the loss or damage is not apparent, notice in writing shall be given within six consecutive days after the day when the goods were handed over to the consignee. No compensation shall be payable for loss resulting from delay in delivery unless notice has been given in writing to the multimodal transport operator within 60 consecutive days after the day when the goods were delivered by handing over to the consignee.

根据《多式联运公约》提出有关国际多式联运的任何诉讼，如果在两年期间内没有提起诉讼或交付仲裁，即超过时效期。但是，如果在货物交付之日后 6 个月内，或于货物未交付时，在应当交付之日后 6 个月内，没有提出书面索赔通知，说明索赔的性质和主要事项，则诉讼在此期限届满后即失去效力。时效期间自多式联运经营人交付货物或部分货物之日的次一日起算，如货物未交付，则自货物应当交付的最后一日的次一日起算。接到索赔要求的人可于时效期间内随时向索赔人提出书面声明，延长时效期间。此种期间可用另一次声明或多次声明，再度延长。

除非一项适用的国际公约另有相反规定，根据《多式联运公约》负有赔偿责任的人即使在上述各项规定的时效期间届满后，仍可在起诉地国家法律所许可的限期内提起诉讼，要求追偿，而此项所许可的限期，自提起此项追偿诉讼的人已清偿索赔要求或接到对其本人的诉讼传票之日起算，不得少于 90 日。

According to *the Multimodal Transport Convention*, any action relating to international multimodal transport under this Convention shall be time-barred if judicial or arbitral proceedings have not been instituted within a period of two years. However, if notification in writing, stating the nature and main particulars of the claim, has not been given within six months after the day when the goods were delivered or, where the goods have not been delivered, after the day on which they should have been delivered, the action shall be time-barred at the expiry of this period. The limitation period commences on the day after the day on which the MTO has delivered the goods or part thereof or, where the goods have not been delivered, on the day after the last day on which the goods should have been delivered. The person against whom a claim is made may at any time during the running of the limitation period extend that period by a declaration in writing to the claimant. This period may be further extended by another declaration or declarations.

Provided that the provisions of another applicable international convention are not to the contrary, a recourse action for indemnity by a person held liable under *the Multimodal Transport Convention* may be instituted even after the expiration of the limitation period provided for in the preceding paragraphs if instituted within the time allowed by the law of the State where proceedings are instituted; however, the time allowed shall not be less than 90 days commencing from the day when the person instituting such action for indemnity has settled the claim or has been served with process in the action against himself/herself.

五、国际货物运输保险

1. 国际货物运输保险概述

保险在国际货物运输中占有重要地位。一旦国际贸易买卖双方就货物名称、数量、价格和运输方式达成协议，其必须就货物跨越国境运输期间可能遇到的风险予以投保。投保人为哪一方，由双方在合同中约定的贸易术语决定。正如本章第一节有关术语的内容所述，若货物成交价为 CIF 价，由卖方投保。再如货物成交价为 FOB 价，则买方更有可能会为了避免货物在运输中的灭失、损坏而进行货物运输投保。下文将主要说明国际海上运输保险合同的主要原则。

投保人对保险标的进行投保的前提是被保险人对保险标的具有可保利益。可保利益，指被保险人对于保险标的的持续存在具有合法的利害关系。被保险人是指保险事故发生时遭受损害并有权接受赔偿的人。被保险人有时候就是投保人，有时候也可能是投保人以外的其他人。按照各国法律的解释，可保利益来自被保险人对保险标的的享有的所有权、占有权；担保物权和债权；依法承担的风险和责任；因标的物的保全可得到利益或期得利益。可保利益必须是确定的，但可以是现有利益，也可以是期得利益；可保利益必须合法，也必须能用金钱计算。

3.2.5　International Cargo Transportation Insurance

1. An Overview of International Cargo Transportation Insurance

Insurance is very important to international cargo transportation. The seller and the buyer, once they have agreed on the description, quantity, price and mode of delivery of the goods, have to arrange insurance to cover the hazards likely to be encountered during the transportation of goods from the seller's country to the buyer's country. As to who arranges for insurance during transportation will depend on the terms of the contract. As gathered from Section 1 on INCOTERMS, where the goods, for instance, have been sold on cost, insurance, freight (CIF) terms, the seller obtains insurance. Where the sale, for instance, is on free on board (FOB) terms, the buyer is likely to take out insurance if he/she wishes to protect himself/herself against loss or damage to goods in the course of transportation. The following part illustrates, using marine insurance, the general principles underlying insurance contracts.

The policy-holder can only take out insurance while insurant has insurable interest in the objects of insurance. Insurable interest exists when an insured person derives a financial or other kind of benefit from the continuous existence of the insured object. A person has an insurable interest in something when loss-of or damage-to that thing would cause the person to suffer a financial loss or other kind of loss. Insurant can be the policy-holder or someone else. Insurable interests come from the insurant's ownership, possess, guarantee, claim, other kinds of risks and responsibility etc. in the objects of insurance. Insurable interests can be interests in existence or in the future, but must be certain, legal and measurable for a price.

2. 国际海上货物运输保险合同

海上保险针对船舶、货物、港口以及运输起点和终点之间的转运期间的任何运输工具或货物的保险。海上保险可分为船身保险和货物保险。海上货物运输保险合同，是指保险人对于被保险人由于海上运输货物遭受保险事故造成的损失和产生的责任负责赔偿，投保人依据约定支付保险费的合同。在国际海上货物运输保险领域，并没有统一法，相反，商事惯例的作用非常显著。因此，海上保险合同主要受合同法一般原则和各国海上保险法的约束。

1) 保险单证

保险单证是保险人与被保险人之间保险合同的证明，也是确定保险人赔偿范围的依据。作为投保人缴纳保险费的回报，保险人在保险单证载明的承保风险造成的损害范围内向被保险人做损害赔偿。保险单证包括保险单和保险凭证。根据我国《海商法》的规定，海上保险合同成立，保险人应当及时向被保险人签发保险单或者其他保险单证，并在保险单或者其他保险单证中载明当事人双方约定的合同内容。海上保险合同的内容主要包括：保险人名称；被保险人名称；保险标的；保险价值；保险金额；保险责任和除外责任；保险期间；保险费。

---

2. International Marine Cargo Insurance Contract

Marine insurance covers the loss or damage of ships, cargo, terminals, and any transport or cargo by which property is transferred, acquired, or held between the points of origin and final destination. Marine insurance may be divided into hull insurance or cargo insurance. Marine cargo insurance contract is the contract between the policy-holder and the insurer; the insurer is liable for the loss and damages happened on the insured cargos transport by sea, while the policy-holder pays the insurance premium according to the contract. There is no uniform law or convention for international marine cargo insurance. However, commercial customs, usage and practices in international marine insurance have played a significant role in regulating marine insurance internationally. Thus, the marine insurance contract is subject to both general principles of contract law and relevant domestic marine insurance law.

1) Insurance Documents

The insurance document evidences a contract between the insurer and the insured which determines the claims which the insurer is legally required to pay. In exchange for payment, known as the premium, the insurer pays for damages to the insured which are caused by covered perils under the policy language. The insurance document includes insurance policy and certificate. Under *the Maritime Code* of the P.R.C., after the establishment of a marine insurance contract, the insurer shall issue to the insured an insurance policy or other certificate of insurance in time, and the contents of the contract shall be contained therein. A contract of marine insurance mainly includes the name of the insurer, the name of the insured, subject matter insured, insured value, insured amount, perils insured against and perils excepted, duration of insurance coverage, insurance premium.

海上货物运输保险合同可以由被保险人背书或者以其他方式转让，合同的权利、义务随之转移。合同转让时尚未支付保险费的，被保险人和合同受让人负连带支付责任。

　　2) 保险合同当事人的权利和义务

　　保险合同当事人必须遵循一个根本原则：绝对诚信原则。该原则要求保险合同双方均本着诚信原则进行交易，尤其要求被保险人一方对所有与承保风险有关的重大事实进行披露，如货物状况、货物的价值等。因为这些情况往往是保险人决定是否承保以及如何收取保险费率时所依据的事实。这种做法与绝大多数其他合同所提出的"货物出门概不退换"即买方注意要求截然相反。在美国，保险公司可以投保人违反绝对诚信原则为由而提起侵权之诉。

　　A contract of marine cargo insurance for the carriage of goods by sea may be assigned by the insured by endorsement or otherwise, and the rights and obligations under the contract are assigned accordingly. The insured and the assignee shall be jointly and severally liable for the payment of the premium if such premium remains unpaid up to the time of the assignment of the contract.

　　2) The Rights and Obligations of the Parties to an Insurance Contract

　　Insurance contracts are governed by the principle of utmost good faith, which requires both parties of the insurance contract to deal in good faith, and in particular it imparts on the insured a duty to disclose all material facts which relate to the risk to be covered, such as disclosing the condition and value of the cargo. The insurer determines whether to deal with the insured or not and how to get the insurance rate based on the facts the insured disclosed. This contrasts with the legal doctrine that covers most other types of contracts, caveat emptor (let the buyer beware). In the United States, the insurer can sue an insured in tort for acting in bad faith.

保险人的权利和义务主要有：发生保险事故造成损失后，保险人应当及时向被保险人支付保险赔偿。保险人赔偿保险事故造成的损失，以保险金额为限。保险标的在保险期间发生几次保险事故所造成的损失，即使损失金额的总和超过保险金额，保险人也应当赔偿。但是，对发生部分损失后未经修复又发生全部损失的，保险人按照全部损失赔偿。对于被保险人故意造成的损失，保险人不负赔偿责任。除合同另有约定外，由下列原因之一造成货物损失的，保险人不负赔偿责任：航行迟延、交货迟延或者行市变化；货物的自然损耗、本身的缺陷和自然特性；包装不当。

被保险人的主要权利和义务如下。

(1) 除合同另有约定外，被保险人应当在合同订立后立即支付保险费；被保险人支付保险费前，保险人可以拒绝签发保险单证。

(2) 被保险人违反合同约定的保险条款时，应当立即书面通知保险人。保险人收到通知后，可以解除合同，也可以要求修改承保条件，或增加保险费。

(3) 一旦保险事故发生，被保险人应当立即通知保险人，并采取必要的合理措施，防止或者减少损失。被保险人收到保险人发出的有关采取防止或者减少损失的合理措施的特别通知的，应当按照保险人通知的要求处理。

The insurer's rights and obligations mainly include: the insurer shall indemnify the insured promptly after the loss from a peril insured against has occurred; the insurer's indemnification for the loss from the peril insured against shall be limited to the insured amount; the insurer shall be liable for the loss to the subject matter insured arising from several perils insured against during the period of the insurance even though the aggregate of the amounts of loss exceeds the insured amount. However, the insurer shall only be liable for the total loss where the total loss occurs after the partial loss which has not been repaired; the insurer shall not be liable for the loss caused by the intentional act of the insured; unless otherwise agreed in the insurance contract, the insurer shall not be liable for the loss of or damage to the insured cargo arising from (a)delay in the voyage or in the delivery of cargo or change of market price; (b)fair wear and tear, inherent vice or nature of the cargo; (c)improper packing.

The insured's rights and obligations mainly include the following points.

(1) Unless otherwise agreed in the insurance contract, the insured shall pay the premium immediately upon conclusion of the contract. The insurer may refuse to issue the insurance policy or other insurance certificate before the premium is paid by the insured.

(2) The insured shall notify the insurer in writing immediately where the insured has not complied with the warranties under the contract. The insurer may, upon receipt of the notice, terminate the contract or demand an amendment to the terms and conditions of the insurance coverage or an increase in the premium.

(3) Upon the occurrence of the peril insured against, the insured shall notify the insurer immediately and shall take necessary and reasonable measures to avoid or minimize the loss. Where special instructions for the adoption of reasonable measures to avoid or minimize the loss are received from the insurer, the insured shall act according to such instructions.

3) 代位与委付

当保险标的发生保险责任范围内的损失是由第三人造成的情况下，被保险人有向第三人要求赔偿的权利，自保险人支付赔偿之日起，相应地转移给保险人。这就是在海上货物保险当中广泛使用的代位。据此，由于第三人在替债务人履行偿债义务后即可取得针对债务人的债权，保险人在替第三人履行赔偿义务后，即取代被保险人取得对第三人的请求赔偿的权利。在被保险人仍然自行行使赔偿请求权时，保险人有权请求被保险人不得损害保险人的代位权。被保险人应当向保险人提供必要的文件和其所需要知道的情况，并尽力协助保险人向第三人追偿。被保险人未经保险人同意放弃向第三人要求赔偿的权利，或者由于过失致使保险人不能行使追偿权利的，保险人可以相应扣减保险赔偿。保险人支付保险赔偿时，可以从应支付的赔偿额中相应扣减被保险人已经从第三人取得的赔偿。保险人从第三人取得的赔偿，超过其支付的保险赔偿的，超过部分应当退还给被保险人。

3) Subrogation and Abandonment

Where the loss of or damage to the subject matter insured within the insurance coverage is caused by a third person, the right of the insured to demand compensation from the third person shall be subrogated to the insurer from the time the indemnity is paid. Subrogation in its most common usage in marine cargo insurance circumstances refers to as the transfer of right of the creditor to the third party who pays the debt of the debtor. Subrogation gives the insurer access to the assured's right of action, while the assured may pursue his/her own claims, the insurer has a right to claim that the assured does not compromise the insurer's subrogated rights. The insured shall furnish the insurer with necessary documents and information that should come to his/her knowledge and shall endeavour to assist the insurer in pursuing recovery from the third person. Where the insured waives his/her right of claim against the third person without the consent of the insurer or the insurer is unable to exercise the right of recourse due to the fault of the insured, the insurer may make a corresponding reduction from the amount of indemnity. In effecting payment of indemnity to the insured, the insurer may make a corresponding reduction therefrom of the amount already paid by a third person to the insured. Where the compensation obtained by the insurer from the third person exceeds the amount of indemnity paid by the insurer, the part in excess shall be returned to the insured.

委付是在发生推定全损的情况下，被保险人为了取得全损保险金额，而把残存货物的所有权转移给保险人。保险人没有必须接受委付的义务，但应当在一段合理期间内通知被保险人其是否接受委付。接受委付不得附条件。委付一旦接受就不能撤回，所有与委付财产有关的权利与义务均随之转移给保险人。

4) 保险责任起讫

《海洋运输货物保险条款》第 3 条规定，保险人的责任起讫是从被保险货物运离保险单所载明的启运地仓库或储存处开始运输时起，至该货物到达保险单所载目的地收货人的最后仓库或储存处，或被保险人用作分配、分派或非正常运输的其他储存处所为止，即通常称之为"仓至仓"条款。此类"仓至仓"条款是海上货物运输保险关于保险责任起讫的通常做法。

3. 国际海上货物运输的保险范围

1) 承保风险

海上货物运输保险的风险包括海上风险和外来风险。

Where the subject matter insured has become a constructive total loss and the insured demands indemnification from the insurer on the basis of a total loss, the subject matter insured shall be abandoned to the insurer. The insurer may accept the abandonment or choose not to, but shall inform the insured of his/her decision whether to accept the abandonment within a reasonable time. The abandonment shall not be attached with any condition. Once the abandonment is accepted by the insurer, it shall not be withdrawn. Where the insurer has accepted the abandonment, all rights and obligations relating to the property abandoned are transferred to the insurer.

4) Commencement and Termination of Cover

Article 3 of *the P.I.C.C. Ocean Marine Cargo Clauses* stipulates: "This insurance attaches from the time the goods hereby insured are taken away from the ware-house or place of storage named in the Policy for the commencement of the transit until the insured goods are delivered to the consignee's final warehouse or place of storage at the destination named in the Policy or to any other place used by the insured for allocation or distribution of the goods or for stores other than in the ordinary course of transit." That is a typical "Warehouse to Warehouses Clause", which is a rule of great generality to the coverage of marine cargo insurance.

3. Scope of International Marine Cargo Insurance

1) Underwriting Risk

In marine cargo insurance, perils are generally of two kinds, which include perils of the sea and extraneous risks.

（1）海上风险。

海上风险是指货物在海上航行的过程中发生的，或与海上运输相关的风险，包括自然灾害和意外事故。自然灾害是指由于自然力量所造成的灾害，如恶劣气候、雷电、海啸、潮汐、地震、洪水、火山爆发。意外事故是由于意外原因引起的事故，如运输工具搁浅、触礁、沉没、碰撞、火灾、与冰山相撞、爆炸、海盗等。

（2）外来风险。

外来风险是由海上风险以外的外来原因造成的风险。可以分为一般外来风险和特别外来风险。一般外来风险主要包括：偷窃、沾污、淡水雨淋、渗透、碰损破碎、串味、生锈、受潮受热、钩损、包装破裂等。特别外来风险主要包括：战争险、罢工险、交货不到险、舱面货物险和拒收险等。

2）损失和费用

（1）全部损失：实际全损与推定全损。

实际全损，指货物全部损失或失去了原有形体、用途或价值，或货物不能再归被保险人拥有。

推定全损，是指被保险货物的实际损失已经不可避免，或者对受损货物的修复费用加上续运到目的地的费用，估计将超过该货物到达目的地后的价值。

（1）Perils of the sea.

Perils of the sea include natural calamities and fortuitous accidents. Natural calamities include the calamities caused by nature, such as atrocious weather, thunder and lighting, tsunami, tidal wave, earthquake, floods, volcanic eruption. Fortuitous accidents mean accidents generated by contingent event, such as ship stranded, striking upon the rocks, ship sinking, ship collision, colliding with icebergs, fire explosion, pirate etc.

（2）Extraneous risks.

Extraneous risks are the ones that are resulted from any causes other than the perils of the sea. They consist of general extraneous risks and special extraneous risks. General extraneous risks include theft or pilferage, contamination, rain, leakage, breakage, clashing, taint of odor, rusting, dampness, heating, hooking, breakage of packing, etc. Special extraneous risks include war risks, strikes, non-delivery of cargo, refusal to receive cargo, etc.

2）Loss and Expenses

（1）Total loss: actual total loss and constructive total loss.

Where after the occurrence of a peril insured against the subject matter insured is lost or is so seriously damaged that it is completely deprived of its original structure and usage or the insured is deprived of the possession thereof, it shall constitute an actual total loss.

Constructive total loss is found in the case where an actual total loss appears to be unavoidable or the cost to be incurred in recovering or reconditioning the goods together with the forwarding cost to the destination named in the policy would exceed their value on arrival.

(2) 部分损失：共同海损与单独海损。

在海上货物运输实践中，共同海损由来已久，它是为了海上航行的整体利益将某些特殊损失公平分配给同一航程的各利益方。构成共同海损的要件如下。

① 船与货面临共同的危险，这种危险是迫在眉睫而且显然是无法避免的，除非主动放弃一部分利益来拯救其他的利益。

② 是船方为避免迫近的危险而有意作出的牺牲和支出的费用。

③ 牺牲和费用是合理的、有效的。如在船舶面临沉没的危险时，船方抛弃一部分价格低而重量大的货物，而使船与货避免了沉没的危险。

单独海损只是船方或货物单方的损失，这种损失由受损方自己承担或根据保险合同由保险人赔偿。

由于保险风险造成的货物损失可分为两类：货物本身遭受的损失以及为营救货物而支出的费用。海上货物运输保险不但承保货物本身遭受的损失，还承保费用。费用主要包括以下两种。

① 单独费用，是指为了防止货物遭受承保风险所导致的损失而由被保险人、其雇员或代理人等人支出的费用。

---

(2) Partial loss: general average and particular average.

General average originated in ancient times as a way to apportion fairly among all parties to a maritime venture any losses incurred by some of the ventures in the interest of preserving the entire venture. The requirements of general average are as follows.

(a) A common danger: a danger in which the vessel, cargo and crew all participate; a danger imminent and apparently inevitable, except by voluntarily incurring the loss of a portion of the whole to save the remainder.

(b) There must be a voluntary jettison, or casting away, of some portion of the joint concern for the purpose of avoiding this imminent peril.

(c) This attempt to avoid the imminent common peril must be reasonable and effective, for example, casting away a portion of heavy but cheap cargo to avoid sinking.

A particular average is a partial loss that is to be borne by only a particular interest (such as the vessel alone or one of the various cargo interests aboard). A particular average is afforded by the injured party or by the insurer through an insurance contract.

Losses sustained by the insured because of the perils come from not only the loss of the goods or the damage done to the goods, but also from the expenses the insured sustained in rescuing the goods in danger. Transportation insurance not only insures the losses caused by perils but also the losses of expenses. The main expenses include the following two charges.

(a) Particular charges. These expenses are the expenses arising from measures properly taken by the insured, the employee and the assignee, etc. for minimizing or avoiding losses caused by the risks covered in the insurance policy.

② 救助费用，指保险货物在海上遇到承保风险时，由保险人和被保险人以外的第三人自愿采取救助措施而获救，由被救方支付救助方一定的报酬，这部分被救助方应当向救助方支付的任何救助报酬、酬金或者补偿就是救助费用。

4. 国际海上货物运输险的保险条款

保险人在某一海上货物运输保险合同中的责任是依据保险单及所记载的保险条款确定的。在保险条款中，保险人将风险、损失和责任按范围不同进行划分，构成保险条款。保险条款不同，所承担的责任不同。我国对外贸易运输中经常使用的是中国人民保险公司制定的海洋运输货物保险条款。此外，国际上常用的是伦敦保险业协会制定的货物保险条款。

1) 中国人民保险公司海洋运输货物保险条款

该条款把承保范围分为三种基本险，平安险、水渍险和一切险。被保险货物遭受损失时，保险公司按照保险单上列明承保险别的条款和规定，负赔偿责任。

(1) 平安险。

承保的范围如下。

(b) Salvage charges. While the insured cargo meets perils in the sea venture, a third party other than the insured, the employee and the assignee, etc. may save it from suffering loss, thus the salved party shall pay the salvor payment. The payment which means any reward, remuneration or compensation for salvage operations to be paid by the salved party to the salvor is salvage charges.

4. International Marine Cargo Insurance Clause

The responsibilities of the insurer lie in the insurance clause. In insurance clause, the insurer classified different insurance policies by peril, loss and liability. With different insurance clause, the insurer undertakes different obligations. In China, Ocean Marine Cargo Clauses of P.I.C.C. is a common choice for the home and foreign trade. Moreover, Institute Cargo Clause of I.C.C. is a more popular choice for traders all over the world.

1) Ocean Marine Cargo Clauses of P.I.C.C.

This insurance is classified into the following three conditions—Free from Particular Average (F. P. A.), With Average (W. A.) and All Risks. Where the goods insured hereunder sustain loss or damage, the Company shall undertake to indemnify therefor according to the insured condition specified in the policy and the provisions of these clauses.

(1) Free from Particular Average (F. P. A.).

This insurance covers the following scope.

① 被保险货物在运输途中由于恶劣气候、雷电、海啸、地震、洪水自然灾害造成整批货物的全部损失或推定全损。当被保险人要求赔付推定全损时，须将受损货物及其权利委付给保险公司。被保险货物用驳船运往或运离海轮的，每一驳船所装的货物可视作一个整批。

② 由于运输工具遭受搁浅、触礁、沉没、互撞、与流冰或其他物体碰撞以及失火、爆炸意外事故造成货物的全部或部分损失。

③ 在运输工具已经发生搁浅、触礁、沉没、焚毁意外事故的情况下，货物在此前后又在海上遭受恶劣气候、雷电、海啸等自然灾害所造成的部分损失。

④ 在装卸或转运时由于一件或数件整件货物落海造成的全部或部分损失。

⑤ 被保险人对遭受承保责任范围内的危险的货物采取抢救、防止或减少货损的措施而支付的合理费用，但以不超过该批被救货物的保险金额为限。

⑥ 运输工具遭遇海难后，在避难港由于卸货所引起的损失以及在中途港、避难港由于卸货、存仓以及运送货物所产生的特别费用。

⑦ 共同海损的牺牲、分摊和救助费用。

⑧ 运输契约订有"船舶互撞责任"条款，根据该条款规定应由货方偿还船方的损失。

(a) Total or constructive total loss of the whole consignment hereby insured caused in the course of transit by natural calamities: heavy weather, lightning, tsunami, earthquake and flood. In case a constructive total loss is claimed for, the insured shall abandon to the Company the damaged goods and all his/her rights and title pertaining thereto. The goods on each lighter to or from the seagoing vessel shall be deemed a separate risk.

(b) Total or partial loss caused by accidents the carrying conveyance being grounded, stranded, sunk or in collision with floating ice or other objects as fire or explosion.

(c) Partial loss of the insured goods attributable to heavy weather, lightning and/or tsunami, where the conveyance has been grounded, stranded, sunk or burnt, irrespective of whether the event or events took place or after such accidents.

(d) Partial or total loss consequent on falling of an entire package or packages into sea during loading, transshipment or discharge.

(e) Reasonable cost incurred by the insured on salvaging the goods or averting or minimizing a loss recoverable under the policy, provided that such cost shall not exceed the sum insured of the consignment so saved.

(f) Losses attributable to discharge of the insured goods at a port of refuge following a sea peril as well as special charges arising from loading, warehousing and forwarding of the goods at an intermediate port of call or refuge.

(g) Sacrifice in and contribution to general average and salvage charges.

(h) Such proportion of losses sustained by the shipowners as is to be reimbursed by the cargo owner under the contract of Affreightment Both to Blame Collision clause.

（2）水渍险。

除了承保平安险的内容外，还负责被保险货物由于恶劣气候、雷电、海啸、地震、洪水自然灾害所造成的部分损失。

（3）一切险。

除承保平安险和水渍险的范围外，还负责被保险货物在运输途中由于外来原因所致的全部或部分损失。

平安险、水渍险和一切险的承保范围是逐步递增的，但值得注意的是，投保一切险并不意味着保险公司承担了一切损失的赔偿责任，比如，战争风险。本保险索赔的时效，以被保险货物在最后卸载港全部卸离海轮后起算，最多不超过两年。

2）伦敦保险业协会货物保险条款

海运货物保险单的承保范围依据由伦敦保险业协会(或美国保险协会)颁发的标准保单。这些海运货物保险单的承保范围被称为"协会货物条款"。虽然有很多不同的条款且不同的货物适用于不同的条款，但通常承保范围最广泛的为"货物保险条款 A"，而"货物保险条款 B"和"货物保险条款 C"的承保范围则较窄。伦敦保险业协会之前的条款——一切险、水渍险、平安险已被这些新颁布的保险条款所取代。

(2) With Average (W. A.).

Aside from the risks covered under F. P. A. condition as above, this insurance also covers partial losses of the insured goods caused by heavy weather, lightning, tsunami, earthquake and/or flood.

(3) All Risks.

Aside from the risks covered under the F. P. A. and W. A. conditions as above, this insurance also covers all risks of loss of or damage to the insured goods whether partial or total, arising from external causes in the cause of transit.

From F. P. A. to All Risks, the coverage becomes wider and wider, but it is important to note that "All Risks" does not mean the insurance covers all risks, such as war. The time of validity of a claim under this insurance shall not exceed a period of two years counting from the time of completion of discharge of the insured goods from the seagoing vessel at the final port of discharge.

2) London Insurance Institute Cargo Clauses (I.C.C.)

The cover under a marine cargo policy is defined by standard policy wordings issued by the Institute of London Underwriters (or the American Institute of Marine Underwriters). These are called Institute Cargo Clauses. While there are numerous clauses and different clauses will apply to different cargoes, normally the widest cover is provided under Institute Cargo Clauses A with more restrictive cover under Institute Cargo Clauses B and Institute Cargo Clauses C. These new clauses replaced the previous Institute Cargo Clauses All Risks, With Average (W.A.) and Free from Particular Average (F.P.A.).

"货物保险条款 A"中，保险人承保除除外责任外的一切风险。除外责任有四类：①一般除外，包括被保险人的故意不法行为；自然渗漏、包装不当、内在缺陷或特性；迟延；船舶所有人、经理人、租船人或经营人破产或不履行债务；原子核武器造成的灭失、损坏或费用。②不适航、不适货除外。③战争除外。④罢工除外。

"货物保险条款 B"中保险人只承保明确列明的风险和损失，未列的风险不予承保。

"货物保险条款 C"中保险人只承保意外事故造成的货物损失，不承保自然灾害及非意外事故的货物灭损。该条款增加了承保陆上风险的规定。投保人可以在投保"货物保险条款 C"的同时投保其他保险条款，如附带货物战争险、货物罢工险。

综 合 练 习

1. 简述国际货物销售合同当事人的义务。

2. 简述国际货物销售合同的违约补救方法。

3. 简述单独海损和共同海损的联系和区别。

4. 简述国际多式联运的责任制度。

5. 简述《国际货约》的主要内容。

Institute Cargo Clauses A covers all risks of loss of or damage to the subject-matter insured except: (a)general exclusion includes loss, damage or expense attributable to wilful misconduct of the assured, ordinary leakage, loss, damage or expense caused by insufficiency or unsuitability of packing or inherent vice, delay, insolvency or financial default of the owners, managers, charterers or operators of the vessel, loss, damage or expense arising from the use of nuclear weapon, etc., (b)unseaworthiness and unfitness exclusion, (c)war exclusion, (d)strikes exclusion.

Institute Cargo Clauses B covers only the risks and losses expressly stated in the insurance clause.

Institute Cargo Clauses C covers loss or damage due to fortuitous accidents. In no case shall this insurance cover the loss or damage due to natural calamities or any other peril other than fortuitous accidents. In addition, Clauses C adds coverage about land conveyance. Policy-holder may take out Clauses C and other kinds of policy clauses, such as Institute War Clause-Cargo and Institute Strikes Clause-Cargo, simultaneously.

Comprehensive Exercises

1. Briefly describe the obligations of the parties to a contract for the international sale of goods.

2. Briefly describe the remedies for the breach of a contract for the international sale of goods.

3. Describe the connections and differences between particular average and general average.

4. Briefly describe the responsibility system of international multimodal transport.

5. Briefly describe the main contents of *the COTIF/CIM*.

第四章 国际知识产权与技术转让法

学习目标

了解知识产权的概念及其分类。

理解知识产权使用许可转让协议的概念、特征和内容。

掌握政府在技术转让中的管制措施以及与技术转让有关的主要国际法规范。

Chapter 4 Law on International Intellectual Property and Technology Transfer

Learning Objectives

To know the concept, classification of intellectual property.

To understand the concept, features and content of license agreement of intellectual property.

To master the government regulations in technology transfer and main sources of international law on transfer of technology.

第一节　知识产权概述

一、知识产权的概念

知识产权是无形财产。它包括想法、创新活动及其他人类创造性的表现形式，受到知识产权法的保护。作为财产，知识产权可以进行交易。授予使用许可是创造知识产权价值的一个重要途径。因为知识产权所有人允许他人使用该知识产权的同时，自己仍拥有对该知识产权的所有权。授予使用许可有利于创造收入来源，将技术传播给更广泛的用户群和潜在的技术开发者，同时也推动和促进技术的进一步开发和商业化。

知识产权法律包括关于专利、实用新型、商业秘密、商标、地理标志、工业品外观设计、集成电路布图设计、非原创性数据库、植物新品种、版权及相关权利的法律。

当多数国家的知识产权法律趋向更大程度的协调一致时，它们依旧保持着国家(或者地区，这取决于这些多数国家是否已经就这样一部区域性的知识产权法律达成一致)的法律在本国或本地区境内领土上有效。因而，在一个地域内得到的知识产权权利只在该地域内有效。

4.1　Introduction to Intellectual Property

4.1.1　Concept of Intellectual Property

Intellectual property is intangible property. It is a collection of ideas, innovations and other expressions of human creativity, protected by law through the intellectual property system. As property, they are tradable assets. Licensing, the right granted by an owner of such an asset to another to use that asset while continuing to retain ownership of that asset, is an important way of creating value with these assets. Licensing creates an income source, disseminates the technology to a wider group of users and potential developers and acts as a catalyst for further development and commercialization.

The intellectual property laws include laws on patents, utility models, trade secrets, trademarks, geographical indications, industrial design, layout-design of integrated circuits, non-original databases, new varieties of plants, copyright and related rights.

While the intellectual property laws of most countries are moving towards greater harmonization, they remain national (or regional depending on whether a group of countries have agreed to such a regional intellectual property law) laws having effect only within the territorial boundaries of the country or the region. Therefore, an intellectual property right obtained within a jurisdiction is only valid in that jurisdiction.

二、知识产权的分类

知识产权是智力的产物，包括发明、文学艺术作品和在商业中使用的符号、名称和图像。它分为工业产权和版权两类。前者包括发明专利、商标、工业品外观设计和地理标志，后者包括文学作品，如小说、诗歌和表演、电影、音乐作品、艺术作品(如素描、油画、绘画、照相和雕刻)，以及建筑设计。与版权相关的权利(即相邻权)包括表演艺术家在其表演中的权利、唱片制作人的权利，以及广播者在其无线电和电视节目中的权利。

知识产权的主要类型如下。

1. 专利

专利是授予一项发明的专有权，无论是一项产品还是一种方法，它必须可在工业中应用(实用的)，是新的(新颖的)，并展示足够的"发明步骤"(非显而易见的)。专利向发明的拥有人提供专利保护。授予的保护有一定期限，一般来说自申请之日起的 20 年。

专利保护意味着一项专利的拥有人有阻止他人制造、使用、提供销售、销售或引进该发明的专有权利。这些专有权利常常在法院获得执行。在多数国家中，法院有权禁止专利侵权。反之，法院也可以根据第三方有效的权利主张宣布一项专利无效。

4.1.2　Classification of Intellectual Property

Intellectual property refers to creations of the mind: inventions, literary and artistic works, and symbols, names, and images used in commerce. It is divided into two categories: industrial property which includes patents for inventions, trademarks, industrial designs and geographical indications and copyright which includes literary works such as novels, poems and plays, films, musical works, artistic works such as drawings, paintings, photographs and sculptures, and architectural designs. Rights related to copyright include those of performing artists in their performances, producers of phonograms, and those of broadcasters in their radio and television programs.

The main types of intellectual property rights are as follows.

1. Patents

A patent is an exclusive right granted for an invention, whether a product or a process, which must be industrially applicable (useful), be new (novel) and exhibit a sufficient "inventive step" (be non-obvious). A patent provides protection for the invention to the owner of the patent. The protection is granted for a limited period, generally 20 years from the filing date.

Patent protection means that the owner of a patent has the exclusive right to prevent others from making, using, offering for sale, selling or importing the invention. These patent rights are usually enforced in a court, which, in most systems, holds the authority to stop patent infringements. Conversely, a court can also declare a patent invalid upon a successful challenge by a third party.

专利所有人有权决定谁可以(或不可以)使用在保护期内的专利发明。专利所有人可以根据协议条款允许或授予他方使用该发明的权利。所有人还可以向其他人出售该发明权,此人将变成专利的新所有人。一旦专利保护期满,发明就进入公有领域,即拥有人不再持有发明的独占权,发明可供他人商业使用而无须所有人的授权或允许。

作为对专利保护的补偿,所有专利所有人均有义务公开揭示与其发明有关的信息,以便丰富人类的技术知识体系。该公有知识整体不断增加,将进一步促进其他人的创造和发明。通过这种方法,专利不仅为所有人提供保护,并且也为以后的研究人员和发明者提供有价值的信息和灵感。

成功获得专利的第一步是提交专利申请书。专利申请书一般包含发明名称以及其在技术领域的描述。它必须包括发明的背景,并以清楚的语言对发明进行详尽表述,以便本领域具有普通理解能力的人员可以使用或复制该发明。为了更好地进行描述,表述时通常还伴有可视材料,例如绘图、设计图或图表等。申请书还包括各种"权利声明",即确定专利保护范围的相关信息。

A patent owner has the right to decide who may (or may not) use the patented invention for the period in which the invention is protected. The patent owner may give permission to, or license, other parties to use the invention on mutually agreed terms. The owner may also sell the right to the invention to someone else, who will then become the new owner of the patent. Once a patent expires, the protection ends, and an invention enters the public domain, that is, the owner no longer holds exclusive rights to the invention, which becomes available for commercial exploitation by others.

All patent owners are obliged, in return for patent protection, to publicly disclose information on their invention in order to enrich the total body of technical knowledge in the world. Such an ever-increasing body of public knowledge promotes further creativity and innovation in others. In this way, patents provide not only protection for the owner but also valuable information and inspiration for future generations of researchers and inventors.

The first step in securing a patent is the filing of a patent application. The patent application generally contains the title of the invention, as well as an indication of its technical field. It must include the background and a description of the invention, in clear language and enough details that an individual with an average understanding of the field could use or reproduce the invention. Such descriptions are usually accompanied by visual materials such as drawings, plans, or diagrams to better describe the invention. The application also contains various "claims", that is, information which determines the extent of protection granted by the patent.

2. 商标

商标是一种特殊标志，它表明由专门的人或企业生产或提供的一定产品或服务。商标有助于消费者识别并购买产品或服务，因为独一无二的商标所指向的产品或服务，其性质和质量符合消费者要求。

商标通过提供排他性权利保护标识所有人，或者排他性地使用标识于产品或服务，或者授权他人使用该标识并获得报酬。不同的商标保护期限不同，但商标都可以通过缴纳相应的费用而不定期地续展。商标权的保护由法院执行，在多数国家，法院有权制止商标侵权。

商标可以包括用于区别特征的图形、符号、三维标记(如物品的外形和包装)、可听标记(如音乐或歌声)、气味或颜色。除商标识别产品或服务的商业来源之外，还有几种其他种类的标识。集体商标由协会所有，协会成员使用集体商标标示自己具有一定质量水平和协会规定的其他要求。如会计师协会、工程师协会以及建筑师协会等就属于这类协会。证明商标则用于说明符合规定的标准，但不具有会员资格。它们可授予任何可证明其产品符合一定规定标准的任何人。

2. Trademarks

A trademark is a distinctive sign, which identifies certain goods or services as those produced or provided by a specific person or enterprise. The trademark helps consumers identify and purchase a product or service because its nature and quality, indicated by its unique trademark, meets their needs.

A trademark provides protection to the owner of the mark by ensuring the exclusive right to use it to identify goods or services, or to authorize another to use it in return for payment. The period of protection varies, but a trademark can be renewed indefinitely on payment of corresponding fees. Trademark protection is enforced by the courts, which in most countries have the authority to block trademark infringement.

Trademarks can include drawings, symbols, three-dimensional signs such as the shape and packaging of goods, audible signs such as music or vocal sounds, fragrances, or colors used as distinguishing features. In addition to trademarks identifying the commercial sources of goods or services, several other categories of marks exist. Collective marks are owned by an association whose members use them to identify themselves with a level of quality and other requirements set by the association. Examples of such associations would be those representing accountants, engineers, or architects. Certification marks are given for compliance with defined standards, but are not confined to any membership. They may be granted to anyone who can certify that the products involved meet certain established standards.

3. 工业品外观设计

工业品外观设计是一件商品的装饰或富有美感的外表。设计可由三维特征(例如物品的形状或外表)或二维特征(例如样式、线条或颜色)组成。工业品外观设计广泛应用于工业产品和手工艺产品：从技术和医疗仪器到手表、珠宝及其他奢侈品；从家庭器皿和电器到运输工具和建筑结构；从纺织品图案到休闲商品。要获得大多数国家的法律保护，工业品外观设计必须是新的或原创的，并且是非功能性的。这意味着，工业品外观设计首先要具有一种美学性质，其所应用的物品的任何技术性特征不受保护。当工业品外观设计受到保护时，所有人——注册该外观设计的个人或实体即享有阻止第三方未经许可复制或仿制该外观设计的排他性权利。

4. 商业秘密

从广义上来说，任何能提供给企业竞争优势的机密性商业信息都可称为商业秘密。商业秘密可能与技术内容有关，例如一种产品的构成或设计，或者一种实施特殊操作所必需的制造方法或技术秘密。作为商业秘密保护的内容，通常包括制造过程、市场调研结果、消费者剖析、供应商和客户名单、价格目录、财务信息、商业计划、商业战略、广告战略、市场营销计划、销售计划和方法、配送方法、设计、图案、建筑平面图、蓝图和地图等。

---

3. Industrial Designs

An industrial design is the ornamental or aesthetic aspect of an article. The design may consist of three-dimensional features, (such as the shape or surface of an article,) or of two-dimensional features, (such as patterns, lines or color). Industrial designs are applied to a wide variety of products of industry and handicraft: from technical and medical instruments to watches, jewelry, and other luxury items; from house wares and electrical appliances to vehicles and architectural structures; from textile designs to leisure goods. To be protected under most national laws, an industrial design must be new or original and non-functional. This means that an industrial design is primarily of an aesthetic nature and any technical features of the article to which it is applied are not protected. When an industrial design is protected, the owner—the person or entity that has registered the design—is assured an exclusive right against unauthorized copying or imitation of the design by third parties.

4. Trade Secrets

Broadly speaking, any confidential business information which provides an enterprise with a competitive edge can qualify as a trade secret. A trade secret may relate to technical matters, such as the composition or design of a product, a method of manufacture or the know-how necessary to perform a particular operation. Common items that are protected as trade secrets include manufacturing processes, market research results, consumer profiles, lists of suppliers and clients, price lists, financial information, business plans, business strategies, advertising strategies, marketing plans, sales plans and methods, distribution methods, designs, drawings, architectural plans, blueprints and maps, etc.

虽然各国的情况不同，但对于如何界定商业秘密通常都存在一些一般性的标准。这些标准如下。

(1) 信息必须是机密或秘密的。众所周知或容易获知的信息是不能作为商业秘密保护的。如果所有人不采取适当的防范措施保护其机密或秘密，甚至很难了解的信息也可能失掉其受保护地位。

(2) 信息还必须具有商业价值，因为它们属于秘密，信息的所有人必须采取合理的步骤保护其机密或秘密性质(如通过与所有能够获取保密信息的人订立保密或不披露协议)。简单地把信息称作商业秘密并不会使它真的成为商业秘密。

商业秘密的所有人可以阻止他人不正当获取、披露或使用它。然而，商业秘密法未赋予其权利去阻止人们以合法途径获取或使用信息。合法途径，即没有使用非法手段，也未违反协议和国家法律。不同于其他形式的知识产权，如专利、商标和工业品外观设计，商业秘密的保护基本上是一种自我保护形式。信息的机密性保护多长，商业秘密的保护时间就持续多长。相关信息一经公开，商业秘密的保护即告终止。

While conditions vary from country to country, but there are some general standards for how to define trade secrets.

(1) They are that the information must be confidential or secret. Information which is generally known or readily ascertainable is not protectable as a trade secret. Even hard-to-learn information may lose its protected status if the owner does not take proper precautions to maintain its confidentiality or secrecy.

(2) The information must have commercial value because it is a secret and the holder of the information must have taken reasonable steps to keep it confidential or secret (e.g. through confidentiality or non-disclosure agreements with all those who have access to the secret information). Simply calling information a trade secret will not make it so.

The owner of a trade secret can prevent others from improperly acquiring, disclosing or using it. However, trade secret law does not give the right to stop people who acquire or use information in a legitimate way, that is, without using illegal means or violating agreements or state laws. Unlike other forms of intellectual property such as patents, trademarks and industrial designs, maintaining trade secrecy is basically a do-it-yourself form of protection. Trade secret protection lasts for as long as the information is kept confidential. Once the relevant information is made public, trade secret protection ends.

5. 版权与相关权利

版权是法律授予作者、艺术家和其他创作者，保护其文学艺术作品的权利。这些作品一般被称为"著作"。与版权最密切相关的权利领域是"相关权利"，它提供与版权相类似或相同的权利，尽管有时期限很有限或期限更短。相关权利的受益者是表演活动中的表演者(如演员和音乐家)，录音中的录音作品(如录音带和光盘)制作者，以及无线电和电视节目的广播组织。

版权所覆盖的作品，包括但不限于：小说、诗歌、戏剧、参考书、报纸、计算机程序、数据库、电影、音乐作曲、舞蹈表演、油画、素描、摄影、雕刻、建筑作品、广告、地图和技术制图。根据版权法，受版权保护作品的创作者及其继承人和继受者(一般称为"权利持有人")享有一定的基本权利。他们享有使用或通过协议条款许可他人使用其作品的专有权利。

5. Copyright and Related Rights

Copyright is the body of laws which grants rights to authors, artists and other composers for protecting their literary and artistic creations, which are generally referred to as "works". A closely-associated field of rights related to copyright is "related rights", which provides rights similar or identical to those of copyright, although sometimes more limited and of shorter duration. The beneficiaries of related rights are performers (such as actors and musicians) in their performances; producers of sound recordings (for example, cassette recordings and compact discs) in their recordings; and broadcasting organizations in their radio and television programs.

Works covered by copyright include, but are not limited to: novels, poems, plays, reference works, newspapers, computer programs, databases, films, musical compositions, choreography, paintings, drawings, photographs, sculptures, architectural works, advertisements, maps, and technical drawings. The creators of works protected by copyright, and their heirs and successors (generally referred to as "rights holders"), have certain basic rights under the copyright law. They hold the exclusive right to use or authorize others to use the work on agreed terms.

一件作品的权利持有人可以禁止或许可他人：①以各种形式复制作品，包括印刷和录音；②将其进行公开表演和向公众传播；③将其广播；④将其翻译成其他语言；⑤将其改编，例如将小说改编成电影剧本。根据相关权利的法律，还可以授予与固定(录音)和复制相似的权利。由于受版权和相关权利法律保护的许多作品类型需要大量发行、传播和投资推广(例如，出版、录音和电影)，创作者常常将其作品的权利转让给最有能力开发其作品并推向市场的公司，从而以付款和/或版税的形式获得报酬(报酬根据作品产生收入的一个比例计算)。

版权的经济权利有一定期限，如 WIPO 相关条约规定，自作品创作和固定时开始，持续到不少于创作者死亡后 50 年。各国家法律可以确定更长的保护期。这一保护期可使创作者及其继承人和继受者在一个合理的时间内获得资金收益。相关权利享有较短期限，正常情况下是表演、录音或广播后的 50 年。版权对表演者的保护，还包括精神权利，即要求对作品标明作者身份的权利，以及反对改变其作品的权利，这种改变可能损害创作者的声誉。

The rights holder(s) of a work can prohibit or authorize: (a)its reproduction in all forms, including printing and sound recording; (b)its public performance and communication to the public; (c)its broadcasting; (d)its translation into other languages; (e)and its adaptation, such as a novel into a screenplay for a film. Similar rights of, among others, fixation (recording) and reproduction are granted under the law of related rights. Many types of works protected under the laws of copyright and related rights require mass distribution, communication, and financial investment for their successful dissemination (for example, publications, sound recordings, and films). Therefore creators often transfer the rights to their works to companies best able to develop and market the works, in return for remuneration, in the form of payments and/or royalties (remuneration based on a percentage of revenues generated by the work).

The economic rights of copyright have a certain period of time , as provided in the relevant WIPO treaties, commencing upon the creation and fixation of the work, and lasting for not less than 50 years after the creator's death. National laws may establish longer terms of protection. This term of protection enables both creators and their heirs and successors to benefit financially for a reasonable period of time. Related rights enjoy shorter terms, normally 50 years after the performance, recording or broadcast took place. Copyright and the protection of performers also include moral rights, which are the right to claim authorship of a work, and the right to oppose changes to the work which could harm the creator's reputation.

版权和相关权利的保护是自动获得的，无须履行注册或其他正式手续。然而，许多国家提供了可选择的作品注册和提交系统。这些系统便于解决诸如涉及有关所有权或创作权、财务手续、销售、分配和权利转让等有争议的问题。许多作者和表演者没有能力或手段请求司法或者行政机关保护其版权和相关权利，特别是在文学、音乐和表演作品在世界范围的使用越来越多的情况下。

因此，建立并加强集体管理组织或组建"协会"，在许多国家正成为必然趋势。这些协会可以通过向其成员提供服务获得行政管理、法律咨询和组织效率等方面的收益。这些服务如收集、管理或分发来自一国和他国的使用某会员作品或表演的版税。录音生产者和广播组织的某些权利也实行集体管理。

三、知识产权使用许可转让的必要性

知识产权资产可由其所有者进行商业性开发，或者许可他人开发。他人开发知识产权的途径之一就是从知识产权所有者那里获得知识产权的使用许可。"使用许可"一词的含义简单来说，就是由知识产权权利所有人授予另一方在经其同意的条款和条件下，为了确定的目的，在指定地域和约定期限内可使用该知识产权的权利。

Copyright and related rights protection is obtained automatically without any need for registration or other formalities. However, many countries provide for a national system of optional registration and deposit of works; these systems facilitate, for example, questions involving disputes over ownership or creation, financing transactions, sales, assignments and transfers of rights. Many authors and performers do not have the ability or the means to pursue the legal and administrative enforcement of copyright and related rights, especially given the increasingly worldwide use of literary, musical and performing works.

As a result, the establishment and enhancement of collective management organizations, or "societies", is a growing and necessary trend in many countries. These societies can provide for their members the benefits of the organization's administrative and legal expertise and efficiency in, for example, collecting, managing, and disbursing royalties gained from the national and international use of a member's work or performance. Certain rights of producers of sound recordings and broadcasting organizations are sometimes managed collectively as well.

4.1.3　Necessity for Transferable Intellectual Property License

Intellectual property assets can be commercially exploited by their owner or with the permission of the owner by others. One way for others to exploit intellectual property is through licensing the intellectual property from the owner. The word "license" simply means permission granted by the owner of the intellectual property right to another to use it on agreed terms and conditions, for a defined purpose, in a defined territory and for an agreed period of time.

　　知识产权使用许可通常可以分为三大类：技术使用许可、出版和娱乐表演使用许可及商标和商品销售使用许可。不过，这些种类并非完全绝对的。本节将不涉及出版和娱乐表演方面的专门使用许可以及商标和商品销售的使用许可，重点介绍技术使用许可，主要包括专利和商业秘密。软件使用许可，在某些国家可能属于专利保护范围，因此可以属于技术使用许可，但不包含在本章范围之内。

　　企业只有以较低的价格持续供应更好的产品和服务才具有竞争力，从而盈利，并在全球化、快速发展、需求日益增长的市场经济中占有优势地位。企业如何满足对新产品或更好的产品和服务的需求并以更有竞争力的价格提供更好的产品和服务呢？经济增长的传统驱动力：土地、劳动力和资本，已不足以为企业提供必需的竞争优势，而竞争优势可使企业之间出现显著差别，否则企业彼此之间将会非常相似。答案就是依赖新技术或改进技术。

　　技术对许多人意味着许多东西。韦氏大字典把技术定义为"知识的实际应用，来自实际应用知识的能力，或完成一项任务的方式，特别是利用技术过程、方法或知识来完成任务的方式"。

License of intellectual property is often considered in three broad categories, technology license, license for publishing and entertainment performance, and licenses for the sale and use of trademarks and commodities. These categories are, however, not watertight compartments. This chapter will not be dealing with aspects specific to publishing and entertainment licenses or to trademark and merchandising licenses. Its focus will be on technology licenses, which mainly involve patents and trade secrets. Software license, which may in some countries be protected by patents and could, therefore, fall within technology license, is outside the scope of this chapter.

Only companies that continue to provide better products and services at a lower price will be competitive, profitable and maintain an edge in a market economy that is globalized, fast developing and constantly demanding. How do companies meet this demand for new or better products and services, and provide these at a competitive price? The traditional drivers of economic growth: land, labor and capital, are no longer sufficient to provide the necessary competitive advantage that makes the difference between enterprises that are otherwise very similar to one another. The answer lies in new or improved technology.

Technology means many things to many people. *The Merriam-Webster's Dictionary* defines technology as "the practical application of knowledge, the capability given by the practical application of knowledge or the manner of accomplishing a task especially using technical processes, methods, or knowledge".

　　大英百科全书将技术定义为"将科学知识应用于人类生活的实际目的，或者如有时所表述的那样，用于改变或操纵人类环境。技术包括使用材料、工具、技术和动力源，使生活更简便或更舒适，工作更有效率。相比而言，科学关心事物如何或为什么发生，而技术则聚焦于使事情发生"。技术的通俗定义是，"技术是对科学信息的实际应用"。因此，从广义上说，技术系指具有发明和技术秘密形式的科学研究与开发的终端产品。为更好地满足市场需求，这些发明和技术秘密用作创造新的或改进的产品和服务的工具或过程。过去常常有把一项专利与一项技术等同起来的情况，现在这种情况很少见。越来越多地，一项技术由许多专利共同组成，而一项产品也由许多技术共同组成，例如相机或汽车。

　　这种技术要么可以由企业自身与他人合作进行研究与开发获得，要么可以通过从他人已开发并投放的市场中得到。通常，谨慎的做法是从别人那里获得技术，而不是自己投入时间和资源去寻找完美的解决方案。例如，如果由于成本、时间、人力资源及其他资产方面的原因，而自己内部不能开发所需技术，使用或采用别人已获得且可以从市场上得到的技术解决方案，这可能是最好的商业办法。有时，甚至有必要获得技术使用许可，这些技术属于行业标准、国家标准或国际标准的组成部分。如果一种新产品或改进产品不可避免地要侵犯他人所拥有的知识产权，那么获得使用许可则是非常必要的。

The Encyclopedia Britannica defines it as "the application of scientific knowledge to the practical aims of human life or, as it is sometimes phrased, to the change and manipulation of the human environment. Technology includes the use of materials, tools, techniques, and sources of power to make life easier or more pleasant and work more productive. Whereas science is concerned with how and why things happen, technology focuses on making things happen". A popular definition of technology is that "technology is the practical use of scientific information". Therefore, broadly speaking, technology refers to end products of scientific research and development in the form of inventions and know-how which are used as tools or processes for creating new or improved products and services that better serve the needs of the market. There used to be a case of equating one patent with one technology, this is rarely the case nowadays. Increasingly, a number of patents together are responsible for a technology and a number of technologies for a product, for example, a camera or a car.

Such technology may be acquired either through research and development undertaken by the company itself, in cooperation with others, or through the market in which others have developed and offered the technology. Often, it is prudent to obtain technology from others instead of investing the time and resources to find the perfect solution oneself. For example, if the necessary technology cannot be developed in-house for reasons of cost, timeframe, human resources and complimentary assets, it may make good business sense to use or adopt a technological solution that has already been found by others and is available on the market. Sometimes, it may even be necessary to obtain licenses for technologies which are part of industry, national or international standards set by standard-setting organizations. A license may be necessary in a situation where a new or improved product inadvertently violates the intellectual property rights owned by another.

此外，如果一家企业已经拥有一种新的或更好的产品或方法，它很清楚地知道可能有其他企业也在寻求这种产品或方法，作为一个不错的商业选择，它可以选择将此项产品或方法进行转让而获得一笔额外收入。实际上，许多企业或是从产品制造转而从事授予专利和技术秘密形式的知识产权使用许可，或是确定单纯以创造知识产权并授出使用许可为目的，而不生产任何产品。换言之，技术已成为产品。如今，甚至最大的企业也不再自己做每一件事情，而是依靠外部资源，不仅包括主要的部件、服务，而且也包括技术。另一些企业自己只开发技术，而后将产品的生产外包给本国或海外的其他公司，为此目的而签订使用许可协议。

由于技术具有无形性，一个人对其使用不会损害他人的使用。换言之，它可同时供许多用户出于同样或者不同目的使用，这种使用不会在任何方面影响其质量或者功能。因此，技术的所有者可以将其技术授予使用许可，让潜在被许可人使用，他希望有多少被许可人就可以有多少，尽可能使其技术的潜在收益最大化，其技术只受到与潜在的被许可人所签订的协议条款约束。从某种意义上来说，一项技术可能成为一系列相关或不相关产品和服务的基础，这些产品由一个或多个国家的一个或多个企业生产，涉及的地域非常广泛。

Furthermore, a company that has come up with a new or better product or process will do well to know that there may be others searching for such a solution and it could be a good business option to transfer that knowledge and earn a bonus from an additional source of income. In fact, a number of companies have either shifted from manufacturing of products to licensing of intellectual property in the form of patents and know-how or have been set up with the sole objective of creating and licensing intellectual property without manufacturing any products. In other words, the technology becomes the product. Today, even the largest companies are no longer doing everything in-house and depend on outside sources not only for key components and services but also for technologies. Some other companies just develop technology and outsource the manufacture of the products to other companies in their own country or abroad by entering into a licensing agreement for this purpose.

Given the intangible character of technology, its use by one does not detract from its use by another. In other words, it can be used simultaneously by many users for the same or different purposes without impacting in any way on its quality or functionality. Therefore, the owner of technology could potentially license the use of his/her technology to as many licensees as he/she wishes, maximizing the earning potential of his/her technology constrained only by the terms of the agreements that he/she enters into with the potential licensees. In a sense, one technology could become the basis for a whole range of related or unrelated products and services made by one or many enterprises in a potentially large number of locations in one or many countries.

第二节　使用许可协议

一、使用许可协议概念

使用许可协议是将技术中的知识产权使用权由许可人转让给被许可人，以使对方在特定时间和地区，以特定方式，生产、使用和销售包含该技术的产品。换言之，许可人将继续拥有对该技术的知识产权，仅仅授予了被许可人对该项技术的规定范围内的使用权利。每一个使用许可协议都是独特的，它反映了许可人和被许可人的特殊需求与期望。可能有多种多样的使用许可协议，但是都受限于双方的需求以及相关法律和法规的规定。

二、使用许可协议的结构

广义而言，使用许可协议涉及①许可使用什么；②以什么价格许可使用(费用和付款时间表)；③许可谁使用；④为何目的使用；⑤许可使用多长时间；以及⑥在什么条件下使用(担保、免责声明、赔偿)。下文将从三个部分讨论使用许可协议的结构，但它们未必都将包括在使用许可协议中。每一个使用许可协议的具体内容更多取决于各自的具体情况。

4.2　License Agreement

4.2.1　Concept of License Agreement

A license agreement transfers from the licensor to the licensee the right to use the intellectual property in the technology and to make, use and sell products embodying the technology, in a specified manner for a specified time in a specified region. In other words, the licensor continues to have the proprietary rights over the technology and has only given a defined right to the use of that technology. Every license agreement is unique, reflecting the particular needs and expectations of the licensor and licensee. An infinite variety of agreements are possible, limited only by the needs of the parties and by the parameters of the relevant laws and regulations.

4.2.2　Structure of a License Agreement

Broadly speaking, a license agreement deals with (a)what is licensed, (b)at what price (cost and payment schedule), (c)to whom, (d)for what purpose, (e)for how long, and (f)under what conditions (warranties, disclaimers, indemnification). The next shall discuss the structure of license agreement divided into three parts. It is, however, not necessary that all of them be included in all license agreements. Much will depend on the particular circumstances of each case.

1. 协议主题

使用许可协议的主题可包括创造，例如发明、保密信息、小说、电视剧、电影、音乐中的创造性表现形式、商品及服务名称、商业标志等。这些主题可以根据知识产权法获得保护。这些法律强调对专利、实用新型、商业秘密、商标、地理标志、工业品外观设计、集成电路布图设计和版权的保护，并反对一定类型的不公平竞争行为。

主题事项是使用许可协议的首要部分，对协议内容具有重要影响。因此，在涉及计算机软件的使用许可协议中，很可能有详细说明允许使用或应用以及保密性要求的条款。在商标使用许可协议中，尤其要注意广告和市场营销中对商标的正确使用，并注意保持该商标下的产品或服务的质量。

由于使用许可协议的主题事项通常包括保密信息和发明，因此不仅要对专利的使用许可给予注意，也应对这些保密信息给予足够注意，包括技术秘密和获得许可的商业秘密。在这方面，协议应该包括一项或多项可替代保密协议的条款，而保密协议是要在谈判前签订的。

---

1. Subject Matter

The subject matter of a license agreement may include creations such as inventions, confidential information, the creativity expressed in novels, plays, movies, music, the names of goods and services, business identifiers, etc. These can be owned and protected under intellectual property laws, which, to reiterate, include patents, utility models, trade secrets, trademarks, geographical indications, industrial designs, layout-design of integrated circuits and copyright, as well as those that protect against certain types of unfair competition.

The subject matter is the first main section of the license agreement and it will have an important influence on the contents of the agreement. Thus, in license agreement involving computer software there are likely to be clauses specifying the permitted use or application and requiring confidentiality to be maintained. In a trademark license agreement, particular attention should be paid to controlling the proper use of the trademark in advertising and marketing, and to maintaining the quality of the product or service bearing the trademark.

As the subject matter of a license agreement often includes confidential information as well as inventions, as much attention as is devoted to the licensing of patents should also be devoted to such confidential information, including know-how and licensed trade secrets. In this connection, it is important to include in the agreement one or more clauses superseding the confidentiality agreement entered into prior to the negotiations.

2. 许可的权利范围

使用许可协议的第二个主要部分是关于使用许可的权利范围。这涉及被许可权利的范围，使用许可是独占性的、唯一性的，或是非独占性的，以及所授予使用许可的地理地域。该范围可能还包括在许可使用期间对技术的改进以及协议的有效期。

被许可权利的性质取决于其主题事项。对于一项专利而言，权利通常包括制造、使用以及销售某项专利产品或使用某项已获专利的方法。不过，也可能有一些不适当的情况，例如，授予销售权，而这是一种非常有限的使用许可，因为被许可人不能从使用许可中获得商业收益。在版权使用许可的情况下，也可以包括复制、展示、修改以及发行的权利。一些使用许可允许被许可人将使用许可中所提到的部分或全部权利授予"分使用许可"，因而可允许被许可人自己进入授予使用许可的生意。在其"范围"部分，使用许可必须明确许可使用什么权利。例如，短期的使用许可不允许被许可人改变设计，而只允许被许可人在特定国家或地区制造或销售产品，这比永久性或者不可撤销的使用许可更受限制。永久性使用许可允许被许可人制造、使用、修改、改进、拷贝、复制、发行、展示、出口、进口以及将上述权利授予世界范围内的其他人"分使用许可"的权利，同时还可以使用与之相关的商标权利。这类使用许可非常接近于出售(让与)知识产权及其所保护的技术的所有权。

---

2. Extent of the Licensed Rights

The second main section of a license agreement relates to the extent of the licensed rights. This refers to the scope of the right being licensed, whether the license is exclusive, sole or non-exclusive, and the geographic territory for which the license is granted. The scope might also include improvements made to the technology during the license and will include the duration of the agreement.

The nature of the rights being licensed depends on the subject matter. For a patent, this would normally be the right to make, use and sell a patented product or use a patented process. There may, however, be circumstances where it would not be appropriate, for example, to grant the right to sell, though this would be a very limited license as the licensee would not be able to receive a commercial benefit from the license. In the case of a copyright license, it may also include the right to reproduce, display, modify and distribute. Some licenses permit the licensee to "sub-license" some or all of the rights conferred in the license, thus permitting the licensee to go into the business himself/herself of licensing the technology. The license must clarify in its "scope" section, what rights are given. For example, a short term license that does not permit the licensee to modify a design, but only to make it and sell it in the certain country or region, is more limited than a perpetual and irrevocable license that permits the licensee to make, use, modify, improve, copy, reproduce, distribute, display, export, import, and sub-license all of the above rights to others worldwide, as well as the right to use the associated trademark in connection therewith. Such a license comes close to being a sale (assignment) of ownership in the intellectual property and the technology it underlies.

1) 独占性、唯一性或非独占性

在某些特殊领域，使用许可可能是独占性的、唯一性的或非独占性的。

非独占性使用许可，即被许可人是与许可人签订使用或开发技术协议的几个被许可人之一，是大多数许可人的首选。许可人通过在几个被许可人之间分散风险、分享报酬，可以不单纯依靠一个被许可人的成功。他可以对技术保持较好的控制，而且，由于有几个被许可人在几个市场及各种产品方面使用并开发该技术，该技术有机会得到进一步地演进和开发。不过，在技术开发早期，由于被许可人需要投入大笔的额外投资金额，大多数潜在的被许可人将至少在一定地域内寻求独占性使用许可。

独占性使用许可通常规定，该权利只授予被许可人，甚至排除许可人在该地域的使用权。唯一性使用许可通常规定，许可人和被许可人在该地域内均可使用该技术，但是其他人不可以。不过，这一区别在实践中可能被模糊，而"独占性"一词有时就用以指实际上的唯一性使用许可。在任何情况下，这两种许可方式均不允许许可人再授予他人使用许可(至少在使用许可已明确规定为独占性和唯一性的地域内)。在该地域内，许可人依赖于被许可人。因此，重要的是保证协议包含适当的激励和惩罚条款，在被许可人不履行其义务时可以保护许可人的利益。这些条款可包括每年交付使用费。如果被许可人不支付使用费，那么惩罚的方式就是终止使用许可协议，或者将独占使用许可转变为非独占使用许可。

---

1) Exclusive, Sole or Non-exclusive

In a particular territory, the license may be exclusive, sole or non-exclusive.

A non-exclusive license, where the licensee is one of several licensees with whom the licensor has entered into agreements for the use and exploitation of the technology, is the preferred option of most licensors. By spreading the risks and rewards to several licensees, the licensor does not depend on the success of one licensee. He/She can maintain a better control over the technology and, by virtue of the fact that several licensees are using and exploiting the technology in several markets and perhaps in a variety of products, give the technology a chance to further evolve and develop. However, in the case of early stage technologies which call for a significant amount of additional investment from the licensee, most potential licensees would seek exclusivity, at least in certain territories.

An exclusive license usually describes the situation where the rights granted to the licensee even exclude the rights of the licensor in the territory. A sole license usually describes the situation where the licensor as well as the licensee can use the technology in the territory, but no one else can. This distinction can be blurred in practice and the term exclusive is sometimes used to mean what is really a sole license. In any event, under both types of license, the licensor is not permitted to grant other licenses (at least in the territory in which the license is expressed to be exclusive or sole). In that territory, the licensor is reliant on one licensee. Accordingly, it is important to ensure that the agreement contains appropriate incentives and/or penalties to protect the licensor in the event of non-performance by the licensee. These might include the payment of an annual minimum royalty. If the licensee does not make the required payment, then the penalties might be termination of the license or conversion of the exclusive license to a non-exclusive license.

2) 最惠被许可人

如果使用许可属于非独占性，那么被许可人可能希望在协议中包含一条最惠被许可人条款。该条款实际上保证，当许可人授予其他被许可人更加优惠的条件时，根据此条款，现被许可人有资格享受与授予其他被许可人相同的优惠条件。

3) 地域

使用许可范围也指地理地域，例如可能被授予世界范围内的使用许可权利，或者是限于特定的国家，甚至一些国家的特定部分(例如某个国家的某个州或地区)。

4) 分使用许可

被许可人，尤其是独占使用许可的被许可人，可能希望享有在其被许可的地域内授予分使用许可的权利。如果这样，应就此进行专门谈判，并在协议中予以说明。同时还应说明，授予任何分使用许可是否需要许可人预先书面批准，选择分被许可人和可能授予分被使用许可所依据的条件。例如，分使用许可协议的条款应在多大程度上与主许可协议的条款相符合。还有一项补充条款，应说明分使用许可在主要的使用许可结束时或由于任何原因失效时，该分使用许可是否终止。

5) 技术改进

当谈及技术"改进"，即我们所熟知的版本、增强和新模式时，最重要的是界定什么是与此项许可有关的改进，以及什么是新技术或新知识产权。

---

2) Most-Favored Licensee

Where the license is non-exclusive, the licensee may wish to include in the agreement a most-favored licensee clause which in effect ensures that in the event that the licensor grants another licensee terms that are more favorable, then, by virtue of this clause, the present licensee would be entitled to terms as favorable as had been granted to the other licensee.

3) Territory

The extent of the license also refers to the geographic territory. For example, worldwide rights could be granted, or the rights could be for specific countries or even specific parts of countries (such as a state or region of a country).

4) Sub-license

The licensee, particularly if the licensee has an exclusive license, may wish to have the right to grant sub-licenses in its territory. If so, this needs to be specifically negotiated and stated in the agreement. It should also be stated if the licensor's prior written approval is required for the granting of any sub-licenses, the choice of sub-licensee and the conditions upon which such sub-licenses may be granted; for example, the extent to which the terms of the sub-license should accord with those of the head license agreement. An additional clause should state whether or not the sub-license comes to an end when the head license is terminated or expires for any reason.

5) Technology Improvements

When dealing with improvements, also known as versions, enhancements, and new models, it is important to define what is an improvement covered by the license, and what is a new technology or new intellectual property.

如果许可人已经成功地进行了商业生产，那么对被许可技术的改进可能不是一个重要问题。不过，如果许可人和／或被许可人正在从事研发活动，或者被许可的技术正处于早期开发阶段，那么在使用许可协议期间，工艺或产品就有可能得到改进。

如果该项技术改进有可能获得专利或者可能受到保护，那么此问题就变得尤为重要。在这种情况下，许可人将希望拥有对被许可人所开发的任何这类技术的使用权，即使他并不需要。该项权利也可能延伸到许可人，他能够将该改进技术授予在其他地域的分使用许可协议的被许可人。该项权利也可能涉及许可人将该改进技术用于其他产品应用方面。此外，还应考虑到被许可人是否可以获得许可人后来所进行的技术改进。

对上述事宜可能做出的一种安排是，双方都应让对方了解，并有权免费使用被许可技术的所有改进，同时许可人有权将被许可人的改进向本地域之外的其他被许可人授予分使用许可，或者对该项改进按预先的规定支付附加许可使用费。

Improvements to the licensed technology are not likely to be a major issue where the licensor is in successful commercial production. Where, however, the licensor and/or the licensee is involved in ongoing research and development, or the licensed technology is at an early stage of development, it is likely that improvements will be made to the process or product during the term of the license agreement.

This is a particularly important issue if the improvements are likely to be patentable or otherwise protectable. In this event, the licensor will want any such technology developed by the licensee, even if he/she does not need it. This right might extend to the licensor being able to grant a sub-license to other licensees in other territories and may involve the licensor using the improvements for other product applications. In addition, consideration will need to be given as to whether the licensee will have access to any subsequent improvements made by the licensor.

A possible arrangement reflecting some of the above is that each party shall keep the other informed of, and shall have the right to use on a royalty-free basis, all improvements made to the licensed technology, and the licensor shall have the right to sub-license the licensee's improvements to its other licensees outside the territory, or the improvements may be subject to an additional royalty to be fixed in advance.

6) 技术协助

根据转让技术的种类，常见的一种协议是向被许可人提供文献、数据和专家等形式的技术协助。

7) 期限

使用许可协议的期限或有效时间可能受被许可权利的主题事项影响。因此，专利使用许可会在被许可的专利有效期满时结束。技术秘密或者商标使用许可协议的有效期可以为 5 年，如果双方中的任何一方没有提前发出书面终止通知，则可自动延长 5 年。技术使用许可的期限，包括专利权、版权、商标权和工业品外观设计计权，取决于市场及双方对收入的估计。

8) 付款

为获取和使用技术而向许可人支付的款项，通常可分为一次性总付和使用费支付。许多协议同时包括上述两种付款方式。

---

6) Technical Assistance

Depending on the kind of technology being transferred, there is often an agreement to provide the licensee with technical assistance in the form of documentation, data and expertise.

7) Term

The term or duration of the license agreement can be influenced by the subject matter of the rights being licensed. Thus, a patent license could end on the expiration of the last to expire of the licensed patents. A know-how or trademark agreement might be for five years, extended automatically for the same period, unless one of the parties gave prior written notice of termination. The term of a technology license including rights to patents, copyright, trademarks, and industrial designs will depend on the market and revenue estimations of the parties.

8) Payment

Payments to the licensor for the acquisition and use of technology are usually classified as lump sums and royalties, and many agreements contain both types of payment.

一次性总付是在发生特定情况时支付。有可能仅在签订协议时一次性总付。如果没有后续的支付，那么就视为全额清付的使用许可。另一方面，也可能在发生特定事件时进行系列性的总付。这样的重大事件可以时间为基础，例如签订协议后一周年或两周年；也可能以行为业绩为基础，例如披露保密信息时或者商业化生产启动时；也可能是行使权利或进行选择之时，例如被许可人将使用许可延伸至其他地理区域或使用领域之时。以时间为基础的付款，具体付款金额双方都知晓并同意。当特定期限过去后，在支付方面不存在风险，被许可人或许可人无须采取进一步行动。而以行为业绩为基础的付款将取决于一定事件的发生情况，例如首次商业销售。如果所提及的事件不发生，被许可人就不会付款，所以明确界定事件是很重要的。

使用费是被许可人向许可人支付的定期付款，它反映该项技术已由被许可人使用。由于使用费将使用情况与货币金额联系在一起，可以有效地体现技术对被许可人的价值。因此，使用费是使用许可协议中最常见的付款方式。使用费包括两个主要成分：使用费基准及使用费率。使用费基准可以是制造成本或是销售被许可产品所创造的利润，也可以是被许可人的毛收入或净销售收入。最常见的许可使用费基准是被许可人的销售。

Lump sums are payable on the happening of a particular event. There may be one sum only, payable on signing the agreement. If there were no further payments, this would be considered a fully-paid-up license. On the other hand, there could be a series of lump sums, payable on the occurrence of specific events, which might be time-based, such as on the first or second anniversary of the signing of the agreement. Events can also be performance-based, such as on the disclosure of confidential information or on the commencement of commercial production. An event could also be the exercise of a right or option such as the licensee extending the license to additional geographical territories or fields of use. Time-based payments are certain in that the amounts are known and agreed, and they are risk-free in that they will be paid when the specified period has elapsed. No further action is required by the licensee or the licensor. Performance-based payments, on the other hand, depend on the occurrence of certain events, such as the first commercial sale. As the payments are not made if the event in question does not occur, it is important to clearly define events.

Royalties are regular payments to the licensor, which reflect the use of the technology by the licensee. As they link use with a monetary amount, they can be a good reflection of the value of the technology to the licensee and, accordingly, royalties are the most usual type of payment in license agreements. Royalties have two key components: the royalty base and the royalty rate. The royalty base could be the cost of manufacturing or the profit from selling the licensed products. Alternatively, the royalty base could be either the gross or the net sales receipts of the licensee. However, the most common royalty base is the licensee's sales.

使用费率的确定，对于双方形成一个好的商业计划是很重要的。因此，使用费率方面的谈判是协议成功的基础。如果费率太高，对被许可人来说，可能意味着该使用许可无利可赚；如果费率太低，可能意味着许可人不能收到足够的回报，这会使许可人减少继续研发的支出。任何一种情况都可能影响双方之间的关系以及协议的成功。

9）侵权

对于已经获得专利或其他知识产权保护的所有或部分技术，防范侵权行为的发生是十分重要的。发生侵权的情况有两种。第一种是第三方使用受保护的技术但没有获得使用许可。这样，被许可人就面临竞争，而且由于侵权的竞争者未付使用费还可能遭受财务上的损失。被许可人，特别是非独占被许可人，会期望许可人采取措施处理侵权行为。第二种侵权情况是第三方声称被许可人使用的一项技术是第三方获得法律保护的。在此情况下，被许可人可能面临不能继续使用已获许可的全部或部分技术的局面。被许可人将再次期望许可人提供支持和帮助。然而，许可人可能会提出争议，被许可人已掌握该技术，而且在任何情况下，在协议签字和商业生产前，被许可人应该已经进行了相关检索，这些检索往往揭示了这些先前已有权利的存在。即使如此，使用许可协议也可以规定，各方应确定许可人是否可能提供一项非侵权技术。

Royalty rate is important that the rate results in a good business proposition for both parties, and so negotiation of the royalty rate is fundamental to the success of the agreement. Too high a rate can mean the license is unprofitable for the licensee. Too low a rate can mean the licensor does not receive an adequate return, which might lead to reduced expenditure on continuing research and development. Either might adversely affect the relationship between the parties and the success of the agreement.

9) Infringement

To all or part of the technology that has the benefit of patent or other intellectual property protection, it is important to prevent any infringement. There are two situations where infringement could occur. The first is where a third party is using the protected technology but does not have a license. Here the licensee is facing competition and is likely to be at a financial disadvantage as the infringing competitor is not paying royalties. The licensee, particularly if he/she is a non-exclusive licensee, will expect the licensor to take steps to deal with the infringement. The second infringement situation is where a third party claims that the licensee is using technology in respect of which the third party has obtained protection. In this situation, the licensee may be faced with the prospect of not being able to continue to use all or some part of the licensed technology. Again the licensee will look to the licensor to provide support and assistance. However, the licensor might argue that it is the licensee who has controlled over the application of the technology and that, in any event, before signing the agreement and commencing production, the licensee should have carried out the relevant searches, which would usually have revealed the presence of these pre-existing rights. Even so, the license agreement might stipulate that parties should ascertain whether possible to provide a non-infringing technique.

10) 产品责任

被许可人通常对所有制造中的缺陷或缺乏质量控制负有责任。许可人可能向被许可人供应组件，在这种情况下，许可人通常对这些组件的任何缺陷负有责任。对于第三方向另一方声称的损失和损害，责任方也应承担。因而，使用许可协议通常要求获得产品责任的保证，保证按照双方同意的价格向许可人和被许可人赔偿。

3. 一般条款

使用许可协议的最后一个主要部分包括其他未涉及的问题：陈述与担保，特殊的许可人和被许可人义务，以及放弃条款、不可抗力、争端解决等。

1) 陈述与担保

陈述与担保是与许可协议的事项或情况有关的声明或保证。一个重要的区别是，陈述往往不是协议条款，而担保是协议条款，违背该条款可能导致受损方终止协议并因损失而起诉索赔。对于陈述或担保的内容并没有限制，通常包括以下内容：①许可人拥有技术，并有权利和权威授予使用许可；②许可使用的材料(例如，文本、软件和/或文件)是原始的而不是拷贝的；③尽许可人所知并确信，许可使用的专利是有效的而且未被第三方侵权。

---

10) Product Liability

The licensee would usually be responsible for any manufacturing defects or for inadequate quality control. The licensor may supply components to the licensee, and, in this event, the licensor would usually be responsible for any defects in those components. The party accepting responsibility would also provide the other party with an indemnity against any claims by a third party for loss or damage. Thus, it is usual for the license agreement to require that product liability insurance indemnifying the licensor and licensee for an agreed value is obtained and maintained.

3. General Conditions

The last main section of a license agreement is intended to embrace the issues that have not been referred to in the above. Thus, they include representations and warranties, specific obligations of both licensor and licensee, as well as issues of waiver, force majeure and dispute settlement.

1) Representations and Warranties

Representations and warranties are statements or assurances about a matter or position relevant to the license agreement. One important distinction is that a representation is not usually a term of the agreement, whereas a warranty is a contractual term, the breach of which could entitle the injured party to terminate the agreement and sue for damages. While there are no restrictions on what might be the subject of a representation or warranty, typical examples include: (a)the licensor owns the technology and has the right and authority to grant the license;(b)that the licensed material (e.g. text, software, and/or documentation) is original and has not been copied;(c)to the best of the licensor's knowledge and belief, the licensed patents are valid and are not being infringed by any third party.

2) 许可人和被许可人的义务

在专利和技术秘密协议中，许可人被要求采取所有必要行动转让技术并帮助被许可人开始商业生产。同样地，被许可人最好在本土成功生产并营销被许可产品。实际上，这是可能引起许多争端的领域。因此，各方明确确定为实现这些目标所需进行的全部行动十分必要，而且这些行动应得到同意并在使用许可协议中予以记录。有时，如果使用许可是独占性的，被许可人有全面义务付出所有合理的努力，或尽最大的努力，以实现使用许可协议和商业成功的目标。

3) 放弃条款

在使用许可协议中，放弃条款意味着一方并不因为没有实施这些权利而失掉其权利。因此，如果被许可人未付许可费，不论之前许可人是否违约，许可人仍旧有权发出另一项终止通知。

4) 不可抗力

使用许可协议中的不可抗力条款用于处理超出一方控制的干预情况，它使该方无法履行其义务。战争、罢工和火灾被视为此类事件。而该条款的好处在于，履行义务的时间可以延迟，直至不可抗力的情况停止或被消除。

---

2) Obligations of Licensor and Licensee

The licensor is expected to take, for example, in a patent and know-how agreement, all necessary actions to transfer the technology and assist the licensee to commence commercial production. Similarly, the licensee is expected to successfully manufacture and market the licensed product in the territory. In practice, this is an area that could give rise to a lot of disputes. It is, therefore, important that the parties clearly identify all actions that are necessary to achieve these objectives, and they should be agreed and recorded in the license agreement. Sometimes, there is an overall obligation on the licensee to use all reasonable efforts, or best efforts if the license is exclusive, to achieve the objectives of the license agreement and commercial success.

3) Waiver Clause

A waiver clause in a license agreement means that a party does not lose its rights because it does not enforce those rights. Thus, if a licensor was entitled to give notice of termination due to nonpayment of royalties, but overlooked or ignored the breach, the licensor could still give notice in respect of another breach of that obligation.

4) Force Majeure

A force majeure clause in a license agreement addresses intervening circumstances beyond the control of a party, which prevents that party from carrying out its obligations. War, strikes and fire are the types of occurrences envisaged, and the benefit of the clause is that the time to carry out an obligation may be delayed until the force majeure circumstance ceases or is removed.

5) 争端解决

进行使用许可协议谈判时，各方必须意识到可能会产生争端，并应提供解决的方法。建立灵活的改正机制就是解决争端的最佳选择。如果不行，则必须确立争端解决机制。当起草争端解决条款时，各方可以提出几种选择。传统上，各方大都同意通过向专门的国内法院提起诉讼解决争端。然而，各方越来越多地选择可替代性争端解决程序(ADR)，例如，仲裁、调解或调解后仲裁。

6) 到期与终止

使用许可协议以两种方式结束。第一种是由于发生了双方约定的情况，协议到期。例如，期限是十年或直到最后一个许可专利失效或到期。当这种情况发生时，协议自动结束。第二种方式是在协议结束前由一方终止该协议。通常要详细陈述可能引发一方有权终止协议的情况，这些情况与没有依某种方式操作和违背协议的条件有关。有的是由于到期、破产或无力偿还而没有付款。当这些情况中的某一种发生时，协议便自动终止，如果另一方在规定时间内没有纠正其行为，最好发出协议终止通知。

5) Dispute Settlement

When negotiating the license agreement, parties should be aware that disputes might arise and provide means for resolving them. Built-in flexibility for amendments should provide means for resolution at first resort. Failing which, mechanisms for dispute resolution must be provided for. When drafting dispute resolution clauses, parties can draw from several options. Traditionally, parties have often agreed to resolve disputes through litigation in a specified domestic court. Increasingly, however, parties opt for alternative dispute resolution (ADR) procedures, such as arbitration or mediation or mediation followed by arbitration.

6) Expiration and Termination

License agreements come to an end in two ways. The first is where the term or period of the agreement expires because of the occurrence of an agreed event. For example, the term is ten years or until the last of the licensed patent lapses or expires. When these events happen, the agreement automatically expires. The second way is that the agreement is terminated by one party before the agreement has expired. The events that can give rise to a party having the right to terminate the agreement are usually set out in detail and relate to a failure to perform in some way and breach of a condition of the agreement. Some examples are failure to make payments when due, bankruptcy or insolvency. While the agreement could terminate automatically when one of these events happens, it is preferable that notice is given, with the agreement terminating if the default is not rectified by the other party within a specified time.

第三节　技术转让中的政府管制

　　当考虑与外国合作伙伴达成使用许可协议时，核实存在哪些可能对其有影响的各种政府法规是很重要的。例如，多数国家至少要求向该国的相关部门注册使用许可协议，但从事此类活动的协议也可能需要经历一个审批过程。在许可人所在国，出于安全或其他原因，对一些技术的交易可能是有限制或有条件的。

　　例如，中国对技术进出口实行统一的管理制度，依法维护公平、自由的技术进出口秩序。根据《中华人民共和国技术进出口管理条例》，技术进出口应当符合国家的产业政策、科技政策和社会发展政策，有利于促进我国科技进步和对外经济技术合作的发展，有利于维护我国经济技术权益。

4.3　Government Regulations in Technology Transfer

　　When considering entering into a license agreement with a foreign partner, it is important to verify the existence of various government regulations that may affect it. For example, most countries would at least require the registration of a licensing agreement with the relevant authorities in that country but there may, in addition, be an approval process that must be followed for engaging in that kind of activity in that country. In the licensor's own country there may be regulations that restrict or make conditional the dealing with certain technologies for security or other reasons.

　　For example, China adopts a uniform system for the administration of technology import and export, and maintains the order for fair and free technology import and export according to law. According to *Regulations on Technology Import and Export Administration of the People's Republic of China*, import and export of technology shall be conducted in compliance with the national policy of industry, the policy of science and technology, and the policy for social development, and shall be conducive to promoting the scientific and technologic progress in China, enhancing the development of foreign economic and technical cooperation, and safeguarding China's economic and technical rights and interests.

　　技术引进方面，国家鼓励先进、适用的技术引进。国务院外经贸主管部门会同国务院有关部门，制定、调整并公布禁止或者限制引进的技术目录。属于禁止引进的技术，不得进口；属于限制引进的技术，实行许可证管理；未经许可，不得引进。引进属于限制引进的技术，应当向国务院外经贸主管部门提出技术引进申请并附有关文件。技术引进项目需经有关部门批准的，还应当提交有关部门的批准文件。技术引进申请经批准的，由国务院外经贸主管部门发给技术引进许可意向书。进口经营者取得技术引进许可意向书后，可以对外签订技术引进合同。进口经营者签订技术引进合同后，应当向国务院外经贸主管部门提交技术引进合同副本及有关文件，申请技术引进许可证。对属于自由引进的技术，实行合同登记管理。引进属于自由进口的技术，合同自依法成立时生效，不以登记为合同生效的条件。引进属于自由引进的技术，应当向国务院外经贸主管部门办理登记。国务院外经贸主管部门应当自收到登记文件之日起 3 个工作日内，对技术引进合同进行登记，颁发技术引进合同登记证。申请人凭技术引进许可证或者技术引进合同登记证，办理外汇、银行、税务、海关等相关手续。

In technology import, the State encourages import of advanced and appropriate technology. The competent foreign trade department under the State Council shall, in conjunction with other relevant departments under the State Council, formulate, regulate and publish catalogues of technologies which prohibited or restricted from import. Technologies prohibited from import shall not be imported. Technologies restricted from import shall be subject to the license administration; any technology for which no license is granted shall not be imported. In respect of import of a technology restricted from import, an application for technology import, together with relevant documents, shall be filed with the competent foreign trade department under the State Council. Where a project of technology import needs to be approved by the relevant department, the documents of approval thereby shall also be submitted. Where an application for technology import is approved, the competent foreign trade department under the State Council shall issue a letter of intent for licensing the technology import. After being granted the letter of intent for licensing the technology import, an import operator may sign a contract for technology import with its overseas counterpart. After signing a contract for technology import, an import operator shall submit to the competent foreign trade department under the State Council a copy of the contract for technology import and relevant documents to apply for the technology import license. Freely importable technologies shall be subject to the contract registration administration. A contract for importing a freely importable technology takes effect from the time when the contract is established according to law, without taking the registration thereof as a condition for the contract to be effective. When a freely importable technology is to be imported, registration shall be made with the competent foreign trade department under the State Council. The competent foreign trade department under the State Council shall register the technology import contract and issue the certificate of registration of the technology import contract within three working days from the date of receipt of the documents. Applicants shall use the technology import license or certificate of registration of technology import contract to go through the foreign exchange, banking, taxation and customs formalities.

　　技术引进合同的让与人应当保证自己是所提供技术的合法拥有者或者有权转让、许可者。技术引进合同的受让人按照合同约定使用让与人提供的技术，被第三方指控侵权的，受让人应当立即通知让与人。让与人接到通知后，应当协助受让人排除妨碍。技术引进合同的受让人按照合同约定使用让与人提供的技术，侵害他人合法权益的，由让与人承担责任。技术引进合同的让与人应当保证所提供的技术完整、无误、有效，能够达到约定的技术目标。技术引进合同的受让人、让与人应当在合同约定的保密范围和保密期限内，对让与人提供的技术中尚未公开的秘密部分承担保密义务。在保密期限内，承担保密义务的一方在保密技术非因自己的原因被公开后，其承担的保密义务即予终止。在技术引进合同有效期内，改进技术的成果属于改进方。技术引进合同期满后，技术让与人和受让人可以依照公平合理的原则，就技术的继续使用进行协商。

　　技术引进合同中，不得含有下列限制性条款。

　　(1) 要求受让人接受并非技术引进必不可少的附带条件，包括购买非必需的技术、原材料、产品、设备或者服务。

The technology supplying party to a technology import contract shall ensure that he/she or it is the legitimate owner of the technology supplied or one who has the right to assign or license the technology. Where the receiving party to a technology import contract is accused of infringement by a third party for using the technology supplied by the supplying party under the contract, the former shall immediately notify the latter. The latter, upon receipt of the notification, shall assist the former in removing the impediment. Where the receiving party to a technology import contract infringes another person's lawful rights and interests by using the technology supplied by the supplying party, the supplying party shall bear the liability therefore. The supplying party to a technology import contract shall ensure the technology it supplies is complete, accurate, effective and capable of achieving the agreed technical object. The receiving and supplying parties to a technology import contract shall be under the obligation to keep confidential the undisclosed part of the technology the supplying party has supplied within the scope of confidentiality and time limit thereof as agreed in the contract. Within the time of confidentiality, the obligation of one party to confidentiality shall terminate immediately after the confidential technology is disclosed for reasons not of his/her or its own. Within the term of validity of a contract for technology import, an achievement made in improving the technology concerned belongs to the party making the improvement. After a technology import contract expires, the technology supplying and receiving parties thereto may negotiate on the continued use of the technology according to the principle of justice and equity.

A technology import contract shall not contain any of the following restrictive clauses.

(1) Requiring the receiving party to accept any additional condition unnecessary for the technology import, including buying any unnecessary technology, raw material, product, equipment or service.

（2）要求受让人为专利权有效期限届满或者专利权被宣布无效的技术支付使用费或者承担相关义务。

（3）限制受让人改进让与人提供的技术或者限制受让人使用所改进的技术。

（4）限制受让人从其他来源获得与让与人提供的技术类似的技术或者与其竞争的技术。

（5）不合理地限制受让人购买原材料、零部件、产品或者设备的渠道或者来源。

（6）不合理地限制受让人产品的生产数量、品种或者销售价格。

（7）不合理地限制受让人利用引进技术生产的产品的出口渠道。

---

(2) Requiring the receiving party to pay exploitation fee for a technology when the term of validity of the patent right in which has expired or the patent right of which has been invalidated, or to undertake other relevant obligations.

(3) Restricting the receiving party from improving the technology supplied by the supplying party, or restricting the receiving party from using the improved technology.

(4) Restricting the receiving party from obtaining technology similar to that supplied by the supplying party from other sources or from obtaining a competing technology.

(5) Unduly restricting the receiving party from purchasing raw material, parts and components, products or equipment from other channels or sources.

(6) Unduly restricting the quantity, variety, or sales price of the products the receiving party produces.

(7) Unduly restricting the receiving party from utilizing the channel for exporting products manufactured using the imported technology.

国家鼓励成熟的产业化技术出口。国务院外经贸主管部门会同国务院有关部门，制定、调整并公布禁止或者限制出口的技术目录。属于禁止出口的技术，不得出口；属于限制出口的技术，实行许可证管理；未经许可，不得出口。出口属于限制出口的技术，应当向国务院外经贸主管部门提出申请。国务院外经贸主管部门收到技术出口申请后，应当会同国务院科技管理部门对申请出口的技术进行审查，并自收到申请之日起 30 个工作日内作出批准或者不批准的决定。限制出口的技术需经有关部门进行保密审查的，按照国家有关规定执行。

技术出口申请经批准的，由国务院外经贸主管部门发给技术出口许可意向书。申请人取得技术出口许可意向书后，方可对外进行实质性谈判，签订技术出口合同。申请人签订技术出口合同后，应当向国务院外经贸主管部门提交相关文件，申请技术出口许可证。国务院外经贸主管部门对技术出口合同的真实性进行审查，并自收到相关文件之日起 15 个工作日内，对技术出口作出许可或者不许可的决定。技术出口经许可的，由国务院外经贸主管部门颁发技术出口许可证。

The State encourages the export of well-developed industrialized technology. The competent foreign trade department under the State Council shall, in conjunction with other relevant departments under the State Council, formulate, regulate and publish catalogues of technologies which are prohibited or restricted from export. Technology prohibited from export shall not be exported, technology restricted from export shall be subject to license administration; and shall not be exported without a license. To export any technology restricted from export, an application shall be filed with the competent foreign trade department under the State Council. The competent foreign trade department under the State Council shall, after receipt of a technology export application, examine the technology in respect of which application for export is filed in conjunction with the science and technology administrative department under the State Council, and decide on approval or disapproval within thirty working days from the date of receipt of the application. Where a technology restricted from export requires confidential examination by the relevant department, the relevant regulations of the State shall be complied with.

Where an application for technology export is approved, the competent foreign trade department under the State Council shall issue a letter of intent for licensing the technology export. After obtaining the letter of intent for licensing the technology export, the applicant may begin substantive negotiation, and conclude a contract for the technology export. After concluding a technology export contract, the applicant shall submit to the competent foreign trade department under the State Council the documents in applying for a license for the exporting technology. The competent foreign trade department under the State Council examines the authenticity of the technology export contract, and decides, within fifteen working days from the date of receipt of the documents, on approval or disapproval of the technology export. Where a technology is licensed for export, the competent foreign trade department under the State Council issues the technology export license.

对属于自由出口的技术，实行合同登记管理。出口属于自由出口的技术，合同自依法成立时生效，不以登记为合同生效的条件。出口属于自由出口的技术，应当向国务院外经贸主管部门办理登记。国务院外经贸主管部门应当自收到相关文件之日起 3 个工作日内，对技术出口合同进行登记，颁发技术出口合同登记证。申请人凭技术出口许可证或者技术出口合同登记证办理外汇、银行、税务、海关等相关手续。

第四节　与技术转让有关的主要国际法规范

技术转让可能影响到专有知识在国家间的管理和流动，从而涉及国际法规范。80 多个国际文件和许多次区域和双边协定包含有关技术转移的内容。它们旨在促进技术准入，有时是促进发展中国家尤其是最不发达国家的技术能力建设。本节将阐述两个主要的国际法文件：《与贸易有关的知识产权协定》和《联合国国际技术转让行动守则(草案)》。

Freely exportable technology shall be subject to the contract registration administration. A contract for exporting a freely exportable technology takes effect from the time when the contract is established according to law, without taking the registration thereof as a condition for the contract to be effective. When a freely exportable technology is to be exported, registration shall be made with the competent foreign trade department under the State Council. The competent foreign trade department under the State Council shall, within three working days from the date of receipt of the documents, register the technology export contract, and issue the certificate of the registration of technology export. Applicants shall use the technology export license or certificate of registration of the technology export contract to go through the foreign exchange, banking, taxation and customs formalities.

4.4　Main Sources of International Law Relating to Technology Transfer

Technology transfer may impact on the management and flow of proprietary knowledge between countries, thereby involving international laws. Over 80 international instruments and numerous sub-regional and bilateral agreements contain measures related to transfer of technology. They aim to promote access to technologies and, in some cases, technology capacity building in developing countries, especially in the least-developed countries. This section looks at the two main international documents: *Agreement on Trade-related Aspects of Intellectual Property Rights (TRIPS)* and *Draft International Code of Conduct on the Transfer of Technology (TOT-Code)*.

一、《与贸易有关的知识产权协定》

乌拉圭回合谈判产生了世界贸易组织协定。该回合谈判于 1994 年结束。在该回合谈判中，《与贸易有关的知识产权协定》被纳入国际贸易法律体系。

一般来说，技术转让被确立为《与贸易有关的知识产权协定》的主要目标和原则，主要体现在协议第 7、8 条。第 7 条规定，知识产权的保护和实施应有助于促进技术革新及技术转让和传播，有助于维护技术知识的创造者和使用者的相互利益，并有助于社会和经济福利及权利与义务的平衡。第 8 条规定，在制定或修改其法律和法规时，各成员可采用对保护公共健康和营养，促进对其社会经济和技术发展至关重要部门的公共利益所必需的措施，只要此类措施与协定的规定相一致。只要与协定的规定相一致，可以采取适当措施以防止知识产权权利持有人滥用知识产权或采取不合理地限制贸易或对国际技术转让造成不利影响的做法。

4.4.1 *TRIPS*

The Uruguay Round of negotiation brought about the WTO Agreement. This Round was end in 1994. In the Uruguay Round, *the TRIPS Agreement* was incorporated into legal system of international trade.

Generally, technology transfer is framed as one of the primary aims of *the TRIPS Agreement*, embodied in *TRIPS* Articles 7 and 8. Article 7 states: "The protection and enforcement of intellectual property rights should contribute to the promotion of technological innovation and to the transfer and dissemination of technology, to the mutual advantage of producers and users of technological knowledge and in a manner conducive to social and economic welfare, and to a balance of rights and obligations." Article 8 states: "Members may, in formulating or amending their laws and regulations, adopt measures necessary to protect public health and nutrition, and to promote the public interest in sectors of vital importance to their socio-economic and technological development, provided that such measures are consistent with the provisions of the Agreement. Appropriate measures, provided that they are consistent with the provisions of the Agreement, may be needed to prevent the abuse of intellectual property rights by right holders or the resort to practices which unreasonably restrain trade or adversely affect the international transfer of technology."

在保护专利技术方面，第 30 条规定，各成员可对专利授予的专有权规定有限的例外，只要此类例外不会对专利的正常利用发生不合理的抵触，也不会不合理地损害专利所有权人的合法权益，同时兼顾了第三方的合法权益。第 31 条涉及未经权利持有人授权的其他使用。根据该条规定，如一成员的法律允许未经权利持有人授权即可对一专利作其他使用，包括政府或经政府授权的第三方使用，则应遵守下列规定。

(1) 授权此种使用应一事一议。

(2) 只有在拟使用者在此种使用之前已经按合理商业条款和条件努力从权利持有人处获得授权，但此类努力在合理时间内未获得成功，方可允许此类使用。在全国处于紧急状态或在其他极端紧急的情况下，或在公共非商业性使用的情况下，成员不受此要求约束。尽管如此，在全国处于紧急状态或在其他极端紧急的情况下，应尽快通知权利持有人。在公共非商业性使用的情况下，如政府或合同方未作专利检索即知道或有显而易见的理由知道一有效专利正在或将要被政府使用或为政府而使用，则应迅速告知权利持有人。

In the protection of patented technology, Article 30 of *the TRIPS Agreement* states: "Members may provide limited exceptions to the exclusive rights conferred by a patent, provided that such exceptions do not unreasonably conflict with a normal exploitation of the patent and do not unreasonably prejudice the legitimate interests of the patent owner, taking account of the legitimate interests of third parties". Meanwhile, Article 31 states: "Other use without authorization of the right holder". Where the law of a Member allows for other use of the subject matter of a patent without the authorization of the right holder, including use by the government or third parties authorized by the government, the following provisions shall be respected.

(1) Authorization of such use shall be considered on its individual merits.

(2) Such use may only be permitted if, prior to such use, the proposed user has made efforts to obtain authorization from the right holder on reasonable commercial terms and conditions and that such efforts have not been successful within a reasonable period of time. This requirement may be waived by a Member in the case of a national emergency or other circumstance of extreme urgency or in cases of public noncommercial use. In situations of national emergency or other circumstances of extreme urgency, the right holder shall, nevertheless, be notified as soon as reasonably practicable. In the case of public non-commercial use, where the government or contractor, without making a patent search, knows or has demonstrable grounds to know that a valid patent is or will be used by or for the government, the right holder shall be informed promptly.

(3) 此类使用的范围和期限应仅限于被授权的目的，如果是半导体技术，则仅能限于公共非商业性使用，或用于救济经司法或行政程序确定为限制竞争行为。

(4) 此种使用应是非专有的。

(5) 此种使用应是不可转让的，除非与享有此种使用的那部分企业或商誉一同转让。

(6) 任何此种使用的授权应主要为供应授权此种使用的成员的国内市场。

(7) 在充分保护被授权人合法权益的前提下，如导致此类使用的情况已不复存在且不可能再次出现，则有关此类使用的授权应终止。在收到有根据的请求的情况下，主管机关有权审议这些情况是否继续存在。

(8) 在每一种情况下应向权利持有人支付适当报酬，同时考虑授权的经济价值。

(9) 与此种使用有关的任何决定的法律效力应经过司法审查或经过该成员中上一级主管机关的独立审查。

---

(3) The scope and duration of such use shall be limited to the purpose for which it was authorized, and in the case of semi-conductor technology shall only be for public noncommercial use or to remedy a practice determined after judicial or administrative process to be restrict-competitive.

(4) Such use shall be non-exclusive.

(5) Such use shall be non-assignable, except with that part of the enterprise or goodwill which enjoys such use.

(6) Any such use shall be authorized predominantly for the supply of the domestic market of the Member authorizing such use.

(7) Authorization for such use shall be liable, subject to adequate protection of the legitimate interests of the persons so authorized, to be terminated if and when the circumstances which led to it cease to exist and are unlikely to recur. The competent authority shall have the authority to review, upon motivated request, the continued existence of these circumstances.

(8) The right holder shall be paid adequate remuneration in the circumstances of each case, taking into account the economic value of the authorization.

(9) The legal validity of any decision relating to the authorization of such use shall be subject to judicial review or other independent review by a distinct higher authority in that Member.

(10) 任何与就此种使用提供的报酬有关的决定应经过司法审查或该成员中上一级主管机关的独立审查。

(11) 如允许此类使用以救济经司法或行政程序确定为限制竞争行为，则各成员无义务适用(2)项和(6)项所列条件。在确定此类情况下的报酬数额时，可考虑纠正限制竞争行为的需要。如导致授权的条件可能再次出现，则主管机关有权拒绝终止授权。

(12) 如授权此项使用以允许利用一专利("第二专利")，而该专利在不侵害另一专利("第一专利")的情况下不能被利用，则应适用下列附加条件。

（ⅰ）与第一专利中的发明要求相比，第二专利中的发明要求应包含重要的、具有巨大经济意义的技术进步。

（ⅱ）第一专利的所有权人有权以合理的条件通过交叉许可使用第二专利具有的发明。

（ⅲ）就第一专利授权的使用不得转让，除非与第二专利一同转让。

---

(10) Any decision relating to the remuneration provided in respect of such use shall be subject to judicial review or other independent review by a distinct higher authority in that Member.

(11) Members are not obliged to apply the conditions set forth in subparagraphs (2) and (6) where such use is permitted to remedy a practice determined after judicial or administrative process to be restrict-competitive. The need to correct restrict-competitive practices may be taken into account in determining the amount of remuneration in such cases. Competent authorities shall have the authority to refuse termination of authorization if and when the conditions which led to such authorization are likely to recur.

(12) Where such use is authorized to permit the exploitation of a patent ("the second patent") which cannot be exploited without infringing another patent ("the first patent"), the following additional conditions shall apply.

(i) The invention claimed in the second patent shall involve an important technical advance of considerable economic significance in relation to the invention claimed in the first patent.

(ii) The owner of the first patent shall be entitled to a cross-licence on reasonable terms to use the invention claimed in the second patent.

(iii) The use authorized in respect of the first patent shall be non-assignable except with the assignment of the second patent.

第 40 条规定了对许可协议中限制竞争行为的控制。各成员同意，一些限制竞争的有关知识产权的许可活动或条件可能对贸易产生不利影响，并可能妨碍技术的转让和传播。本协定的任何规定，均不得阻止各成员在其立法中明确规定，即在特定情况下可构成对知识产权的滥用并对相关市场中的竞争产生不利影响的许可活动或条件。如以上所规定的，在与本协定其他规定一致的条件下，一成员可按照该成员的有关法律法规，采取适当的措施以防止或控制此类活动，包括诸如排他性返授条件、阻止对许可效力提出质疑的条件和强制性一揽子许可等。应对方的请求，每一成员应与任一其他成员进行磋商，只要该其他成员有理由认为被请求进行磋商的成员的国民或居民的知识产权所有权人正在采取的做法违反请求进行磋商成员的相关法律法规，并希望在不妨害根据法律采取任何行动及不损害两成员中任一成员作出最终决定的充分自由的情况下使该立法得到遵守。被请求的成员应对请求成员的磋商给予充分和积极的考虑，并提供充分的机会，在按照国内法和请求成员就保障其机密性达成相互满意的协议的前提下，通过提供与所涉事项有关的、可公开获得的非机密信息和可获得的其他信息进行合作。如一成员的国民或居民在另一成员领土内因被指控违反该另一成员相关法律法规而被起诉，则该另一成员应按与前述条件相同的条件给予该成员磋商的机会。

Article 40 of *the TRIPS* is the control of restrict-competitive practices in contractual licences. Accordingly, Members agree that some licensing practices or conditions pertaining to intellectual property rights which restrain competition may have adverse effects on trade and may impede the transfer and dissemination of technology. Nothing in the Agreement shall prevent Members from specifying in their legislation licensing practices or conditions that may in particular cases constitute an abuse of intellectual property rights having an adverse effect on competition in the relevant market. As provided above, a Member may adopt, consistently with the other provisions of the Agreement, appropriate measures to prevent or control such practices, which may include for example exclusive grant-back conditions, conditions preventing challenges to validity and coercive package licensing, in the light of the relevant laws and regulations of that Member. Each Member shall enter, upon request, into consultations with any other Member which has cause to believe that an intellectual property right owner that is a national or resident of the Member to which the request for consultations has been addressed is undertaking practices in violation of the requesting Member's laws and regulations on the subject matter, and which wishes to secure compliance with such legislation, without prejudice to any action under the law and to the full freedom of an ultimate decision of either Member. The Member addressed shall accord full and sympathetic consideration to, and shall afford adequate opportunity for, consultations with the requesting Member, and shall cooperate through supply of publicly available non-confidential information of relevance to the matter in question and of other information available to the Member, subject to domestic law and to the conclusion of mutually satisfactory agreements concerning the safeguarding of its confidentiality by the requesting Member. A Member whose nationals or residents are subject to proceedings in another Member concerning alleged violation of that other Member's laws and regulations on the subject matter shall, upon request, be granted an opportunity for consultations by the other Member under the same conditions as those foregoing.

第 66 条第 2 款专门规定了技术转让方面发达国家对最不发达国家的优惠。根据该条，发达国家成员应鼓励其领土内的企业和组织，以促进和鼓励向最不发达国家成员转让技术，使这些成员能够建立一个良好和可行的技术基础。

二、《联合国国际技术转让行动守则(草案)》

《联合国国际技术转让行动守则(草案)》是在联合国贸易和发展会议的主持下于 1976 年至 1985 年间谈判形成的。守则草案尚未获联合国大会通过。

《行动守则》的目的如下。

(1) 国际技术转让中的当事人，系指任何公法或私法意义上的自然人或法人，包括个人和集合体。如公司包括股份有限公司、有限公司和其他公司、商号、合伙及其他组织，或由它们组成的任何联合体，不论它们是由国家、政府机构、法人或个人建立、所有或控制；不论它们在何处经营；也不论它们是从事通常被视为商业性质的国际技术转让的交易的国家、政府机构、国际组织、地区及其次地区组织。"当事人"一词除包括上述实体外，还包括公司的分公司、子公司和附属公司、合营企业或其他法律实体，不论它们之间的经济关系和其他关系如何。

Article 66(2) of *the TRIPS Agreement* is specifically concerned with technology transfer, requiring developed countries to take measures to transfer technology to least-developed countries. Developed country Members shall provide incentives to enterprises and institutions in their territories for the purpose of promoting and encouraging technology transfer to least-developed country Members in order to enable them to create a sound and viable technological base.

4.4.2　*TOT-Code*

The Draft International Code of Conduct on the Transfer of Technology (TOT-Code) was negotiated under the auspices of the United Nations Conference on Trade and Development between 1976 and 1985. The draft Code has not been adopted by the United Nations General Assembly.

The purposes of the Code of Conduct are as follows.

(1) "Party" means any person, either natural or legal, of public or private law, either individual or collective, such as corporations, companies, firms, partnerships and other associations, or any combination thereof, whether created, owned or controlled by States, government agencies, legal persons, or individuals, wherever they operate, as well as States, government agencies and international, regional and sub-regional organizations, when they engage in an international transfer of technology transaction which is usually considered to be of a commercial nature. The term "party" includes, among the entities enumerated above, incorporated branches, subsidiaries and affiliates, joint ventures or other legal entities regardless of the economic and other relationships between and among them.

(2) 国际技术转让中的受方，系指在一项技术转让中获得使用或利用的许可，购买或者以其他方式获得一项财产或非财产性质的技术，以及与此相关的权利的当事人。

(3) 国际技术转让中的供方，系指在一项技术转让中许可、出售、转让或以其他方式提供一项财产或非财产性质的技术以及与此相关的权利的当事人。

根据《行动守则》，技术转让系指制造某件产品、应用某种制作方法或提供某项服务的系统知识的转让，特别是指下述安排之一。

① 一切形式的工业产权的让与、出售和许可。商标、服务标记和商号，当其不是技术转让的一部分时，不在此列。

② 提供可行性研究报告、计划书、设计图、模型、说明书、指南、配方、基本的或具体的工程设计、技术规范和培训设备，以及提供技术咨询和技术管理人员的服务及员工培训等技术专长和专业知识。

③ 提供工厂设备的安装、操作及运行所必需的技术知识和交钥匙工程。

④ 提供获取、安装及使用已经以购买、租赁或其他方式取得的机器、设备、中间产品(半成品)和／或原材料所必需的技术知识。

---

(2) "Acquiring party" means the party which obtains a license to use or to exploit, purchases or otherwise acquires technology of a property or non-property nature and/or rights related thereto in a transfer of technology.

(3) "Supplying party" means the party which licenses, sells, assigns or otherwise provides technology of property or non-property nature and/or rights related thereto in a transfer of technology.

Transfer of technology under the Code is the transfer of systematic knowledge for the manufacture of a product, for the application of a process or for the rendering of a service, particularly in each of the following cases.

(a) The assignment, sale and licensing of all forms of industrial property, except for trademarks, service marks and trade names when they are not part of transfer of technology transactions.

(b) The provision of know-how and technical expertise in the form of feasibility studies, plans, diagrams, models, instructions, guides, formulae, basic or detailed engineering designs, specifications and equipment for training, services involving technical advisory and managerial personnel, and personnel training.

(c) The provision of technological knowledge necessary for the installation, operation and functioning of plant and equipment, and turnkey projects.

(d) The provision of technological knowledge necessary to acquire, install and use machinery, equipment, intermediate goods and/or raw materials which have been acquired by purchase, lease or other means.

⑤ 提供工业与技术合作协议的技术内容。仅涉及货物销售或租赁的交易不属于技术转让。

《行动守则》应普遍适用于进行技术转让交易的一切当事人，以及一切国家和国家集团，不论其政治、经济制度及发展水平如何。

《行动守则》的目标如下。

(1) 制定普遍公平的标准，作为技术转让交易当事人间及有关各国政府间关系的基础，同时考虑到它们的合法利益，并对发展中国家实现经济和社会的发展目标的特殊需要给予应有的承认。

(2) 促进当事人间及其政府间的相互信任。

(3) 鼓励交易各方当事人应在谈判地位均等、任何一方不滥用其优势地位的条件下进行技术转让交易，尤其在涉及发展中国家的技术转让交易时更应如此，以便达成彼此满意的协议。

(4) 便利和促进技术情报，特别是关于替换技术的情报的国际流通，作为一切国家，尤其是发展中国家，评价、选择、修改、发展和利用技术的前提条件。

(e) The provision of technological contents of industrial and technical cooperation arrangements. It does not extend to the transactions involving the mere sale or mere lease of goods.

The Code of Conduct is universally applicable in scope and is addressed to all parties to transfer of technology transactions and to all countries and groups of countries, irrespective of their economic and political systems and their levels of development.

The Code of Conduct is based on the following objectives.

(1) To establish general and equitable standards on which to base the relationships among parties to transfer of technology transactions and governments concerned, taking into consideration their legitimate interests, and giving due recognition to special needs of developing countries for the fulfillment of their economic and social development objectives.

(2) To promote mutual confidence between parties as well as their governments.

(3) To encourage transfer of technology transactions, particularly those involving developing countries, under conditions where bargaining positions of the parties to the transactions are balanced in such a way as to avoid abuses of a stronger position and thereby to achieve mutually satisfactory agreements.

(4) To facilitate and increase the international flow of technological information, particularly on the availability of alternative technologies, as a prerequisite for the assessment, selection, adaptation, development and use of technologies in all countries, particularly in developing countries.

(5) 便利和促进财产及非财产性技术的国际流通，以加强一切国家，尤其是发展中国家的科学技术力量的稳固增长，增加它们在世界生产和贸易中的参与。

(6) 增进技术对识别和解决一切国家，尤其是发展中国家中社会经济问题的作用，包括发展国民经济基本因素的作用。

(7) 通过制定国际准则，便利国内有关技术转让的政策、法律和法规的制定、通过及执行。

(8) 促使在涉及技术转让不同要素的信息方面作出适当安排，例如对技术交易进行技术上、机构设置上和财务上的评估所需要的信息，这样可以避免作出不适当或不必要的包装。

(9) 具体规定技术转让交易当事人应该/应当避免采取的限制性(商业)措施。

(10) 列出技术转让交易当事人应该承担的一些适当的责任和义务，并且考虑到它们的合法利益及谈判地位的差异。

《行为守则》的原则如下。

(1) 《行为守则》普遍适用于技术转让领域。

---

(5) To facilitate and increase the international flow of property or non-property technology for strengthening the growth of the scientific and technological capabilities of all countries, in particular developing countries, so as to increase their participation in world production and trade.

(6) To increase the contributions of technology to the identification and solution of social and economic problems of all countries, particularly the developing countries, including the development of basic sectors of their national economies.

(7) To facilitate the formulation, adoption and implementation of national policies, laws and regulations on the subject of transfer of technology by setting forth international norms.

(8) To promote adequate arrangements in terms of information concerning the various elements of the technology to be transferred, such as that required for technical, institutional and financial evaluation of the transaction, thus avoiding undue or unnecessary packaging.

(9) To specify restrictive (business) practices from which parties to technology transfer transactions (shall) (should) refrain.

(10) To set forth an appropriate set of responsibilities and obligations of parties to transfer of technology transactions, taking into consideration their legitimate interests as well as differences in their bargaining positions.

The Code of Conduct is based on the following principles.

(1) The Code of Conduct is universally applicable in scope.

（2）各国有权以符合其国际义务的方式并考虑到所有有关当事人的合法利益，采取一切适当措施便利及规范技术转让，鼓励在协商一致、公平合理的前提和条件下的技术转让。

（3）便利和规范技术转让交易，应当承认国家主权和政治独立(包括对外政策和国家安全的要求)原则以及国家主权平等的原则。

（4）各国应当就国际技术转让进行合作以推动整个世界，尤其是发展中国家经济增长。这种合作应不考虑政治、经济和社会制度的任何差异，此为维护国际和平与安全、促进国际经济的稳定和进步、增进各国的共同福利和摒弃基于上述差异的歧视行为的国际合作重要因素。对守则作出的解释，绝不可与《联合国宪章》的规定相背离，或者对遵奉此规定采取的行动有损害。在技术转让中理应按照守则的有关规定给予发展中国家以特殊待遇。

（5）技术转让交易当事人各自的责任与非作为当事人的政府各自的责任之间，应当明确区分。

---

(2) States have the right to adopt all appropriate measures for facilitating and regulating the transfer of technology, in a manner consistent with their international obligations, taking into consideration the legitimate interests of all parties concerned, and encouraging transfers of technology under mutually agreed, fair and reasonable prerequisites and conditions.

(3) The principles of sovereignty and political independence of States (covering, inter alia, the requirements of foreign policy and national security) and sovereign equality of States, should be recognized in facilitating and regulating transfer of technology transactions.

(4) States should cooperate in the international transfer of technology in order to promote economic growth throughout the world, especially that of the developing countries. Cooperation in such transfer should be irrespective of any differences in political, economic and social systems; this is one of the important elements in maintaining international peace and security and promoting international economic stability and progress, the general welfare of nations and international cooperation free from discrimination based on such differences. Nothing in the Code may be construed as impairing or derogating from the provisions of the Charter of the United Nations or actions taken in pursuance thereof. It is understood that special treatment in transfer of technology should be accorded to developing countries in accordance with the provisions in the Code on the subject.

(5) The separate responsibilities of parties to transfer of technology transactions, on the one hand, and those of governments when not acting as parties, on the other hand, should be clearly distinguished.

（6）技术供方和受方的共同利益应不断增长，以维持和促进国际技术流通。

（7）便利和增加在协商一致、公平合理前提和条件下取得技术的机会，这是技术转让和发展过程中的根本要素，对发展中国家尤为如此。

（8）承认对依国内法授予的工业产权权利的保护。

（9）技术供方在技术受让国从事经营活动时，应当尊重该国的主权和法律，适当考虑到该国声明的发展政策和优先项目，并努力对受让国的发展提供实质性帮助。双方当事人在相互接受的前提和条件下谈判、签订和履行技术转让协议的自由，应基于对上述原则及本守则规定的其他原则的尊重。

为了规范技术转让中的限制性商业做法，《行动守则》草案列举了以下具体的限制性做法。

1）排他性回授条款

要求受方在排他基础上，或者在无供方补偿或互惠的条件下，而将源于受让技术的改进技术转让给或回授给供方，或供方指定的任何其他企业；或者当这种做法构成供方对其支配市场地位的滥用时。

---

(6) Mutual benefits should accrue to technology supplying and acquiring parties in order to maintain and increase the international flow of technology.

(7) Facilitating and increasing the access to technology, particularly for developing countries, under mutually agreed fair and reasonable prerequisites and conditions, are fundamental elements in the process of technology transfer and development.

(8) Recognition of the protection of industrial property rights granted under national law.

(9) Technology supplying parties when operating in an acquiring country should respect the sovereignty and the laws of that country, act with proper regard for that country's declared development policies and priorities and endeavour to contribute substantially to the development of the acquiring country. The freedom of parties to negotiate, conclude and perform agreements for the transfer of technology on mutually acceptable prerequisites and conditions should be based on respect for the foregoing and other principles set forth in the Code.

To regulate the restrictive business practices involving the transfer of technology, the Code of Conduct lists the practices.

1) Exclusive Grant-back Provisions

Requiring the acquiring party to transfer or grant back to the supplying party, or to any other enterprise designated by the supplying party, improvements arising from the acquired technology, on an exclusive basis (or) without offsetting consideration or reciprocal obligations from the supplying party, or when the practice will constitute an abuse of a dominant market position of the supplying party.

2) 对有效性持异议

不合理地要求受方不能对转让中包含的专利及其他形式的发明保护的有效性或者对供方声明或取得的其他这类转让标的有效性提出异议，承认任何因这样的异议引起的涉及当事人双方权利和义务的问题应由适当的适用法律以及与此法律一致的协议条款来确定。

3) 排他交易

非为保证合法利益的获得，特别是非为保证转让技术的保密性或者保证全力帮助或促进的义务所必需，而限制受让方就有关相似或竞争性技术或产品签订销售、代理或制造协议或者取得竞争技术的自由。

4) 对研究的限制

不合理地限制受方从事旨在吸收和修改转让技术以使其适于当地条件的研究和发展工作或者制定实施与新产品、新工艺或新设备有关的研究和开发方案。

5) 对人员使用的限制

在为保证技术转让的效率及使技术投入使用所必需的期限外，或者在此期限后当充分培训的当地人员可以找到或当地人员已被培训的情况下，或者对技术受让国人员的使用不利的情况下，不合理地要求受方雇用供方指派的人员。

---

2) Challenges to Validity

Unreasonably requiring the acquiring party to refrain from challenging the validity of patents and other types of protection for inventions involved in the transfer or the validity of other such grants claimed or obtained by the supplying party, recognizing that any issues concerning the mutual rights and obligations of the parties following such a challenge will be determined by the appropriate applicable law and the terms of the agreement to the extent consistent with that law.

3) Exclusive Dealing

Restrictions on the freedom of the acquiring party to enter into sales, representation or manufacturing agreements relating to similar or competing technologies or products or to obtain competing technology, when such restrictions are not needed for ensuring the achievement of legitimate interests, particularly including securing the confidentiality of the technology transferred or best effort distribution or promotional obligations.

4) Restrictions on Research

Unreasonably restricting the acquiring party either in undertaking research and development directed to absorb and adapt the transferred technology to local conditions or in initiating research and development programs in connection with new products, processes or equipment.

5) Restrictions on Use of Personnel

Unreasonably requiring the acquiring party to use personnel designated by the supplying party, except to the extent necessary to ensure the efficient transmission phase for the transfer of technology and putting it to use or thereafter continuing such requirement beyond the time when adequately trained local personnel are available or have been trained; or prejudicing the use of personnel of the technology acquiring country.

6) 固定价格

不公平地强迫受方在技术转让所涉及的相应市场内就使用供方技术制造的产品或提供的服务遵守价格规则。

7) 对修改的限制

不合理地阻止受方修改进口技术以适应当地条件或对之进行革新，或者当受方基于自己的责任并且在没有使用技术供方的名字、商标、服务标记或商号情况下进行修改时，强迫受方采用其不愿采用或不必要的设计或规格变动，除非这种修改不适当地影响到提供给供方、供方指定的人或其他被许可人的产品或制造产品的工艺，或者被用作供应供方客户的产品的零部件。

8) 排他的销售或代理协议

要求受方授予供方或其指定的任何人以专卖权或独家代理权，除非在从合同或制造协议中当事人各方同意由供方或供方指定的任何人来分配技术转让协议下的全部或部分产品。

6) Price Fixing

Unjustifiably imposing regulation of prices to be charged by acquiring parties in the relevant market to which the technology was transferred for products manufactured or services produced using the technology supplied.

7) Restrictions on Adaptations

Restrictions which unreasonably prevent the acquiring party from adapting the imported technology to local conditions or introducing innovations in it, or which oblige the acquiring party to introduce unwanted or unnecessary design or specification changes, if the acquiring party makes adaptations on his/her own responsibility and without using the technology supplying party's name, trade or service marks or trade names, and except to the extent that this adaptation unsuitably affects those products, or the process for their manufacture, to be supplied to the supplying party, his/her designators, or his/her other licensees, or to be used as a component or spare part in a product to be supplied to his/her customers.

8) Exclusive Sales or Representation Agreements

Requiring the acquiring party to grant exclusive sales or representation rights to the supplying party or any person designated by the supplying party, except as to subcontracting or manufacturing agreement wherein the parties have agreed that all or part of the production under the technology transfer agreement will be distributed by the supplying party or any person designated by him/her.

9) 附带条件的安排

不当地迫使受方接受其不愿接受的额外技术、未来的发明及改进、货物或服务，或者不当地限制技术、货物或服务的来源，以此作为购买供方要求提供的技术的条件，而该技术并不是当受方使用供方的商标或服务标记或其他标记时为保持产品或服务的质量所必需的，也不是当充分达到部件的规格要求有困难或涉及公开的未包含在协议中的额外技术时，为完成某项已被担保的特殊性能的义务所要求的。

10) 共享专利或交叉许可协议及其他协议

以技术供方之间的共享专利或交叉许可协议或其他国际技术转让交流协议中对地域、数量、价格、客户或市场的限制，不当地减少受方接近新的技术进步的机会，或者导致滥用某一行业或市场的支配力量，从而造成对技术转让的不利影响。附于合作协议的适当限制，如合作研究安排，不在此列。

---

9) Tying Arrangements

Unduly imposing acceptance of additional technology, future inventions and improvements, goods or services not wanted by the acquiring party or unduly restricting sources of technology, goods or services, as a condition for obtaining the technology required when not required to maintain the quality of the product or service when the supplier's trade or service mark or other identifying item is used by the acquiring party, or to fulfill a specific performance obligation which has been guaranteed, provided further that adequate specification of the ingredients is not feasible or would involve the disclosure of additional technology not covered by the agreement.

10) Patens Pool or Cross-licensing Agreements and Other Agreements

Restrictions on territories, quantities, prices, customers or markets arising out of patent pool or cross-licensing agreements or other international transfer of technology interchange agreements among technology suppliers which unduly limit access to new technological developments or which would result in an abusive domination of an industry or market with adverse effects on the transfer of technology, except for those restrictions appropriate and ancillary to cooperative agreements such as cooperative research agreements.

11) 对广告宣传的限制

不合理地规定对受方进行广告宣传的限制。但是，当广告宣传利用了供方的名字、商标或服务标记、商号或其他标记时而为防止损害供方的商誉或信誉所必需的，或者供方当可能由其承担产品责任时基于避免此责任的合法理由所要求的，或者适当情况下为了安全的目的或为了保护消费者的利益，或者为了保证转让技术的保密性所必需的对广告宣传的限制，不在此列。

12) 工业产权期满后的付款义务和其他义务

因继续使用已失效、被撤销或有效期满的工业产权而要求付款或强加其他义务。承认对任何其他问题，包括与此技术相关的其他付款义务，应依照适当的适用法以及与该法一致的协议条款来解决。

---

11) Restrictions on Advertising

Unreasonably regulating the advertising or publicity by the acquiring party except where restrictions of such publicity may be required to prevent injury to the supplying party's goodwill or reputation where the advertising or publicity makes reference to the supplying party's name, trade or service marks, trade names or other identifying items, or for legitimate reasons of avoiding product liability when the supplying party may be subject to such liability, or where appropriate for safety purposes or to protect consumers, or when needed to secure the confidentiality of the technology transferred.

12) Payments and Other Obligations after Expiration of Industrial Property Rights

Requiring payments or imposing other obligations for continuing the use of industrial property rights which have been invalidated, cancelled or have expired recognizing that any other issue, including other payment obligations for technology, shall be dealt with by the appropriate applicable law and the terms of the agreement to the extent consistent with that law.

13) 协议期满后的限制

双方当事人在谈判和签订技术转让协议时，应当配合当事人所在各国，特别是技术受让国的经济和社会发展目标；在谈判、签订和履行技术转让协议时，应当遵循公平和诚实的商业做法，考虑到个案的特殊情况，应当认识到特定的环境，主要包括技术发展阶段、当事人的经济和技术能力，以及当事人之间技术转让的性质和类型。

技术转让协议应规定可被双方接受的合同义务，包括与支付有关的义务，此外，在适当情况下还应包括：①获得改进技术的途径；②保密责任；③争议解决与法律适用；④对技术的描述；⑤适用性；⑥转让技术的权利；⑦质量标准和商誉；⑧性能担保；⑨文件的交递；⑩培训员工以及提供附属设备、零部件；⑪责任。

13) Restrictions after Expiration of Agreement

When negotiating and concluding a technology transfer agreement, the parties should be responsive to the economic and social development objectives of the respective countries of the parties and particularly of the technology acquiring country, and when negotiating, concluding and performing a technology transfer agreement, the parties should observe fair and honest business practices and take into account the specific circumstances of the individual case and recognition should be given to certain circumstances, mainly the stage of development of technology, the economic and technical capabilities of the parties, the nature and type of the transaction such as any ongoing or continuous flow of technology between the parties.

The technology transfer agreement should provide for mutually acceptable contractual obligations, including those relating to payments and, where appropriate, inter alia, the following: (a)access to improved technology, (b)confidentiality responsibility, (c)dispute settlement and applicable law, (d)description of the technology, (e)suitability for use, (f)rights to the technology transferred, (g)quality levels and goodwill, (h)performance guarantees, (i)transmission of documentation, (j)training of personnel and provision of accessories, spare parts and components, (k)liability.

考虑到发展中国家，尤其是最不发达国家的需要和问题，发达国家政府应直接地或通过合适的国际组织采取适当措施，以便利和鼓励发展中国家建立并增强其科学技术能力，协助并与其合作努力实现其经济和社会目标。

发达国家政府应当依照国内政策、法律和规章采取措施，鼓励并尽力推动各国的企业和组织，单独地或与发展中国家，尤其是最不发达国家的企业和组织合作，除其他努力外，还应作出下列努力：①帮助发展中国家的企业提高技术能力，包括提供受方要求的特别培训；②从事适合发展中国家需要的技术的开发；③在发展中国家从事惠及该国的研究和开发活动，增进发达国家和发展中国家的企业及科学技术组织之间的合作；④协助发展中国家的企业和组织实施旨在发展和改进适于发展中国家条件和特别需要的新技术及现有技术的计划。

Taking into consideration the needs and problems of developing countries, particularly of the least developed countries, according to the Code of Conduct, governments of developed countries should take adequate specific measures, directly or through appropriate international organizations, in order to facilitate and encourage the initiation and strengthening of the scientific and technological capabilities of developing countries so as to assist and cooperate with them in their efforts to fulfill their economic and social objectives.

Governments of developed countries should take measures in accordance with national policies, laws and regulations to encourage and to endeavour to give incentive to enterprises and institutions in their countries, either individually or in collaboration with enterprises and institutions in developing countries, particularly those in the least developed countries, to make special efforts, inter alia, (a)to assist in the development of technological capabilities of the enterprises in developing countries, including special training as required by the acquiring party; (b)to undertake the development of technology appropriate to the needs of developing countries; (c)to undertake R & D activity in developing countries of interest to such countries, as well as to improve cooperation between enterprises and scientific and technological institutions of developed and developing countries; (d)to assist in projects by enterprises and institutions in developing countries for the development and adaptation of new and existing technologies suitable to the particular needs and conditions of developing countries.

　　为了促进旨在加强一切国家技术力量的国际技术广泛流通，考虑到守则的目标和原则，以及为了推动守则的有效实施，守则草案鼓励开展双边或多边、次区域、地区或地区间范围内的国际合作，合作方式可以包括：①交换关于技术和技术替代品的效力和描述的有效信息；②交换关于探索解决涉及技术转让的问题，特别是技术转让中限制性商业做法问题的经验的有效信息；③交换与技术转让有关的国内立法发展的信息；④推动缔结为技术供方和受方政府提供平等待遇的国际协议；⑤进行磋商，以促使与技术转让有关的国内立法和政策在适当情况下进一步协调一致；⑥在适当情况下推动旨在寻求、获得和传播技术的共同计划；⑦推动为实现发展目标修改和改进技术的计划；⑧推动有利于当地技术进步的科学技术资源和能力的发展；⑨通过国际协定采取行动，尽可能避免对技术转让交易所产生的各项收益和付款重复征税。

With a view to facilitating an expanded international flow of technology for strengthening the technological capabilities of all countries, taking into account the objectives and principles, and to promoting the effective implementation of its provisions, the Code encourages international collaboration between governments at the bilateral or multilateral, sub-regional, regional or interregional levels may include the following measures: (a)Exchange of available information on the availability and description of technologies and technological alternatives; (b)Exchange of available information on experience in seeking solutions to problems relating to the transfer of technology, particularly restrictive business practices in the transfer of technology; (c)Exchange of information on development of national legislation with respect to the transfer of technology; (d)Promotion of the conclusion of international agreements which should provide equitable treatment for governments of both technology supplying and acquiring parties; (e)Consultations which may lead to greater harmonization, where appropriate, of national legislation and policies with respect to the transfer of technology; (f)Promotion, where appropriate, of common programs for searching for, acquiring and disseminating technologies; (g)Promotion of programs for the adaptation and development of technology in the context of development objectives; (h)Promotion of the development of scientific and technological resources and capabilities stimulating the development of indigenous technologies; (i)Action through international agreements to avoid, as far as possible, imposition of double taxation on earnings and payments arising out of transfer of technology transactions.

综 合 练 习

1. 技术转让中可作为转让标的的知识产权有哪些？

2. 技术许可协议的基本内容是什么？

3. 怎样理解 TRIPS 成员在 TRIPS 下承担的义务与其在其他重要的多边知识产权公约下所承担的义务的关系？

4. 怎样理解发展中国家和发达国家对于规制限制性商业做法的态度差异？

5. 法律是否禁止所有限制性商业做法？

Comprehensive Exercises

1. How many types of intellectual properties fall into the subjects of technology transfer?

2. What is the basic content of technology license agreement?

3. How to understand the relationship between the obligations a member shall assume under *the TRIPS* for the protection of intellectual property and those under the most important existing multilateral intellectual property treaties?

4. How to understand the difference in the attitudes towards the regulation of restrictive business practices between developing countries and developed countries?

5. Are all restrictive business practices prohibited by laws?

第五章 国际服务贸易法律制度

学习目标

了解《服务贸易总协议》的背景。

掌握国际服务贸易的概念、内涵和范围。

掌握《服务贸易总协议》的主要内容。

Chapter 5　Legal System on International Trade in Services

Learning Objectives

To know the background of *the GATS*.

To grasp the concept, connotation and scope of international trade in services.

To grasp the principal content of *the GATS*.

第一节 服务贸易的概念

服务贸易是指服务提供者向消费者出售和交付服务这种无形商品的交易活动。从法律上讲，在不同国家或经济体的服务提供者和消费者之间发生的服务交易活动则称为国际服务贸易。最早的规范国际服务贸易的多边规则主要体现在《服务贸易总协议》中。

《服务贸易总协议》没有对服务或服务部门作出概念界定，而是在其第一部分列举了服务贸易的四种"提供方式"。(1)跨境服务，指从一成员方境内向另一成员方境内提供服务，不需要服务提供者和消费者的实际流动，如电信服务。(2)境外消费，指在一成员方境内向来自任何其他成员方的消费者提供服务，需要消费者前往服务提供者境内接受服务，如旅游。(3)商业存在，指一成员方的服务提供者通过购买或租用经营场所等方式，在其他任何成员方境内以商业存在的形式提供服务，比如一国保险公司在另一国开设子公司。(4)自然人流动，是指一成员方的服务提供者通过在其他成员方境内以自然人存在的形式提供服务，如会计师、医生或教师等。

5.1 Concept of Trade in Services

Trade in Services refers to the sale and delivery of an intangible product, called a service, from a producer to a consumer. Trade in services takes place between a producer and a consumer that is, in legal terms, based in different countries or economies, this is called International Trade in Services. The first and principal set of multilateral rules governing international trade in services is now found in *the General Agreement on Trade in Services (GATS)*.

The GATS does not define either service or service sector. It does so in terms of "modes of supply" in Part I. Four modes are described as follows: (1)Cross-border: the cross-border supply of services refers to the supply of a service from the territory of one member into the territory of any other member, which does not require the physical movement of either the supplier or the consumer (such as telecommunications). (2)Consumption abroad: the consumption abroad refers to the supply of a service in the territory of one member to the service of a consumer from any other member, which requires the consumer to go to the supplier (such as tourism). (3)Commercial presence: it means a service is supplied by a service supplier from one member state by means of a commercial presence, including through buying or lease of premises, in another member's territory (e.g. domestic subsidiaries of foreign insurance companies). (4)Movement of natural persons: it refers to a service supplied in the territory of a member state by a service supplier from another member state by means of the temporary presence of natural persons of another member state (e.g. accountants, doctors or teachers).

根据世界贸易组织服务部门分类表，服务部门分为 12 个：商业服务；通信服务；建筑与相关工程服务；分销服务；教育服务；环境服务；金融服务；健康与社会服务；旅游及相关服务；娱乐、文化与体育服务；交通运输服务；其他服务。

第二节 《服务贸易总协议》的历史背景与基本宗旨

一、《服务贸易总协议》的历史背景

《服务贸易总协议》(GATS)是第一个规范服务贸易的多边贸易协定，是多边贸易谈判"乌拉圭回合"(1986—1993 年)的主要成果之一。这距《1947 年关税与贸易总协定》的达成与实施已经过去了近半个世纪。

According to the Service Sectoral Classification List of the WTO, the 12 core service sectors are: Business Services; Communication Services; Construction and Related Engineering Services; Distribution Services; Educational Services; Environmental Services; Financial Services; Health-related and Social Services; Tourism and Travel-related Services; Recreational, Cultural and Sporting Services; Transport Services; Other Services not Included Elsewhere.

5.2 Historical Background and Basic Purposes of *GATS*

5.2.1 Historical Background of *GATS*

The General Agreement on Trade in Services (GATS) is the first multilateral trade agreement to cover trade in services. Its creation was one of the major achievements of the Uruguay Round of trade negotiations, from 1986 to 1993. This was almost half a century after the entry into force of *the General Agreement on Tariffs and Trade (GATT) of 1947*.

关于服务贸易问题达成协定的必要性，很久以来一直存在争议。从旅馆业、餐饮业到一些个人服务，传统上认为大部分的服务贸易活动都在国内展开，没有必要运用贸易政策和手段去调整。而如铁路运输、电信等部门，因其在重要基础设施建设方面意义重大，在一定情况下具有自然垄断地位，通常认为是政府所有并控制的领域。至于健康、教育和基础保险服务等第三类重要的服务部门，由于对促进社会融合、增强地区凝聚力具有重要作用，很多国家都视其为政府责任并加以严格规制，并没有任由市场进行激烈竞争。

不过，有的服务部门，特别是国际金融和海运服务等，因其对商品贸易具有天然的补充作用，已开放几个世纪之久。其他主要服务部门由于近几十年来在技术和规则方面已发生了根本改变，已能够向私人开放市场，减少甚至消除现存的准入壁垒。互联网的出现，衍生出许多可跨国交易的服务产品，如电子银行业、远程教育等。而在 20 年前，这些服务产品还闻所未闻。不仅如此，互联网还消除了诸如软件开发、顾问及咨询等专业服务领域中给相距遥远的专业服务提供者以及服务使用者造成不便的距离障碍。目前，越来越多的国家政府已经将过去垄断的服务部门向市场开放，允许竞争。电信便是其中的一例。

The need for a trade agreement in services has long been questioned. Large segments of the service economy, from hotels and restaurants to personal services, have traditionally been considered as domestic activities that do not lend themselves to the application of trade policy and instruments. Other sectors, from rail transport to telecommunications, have been viewed as classical domains of government ownership and control, given their infrastructural importance and the perceived existence, in some cases, of natural monopoly situations. A third important group of sectors, including health, education and basic insurance services, are considered in many countries as governmental responsibilities, given their importance for social integration and regional cohesion, which should be tightly regulated and not be left to the rough and tumble of markets.

Nevertheless, some service sectors, international finance and maritime transport in particular, have been largely open for centuries as the natural complements to merchandise trade. Other large sectors have undergone fundamental technical and regulatory changes in recent decades, opening them to private commercial participation and reducing, even eliminating, existing barriers to entry. The emergence of the internet has helped to create a range of internationally tradable product variants, from e-banking to distance learning, that were unknown only two decades ago, and has removed distance-related barriers to trade that had disadvantaged suppliers and users in remote locations (relevant areas include professional services such as software development, consultancy and advisory services, etc.). A growing number of governments have gradually exposed previous monopoly domains to competition; telecommunication is a case in point.

对于一些最具活力和创新性的经济部门来说，以公共服务的传统体制来运行已越来越不合时宜，政府明显缺乏创业精神和财政资源去充分挖掘当下服务贸易蕴含的增长潜力。

国际服务贸易不断发展的态势迫切需要能够获得各国广泛承认的规则。

在 1982 年的关税与贸易总协定部长级会议，经过激烈讨论，首次将服务贸易列入工作计划，并请各缔约方考虑就服务采取多边行动是否适合和必要。总体来说，美国与欧共体希望将服务贸易纳入《关税与贸易总协定》，而发展中国家对此持反对态度。1986 年乌拉圭回合启动，成立了专门的服务贸易谈判工作小组，以便在保证透明度和逐步自由化的条件下扩大服务贸易谈判。乌拉圭回合中，虽然将非歧视原则以及比较优势等原则扩展至服务交换领域的目标并没有完全实现，但谈判仍促成了《服务贸易总协议》的产生，提供了以部门为基础的协定框架。

The traditional framework of public services increasingly proved inappropriate for operating some of the most dynamic and innovative segments of the economy, and governments apparently lacked the entrepreneurial spirit and financial resources to exploit fully existing growth potential of trade in services.

Given the continued momentum of world service trade, the need for internationally recognized rules became increasingly pressing.

In the GATT Ministerial Meeting of 1982, after the heated discussion, the subject of services was for the first time placed on the agenda, and contracting parties were invited to consider whether any multilateral action in respect of services was appropriate and desirable. Generally the United States and the European Community were in favor of including services in *the GATT* system, while the developing countries were opposed. When the Uruguay Round was launched in 1986, a separate group on Negotiations on Services was created with a view to expansion of such trade under the conditions of transparency and progressive liberalization. The attempt in the Uruguay Round to impose the principles of nondiscrimination and comparative advantage on exchange of services was partly successful, but the negotiations achieved *the GATS*, which provides a framework for sector-specific agreements.

二、《服务贸易总协议》的基本宗旨

根据其序言，《服务贸易总协议》的宗旨是在透明度和逐步自由化的前提下，扩大服务贸易，并以此来促进贸易各方和发展中国家的经济增长，因此，扩大服务贸易不仅是目的，而且是促进经济增长和发展的手段。序言明确指出，应促进发展中国家更多地参与国际服务贸易，并考虑最不发达国家的特殊经济状况和发展及其贸易和金融的需要，从而进一步强调了服务贸易与促进发展的联系。《服务贸易总协议》对于国际服务贸易的贡献主要体现在两个方面：第一，确保增加有关服务贸易规则和法规的透明度和可预知性；第二，通过连续回合的谈判促进服务贸易的逐步自由化。在《服务贸易总协议》框架中，逐步自由化意味着应促进市场开放，在更多服务部门中给予外国服务以及服务提供者国民待遇。同时，《服务贸易总协议》也明确承认，各国政府有权管理服务贸易，有权制定符合国内政策目标的法规，发展中国家可以根据需要行使这些权利。

5.2.2   Basic Purposes of *GATS*

As stated in its preamble, the purposes of *the GATS* are to contribute to trade expansion under the conditions of transparency and progressive liberalization and as a means of promoting the economic growth of all trading partners and the development of developing countries. Trade expansion is thus not seen as an end in itself but as an instrument to promote growth and development. The link with development is further reinforced by explicit references in the preamble to the objective of increasing participation of developing countries in services trade and to the special economic situation and the development, trade and financial needs of the least-developed countries. *The GATS*' contribution to world service trade rests on two main pillars. One is ensuring increased transparency and predictability of relevant rules and regulations, the other is promoting progressive liberalization of the trade in services through successive rounds of negotiations. Within the framework of the Agreement, the latter concept is tantamount to improving market access and extending national treatment to foreign services and service suppliers across an increasing range of sectors. Rather, the Agreement explicitly recognizes governments' right to regulate, and introduce new regulations, to meet national policy objectives and the particular need of developing countries to exercise this right.

第三节 《服务贸易总协议》的基本框架与内容

《服务贸易总协议》由三个相互关联的部分组成：①协议本身，主要规定适用于所有世界贸易组织成员的规则，常称作框架协定；②处理具体部门事项的附件；③具体承诺表，由各成员在多边贸易谈判"乌拉圭回合"中达成。

框架协议第一部分的适用对象覆盖了服务贸易各部门，但不涉及行使政府职能而提供的服务。协议规定了四种服务提供模式：跨境服务、境外消费、商业存在和自然人流动。各种模式相互间还可能存在商业联系，比如，一家依"商业存在"模式在甲国成立的外国公司，可能雇用来自乙国的国民（"自然人流动"模式）向乙国、丙国及其他国家提供"跨境服务"。同样，到甲国进行商务考察（"自然人流动"模式）可能是为向该国提供跨境服务所必需的，或者旨在增强在该国设立的分支机构的经营能力（"商业存在"模式）。

5.3　Basic Framework and Content of *GATS*

The GATS is made up of three interrelated components: (a)the agreement itself, often called the Framework Agreement, which contains the rules applicable to all the members of the World Trade Organization; (b)the sectoral annexes that deal with issues unique to particular economic sectors; and (c)the national schedules of specific commitments each member has agreed to undertake, which were agreed to mainly through negotiations undertaken as part of the Uruguay Round of Multilateral Trade Negotiations.

The Part I of the Framework Agreement covers all trade in services in any sector except those supplied in the exercise of governmental functions. The Agreement distinguishes between four modes of supplying services: (A)cross-border, (B)consumption abroad, (C)commercial presence, (D)movement of natural persons. Commercial linkages may exist among all four modes of supply. For example, a foreign company established under mode C in Country A may employ nationals from Country B (mode D) to export services cross-border into Countries B, C etc. Similarly, business visits into Country A (mode D) may prove necessary to complement cross-border supplies into that country (mode A) or to upgrade the business capacity of a locally established office (mode C).

框架协议的第二部分确定了最惠国待遇、透明度以及避免滥用垄断地位的基本原则。第三部分规定了以部门为单位给予的市场准入以及国民待遇。其余部分对定期谈判回合、附表的约束力、将争端诉诸《关于争端解决规则与程序的谅解》以及服务贸易理事会的设立进行了规定。

一、《服务贸易总协议》的适用范围

《服务贸易总协议》适用于各成员影响服务贸易的措施，包括了中央、地区或地方政府采取的措施以及由获授权的非政府机构采取的措施。这里的"措施"，指成员的任何措施，不论采取法律、法规、规章、程序、决定、行政行为或其他任何形式，包括下列方面的措施：①服务的购买、支付和使用；②与服务提供有关的、成员要求向公众提供的服务的准入和使用；③一成员的自然人或法人为提供服务在另一成员境内的存在，包括商业存在。"措施"的定义对于水平不同的各成员熟悉《服务贸易总协议》的基本概念非常重要，可防止各成员在自身未察觉的情况下违反《服务贸易总协议》义务，并有助于他们有效展开与贸易伙伴的谈判。

Part Ⅱ of the Framework Agreement sets down the basic principles—MFN, transparency, and avoidance of abuse of dominant position. Part Ⅲ then provides for specific commitments by sector for market access and national treatment. The remaining parts provide for periodic negotiating rounds, binding or unbinding of schedules, dispute settlement by recourse to *the Understanding on Rules and Procedures Governing the Settlement of Disputes*, and creation of the Council on Trade in Service.

5.3.1　Scope and Application of *GATS*

The GATS applies to measures by its members affecting trade in services. It does not matter in this context whether a measure is taken at central, regional or local government level, or by non-governmental bodies exercising delegated powers. The relevant definition covers any measure, whether in the form of a law, regulation, rule, procedure, decision, administrative action, or any other form in respect of: (a)the purchase, payment or use of a service; (b)the access to and use of, in connection with the supply of services which are required by those Members to be offered to the public generally; (c)the presence, including commercial presence, of natural or legal persons of a Member for the supply of a service in the territory of another Member. This definition is important to familiarize staff at all levels with basic concepts of *the GATS* to prevent them from acting, unintentionally, in contravention of obligations under *the GATS* and enable them to negotiate effectively with trading partners.

《服务贸易总协议》将国际服务部门分为 12 个核心部门和 160 个分部门，各成员可在承诺表中对这些部门的市场准入和国民待遇作出具体承诺。不过，协议覆盖部门的范围虽然全面，但仍然存在特殊部门的例外。依协议有关航空运输服务的附件规定，协议仅适用于影响航空器维修及保养服务、空运服务的销售与营销服务和计算机订位系统服务方面的措施，与航权行使直接相关的服务则不在适用之列。另一个不在协议适用范围内的是为行使政府职权而提供的服务，具体是指既不依据商业基础提供，也不与一个或多个服务提供者竞争的任何服务，典型的例子如警察、消防、金融政策执行、税收和海关管理等。

二、一般义务和纪律

　　框架协议对最惠国待遇和透明度的规定，是适用于所有成员的一般性原则。

　　Under the classification system of *the GATS*, 12 core service sectors and 160 sub-sectors may be included in a Member's schedule of commitments with specific market access and national treatment obligations. There is only one sector-specific exception to the Agreement's otherwise comprehensive coverage. Under *the GATS* Annex on Air Transport Services, only measures affecting aircraft repair and maintenance services, the selling and marketing of air transport services, and computer reservation system (CRS) services have been included. Measures affecting air traffic rights and directly-related services are excluded. Another blanket exemption applies to services supplied in the exercise of governmental authority. The relevant definition specifies that these services are supplied neither on a commercial basis, nor in competition with one or more service suppliers. Typical examples may include police, fire protection, monetary policy operations, and tax and customs administration.

5.3.2　General Obligations and Disciplines

　　Two general principles in the Framework Agreement apply to all the WTO members: most-favored-nation (MFN) treatment and transparency.

作为第二次世界大战后多边贸易体制得以形成的基础，最惠国待遇原则试图构建以规则为基础的框架机制，确保各方享有贸易权利以及行使不依附于贸易参与者个体的经济或政治实力，努力消除以实力为依托的政策之间产生的摩擦以及扭曲效应。更确切地说，最惠国待遇原则要求给予一国的准入条件必须自动给予多边贸易体制的所有其他参与者，这使得更有谈判影响力的主要贸易伙伴在谈判中所做让步能惠及每一个贸易参与者，而不需要再另行谈判。在《服务贸易总协议》中，给予最惠国待遇的义务适用于任何影响该协定下服务贸易各部门的措施，不论成员方是否作出开放服务贸易部门的具体承诺。当然，为了获得广泛的接受，《服务贸易总协议》也允许成员在加入时提出保留，列入各成员不愿承担最惠国待遇的措施清单，这些措施的期限原则上不超过 10 年。不过，成员政府出于各种原因，往往会大范围介入服务市场，如为实现社会政策目标或存在自然垄断等，考虑到这一点，《服务贸易总协议》力图确保相关措施不致减损最惠国待遇这样的一般性义务。

The most-favored-nation (MFN) principle is a cornerstone of the multilateral trading system conceived after World War II. It seeks to replace the frictions and distortions of power-based policies with the guarantees of a rules-based framework where trading rights do not depend on the individual participants' economic or political clout. Rather, the best access conditions that have been conceded to one country must automatically be extended to all other participants in the system. This allows everybody to benefit, without additional negotiating effort, from concessions that may have been agreed between large trading partners with much negotiating leverage. In the context of *the GATS*, the MFN obligation is applicable to any measure that affects trade in services in any sector falling under the Agreement, whether specific commitments have been made or not. Exemptions could have been sought at the time of the acceptance of the Agreement. They are contained in country-specific lists, and their duration must not exceed ten years in principle. However, given strong government involvement in many service markets—for various reasons, including social policy objectives or the existence of natural monopolies—*the GATS* seeks to ensure that relevant measures do not undermine general obligations, such as MFN treatment.

因此，对已作出特定承诺的服务部门，协议要求各成员应确保其影响服务贸易的所有一般性适用措施以公平、合理和客观的方式实施(第 6 条第 1 款)。乌拉圭回合谈判期间，一些工业化国家服务业谈判代表认为实行无条件的最惠国待遇将导致"搭便车"问题，使有的国家不用改变其服务业一直存在的严格法律管制，而其服务提供者却能进入在法律上对服务业给予更多开放的国家。为迫使封闭市场的国家开放服务业市场，服务业谈判代表提出了最惠国待遇豁免并得以实施。通过设立《服务贸易总协议》附件的形式，世界贸易组织各创始成员可在协议生效时提交最惠国义务例外清单，并规定新的豁免申请，应依世界贸易组织有关普通豁免程序处理。最惠国待遇豁免的期限一般不超过10 年，需定期审查，并在以后的贸易谈判回合中重新谈判。

Thus, each member is required to ensure, in sectors where commitments exist, that measures of general application are administered impartially and in a reasonable and objective manner (Article 6(1)). During the Uruguay Round negotiations, the representatives of service industries in a number of industrialized nations argued that unconditional MFN treatment would allow states with restrictive laws governing services to keep those laws in places while their own service suppliers would get a "free ride" into the markets of states with more than open laws. To force states with closed markets to open them, the representatives of service industries successfully advocated the use of MFN exemptions. An annex was added to *the GATS* that (a) allowed the original WTO members to submit a list of MFN exemptions that became effective when *GATS* came into force and (b) provide that any later applications for exemptions will be considered using the ordinary WTO waiver procedures. The MFN exemptions are to be limited in time lasting no longer than ten years and subject to periodic review and to negotiations in future rounds.

　　框架协议对于成员方透明度的基本义务作出规定，要求立即公布有关影响协定实施的所有普遍适用的措施，或最迟应在此类措施生效时公布。相比其他经济领域，法规作为贸易保护手段或国内政策工具，对服务贸易的影响更为明显，这使得透明度义务的履行尤为必要。成员还有设立咨询点的一般义务，对其他成员的要求予以答复。此外，发达国家应建立联系点，应发展中国家服务提供者的要求提供有关信息。如果新增或修改的法律、法规或行政指导原则对于作出具体承诺的服务贸易部门构成重大影响的，成员方还必须通知服务贸易理事会。

　　除最惠国待遇和透明度的基本义务外，框架协议还规定了适用于服务贸易的其他一般标准。

The transparency provision in the Framework Agreement requires members to publish promptly，or at the latest by the time of their entry into force, "all relevant measures of general application" that affect operation of the Agreement. These transparency obligations are particularly relevant in the service area where the role of regulation—as a trade protective instrument and/or as a domestic policy tool—tends to feature more prominently than in most other segments of the economy. Members also have a general obligation to establish an enquiry point to respond to requests from other members. Moreover, developed countries are to establish contact points to which developing country service suppliers can turn for relevant information. Members must also notify the Council for Trade in Services of new or changed laws, regulations or administrative guidelines that significantly affect trade in sectors subject to specific commitments.

In addition to its core obligations of MFN treatment and transparency, the Framework Agreement establishes other general criteria governing trade in services.

1. 相互承认标准

尽管已有最惠国待遇要求，《服务贸易总协议》第 7 条仍规定了成员以适用标准或颁发执照、许可证等方式，承认服务提供者在国外已经获得的教育或其他资格。这种承认可以自动给予，也可通过有关国家间的协议获得。不过，承认必须以非排他的方式实施，也就是说，签署协议的成员应向其他有兴趣的成员提供机会，就其加入该协议展开谈判；如果是成员自动地给予承认，应向其他成员提供机会，以证明在其境内取得的资格也应予以承认。协议第 7 条还规定，承认不得作为贸易伙伴之间的歧视手段或成为服务贸易的一种隐蔽性限制。

2. 垄断和商业惯例

各成员可以赋予某服务提供者垄断权利，但应确保该服务提供者在提供垄断服务时，不违背该成员承担的最惠国待遇义务及其具体承诺。对于其他抑制竞争，进而限制服务贸易的商业惯例，《服务贸易总协议》要求各成员与其他成员进行磋商，以期取消这样的商业惯例。

---

1. Mutual Recognition Criteria

Notwithstanding the MFN requirement, Article 7 of *the GATS* provides the scope for the Members, when applying standards or granting licenses, certificates, etc., to recognize education and other qualifications a supplier has obtained abroad. This may be done on an autonomous basis or through agreement with the country concerned. However, recognition must not be exclusive, i.e. other Members are to be afforded an opportunity to negotiate their accession to agreements or, in the event of autonomous recognition, to demonstrate that their requirements should be recognized as well. Article 7 also requires that recognition not be applied as a means of discrimination between trading partners or as a disguised trade restriction on trade in services.

2. Monopolies and Business Practices

Each member may grant monopoly rights to a service supplier, but in doing so, it must not allow the supplier to act in a manner inconsistent with the MFN obligation and its specific commitments. As for other business practices which restrain competition and thereby restrict trade in services, *the GATS* requires each member to consult with any other members with a view to eliminating such practices.

3. 发展中国家的更多参与

为鼓励发展中国家更多地参与服务贸易，《服务贸易总协议》授权发达国家和发展中国家展开谈判，促成类似关税与贸易总协定下普遍优惠制和南南合作的制度，旨在提升发展中国家参与服务贸易的能力、效率以及竞争力。

4. 区域经济一体化

《服务贸易总协议》致力于促成服务贸易和劳动力流动方面的区域经济一体化，对成员之间达成的服务一体化协议，要求其应涵盖大多数服务部门并消除成员之间全部或绝大部分歧视性措施。参与一体化协议的成员方应向服务贸易理事会"通知"此类协议并经服务贸易理事会审查和批准。

---

3. Increasing Participation of Developing Countries

To encourage the participation of developing countries, *GATS* authorizes developed and developing countries to enter into negotiations similar to those that produced GATT's General System of Preferences and South-South Preferences targeted at improving the capacity, efficiency, and competitiveness of the developing countries.

4. Regional Economic Integration

The GATS seeks to encourage regional economic integration both in trade in services and in the movement of labor. A service integration agreement among the members is required to have substantial sectoral coverage and must provide for the elimination of all or substantially all discrimination among the parties in the sectors it covers. The participating member parties have to "notify" the Council for Trade in Services of their proposed agreement for the Council's review and approval.

5. 国内规章

《服务贸易总协议》要求，各成员方应在其作出具体承诺的领域，保证各种影响服务贸易的一般适用法律、规章和措施以合理、客观和公正的方式实施，不允许现有的有关执照、资格的要求对服务贸易构成不必要的负担或限制，或以不透明的方式实施。如果服务贸易理事会在这些领域采用有关国际组织①的国际标准时，则要求各成员方有关执照、资格的要求应与之相符。

三、一般例外和安全例外

《服务贸易总协议》规定了例外条款，允许成员方在满足一定条件时背离《服务贸易总协议》下应履行的义务和作出的承诺。一般而言，例外包括一般例外和安全例外。

成员方援引和实施的一般例外措施如下。

(1) 为维护公共道德和公共秩序所必需的措施。

---

5. Domestic Regulations

In sectors where specific commitments are undertaken, *the GATS* requires its members to ensure that all laws, regulations and measures of general application affecting trade in services are administered in a reasonable, objective, and impartial manner. It forbids them from applying their existing licensing, qualification requirements in a burdensome, restrictive, or nontransparent manner; and, as soon as the Council for Trade in Services adopts international standards of relevant international organizations in these areas, it will require them to bring their practices into compliance with those standards.

5.3.3　General Exceptions and Security Exceptions

The GATS provides for exceptions provision allowing Members to deviate, under certain conditions, from obligations and commitments under *the GATS*, principally including general exceptions and security exceptions.

The following general exceptions are measures adopted and enforced by Members.

(1) Measures which are necessary to protect public morals or to maintain public orders.

---

① "有关国际组织"是指其成员资格至少对世界贸易组织的成员或有关机构开放的国际组织。

(2) 为保护人类、动物或植物的生命或健康所必需的措施。

(3) 为确保遵守与《服务贸易总协议》不相抵触的与下述问题相关的法律和法规所必需的措施：防止欺骗和欺诈行为或处理服务合同违约而产生的影响；保护与个人信息处理和传播有关的个人隐私及保护个人记录和账户秘密性；安全。

(4) 为保证对其他成员方的服务或服务提供者平等或有效地课征或收取直接税而给予的差别待遇(即国民待遇例外，与协议第 17 条关于国民待遇的规定不一致)。

(5) 源于该成员方受其约束的避免双重征税协议或任何其他国际协议或安排中的避免双重征税的规定的差别待遇(即最惠国待遇例外，与协议第 2 条关于最惠国待遇的规定不一致)。

此外，上述措施的实施不在情形类似的国家间构成任意的或不合理的歧视手段，或构成对服务贸易的变相限制。

---

(2) Measures which are necessary to protect human, animal or plant life or health.

(3) Measures which are necessary to secure compliance with laws or regulations which are not inconsistent with the provisions with this Agreement including those relating to the prevention of deceptive and fraudulent practices or to deal with the effects of a default on service contracts, or relating to the protection of the privacy of individuals in relation to the processing and dissemination of personal data and the protection of confidentiality of individual record and account, or relating to safety.

(4) Measures which are inconsistent with Article 17, provided that the difference in treatment is aimed at ensuring the equitable or effective imposition or collection of direct taxes in respect of services or service suppliers of other Members.

(5) Measures which are inconsistent with Article 2, provided that the difference in treatment is the result of the agreement on the avoidance of double taxation or provisions on the avoidance of double taxation in any other international agreement or arrangement by which the Member is bound.

Moreover, a measure under the above paragraphs from (1) to (5) shall not be applied in a manner which would constitute a means of arbitrary or unjustifiable discrimination between countries where like conditions prevail, or a distinguished restriction on trade in services.

除一般例外以外，《服务贸易总协议》还规定了与国家和国际安全有关的安全例外。《服务贸易总协议》第14条第2款对安全例外作出规定，该协议不得做如下解释。

(1) 要求任何成员方提供其认为公开后会违背其基本安全利益的任何材料。

(2) 阻止任何成员方采取其认为保护其基本安全利益所必需的行动，此类行动与下列情形有关：为供应军事设施而直接或间接提供的服务；可分裂与可融合的物质，或用以制造此类物质的原料；战时或在其他国际关系处于紧急状态时采取的措施。

(3) 阻止任何成员方为履行《联合国宪章》下维护国际和平与安全的义务而采取的行动。

通过安全例外的规定，《服务贸易总协议》允许各成员方基于国家或国际安全利益援引或实施与协议义务不符的措施。世界贸易组织成员方有时会采取针对其他成员方的单边或双边措施以维护国家或国际安全与和平，并从《服务贸易总协议》第14条第2款的规定中为此类措施寻求法律依据。

In addition to the General Exceptions, *the GATS* also provides for the Security Exceptions, the exceptions relating to national and international security. Article 14(2), entitled Security Exceptions, states in its first paragraph: Nothing in this Agreement shall be construed as follows.

(1) To require any Member to furnish any information, the disclosure of which it considers contrary to its essential security interests.

(2) To prevent any Member from taking any action which it considers necessary for the protection of its essential security interests relating to the supply of services as carried out directly or indirectly for the purpose of provisioning a military establishment, or relating to fissionable and fissionable materials or the materials from which they are derived, or taken in time of war or other emergency in international relations.

(3) To prevent any Member from taking any action in pursuance of its obligations under *the United Nations Charter* for the maintenance of international peace and security.

The GATS thus allows Members to adopt and enforce measures, in the interests of national or international security, otherwise inconsistent with *GATS* obligations. On occasion, the WTO Members take unilateral or multilateral measures affecting trade in services against other Members, as a means to achieve national or international security and peace. Members taking such measures can seek justification for these measures under Article 14(2).

四、具体承诺

《服务贸易总协议》旨在通过国与国之间就服务部门的开放展开谈判，促成世界贸易组织成员方向全球开放其具体的服务部门。通过谈判或主动提出方案，一成员方可以将其承诺开放的部门或分部门列入服务贸易减让表作为《服务贸易总协议》的附件，并给予其他成员方服务和服务提供者不低于减让表所承诺的待遇。《服务贸易总协议》要求，各成员方对其已作出市场准入承诺的部门，不能在部分区域或其全境维持或采取以下 6 类限制措施，除非其在减让表中明确列出。

(1) 限制服务提供者的数量，不论通过数量配额、垄断和专营服务提供者的方式限制，还是通过经济需求检测要求的方式限制。

(2) 以数量配额或经济需求检测要求的形式限制服务交易或资产的总值。

(3) 以数量配额或经济需求检测要求的形式，限制服务网点总数或以指定数量单位表示的服务产出总量。

5.3.4　Specific Commitments

The GATS is designed to open up specific service sectors of the WTO members' markets to international access on a sector-by-sector and a state-by-state basis. Following negotiations or on its own initiative, a member is to submit a schedule of specific commitments for annex to *the GATS* that lists the sectors or subsectors it is opening to market access, which is defined as giving services and service suppliers of other members "treatment no less favorable" than that is listed in the member's schedule. *The GATS* requires that, in sectors where market-access commitments are undertaken, six categories of limitation measures which a member shall not maintain or adopt either on the basis of a regional subdivision or on the basis of its entire territory, unless otherwise specified in its schedule, are defined as:

(1) limitations on the number of service suppliers whether in the form of numerical quotas, monopolies, exclusive service suppliers or the requirements of an economic needs test.

(2) limitations on the value of service transactions or assets in the form of numerical quotas or the requirements of an economic needs test.

(3) limitations on the total number of service operations or the total quantity of service output expressed in terms of designated numerical units in the form of quotas or the requirements of an economic needs test.

(4) 以数量配额或经济需求检测要求的形式，限制特定服务部门或服务提供者可雇用的、为提供特定服务所必需且直接相关的自然人总数。

(5) 限制或要求服务提供者通过特定类型的法律实体或合营企业提供服务的措施。

(6) 通过限制外国股权最高百分比，或限制单笔或总体外国投资总额的方式限制外国资本的参与。

除市场准入以外，各成员方必须遵守的另一具体义务是国民待遇，即成员方给予任何其他成员方的服务和服务提供者的待遇不得低于其给予本国同类服务和服务提供者的待遇。履行国民待遇义务，意味着应取消所有改变竞争条件、所有使外国服务或服务提供者处于不利地位的歧视性措施。另外，也可列入其他限制措施，作为实施与国民待遇义务不符的措施的正当性依据，如歧视性补贴和税收措施、居留要求等。适用国民待遇规定，并不要求外国服务和服务提供者获得的待遇在形式上与给予本国的同类服务和服务提供者相同，而在于两者能够获得平等的竞争机会。

---

(4) limitations on the total number of natural persons that may be employed in a particular service sector or that a service supplier may employ and who are necessary for, and directly related to, the supply of a specific service in the form of numerical quotas or the requirements of an economic needs test.

(5) measures which restrict or require specific types of legal entity or joint venture through which a service supplier may supply a service.

(6) limitations on the participation of foreign capital in terms of maximum percentage limit on foreign shareholding or the total value of individual or aggregate foreign investment.

Apart from market access, the other specific obligation the member must observe is national treatment, which is giving services and service suppliers of other members "treatment no less favorable" than what the member grants its own like services and services suppliers. National treatment implies the absence of all discriminatory measures that may modify the conditions of competition to the detriment of foreign services or service suppliers. Again, limitations may be listed to provide cover for inconsistent measures, such as discriminatory subsidies and tax measures, residency requirements, etc. National treatment obligation applies regardless of whether or not foreign services and service suppliers are treated in a formally identical way by their national counterpart. What matters is that they are granted equal opportunities to compete.

每一个世界贸易组织成员都应以附件形式向《服务贸易总协议》提交具体承诺减让表，在表中对其开放的服务部门作出承诺。对列入减让表的服务部门，必须规定：①市场准入的规定、限制和条件；②国民待遇的条件和资格；③有关附加承诺的承诺；④实施具体承诺的时间表；⑤具体承诺的生效日期。成员方没有义务开放其全部服务部门，有初步研究表明，发展中国家仅开放了约五分之一的服务部门，而发达国家则开放了三分之二左右的服务部门。不过，《服务贸易总协议》从无到有，只是服务贸易多边体制规则化的开始，需要继续展开谈判，促成国际服务贸易的自由化。如果《服务贸易总协议》未来能够取得和《关税与贸易总协定》以往一样多的丰硕成果，国际服务贸易很可能在未来数十年中得到巨大的发展。

五、逐步自由化

鼓励成员方开放尽可能多的服务部门是《服务贸易总协议》的长期目标。为达成目标，《服务贸易总协议》成员应在《世界贸易组织协定》生效日后不迟于 5 年内开始多轮定期谈判，逐步实现更高水平的自由化。谈判应以减少或消除对服务贸易产生不利影响的措施为方向，促进所有参与方互利共赢，确保权利义务的总体平衡。

Each WTO member is required to submit for annex to *GATS* a schedule of specific commitments regarding the service sectors that it has opened to international market access. For each such sector, its Schedule must specify (a) terms, limitations, and conditions on market access, (b)conditions and qualifications on national treatment, (c)undertakings relating to additional commitments, (d)the time frame for implementing its commitments, and (e)the date of entry into force of its commitments. Members are not required open all of their service sectors and one preliminary study illustrates that developing countries have only opened about one-fifth of their service sectors and developed countries about two-thirds of theirs. Nevertheless, *the GATS* is new and it is but a first step. It requires that negotiations continue to liberalize the international trade in services. If *the GATS* is as successful in the future as *GATT* has been in the past, it seems likely that international trade in services will grow dramatically in the decades to come.

5.3.5 Progressive Liberalization

The long-term objective of *the GATS* is to encourage its members to open as many of their service sectors to market access as possible. In pursuance of the objectives of this Agreement, members shall enter into successive rounds of negotiations, beginning not later than five years from the date of entry into force of *the WTO Agreement* and periodically thereafter, with a view to achieving a progressively higher level of liberalization. Such negotiations shall be directed to the reduction or elimination of the adverse effects on trade in services of measures as a means of providing effective market access. This process shall take place with a view to promoting the interests of all participants on a mutually advantageous basis and to securing an overall balance of rights and obligations.

逐步自由化虽然是《服务贸易总协议》的重要目标，但成员方并不受其在服务贸易减让表中所作承诺的永久约束。一成员方在其某项承诺生效之日起 3 年后的任何时间可修改或撤销该承诺，但应提前 3 个月通知服务贸易理事会；如果受此修改或撤销影响的成员方请求，该修改成员方必须进行谈判，以期对必要的补偿性调整达成协议。

六、组织机构和争端解决

《服务贸易总协议》的运作实施由世界贸易组织所有成员代表组成的服务贸易理事会负责监督，其下设有附属机构，包括部门委员会，负责相应部门附件的运作实施。

服务贸易理事会在世界贸易组织框架内执行被赋予的职责，因此，对发展中国家提供与服务贸易有关的技术援助应由经服务贸易理事会决定，由秘书处以多边方式提供。此外，就有关《服务贸易总协议》的事项展开协商以及解决争端均适用世界贸易组织的《关于争端解决规则与程序的谅解》。

Although progressive liberalization is the goal of *GATS*, members are not permanently bound to the commitments they make in their Schedules. A member may modify or withdraw it after a period of three years from the entry into force of a commitment. Before doing so, the member must give the Council for Trade in Services at least three months notice; and, if a member affected by the proposed modification or withdrawal asks, the modifying member must participate in negotiations to agree on appropriate compensatory adjustments.

5.3.6 Organizational Bodies and Dispute Settlement

The operation of *the GATS* is overseen by a Council for Trade in Services made up of representatives of all the WTO members. Subordinate to the Council are several bodies, including sectoral committees responsible for the operation of the different sectoral annexes.

The Council for Trade in Services is meant to function that may be assigned to it within the WTO structure. Thus, technical assistance to developing countries on matters related to trade in services shall be provided at the multilateral level by the Secretariat and shall be decided upon by the Council for Trade in Services. And both consultations and dispute settlements related to *GATS* are governed by the WTO's *Understanding on Rules and Procedures Governing the Settlement of Disputes*.

七、附件

与国际货物贸易相比，服务贸易更具多样化特点。比如电话公司、银行、航空公司和会计师事务所提供服务的方式存在很大差异。《服务贸易总协议》附件便体现了此等多样性。

(1) 关于自然人移动的附件。该附件要求成员方就自然人为提供服务在一国境内短期停留的权利进行谈判。

(2) 关于电信服务的附件。电信服务附件涉及电信服务的跨境竞争、市场开放、公共电信传送网络和终端开放等内容，确认了电信服务部门作为远程经济活动部门和其他经济活动的传送手段的双重属性。

(3) 关于金融服务的附件。该附件中的金融服务，是指一成员方的金融服务提供者所提供的任何具有金融性质的服务，包括所有保险及其相关服务，以及所有银行和其他金融服务(保险除外)。有关金融服务的附件承认各成员方有权对金融交易采取类型和层次不一样的审查措施，只要不是基于拒绝给予国民待遇和市场准入的意图，就不构成对《服务贸易总协议》的违反。不仅如此，金融服务附件还允许其他国家为确保其金融系统完善和稳定而采取审慎措施。

5.3.7　*GATS* Annexes

Unlike international trade in goods, trade in services is much more diverse. Telephone companies, banks, airlines and accountancy firms provide their services in quite different ways. The GATS annexes reflect some of the diversity as follows.

(1) Movement of natural persons. This annex deals with negotiations on individuals' rights to stay temporarily in the country for the purpose of providing a service.

(2) Telecommunications. The annex on telecommunications contemplated competition across frontiers, and access not just to the market in general but to public telecommunications transport networks and terminals. The telecommunications services sector is seen both as distant sector of economic activity and as the underlying transport means for other economic activities.

(3) Financial services. Under this annex, a financial service is any service of a financial nature offered by a financial service supplier of a member. Financial services include all insurance and insurance-related services, and all banking and other financial services (excluding insurance). The annex on financial services acknowledges that, if members impose different kinds or levels of scrutiny of financial transactions without the motive of denying national treatment or market access, they will not thereby be violating *the GATS*. Further, the annex permits recognition of another country's prudential measures to ensure the stability and integrity of the financial system.

（4）关于航空运输服务的附件。在航空运输服务附件中，交通权以及和交通权行使直接相关的服务部门不在《服务贸易总协议》调整范围内，《服务贸易总协定》适用于航空器的修理和保养服务、航空运输服务的销售和营销以及计算机订位系统服务。

综 合 练 习

1. 举例说明《服务贸易总协议》规定的各种服务提供方式。

2. 《服务贸易总协议》与《1994 年关税与贸易总协定》中国民待遇义务的区别是什么？

3. 成员方采取影响服务贸易的措施能否背离其《服务贸易总协议》下最惠国待遇义务？

4. 哪些针对具体服务部门的限制措施可列入具体承诺减让表作为《服务贸易总协议》的附件？

5. 简述《服务贸易总协议》基本内容。

---

(4) Air transport services. Under the annex on air transport services, traffic rights and services directly related to the exercise of traffic rights are excluded from the coverage of *the GATS*. However, the annex specifies that *the GATS* applies to aircraft repair and maintenance services, selling and marketing of air transport services and computer-reservation services.

Comprehensive Exercises

1. Give an example of each mode of supply of services provided for in *the GATS*.

2. What are the differences between the national treatment obligation of *the GATS* and that of *GATT1994*?

3. Can members exempt measures affecting trade in services from the application of the MFN treatment obligation of *the GATS*?

4. What limitation measures applying to specific service sectors can be included in the schedule of specific commitments for the annex to *the GATS*?

5. Give a briefing of the basic content of *the GATS*.

第六章　国际贸易管理法律制度

学习目标

了解国际贸易管理法的概念、特征。

掌握我国进出口管理法律制度。

理解世界贸易组织的基本原则。

掌握世界贸易组织的关税措施、反倾销措施、补贴与反补贴措施等多边规则。

Chapter 6　Legal System on International Trade Administration

Learning Objectives

To know the concept, characteristics of the international trade administration law.

To master China's Legal System on imports and exports administration.

To understand the basic principle of WTO.

To master the multilateral rules of WTO on tariffs, anti-dumping measures, subsidies and countervailing measures, etc.

第一节　国际贸易管理法律制度概述

一、国际贸易管理法的概念

国际贸易是国际经济不可分割的重要组成部分。第二次世界大战以来，随着国际贸易在各国经济发展中作用的凸显，从国内到国际产生了一系列的调整贸易关系的法律。国际贸易管理法就是指主权国家或国际组织对于国际贸易的行为，包括产品、技术、服务贸易的进口与出口，进行管理、控制和服务的法律制度。一般体现为一国所签署的国际贸易条约及其涉外贸易法律制度。

二、国际贸易管理法的特征

与商事交易法相比，国际贸易管理法表现出强制性、层次性、统一性和多边性的特点。

6.1 Introduction to Legal System on the International Trade Administration

6.1.1 Concept of the International Trade Administration Law

International trade is an integral and important part of the international economy. Since World War II, with the important role of international trade in the economic development of countries, there arrives a series of laws relating to adjustment of trade relations from domestic to international range. The international trade administration law covers international trade business of sovereign states or international organizations. It is generally agreed that the international trade administration law is the body of rules and norms that regulates the cross-border transaction in goods, technologies and services between parties, including international trade treaties signed by a country and its foreign trade legal system.

6.1.2 Characteristics of the International Trade Administration Law

Compared with the commercial transactions law, the international trade administration law includes characteristics of mandatoriness, hierarchy, unity and multilaterality.

1. 强制性

无论是国家还是国际经济组织，其管理贸易的法律都属于强制性法律规范，任何人不得随意改变。

2. 层次性

一方面，有全球性的组织、区域性的组织以及国家这些不同层次的管理主体。另一方面，有几乎适用于所有国家的国际性规范和适用于特定国家范围的区域性规范、双边条约和国家立法。

3. 统一性

虽然各国的贸易立法不尽相同，但其遵循的总原则是一致的，这使得国际贸易能够在共同的原则基础上进行。

4. 多边性

多边性是关税与贸易总协定成立以来取得的最大成就。国与国之间的贸易纠纷不再仅仅局限于两国范围内解决，而可以依据共同的规则在多边体制中解决，这就避免了不稳定性，增加了可预见性，从而促进了国际贸易平衡发展。

---

1. Mandatoriness

Whether nations or international economic organizations, their trade administration laws are mandatory laws and regulations, any person can not change them.

2. Hierarchy

On the one hand, there are different levels of the management body, such as global organizations, regional organizations and states. On the other hand, there are international norms applicable to almost all countries, regional norms, treaties and national legislation applicable to the specific nation.

3. Unity

The trade administration legislation in different countries varies, but general principles followed by them are the same, which makes international trade on the basis of the common principles.

4. Multilaterality

The multilateral nature had been the greatest achievement since the GATT was established. Trade disputes between countries are no longer resolved within the two countries range, but also resolved in the multilateral system on the basis of common rules, such resolutions avoid the instability and increase the predictability of international trade resulting the development of international trade balance.

三、国际贸易管理法的渊源

法的渊源是指作为立法和司法效力依据的宪法、条约、法规或惯例。国际贸易管理法的渊源是指对国际贸易活动进行裁决的依据，包括国际条约、公约和国内法。

1. 国际贸易管理的国内法

国内法是国际贸易管理法的主要渊源，它通常是指由特定国家政府对其对外贸易活动进行管理的法律法规的总称。每个国家都会通过立法对跨境交易进行管理，例如，通过立法对商品和服务的进出口进行管理。在国家对对外贸易进行管理的过程中，最常用的是关税和非关税措施。

虽然国际条约或公约的数量日益增加，但国内法在可预见的未来仍将是国际贸易管理法的重要渊源，其原因在于，一方面，虽然国际条约或公约所确立的原则日益为越来越多的国家所认同，但并非全球所有国家都会立即接受这些原则；另一方面，国际贸易管理法领域的众多规则都在不断发展，国家立法机构需要通过国内法确保这些规则实施的有效性。

6.1.3　Sources of the International Trade Administration Law

Source in legal sense refers to something such as a constitution, treaty, statute, or custom that provides authority for legislation and for judicial decisions. Sources of the international trade administration law are what international tribunals rely upon in determining the content of the international trade administration law, and they include international treaties and conventions and national law.

1. Domestic Law of the International Trade Administration

National law is usually the most extensive way of law-making, and one of the most important sources of the international trade administration law. It refers to all rules and norms by a specific state. The government of a country usually controls over international trade by its own foreign trade law. Each state has established its own legal system governing cross-border transactions. For instance, importing and exporting are governed by the law and regulations of the countries through which goods and services pass. Nations regulate international trade in many ways. The most common methods are tariffs and non-tariffs measures.

Although there are increasing numbers of international treaties or conventions, national law is and will be an important source of the international trade administration law in the foreseeable future, chiefly because, on the one hand, though the principles of international treaties or conventions are universally recognized, they are not accepted by all countries in the world; on the other hand, many rules in the international trade administration law are continuously developed, and state legislature is needed to assure efficient enforcement and authority to the rules.

2. 国际贸易管理的国际法

国际贸易管理的国际法制度是指调整国家与国家之间贸易关系的国际条约、国际贸易组织的宣言、决议等文件所形成的制度体系。依据世界贸易组织的目标，制定国际贸易管理的国际法律制度的目的在于：国家间的贸易和经济联系应致力于提高人民的生活水平，保证充分就业和大幅度稳步提高实际收入和有效需求，扩大货物与服务的生产和贸易，为持续发展之目的而扩大对世界资源的充分利用的同时，寻求保护和维护环境，并以符合不同经济发展水平下各自需要的方式，加强采取各种相应的措施。

国际贸易管理法的国际法渊源主要包括两种制度形式，即国际条约和国际贸易组织的宣言、决议等文件。

2. International Law of the International Trade Administration

International law of the international trade administration is the system of international treaties, or declarations, resolutions and other documents of the international trade organization to adjust the trade relations between countries. In accordance with the objectives of the WTO, the development of the international legal regime for international trade administration aims: nation's relations in the field of trade and economy should be conducted with a view to raising standards of living, ensuring full employment and a large and steadily growing volume of real income and effective demand, and expanding the production of and trade in goods and services, while allowing for the optimal use of the world's resources in accordance with the objective of sustainable development, seeking both to protect and preserve the environment and to enhance the means for doing so in a manner consistent with their respective needs and concerns at different levels of economic development.

Sources of international law of the international trade administration mainly consist of two parts: international treaties and the declarations, resolutions and other documents of the international trade organization.

(1) 国际条约是两个或两个以上的主权国家之间订立的具有法律约束力的协议。公约是作为国际组织的成员国间订立的具有法律约束力的协议。在国际贸易管理领域，一些条约的目的在于促进缔约国间的贸易自由化，如《关税与贸易总协定》。条约和公约对缔约国均具有法律约束力，因为其建立在协商一致的基础上，同时，如果一缔约国不遵守其在公约或条约中的义务，其他缔约国亦不会履行其承诺。条约或公约的各项条款构成缔约国国内法的一部分，对于某一特定的条约或公约，仅对其缔约国具有约束力。还有一些条约(在订立后)并不立即生效或仅适用于特定的缔约国之间。有鉴于此，很多具有统一法性质的公约或条约仅仅实现了有限程度或特定区域内的统一。

一些重要的条约或公约成为国际贸易管理法的渊源，它们包括但不限于：《北美自由贸易协定》《世界贸易组织协定》等。

(2) 国际贸易组织的文件，包括国际贸易组织本身赖以产生、存在和运作的规范性文件。这类基本文件一般明确表明各签约方建立组织的意图，并对拟建立的机构的宗旨、组织结构、职能范围、活动程序、成员的权利义务等重大问题进行了规定，是国际贸易组织的章程。

---

(1) International treaties are legally binding agreements between two (bilateral treaties)or more states (multilateral treaties). Conventions are legally binding agreements between states sponsored by the international organizations. In the field of the international trade administration, the purpose of some treaties is to liberalize trade between the contracting states such as *the GATT*. Both are binding upon states because of a shared sense of commitment, and because one state fears that if it does not respect its promises in conventions or treaties, the others will not respect their promises too. The provisions of the treaties or conventions become part of the national law of the contracting states. For a specific treaty or convention, only the contracting states are bound by it. A number of treaties are, for instance, not yet in force or at present only applied by a limited number of countries. For that reason many unifying law treaties or conventions achieve only a limited or a regional unification.

There are some important international treaties or conventions as the source of the international trade administration law. They include but not limited to: *the North America Free Trade Agreement (NAFTA), WTO Agreements*, etc.

(2) Documents of the international trade organization include the documents about the emergence, existence and operation of the international trade organization which itself depends on. Such documents show clearly the intent and purpose that the signatories establish the organization. These documents are the statutes of the international trade organization, which provide the purpose of the proposed institutions, organizational structure, scope of functions, activities program, the rights and obligations of the members.

第二节　国际贸易管理的国内法制度

一、国际贸易管理的国内法制度概述

进口和出口的货物、服务和技术，在一定程度上，由国家贸易管理法进行规定。这样的规定，通常为了促进一国经济目标的实现。一国制定国家贸易管理法的目的在于通过促进出口或减少进口消费以维持本国的贸易平衡；保护国家资源；通过抑制供给或促进国内产业的增长以维持特定商品的国际市场价格。除了上述经济目标以外，控制进出口法规的实施还服从于国家的特定政治和国家安全目标，表现在对政治同盟内国家之间的贸易往来进行鼓励而对潜在的敌国进行贸易制裁，以达到限制其国家的军事能力，对其实施制裁，或促使它改变其政策的目的。例如，美国就是通过贸易制裁实现其外交政策和国家安全目标的主要倡导者，保持着对许多国家进行经济制裁的不良记录。

国家通过法律法规对货物、技术和服务的进出口进行管理和控制的手段是多种多样的，主要包括关税、非关税壁垒和出口限制措施。

6.2　Domestic Law of the International Trade Administration

6.2.1　Introduction to Domestic Law of the International Trade Administration

Imports and exports of goods, services and technologies are, to some degree, regulated by the domestic trade administration laws. Such regulations usually aim at the economic objectives for the nation. One possible economic objective might be to affect the balance of the trade, perhaps by promoting exports or by reducing consumption of imports. Other economic objectives might be to conserve national resources, maintain world price of a commodity by withholding supplies or foster growth in a domestic industry. However, domestic regulations on imports and exports are used to implement not only economic policy but also political and national security objectives. These regulations can be used to encourage trade with political ally or to discourage the trade with a potential foe, to limit the military capacity of another country, or to sanction a country or induce it to change its policies. For instance, the U.S. is the leading proponent of export sanctions to accomplish foreign policy and national security objectives and punish other states. Although these economic sanctions have a poor track record, the U.S. maintains them against many countries.

Importing and exporting is governed by the law and regulations of the countries through which goods, technologies or services pass. Nations regulate trade in many ways. The most common methods are tariffs, non-tariff barriers and export restrictions.

二、关税

关税是一国政府对进出口货物所征收的税收。各个国家都有不同的关税管理规定，主要包括五种类型：财政关税、从价税、从量税、禁止性关税和保护性关税。财政关税亦称收入关税，是以增加国家财政收入为主要目的而征收的关税。例如，不种植香蕉的国家可能会对进口香蕉征税，然后政府从经营香蕉进口业务的企业获得相应的收入。从价关税是以进口商品价格为标准征收的关税，按商品价格的一定百分比征收。从量关税与商品价格无关，而是以货物的计量单位(数量、重量、体积)为计征标准而计算征收的一种关税。禁止性关税是指对某些商品加重课征，使进口品在国内的价格高于本国生产的同种商品，从而实质上禁止进口，使进口行为得不偿失。保护性关税是一种通过提高进口商品价格来应对国外市场竞争的保护性措施，使得国内企业能够与承担了更高税负的进口产品企业相竞争。

关税主要是针对进口商品征收的国内税。关税的征收使得国内产品拥有了相对于同类进口产品的价格优势，同时增加了政府的财政收入。乌拉圭回合谈判的成果之一就是各成员方承诺削减关税并将其海关税率约束在难以提高的水平。目前在多哈回合谈判中主要集中于农产品和非农产品的市场准入。

6.2.2 Tariffs

A tariff is a tax placed on imported or exported goods. Each country has separate regulations, but there are five main types of tariffs: revenue, *ad valorem*, specific, prohibitive and protective. A revenue tariff increases government funds. For example, countries that do not grow bananas may create a tax on importing bananas. The government would then make money from businesses that import the fruit. An *ad valorem* tariff means that the tax applies to a percentage of the import's value. A specific tariff, on the other hand, means that the tax is not concerned with the estimated value of the imported goods, but rather is based on specific amount of the goods. This type may apply to the number of goods imported or to the weight, volume or other measurement of the goods. A prohibitive tariff is one that high cost keeps the item from being imported. A protective tariff is used to raise the price of imported goods as a protective measure against the competitors from foreign markets. A higher tax allows a local company to compete with foreign competition.

Tariffs are mainly domestic taxes imposed on imported goods. Tariffs give a price advantage to locally-produced goods over similar goods which are imported, and they raise revenues for governments. One result of the Uruguay Round was countries' commitments to cut tariffs and to "bind" their customs duty rates to levels which are difficult to raise. The current negotiations under the Doha Agenda continue efforts in agriculture and non-agricultural market access.

三、非关税壁垒

非关税壁垒是指除关税以外的一切措施。很多非关税壁垒源自国家安全和公众健康保护规则，其他的则涉及环境保护、消费者权益保护、产品标准和政府采购，这些措施往往是基于对合法的消费者和公共利益进行保护而创设的。相对于关税措施而言，非关税壁垒由于其隐蔽性的特点，对国际贸易的阻碍更大。与关税措施不同，非关税壁垒往往以政府法规或行业规定的形式被掩盖起来，外国公司往往难以理解。国家通过这些非关税壁垒来保护本国的经济、社会和政治利益。进口货物往往会因为健康和安全方面的原因被禁止进口。进口货物通常必须注明原产国并以进口国的语言进行标记，以便消费者了解他们所购买的进口货物。常见的非关税壁垒包括：技术性贸易壁垒或产品标准，表现为安全标准、电气标准和环保标准。例如，德国生产的汽车如果要进入美国市场必须符合美国的排放标准而非欧洲的同类标准。配额措施，是指通过法律规定对某些敏感商品的进口进行数量或金额上的控制。与关税措施不同，除一些特殊情况外，并非所有国家都认为配额措施是国家管理国际贸易的合法手段。贸易禁运，是指完全或几乎完全禁止与某一特定国家进行贸易，这种措施往往通过军事手段实施并出于某种政治目的。例如，1990 年伊拉克入侵科威特后，国际社会就精心策划了对伊拉克的贸易禁运，这一措施在 2003 年春季美国发动伊拉克战争后得到了进一步加强。抵制，通常是指因为政治或其他原因，拒绝与来自某一特定国家的某些公司进行贸易或商业往来。

6.2.3 Non-tariff Barriers

Non-tariff barriers are all barriers to importing and exporting other than tariffs. Many of these barriers arise out of state safety and health regulations. Others concern the environment protection, customer protection, product standards and government procurement. Many of the relevant rules are created for legitimate consumer and public protection reasons. Non-tariff barriers are generally a greater barrier to trade than tariffs, because they are more insidious. Unlike tariffs, non-tariff barriers are often disguised in the form of government rules or industry regulations and are often not understood by foreign companies. Countries impose non-tariff barriers to protect their national economic, social, and political interest. Imports might be banned for health and safety reasons. Imported goods usually have to be marked with the country-of-origin and labeled in the local language so that consumers know what they are buying. One form of non-tariff barriers is the technical barrier to trade, or product standard. Examples of product standards include safety standards, electrical standards and environmental standards. For example, German cars should be complied with the U.S. emission standards not mandated in Europe. A quota is a restriction imposed by law on the quantities or amounts of goods, or of a particular type of goods, allowed to be imported. Unlike tariffs, quotas are not internationally accepted as a lawful means regulating trade except in some special case. An embargo is a total or near total ban on trade with a particular country, sometimes enforced by military action and usually imposed for political purpose. An internationally orchestrated embargo was used against Iraq after its invasion on Kuwait in 1990.This embargo was strengthened by the U.S. invasion on Iraq in the spring of 2003. A boycott is a refusal to trade or do business with certain firms, usually from a particular country, on political or other grounds.

　　关税和非关税壁垒对企业的贸易和投资决策有着巨大的影响。反过来，企业的这些决定又反映了世界贸易和国际投资流动的方向和趋势。例如，当日本企业了解到墨西哥制造的产品在北美地区销售将面临更低的关税和更少的非关税壁垒时，日本公司就迅速寻求在墨西哥建立生产基地，以便利用这些贸易法律变化带来的优势。具有海外投资愿望的中国企业也应对外国的贸易管制手段给予应有的重视，并迅速采取措施，开拓国外市场。

四、出口限制

　　出口限制是政府控制贸易的另一重要手段。出口限制或限制出口，是指政府对出口到某一或某些特定国家的货物数量进行控制。例如，如果没有获得美国或加拿大政府的授权，某些高科技电脑可能无法从美国或加拿大运到另一个国家。政府实施出口管制措施的目的在于实现财政收入、发展和社会政策等目标。尤其是一些国家的政府通过对金属和矿物的出口限制来实现环境保护和自然资源保护的目标。例如，中国政府不允许出口某些原料，这些相关出口限制措施的主要目的是保护环境和节约自然资源，中国的出口商在这些原材料的销售合同签订之前，就必须考虑他们是否能够获得将货物出口的许可。

Tariff and non-tariff barriers have a tremendous influence on how firms make their trade and investment decisions. These decisions in turn are reflected in the patterns of world trade and the flows of investment capital. For example, when Japanese firms learned that Mexican-made products could be traded in North America with lowered tariffs and non-tariff barriers, companies from Japan quickly sought to establish manufacturing facilities in Mexico to take advantage of changes in trade laws. Chinese firms who wish to invest abroad have to pay due attention to the means of trade controls by foreign countries, and take quick measures to penetrate foreign markets.

6.2.4　Export Restrictions

Export restrictions are another important type of control over trade by government. Export restrictions, or a restriction on exportation, are limitations on the quantity of goods exported to a specific country or countries by a government. For instance, high-tech computers might not be shipped from the United States or Canada to another country without license from the U.S. or Canadian governments. Governments apply export restrictions to achieve several policy objectives. These include fiscal revenue, development and social policies. Specifically, several governments have applied export restrictions on metals and minerals for objectives such as environmental protection and the conservation of natural resources. For instances, Chinese government does not allow some raw materials to be exported. The chief aim of such export policies is to protect the environment and conserve natural resources. Before signing a contract for the sale of these raw materials, Chinese exporter must consider whether they will be able to obtain licensing for the shipment.

一国实施出口限制措施可能出于以下目的。

(1) 防止某些货物因出口利润更高而大量输出导致国内市场供应短缺。

(2) 控制因某种货物的大量出口对进口国的国内市场造成影响以避免进口国对其征收反倾销税。

(3) 作为外交政策，例如贸易制裁的一个组成部分。

(4) 约束和限制武器扩散或被用于恐怖主义、核利用、生化武器等其他用途。

(5) 约束和限制与被贸易禁运国家的贸易。

五、国家服务进出口贸易制度

在国际贸易的实践中，基于国际贸易在经济发展中的重要地位与作用，各国均采取金融、关税等各种不同的措施服务和鼓励国际贸易的进行，即国家服务进出口贸易的制度。常见的措施如下。

A country may implement export restrictions for the following purposes.

(1) To prevent a shortage of goods in the domestic market because it is more profitable to export.

(2) To manage the effect on the domestic market of the importing country, which may otherwise impose anti-dumping duties on the imported goods.

(3) As part of foreign policy, for example as a component of trade sanctions.

(4) To limit or restrict arms or dual-use items that may be used in proliferation, terrorism, or nuclear, chemical and biological warfare.

(5) To limit or restrict trade to the embargoed nations.

6.2.5　National Service Trade System

Basing on the importance and effect of international trade to economy, many nations use different measures, both finance and customs, to serve and encourage international trade, which is the national service trade system in international trade. The common measures are:

1. 建立和完善为对外贸易服务的金融机构和措施

许多国家专门研究建立支持进出口的金融机制，如设立进出口银行等专门金融机构为进出口企业提供信贷；政府为进出口企业提供担保、利息补贴和保险；通过设立对外贸易发展基金、风险基金，增加贷款规模；扩大对进出口企业的贷款利率浮动范围；放宽出口打包、抵押贷款及多种保函的条件；建立保证进出口的金融融资渠道和出口保险机制，增加对外保险的险种及降低保险金额等；利用金融机构为贸易公司提供金融服务。其中最常使用的措施是出口信贷。出口信贷是西方国家的银行对本国出口企业提供的一种信贷，是鼓励出口的一种重要措施。出口信贷包括卖方信贷和买方信贷。

2. 设置权威性的机构通过补贴扩大出口

一些国家为了扩大本国的进出口贸易，专门设置权威性的机构，通过补贴、减免税等方式扩大出口。出口补贴方式包括直接补贴和间接补贴两种。直接补贴是指一国政府或同业协会对某些商品的出口向当地出口厂商直接付给现金补贴，以弥补出口商品的贸易损失或提高其对国外市场的竞争能力。

1. Building and Consummating Financial Organization and Measures to Serve International Trade

Many nations lay special focus on the research of building financial mechanism supporting international trade, such as setting up special financial organizations (export-import bank) to provide credit for trading companies, with government providing assurance, interest subsidy and insurance; constructing development and risk fund for international trade, expanding the loan range; enlarging the floating range of loans to trading companies; broadening conditions for packing and mortgage loan as well as assure letter; building financing channels and export insurance mechanism, increasing insurance category and reducing insurance fees; using financial organizations to support trading companies by providing financial service, one of the most common-used measures is export credit loan. Export credit loan is one of the most important measures adopted by banks in western countries to encourage domestic export. Export credit loan includes selling party loan and buying party loan.

2. Establishing Authoritative Organization to Expand Exports through Increasing Subsidy

By providing subsidy and reducing tax, some countries construct authoritative organizations to expand trading, especially the exports. Export subsidy includes both direct and indirect subsidy. Direct subsidy refers to government and craft union providing direct cash subsidy to the export company, balancing the trading loss for exporting goods and enhancing competition for foreign market.

3. 成立专门机构开展对外贸易促进活动

许多国家成立了专门的机构或进出口商会，开展对外联系，举办展览，提供信息、咨询、人员培训和其他对外贸易的促进活动。

4. 通过国内立法为本国企业创造更好的贸易条件

一些外贸法比较发达的国家，通过国内法抵制由于贸易保护主义而产生的各种形式的贸易壁垒，从而为本国企业赢得更好的贸易条件。如美国"301 条款"就是非常典型的制度代表。根据美国《1988 年综合贸易与竞争法》的规定，301 条款分为三种：一般 301 条款、特殊 301 条款及超级 301 条款。

5. 为进出口贸易建立提供信息、交易和管理的新渠道

许多国家利用先进的科学技术手段建立 EDI 网络，为进出口贸易提供信息、交易和管理的新平台。各国普遍建立了数量众多的服务于国际贸易的网站，既有官方的，也有民间的。这样，一是可利用电子商务网创造贸易机会，扩大企业出口和销售，提高文件传递和处理速度，减少中间环节，提高资金周转速度和贸易各方的合作能力，降低交易成本等；二是为企业创造条件，推动企业进行国际竞争；三是利用电子商务网及时了解重点行业和出口商品的贸易情况，从而为企业提供参与国际贸易的机会及途径，推动国际贸易的发展。

---

3. Setting up Special Organizations to Facilitate International Trade Activities

Many nations set up special organizations or import and export chamber of commerce, providing external contact, hosting exhibitions, offering information, consulting, training and other trade facilitating activities.

4. Developing Legislation to Facilitate Trading Conditions for Domestic Companies

Using domestic laws to counteract various trading barriers coming from trade protectionism, some nations with advanced trade laws gained better trading conditions for their domestic companies. Taking the U.S. 301 terms for example, according to *Omnibus Trade and Competitiveness Act of 1988*, the 301 terms include: regular, special, and super 301 terms.

5. Providing New Channels of Information, Trading and Management for Import and Export Trade

Using modern technology, many nations developed EDI network to provide information, trading and management for import and export trade. Each nation has built numerous websites to serve the international trade, both official and non-official. These methods can provide several advantages for the international trade. Firstly, using electrical commercial network, we can expand the export and sale, enhance the speed of document transferring and processing, reduce intermediate process, and lower the competition cost as well as increase the cash flow and cooperation skill among companies. Secondly, offering conditions for companies to participate in international competition. Thirdly, by using electrical commercial network, we can learn about the status quo of main industry and export goods, and offer opportunities and approaches for companies to participate in the international trade and facilitate the development of the international trade.

六、中国的进出口管理法律制度

中国管理进口出口货物、技术和服务的法律制度，包括中国国内的法律以及由中国签署或加入的国际条约，如《世界贸易组织协定》。从 1949 年到 1994 年，中国的对外贸易管理发生了很大的变化，1994 年《中国对外贸易法》的颁布是我国对外贸易管理立法的一个里程碑。然而，2001 年 12 月 11 日中国加入世界贸易组织后，《中国对外贸易法》与世界贸易组织多边协议的冲突日益显露。为填补原《中国对外贸易法》的空白，修正其与世界贸易组织多边协议的不符之处，从而在新形势下更好地促进中国对外贸易的发展，全国人民代表大会于 2004 年 4 月 6 日颁布了修订后的《中华人民共和国对外贸易法》，2004 年 7 月 1 日起生效。另外，还颁布了一系列与对外贸易有关的行政法规，如：货物进出口管理条例(2001)、技术进出口管理条例(2002)、进出口货物原产地规则(2005)、禁止或限制进口技术目录(2007)。除此之外，《世界贸易组织协定》、中国加入世界贸易组织议定书以及加入工作组报告也是中国进出口管理法律制度的组成部分。

6.2.6　China's Legal System on Imports and Exports Administration

China's administration on imports and exports of goods, technologies and services are embodied in China's domestic laws as well as the international treaties signed or acceded to by China, such as *the WTO Agreements*. From 1949 to 1994, great changes took place in this field. And in 1994, the milestone legislation for regulations on foreign trade—*the Foreign Trade Law of the People's Republic of China* was promulgated. However, after China's entry into the WTO on December 11, 2001, some gaps were revealed between *Foreign Trade Law of the People's Republic of China* and *the WTO Agreements*. In order to bridge the gaps and to facilitate the trade of China under new circumstances, on April 6, 2004, the National People's Congress promulgated the revision of *the Foreign Trade Law of the People's Republic of China*, which took effect on July 1, 2004. Besides, a number of regulations and measures related to the regulation of foreign trade were passed, including but not limited to, *Regulations on Imports and Exports of Goods(2001), Regulations on Technology Import and Export Administration of the People's Republic of China(2002), Regulations on Origins of Goods for Imports and Exports(2005), Schedule for Prohibitive and Restrictive Technologies to be Imported(2007)*. Moreover, as a WTO member state, *the WTO Agreements* as well as the Protocol on the Accession of the People's Republic of China and the Report of the Working Party on the Accession of China in document are integral parts of China's administration on imports and exports.

经国务院授权，中国负责对进出口贸易进行管理的主管机关是中华人民共和国商务部，对外贸易实行分级管理。各省、市、自治区经贸厅(委)对同级地方人民政府和商务部负责，并根据授权，对本地区的外贸进行行政管理和督促检查。

第三节　关税与贸易总协定和世界贸易组织的法律制度

一、关税与贸易总协定/世界贸易组织概述

在过去的 60 年里，世界各国致力于消除贸易保护主义的国内立法和促进商品的自由贸易的国际合作，促成了国际贸易的大幅增长。20 世纪 30 年代许多领域的大萧条是贸易保护主义的直接后果。美国通过 1930 年《赫尔利–斯姆特关税法案》对超过 900 种商品提高关税时，引发了世界其他主要贸易国家的竞相报复。第二次世界大战期间，贸易保护主义因其破坏性受到了广泛反对，世界各国迫切希望建立一个全面解决全球政治经济问题的多边体制。

In China, the competent authority in charge of administration on imports and exports is the Ministry of Commerce of the People's Republic of China, receiving the delegation from the State Council. At the provincial level, the bureau of commerce or bureau of foreign trade is responsible for regulating imports and exports affairs within its own region. They shall account for the local government at the same level as well as the Ministry of Commerce.

6.3　Legal System on the GATT and WTO

6.3.1　An Overview of the GATT and WTO

International trade has grown dramatically in the past sixty years. This is largely because the world's nations have cooperated in eliminating protectionist domestic legislation and in promoting the free exchange of goods. The Great Depression of the 1930s in many ways was a direct consequence of protectionism. When the United States raised tariffs on more than 900 items with *the Hawley-Smoot Tariffs Act* of 1930, the other major trading nations of the world reciprocated with similar increases. During World War II, the protectionist sentiments of the 1930s were rejected as destructive, and they were swept aside in a rush to arrange a comprehensive network of multilateral agreements to settle the world's political and economic problems.

1943 年，反法西斯同盟国家呼吁创设一套全面的国际制度，以鼓励贸易自由化和多边经济合作。1944 年 7 月，在布雷顿森林召开的联合国货币金融会议决定建立一个致力于贸易自由化和多边经济合作的体制。布雷顿森林体系原计划成立三个国际组织作为其核心：国际货币基金组织(IMF)、国际复兴开发银行(IBRD，世界银行)和国际贸易组织(ITO)。相对于前两个组织，国际贸易组织发展不顺。虽然国际贸易组织没有能够成立，但是发达的市场经济国家在 1947 年签订了《关税与贸易总协定》。《1947 年关税与贸易总协定》是一个多边条约，条约规定了缔约国以"互惠互利"为基础，开展有关"关税和其他贸易障碍的大幅度削减"的谈判。在其他国家陆续加入后，《1947 年关税与贸易总协定》规范了绝大部分全球贸易。

为使《1947 年关税与贸易总协定》能够适应国际贸易的发展，各主要缔约方先后完成了被称为"回合"的八轮多边贸易谈判。第八轮乌拉圭回合的谈判成果使得关税与贸易总协定体制发生了重大变化，以一个全新的机构——世界贸易组织取代了原先非正式的关税与贸易总协定。

In 1943, the nations fighting Germany, Italy, and Japan called for the creation of an integrated international system to encourage trade liberalization and multilateral economic cooperation. The negotiators who met for the United Nations Monetary and Financial Conference in Bretton Woods in July 1944 were determined to create a system that would promote trade liberalization and multilateral economic cooperation. As originally planned, the Bretton Woods System was to have had at its core three major international organizations: the International Monetary Fund (IMF), the International Bank for Reconstruction and Development (IBRD or World Bank), and the ill-fated International Trade Organization (ITO). Instead of creating an ITO, the developed market-economy countries entered into an accord in 1947 called *the General Agreement on Tariffs and Trade (GATT 1947)*. *GATT 1947* was a multilateral treaty that set out the principles under which its contracting states, on the basis of "reciprocity and mutual advantage", were to negotiate "a substantial reduction in customs tariffs and other impediments to trade". With the addition of other states in subsequent years, *GATT 1947* came to govern almost all of the world's trade.

To keep *GATT 1947* up-to-date, the contracting parties regularly participated in multilateral trade negotiations, informally called rounds. Eight rounds of multilateral trade negotiations were held and finished. The eighth round (called the Uruguay Round) brought about a major change in the institutional structure of the GATT, replacing the informal GATT institution with a new institution: the World Trade Organization.

关税与贸易总协定/世界贸易组织建立起了一个有组织的多边体制，为国际贸易法的顺利发展提供了稳定的国际政治、经济、法律环境。其主要目的是通过消除各种人为的障碍和各国施加的贸易保护目的限制措施，实现无扭曲的国际贸易。

依据国际条约建立起来的关税与贸易总协定/世界贸易组织规则已经成为国际贸易法律的指导原则，任何成员方的管理国际贸易的国内法规都必须依据关税与贸易总协定/世界贸易组织规则制定。作为缔约方，成员方的立法机构和政府机构都应按照关税与贸易总协定/世界贸易组织的基本原则来设置关税税率和实施进口管制措施。

二、世界贸易组织的基本原则——非歧视原则

世界贸易组织最基本的原则是国际贸易的开展不应存在歧视，这一原则的具体形式是最惠国待遇原则和国民待遇原则。

1. 最惠国待遇原则——给予外国贸易伙伴相同的待遇

根据世界贸易组织协议，各成员方需要对所有贸易伙伴一视同仁而不能采取歧视措施。例如，仅对来自一个或几个特定国家的进口产品给予较低的关税税率。

GATT/WTO provides an organized global structure to improve the political, economic, and legal climate for trade. Its primary goal is to achieve distortion-free trade through the removal of artificial barriers and restrictions imposed by self-serving national governments.

GATT/WTO rules are created by international agreements and become guiding principles of international trade law, upon which a WTO member party's own trade regulations are to be based. As the agreement states, their national legislatures and government agencies will comply with GATT/WTO principles in setting tariffs and regulating imports.

6.3.2 Principle of the WTO—Nondiscrimination

The most fundamental principle of WTO is that international trade should be conducted without discrimination. This principle is given concrete form in the most-favored-nation treatment (MFN) and national treatment.

1. Most-Favored-Nation Treatment (MFN): Treating All the Foreign Trading Partners Equally

Under the WTO agreements, countries cannot normally discriminate between their trading partners. Grant someone a special favor (such as a lower customs duty rate for one of their products) and you have to do the same for all the WTO members.

这一原则被称为最惠国待遇(MFN)。因其重要性，最惠国待遇原则被写入了规范货物贸易的《关税与贸易总协定》第一条之中。尽管具体规定略有不同，但最惠国待遇也是《服务贸易总协议》和《与贸易有关的知识产权协定》的重要条款。上述三个协定/协议涵盖了世界贸易组织规范国际贸易的三大领域。

《关税与贸易总协定》第 1 条规定："一缔约方对来自或运往其他国家的产品所给予的利益、优待、特权或豁免，应当立即无条件地给予来自或运往所有其他缔约方的相同产品。"最惠国待遇原则要求成员方的关税措施应对所有贸易伙伴同样适用。这意味着：一方应保证把给予任何特定国家的贸易优惠(如消除贸易壁垒或开放国内市场)同时给予同一商品或服务的其他成员方，而不论该商品或服务所属国家的强弱或经济发展水平如何。

最惠国待遇原则存在若干例外，它不适用于以下情况。

(1) 为反倾销和反补贴采取的措施。

(2) 关税同盟和自由贸易区的设立。

(3) 为保护公众健康、安全、福利和国家安全而采取的措施。

除此之外，世界贸易组织规定了发展中国家例外，为了促进和保护发展中国家的经济，鼓励发达国家采取措施，给予发展中国家更优惠的特殊和差别待遇。

This principle is known as most-favored-nation treatment (MFN). It is so important that it is the first article of *the General Agreement on Tariffs and Trade (GATT)*, which governs trade in goods. MFN is also a priority in *the General Agreement on Trade in Services (GATS)* and *the Agreement on Trade-Related Aspects of Intellectual Property Rights (TRIPS)*, although in each agreement the principle is handled slightly differently. Together, those three agreements cover all three main areas of trade handled by the WTO.

Article 1 of *GATT* provides: "Any advantage, favour, privilege or immunity granted by any contracting party to any product originating in or destined for any other country shall be accorded immediately and unconditionally to the like product originating in or destined for the territories of all other contracting parties." The MFN rule requires each member to apply its tariff rules equally to all other members. It means that every time a country lowers a trade barrier or opens up a market, it has to do so for the same goods or services from all its trading partners—whether rich or poor, weak or strong.

Some exceptions are allowed. The rule does not apply to:

(1) The use of measures to counter dumping and subsidization.

(2) The creation of customs unions and free trade areas.

(3) Restrictions that protect public health, safety, welfare, and national security.

In addition to these three exceptions to the MFN rule and the principle of nondiscrimination, WTO provides for a special exception in the case of developing countries. In order to promote and protect the economies of developing countries, WTO encourages the developed countries not to demand reciprocity from them in trade negotiation, and it authorizes developed countries to adopt measures that give more favourable and differential treatment to developing countries.

2. 国民待遇原则——给予外国生产者与本国生产者相同的待遇

国民待遇原则是世界贸易组织非歧视原则的另一体现。《关税与贸易总协定》第 3 条规定："缔约各方认为，国内税和其他国内费用，影响产品的国内销售、推销、购买、运输、分配或使用的法令、条例和规定，以及对产品的混合、加工或使用须符合特定数量或比例要求的国内数量限制条例，在对进口产品或国产产品实施时，不应用来对国内生产提供保护。一缔约方领土的产品输入到另一缔约方领土时，不应对它直接或间接征收高于对相同的国产产品所直接或间接征收的国内税或其他国内费用。同时，缔约方不应对进口产品或国产产品采用其他与本条第 1 款规定的原则有抵触的办法来实施国内税或其他国内费用。一缔约方领土的产品输入到另一缔约方领土时，在关于产品的国内销售、推销、购买、运输、分配或使用的全部法令、条例和规定方面，所享受的待遇应不低于相同的国产产品所享受的待遇。"

---

2. National Treatment: Treating Domestic and Foreign Producers Equally

The national treatment rule is the second manifestation of the principle of nondiscrimination that appears in WTO. Article 3 of *GATT* provides: "The contracting parties recognize that internal taxes and other internal charges, and laws, regulations and requirements affecting the internal sale, offering for sale, purchase, transportation, distribution or use of products, and internal quantitative regulations requiring the mixture, processing or use of products in specified amounts or proportions, should not be applied to imported or domestic products so as to afford protection to domestic production. The products of the territory of any contracting party imported into the territory of any other contracting party shall not be subject, directly or indirectly, to internal taxes or other internal charges of any kind in excess of those applied, directly or indirectly, to like domestic products. Moreover, no contracting party shall otherwise apply internal taxes or other internal charges to imported or domestic products in a manner contrary to the principles set forth in paragraph 1. The products of the territory of any contracting party imported into the territory of any other contracting party shall be accorded treatment no less favorable than that accorded to like products of national origin in respect of all laws, regulations and requirements affecting their internal sale, offering for sale, purchase, transportation, distribution or use."

　　国民待遇原则旨在确保进口产品在进入国内市场时至少能享有国内相同产品的同等待遇。这一规定同样适用于来自外国的服务、商标、版权和专利。尽管具体规定略有差异，国民待遇原则在世界贸易组织三大协定/协议中均有规定(《关税与贸易总协定》第 3 条，《服务贸易总协议》第 17 条，《与贸易有关知识产权协定》第 3 条)。与最惠国待遇原则相比，国民待遇寻求国产商品和进口商品的平等待遇，而最惠国待遇原则寻求不同出口国的产品之间的平等待遇；国民待遇原则只涉及来自某一外国生产者的产品、服务、知识产权在进入成员方国内市场后所涉及的税费和管制措施。因此，对进口产品征收关税本身并不会被视为对国民待遇原则的违反，尽管国内相同产品无须缴纳该项税费。

The national treatment provisions of *GATT* intend to ensure that imported and locally-produced goods should be treated equally—at least after the foreign goods have entered the market. The same should apply to foreign and domestic services, and to foreign and local trademarks, copyrights and patents. This principle of national treatment (giving others the same treatment as one's own nationals) is also found in all the three main WTO agreement (Article 3 of *GATT*, Article 17 of *GATS* and Article 3 of *TRIPS*). Although once again the principle is handled slightly differently in each of these. In contrast to the MFN rule, which requires nondiscrimination at a country's border, the national treatment rule requires a country to treat products equally with its own domestic products once they are inside its borders. National treatment only applies once a product, service or item of intellectual property has entered the market. Therefore, charging customs duty on an import is not a violation of national treatment even if locally-produced products are not charged an equivalent tax.

三、货物贸易的多边协议

1. 《农产品协议》

在乌拉圭回合及多哈发展议程中，农产品贸易问题一直是焦点。《农产品协议》确立了"发起农业贸易改革进程"的准则。其最终目标是，实现完全以市场为导向而不受任何限制和扭曲的自由贸易。它要求世界贸易组织成员解除对农产品贸易的非关税壁垒(包括配额、税收和关税、许可证制度)，取而代之的是采取关税措施，以确保同样水平的保护。这就是所谓的"单一关税保护"。而对于国内支持措施的采取上，发达国家和发展中国家成员都应当着力减少措施对农产品价格所带来的影响。协议实施期间，对于农产品出口补贴上，发达国家同意减少 36%的出口补贴份额，与之相应的是，发展中国家减少 24%。上述补贴措施均已在《农产品协议》中进行了明确规定。《农产品协议》已逐步确立了成员各方的义务。

6.3.3　Multilateral Agreements on Trade in Goods

1. *Agreement on Agriculture*

Agricultural issues played a central role in the Uruguay Round and Doha Development Agenda. *The Agreement on Agriculture* establishes guidelines for "initiating a process of reform of trade in agriculture". Its ultimate goal is the establishment of a market-oriented system for trade in agricultural products that is free of restrictions and distortions. It requires the WTO members to replace non-tariff barriers to international agricultural products trade (including quotas, levies and licenses) with tariffs that provide substantially the same level of protection. This is known as "tariffication". For domestic support measures, both developed and developing members should reduce the monetary impact of measures. For export subsidies for agricultural products, the developed states have agreed to reduce export subsidies by 36 percent and developing states by 24 percent during the implementation period. These measures are defined in *the Agreement on Agriculture* as subsidies. *The Agreement on Agriculture* provides for the gradual phasing in of member obligations.

2. 《反倾销协议》

《反倾销协议》(《1994 年关税与贸易总协定》第 6 条)规定了成员方可采取反倾销措施的程序。现有协议中对倾销作了如下定义：一国商品以低于其正常价值的价格进入另一国市场，并对该国相应产业造成了实质性损害或形成实质性威胁，或实质性阻碍了进口国相应产业的建立。

对于产品进口时是否低于其正常价值，可以参照如下标准。

(1) 低于正常贸易过程中在出口国供国内消费时的可比价格。

(2) 如无此国内价格，则低于正常贸易过程中同类产品出口至第三国的最高可比价格。

(3) 低于该产品在原产国的生产成本加上合理的销售成本和利润。

---

2. Anti-dumping Agreement

Anti-dumping Agreement (formally the Agreement on Implementation of Article 6 of *GATT 1994*) sets out the procedures by which members may take measures to counter dumping. The current Agreement defines dumping in the following way: Products of one country are introduced into the commerce of another country at less than its normal value, and it causes or threatens material injury to, or materially retards the establishment of a domestic industry in the importing country.

There are three standards to determine whether a product is introduced into the commerce of an importing country at less than its normal value.

(1) If the export price of the product exported from one country to another is less than the comparable price, in the ordinary course of trade, for the like product when destined for consumption in the exporting country.

(2) If there is no such domestic price, the price of the product is less than the highest comparable price for the like product for export to any third country in the ordinary course of trade.

(3) The cost of production of the product in the country-of-origin plus a reasonable addition for selling cost and profit.

成员方如要采取反倾销措施(如征收反倾销税)，必须先开展反倾销调查，并已确定倾销产品造成了实质性损害或构成实质性威胁，或实质性阻碍了进口国产业的建立。在进行反倾销调查时，主管当局应当遵循程序规定。当局须给予利益各方就反倾销调查进行通知，且相关利益关系方应当被给予充分的机会提供证据、进行答辩、反驳指控。随着调查的进行，主管当局可就是否倾销作出初步裁定，并决定是否有必要采取临时措施(如临时反倾销税，或相当于临时估计的反倾销税额度的保证金)，以防止在调查期间对产业造成损害。如经过调查，确定了倾销、损害，以及二者之间真实存在的因果联系，则相关当局可作出终极裁决，并就此征收反倾销税。反倾销税的税额不应高于倾销产品的正常价格与倾销价格之间的差额。一方面，反倾销税应一直有效，直至能够抵消倾销造成的损害；另一方面，征收反倾销税不应超过 5 年的期限，除非有关当局于到期前重新发起审查并确定继续采取措施，否则该项税收将自动终止。

Members that wish to take anti-dumping measures (such as the imposition of offsetting duties) to counter dumping must first conduct an investigation and determine that the dumped product causes or threatens to cause material injury or materially retard the establishment of a domestic industry in the importing country. When carrying out an investigation, the authorities must follow some procedures. The authorities must give all interested parties notice of the investigation, the opportunity to present written evidence, and the opportunity to examine and rebut adverse evidence. After the investigation has been initiated, a preliminary determination may be made of dumping if the authorities believe that such measures are necessary to prevent injury being caused during the investigation. Provisional measures (the imposition of a provisional anti-dumping duty or the deposit of a security equal to a provisionally estimated anti-dumping duty) may be imposed. Final anti-dumping duties may be imposed of the discretion of the authorities concerned upon the completion of an investigation and a final determination that dumping, injury and a causal link between them exist. The monetary amount of an anti-dumping duty may not exceed the difference between a product's normal value and the price at which it is actually exported. On the one hand, such a duty may remain in force as long as it is necessary to counteract dumping that is causing injury; on the other hand, reviews must be held periodically and if no review is conducted for a 5-year, the duty will automatically terminate.

3. 《补贴与反补贴措施协议》

补贴是指由一国政府或任何公共机构提供的用于某一或某些企业、行业的财政支持。当某国政府将补贴不当地用于刺激其出口并对其他国家造成危害时，该类补贴为《1994 年关税与贸易总协定》所禁止。如果对某国的国内市场造成不合理的影响，则该国可以采取征收反补贴税的措施用以抵消其补贴带来的不利影响。但是采取上述反补贴措施必须符合正当、合理、适度等条件。

《补贴与反补贴措施协议》(又称《SCM 协议》)取代了 1979 年在东京回合中达成的《补贴守则》。《SCM 协议》明确地阐释了其原则性规定(如成员国义务)仅适用于下列特定补贴：①针对特定企业或行业的补贴；②针对特定企业群或行业群的补贴；③针对某特定区域内的企业补贴。

上述原则不适用于下列补贴：①非特定性补贴；②协议中规定的特定补贴；③农业补贴(由《农产品协议》所规定)。由《SCM 协议》规制的特定补贴可以分为以下三类：禁止性补贴(红色补贴)；可诉性补贴(黄色补贴)；不可诉补贴(绿色补贴)。

---

3. *Agreement on Subsidies and Countervailing Measures*

A subsidy is a financial contribution made by a government (or other public body) that confers a benefit on an enterprise, a group of enterprises, or an industry. When improperly used by a government to promote its export trade to the detriment of another state, subsidies are forbidden by *GATT 1994*. If subsidies have an unreasonable impact on another country's internal market, that country can impose countervailing duties to offset their impact, but only if it follows certain conditions to ensure that its reaction is justified, appropriate, and not excessive.

The Agreement on Subsidies and Countervailing Measures, or *SCM Agreement*, replaces *the 1979 Subsidies Code* concluded at the Tokyo Round. *The SCM Agreement* clearly states that its "disciplines" (such as member state obligations) apply only to "specific" subsidies—that is, subsidies that target (a)a specific enterprise or industry, (b)specific groups of enterprises or industries, or (c)enterprises in a particular region.

The disciplines do not apply to (a)nonspecific subsidies, (b)certain specific subsidies defined in the agreement, and (c)agricultural subsidies (which are governed by *the Agreement on Agriculture*). Specific subsidies (such as those regulated by *the SCM Agreement*) are divided into three categories: (a)prohibited subsidies (informally referred to as red subsidies), (b)actionable subsidies (yellow), and (c)non-actionable subsidies (green).

禁止性补贴(红色补贴)会扭曲国际贸易，世界贸易组织成员被禁止使用或者维持该类补贴。可诉性补贴(黄色补贴)是否对国际贸易产生扭曲影响，取决于如何使用此类补贴，因此被称为黄色补贴。不可诉补贴(绿色补贴)由不特定补贴和特定基础性补贴构成，之所以称其为绿色补贴，是因为该类补贴得以允许并且不具争议性。

世界贸易组织成员主张其国内行业因禁止性补贴或者可诉性补贴受到损害时通常有四种选择：①保持现状；②要求磋商；③寻求世界贸易组织救济；④征收反补贴税。如果贸易受损成员选择不采取任何措施，则世界贸易组织或其成员都不能对其进行干涉。

除了寻求世界贸易组织授权的救济之外，成员可以自主征收反补贴税，该征收措施需要符合《SCM 协议》中的程序规定(这些程序规定也见于《反倾销协议》的反倾销措施中)。一方面，成员之所以选择自主征收反补贴税而不是寻求世界贸易组织授权救济，主要原因在于其相关行政部门对于反补贴税的征收更具主动权。另一方面，资源有限的国家通常选择世界贸易组织资助的程序，因为其更为经济。

Prohibited subsidies are presumed to be trade distorting, and the WTO members are forbidden to grant or maintain them. Actionable subsidies (yellow subsidies) are subsidies that may or may not be trade distorting, depending upon how they are applied (thus the reason for their designation as yellow). Non-actionable subsidies (green subsidies) consist of nonspecific subsidies and certain specific infrastructural subsidies. They are known as green subsidies because, as a general rule, they are permissible and unchallengeable.

A WTO member that believes that its domestic industries have been injured by either prohibited subsidies or actionable subsidies is given four options: (a)doing nothing, (b)requesting consultations, (c)seeking a remedy from the WTO, (d)independently imposing countervailing duties. If an injured member chooses to do nothing, neither the WTO nor any other member is entitled to intervene.

As an alternative to seeking a WTO-authorized remedy, a member may independently impose countervailing duties so long as it follows the procedures specified in *the SCM Agreement* (which are the same as those used in the *Anti-dumping Agreement* for the adoption of anti-dumping measures). On the one hand, the reason a member may prefer to adopt countervailing duties independently instead of seeking a WTO-authorized remedy is that its administrative agencies will have greater control over the process. On the other hand, a member with limited resources will find the WTO-funded process more economical.

4. 《原产地规则协议》

《原产地规则协议》是用于确定产品生产地的标准。该协议中的规则是一系列贸易措施的必要组成部分,该系列措施包括配额、优惠关税、反倾销措施、反补贴税(用于抵销出口补贴)等措施。《原产地规则协议》也被用于制定贸易政策,并在产品上贴有"某国制造"标签。

《原产地规则协议》要求世界贸易组织成员保证:其原产地规则透明;对国际贸易没有限制性、扭曲性、破坏性影响;以一致、统一、公正和合理的方式实施;并以正面标准加以规定。从长远来看,该协议旨在建立世界贸易组织成员通用的原产地规则,以特惠贸易除外。比如,某些国家建立自由贸易区,并且根据自由贸易协定适用不同的原产地规则。为了使《原产地规则协议》客观、透明和可预测,该协议在 1998 年建成了协调工作机制。上述工作由《原产地规则协议》委员会负责。该工作机制的产物就是在非特惠贸易情况下适用于所有世界贸易组织成员的《原产地规则协议》。

4. *Agreement on Rules of Origin*

Agreement on Rules of Origin are the criteria used to define where a product was made. The rules are an essential part of trade rules including: quotas, preferential tariffs, anti-dumping actions, countervailing duty (charged to counter export subsidies), and more. *Rules of Origin* are also used to compile trade policies, and for "made in…", labels that are attached to products.

Agreement on Rules of Origin requires the WTO members to ensure that their rules of origin are transparent; that they do not have restrictive, distorting or disruptive effects on international trade; that they are administered in a consistent, uniform, impartial and reasonable manner; and that they are based on a positive standard. For the longer term, the agreement aims for common rules of origin among all WTO members, except in some kinds of preferential trade—for example, countries setting up a free trade area are allowed to use different rules of origin for products traded under their free trade agreement. The agreement establishes a harmonization work program, to be completed in 1998, based upon a set of principles, including making *Agreement on Rules of Origin* objective, transparent and predictable. The work is being conducted by a Committee on *Agreement on Rules of Origin*. The outcome will be a single set of *Agreement on Rules of Origin* to be applied under non-preferential trading conditions by all the WTO members in all circumstances.

5. 《技术贸易壁垒协议》

《技术贸易壁垒协议》(又称为《TBT 协议》)规定世界贸易组织成员在符合下列情况时设计、使用、适用技术的规范和标准：①为人类、动物、植物及环境的生命健康提供适当的保护；②杜绝欺诈行为；③排除多余的贸易壁垒。

包括农业和工业产品在内，所有产品均适用于《TBT 协议》，但下列两种情况除外：与政府制造或消费要求有关的采购条款(由《政府采购协议》规定)、卫生检验检疫措施(由《实施卫生与植物卫生措施协议》规定)。《TBT 协议》的主要条款如下。

(1) 世界贸易组织成员必须就技术规范、标准、评定程序等信息设立相关办事机构，并且其他成员或相关方可以获得上述信息。

(2) 就技术规范、标准及评定程序的适用，世界贸易组织成员应当保证给予从其他成员进口的商品享受的待遇不低于本国或第三国类似产品享受的优惠待遇。

(3) 技术规范、标准、评定程序不能被用于准备、使用或适用不必要的国际贸易壁垒。

---

5. Agreement on Technical Barriers to Trade

Agreement on Technical Barriers to Trade (TBT Agreement) establishes rules governing the way WTO members draft, adopt, and apply technical regulations and standards to ensure that they (a)provide an appropriate level of protection for the life and health of humans, animals, and plants, as well as for the environment; (b)prevent deceptive practices; (c)do not create unnecessary obstacles to trade.

All products, including agricultural and industrial products, are covered by the TBT Agreement, but purchasing specifications related to the production or consumption requirements of governmental bodies (which are covered by *the Agreement on Government Procurement*) and sanitary and phytosanitary measures (which are covered by *the Agreement on the Application of Sanitary and Phytosanitary Measures*) are not. The main provisions of *the TBT Agreement* are as follows.

(1) The WTO members must establish one or more offices where information and assistance about technical regulations, standards, and conformity assessment procedures can be obtained by other members and any interested parties.

(2) With respect to the application of technical regulations, standards, and conformity assessment procedures, the WTO members shall ensure that products imported from other members shall be accorded no less favorable treatment than like national products or like products originating in any other state.

(3) Technical regulations, standards, and conformity assessment procedures are not to be prepared, adopted, or applied so as to create unnecessary obstacles to international trade.

6. 《实施卫生与植物卫生措施协议》

《实施卫生与植物卫生措施协议》是对《技术贸易壁垒协议》的补充，规定了世界贸易组织成员在保护人类、动物、植物生命和健康方面可采用的措施。但在运用这些措施时，不得在情形相同的成员方之间造成任意或不正当的歧视，或对国际贸易构成变相的限制。

7. 《海关估价协议》

当货物越过国境时，进口国海关按照货物价值的百分比征收关税。《海关估价协议》用于调整世界贸易组织成员确定货物价值的方式。其力图提供一套公正、中立和统一的海关估价体系，建立海关估价的基本方法和备用方法。海关估价的基本方法是计算进口货物的交易价值，交易价值是以货物出口到进口国时进口货物的实际价格或应付价格为基础计算的。

------

6. *Agreement on the Application of Sanitary and Phytosanitary Measures*

Agreement on the Application of Sanitary and Phytosanitary Measures (SPS Agreement) is meant to complement *the Agreement on Technical Barriers to Trade* by defining the measures that may be taken by the WTO members to protect the life and health of humans, animals, and plants. Members may protect the life and health of living things, but they may not do so as a disguised means for restricting international trade, nor may they act arbitrarily to unjustifiably discriminate between members where identical or similar conditions exist.

7. *Rules on Customs Valuation*

When goods cross an international frontier, they are charged a tariff that is based on a percentage of their value. *Rules on Customs Valuation* is designed to harmonize the methods used by the WTO members to determine the value of those goods. Its detailed rules are meant to provide for a fair, neutral, and uniform system of customs valuation. A primary method and fallback methods are established.The primary method of customs valuation is to figure the transaction value of the imported item. This is based on the price actually paid or payable for the goods when sold for export to the country of importation.

8. 《进口许可程序协议》

《进口许可程序协议》的目的是制定客观公正的许可程序，简化进口申请的形式和程序，以确保进口货物不至于因为申请书填写中的小错误而被拒绝批准，确保货物不会因为在价值、数量或重量方面的微小偏差而被禁止进口。

9. 关税约束及减让

在乌拉圭回合谈判末期，各成员方提交了作为《1994 年关税与贸易总协定马拉喀什议定书》附件的关税减让表，这是在降低关税税率方面具有法律约束力的协议。

根据上述协议，发达国家在从 1995 年 1 月 1 日起的 5 年内对绝大部分工业品的关税税率削减 40%，所有工业产品的加权平均关税税率从 6.3%降到 3.8%。发达国家给予免税待遇的进口工业产品总值从 20%提高到 44%。发达国家将进一步缩小适用高税率的产品范围。乌拉圭回合一揽子协议在谈判结束后得到了进一步发展，1997 年 3 月 26 日，代表世界贸易总额 92%的 40 多个世界贸易组织成员达成《信息技术协议》，承诺在 2000 年之前消除信息技术产品的关税和费用，并承诺每一缔约国应按最惠国待遇原则把这一减让适用于所有其他世界贸易组织成员方，即使该成员方并非《信息技术协议》的缔约国。

---

8. *Agreement on Import Licensing Procedures*

Agreement on Import Licensing Procedures seeks to ensure that licensing procedures are neutral. That is, forms and procedures must be simple, licenses are not to be denied because of minor errors in completing an application, and imports are not to be barred from entry into a member state because of minor deviations in the value, quantity, or weight designated on the license.

9. Tariffs: More Bindings and Closer to Zero

At the end of the Uruguay Round, individual countries listed their commitments in schedules annexed to *Marrakesh Protocol to the General Agreement on Tariffs and Trade 1994*. This is the legally binding agreement for the reduced tariff rates.

Developed countries' tariff cuts are for the most part being phased in over five years from January 1, 1995. The result will be a 40% cut in their tariffs on industrial products, from an average of 6.3% to 3.8%. The value of imported industrial products that receive duty-free treatment in developed countries will jump from 20% to 44%. Developed countries will further narrow the scope of products with high tax rates. The Uruguay Round package has now been improved. On March 26, 1997, 40 countries accounting for more than 92% of world trade concluded *the Information Technology Agreement*. They agreed to eliminate import duties and other charges on information technology products by 2000. Each participating country should apply its commitments equally to exports from all the WTO members, even from members that did not make commitments in the Agreement.

综 合 练 习

1. 根据 2004 年《中华人民共和国对外贸易法》的规定，我国负责管理进出口贸易的是哪个部门？

2. 简述关税与贸易总协定和世界贸易组织的区别。

3. 简述《1994 年关税与贸易总协定》的基本原则。

Comprehensive Exercises

1. Under *the Foreign Trade Law of The People's Republic of China 2004*, which department is responsible for the administration of imports and exports trade in China?

2. Briefly explain the difference between GATT and WTO.

3. Briefly explain the basic principles of *GATT 1994*.

第七章 国际税法

学习目标

了解国际税收管辖权的概念以及分类。

了解国际双重征税的概念以及类型。

掌握避免国际双重征税的方法。

了解国际逃税和国际避税之间的区别。

掌握规制国际逃税与避税的主要法律措施。

了解主要的多边税收协定。

Chapter 7　International Tax Law

Learning Objectives

To know the concept and classification of jurisdiction to international tax.

To know the concept and type of international double taxation.

To grasp the methods for relief from international double taxation.

To know the differences between international tax evasion and tax avoidance.

To grasp the main solutions to tackling international tax evasion and tax avoidance.

To know the main multilateral tax treaties.

全球化以及持续发展的跨国投资与贸易意味着潜在的税收管辖冲突，在特定情况下也意味着税收管辖真空。税收管辖权冲突问题的核心在于不同国家都主张税收管辖权，即两个或多个国家基于主权对同一事项或同一纳税人进行征税。在各国税法存在差异的情况下，纳税人的不当行为可能会加剧管辖冲突。虽然关于由哪个国家行使税收管辖权的问题重要且存在争议，但基于对课税基础流失的合理关切，税收管辖权冲突能够并且也常常通过一国税法单边或者双边税收协定解决，有时甚至通过多边税收协定解决。通常的解决之道是使用统一定义或避免双重征税。

第一节 税收管辖权

在大多数国家，税收管辖权立足于国内立法程序，是国家主权的体现。这有利于强化税收管辖相关问题的敏感性。国际法对征税的立法管辖未作任何限制。原则上，国际税收协定并不限制缔约方的立法管辖权(尽管可能会限制适用根据该管辖权制定的税收规则)。只有在极少数情况下，此类税收安排才可能直接影响到立法管辖权。

Globalization and increased transnational investment and trade imply a potential conflict of tax jurisdictions or, in certain circumstances, a jurisdictional vacuum. Central to the question of jurisdictional conflict is the issue of the jurisdiction to tax: the sovereign right of two or more jurisdictions to levy tax on one and the same event or one and the same taxpayer. Where there are mismatches between national tax laws, the jurisdictional conflict can be exacerbated by improper conduct on the part of taxpayers. Jurisdictional conflicts can be, and often are, relieved unilaterally under national tax laws, or bilaterally and sometimes even multilaterally under tax treaties, although the question as to which jurisdiction should bear the burden of relief is important and not uncontroversial, due to legitimate concerns about the erosion of the tax base. This is generally achieved through the elimination of definitional mismatches or the relief of double taxation.

7.1　Jurisdiction to Tax

In most countries, the jurisdiction to tax is based on the domestic legislative process, which is an expression of national sovereignty, thus heightening the sensitivity of the surrounding issues. There are no restrictions under international law to the legislative jurisdiction to impose and collect taxes. In principle, international tax agreements do not restrict the contracting parties' legislative jurisdiction (although they may restrict the application of tax rules enacted pursuant to that jurisdiction). It is only in rare situations that such tax arrangements may impact directly on the legislative jurisdiction.

然而，一国立法管辖权却要受到跨国实施的明显限制。也就是说，不受限制地行使征税权只局限在一国境内，无法在他国实施。因此，相关国家与应纳税人和/或应税所得之间是否有充分的关联性，是大多数国家能否行使税收管辖权的重要根据。

一、居民税收管辖权

基于相关国家与应纳税人之间的充分联系而制定的税法，采用的是居民税收管辖权原则。实行该原则的国家对其居民(有时也对其国民)在世界范围内的全部所得征税，而不论其来源于何处。

为了行使居民税收管辖权，一国必须制定一套规则以区分个人和法人，以及居民和非居民。具体区分规则如下。

Nevertheless, the impact of a country's legislative jurisdiction is restricted by the obvious limitations on its enforcement powers beyond its own national boundaries. In other words, the unrestricted exercise of the right to tax is limited to the territory of one country and cannot be implemented in other countries. Thus, most countries exercise their jurisdiction to tax by reference to factors that assume a sufficient connection between the relevant country and the taxable person and/or the taxable income.

7.1.1 Residence-based Taxation

Taxation systems based on a sufficient connection between the relevant country and the taxable person apply the principle of "residence-based taxation". Countries applying such a principle tax their residents (and sometimes their nationals) on their worldwide income, wherever derived.

To exercise residence jurisdiction, a country must provide rules that classify individuals and legal entities either as residents or as nonresidents. The rules for determining the residence of individuals and legal entities are discussed below.

1. 个人的居民身份

在很多国家，居民身份是用一种很宽泛的"事实与境况"判定方法来判定的。实际上，政府总是寻求以客观的表征来判定居民身份，看个人是否通过加入一国的经济和社会生活从而确立了对此国的忠诚。这种忠诚的最重要的表征可能就是在该国拥有住所或居所供此纳税人使用。一般而言，永久性住所是指适合常年使用的处所(人可以居住的建筑或构造)，居住者对其日常维护，不论是否具有所有权。不适合常年使用以及仅用于度假目的的处所，都不可视为永久性住所。并且，棚屋或者不含通常可供居住设施(如厨具、浴室等)的建筑或构造，通常也不被认为是永久性住所。一个人可能拥有两个或者两个以上的永久性住所。此外，永久性住所通常还包括配偶所有或租赁的居所。

---

1. Individual Resident Status

In many countries, residence is determined under a very broad facts-and-circumstances test. In effect, the government seeks to determine from objective manifestations whether an individual has established his or her allegiance to the country by joining its economic and social life. The most significant manifestation of allegiance is probably the maintenance in the country of a dwelling or abode that is available for the taxpayer's use. In general, a permanent place of abode is a residence (a building or structure where a person can live) that is suitable for year-round use and he/she maintains whether he/she owns it or not. A structure that is not suitable for year-round use and that he/she uses only for vacations is not a permanent place of abode. Also, a barracks or any structure that does not contain facilities ordinarily found in a dwelling, such as facilities for cooking, bathing, etc., is not generally considered to be a permanent place of abode. It is possible for him or her to have more than one permanent place of abode. Additionally, a permanent place of abode generally includes a residence the spouse owns or leases.

然而，个人的居民身份与从事取得所得的活动的地点、家庭地点、在该国所维持的社会联系、个人的签证和移民情况以及个人在该国的实际停留情况也有关系。有的国家依据个人在该国的停留时间来判定居民身份。一种常用的方法是，个人如果一年内在某国停留时间超过 183 天即成为该国的居民。183 天的标准在对边界控制比较严的国家可能得以执行。然而，对于个人频繁出入境而无边防检查的国家的税务机关来讲，此方法则极难执行。在多数国家，除非个人负有举证责任证明本人在 183 天期间内不在本国，否则这项标准不能有效地运作。

2. 法人的居民身份

　　公司的居民身份一般依据其注册地或者管理地来判定。注册地标准为政府和纳税人提供了简单性和确定性。它也允许纳税人自由选择其最初的注册地。在以避税港来吸引投资者的国家，法律确保注册公司的手续便捷以及费用低廉。

　　一般来讲，一个公司对其组建地点的任何变更，都会招致对其资产所产生收益的征税。这些资产包括市场价值可能很高的无形资产。因此，注册地标准制约了公司通过转换其居民国而避税的能力。许多国家都采用注册地标准。

Also relevant, however, might be the place where the individual engages in income-producing activities, the location of his or her family, the social ties maintained in the country, the individual's visa and immigration status, and the individual's actual physical presence in the country. Some countries test the number of days of presence in the country for determining residence. A common rule is that an individual who is present in a country for at least 183 days of the taxable year is a resident for that year. The 183-day test is probably enforceable in countries that exercise tight control over their borders. It is extremely difficult for the tax authorities of a country to enforce, however, when many individuals are frequently entering and leaving the country without border checks. In most countries, the test probably can not operate effectively unless the burden of proof is put on the individual to prove that he or she is not present for the 183-day period.

2. Resident Status of Legal Person

The residence of a corporation is generally determined either by reference to its place of incorporation or its place of management. The place-of-incorporation test provides simplicity and certainty to the government and the taxpayer. It also allows a taxpayer to freely choose its initial place of residence. Countries that market themselves as tax havens typically offer convenient and inexpensive arrangements for incorporating under their laws.

In general，a corporation cannot freely change its place of incorporation without triggering a tax on the gains that may have accrued on its property, including intangible property that may have a very high market value. Consequently, the place-of-incorporation test places some limits on the ability of corporations to shift their country of residence for tax avoidance purposes. Many countries use the place-of-incorporation test.

管理地标准在适用的确定性上就稍逊一筹。对于从事国际业务的多数公司来讲，在任一纳税年度内管理活动可以在几个国家进行。在实践中，多数采用此种标准的国家都使用可操作的判定方法来确定管理地，例如公司总部地点或者公司董事会开会的地点。英国和其多数前殖民地都采用管理地标准。某些国家，比如加拿大既采用注册地标准又采用管理地标准。

管理地标准很容易被用于避税目的，因为变更管理地可以在不引发征税的情况下完成。有的国家依据公司股东的居民身份来判断公司的居民身份。如果普遍适用公司股东居民身份标准的话，那么在多国居民持有公司大块股份，或者公司上市公开交易、股东身份难以判定的情况下，将会产生严重的问题。

对于除公司外的法律实体，其居民身份一般是通过注册地或者管理地标准来判定的。判定合伙企业的居民身份有时比较困难，因为合伙企业可以以非正式的形式设立。在许多国家，合伙企业是作为透明体或者通透实体来处理的，也就是说，合伙人就其在合伙企业的所得中的份额纳税。对于这些国家，合伙企业的居民身份通常并无关紧要，因为合伙企业并不是纳税实体。

The place-of-management test is less certain in its application. For many corporations engaged in international operations, management activities may be conducted in several countries during any particular taxable year. In practice, most countries using that test employ practical tests, such as the location of the company's head office or the place where the board of directors meet, to determine the place of management. The place-of-management test is used by the United Kingdom and many of its former colonies. Some countries, such as Canada, use both the place-of-incorporation test and the place-of-management test.

A place-of-management test is easily exploited for tax avoidance reasons because a change in the place of management generally can be accomplished without triggering any tax. Some countries test the residence of a corporation by reference to the residence of its shareholders. A general application of a residence-of-the-shareholders test would present serious problems when residents of more than one country hold large blocks of stock in the company or when the stock of the company is publicly traded and the identity of the shareholders is difficult to determine.

For legal entities other than corporations, residence is generally determined either under a place-of-incorporation test or a place-of-management test. Determining the residence of a partnership is sometimes difficult because of the informality with which a partnership can be established. In many countries, partnerships are treated as transparent or as flow-through entities; that is, the partners are taxed on their shares of the income of a partnership. For these countries, the residence of a partnership is usually irrelevant because the partnership is not a taxable entity.

二、所得来源地税收管辖权

基于相关国家与应税所得之间的充分联系而制定的税法，采用的是所得来源地税收管辖权原则。实行该原则的国家对在来源于其境内的所得征税，而不论该居民的住所在何地。

根据此原则，一国的征税权源于其与该所得之间的关系。比如，一国可援引所得来源地税收管辖原则对其领土范围内从事矿藏开采获取的所得征税。通常来说，只有在国家致力于创造商业机会容许纳税人在该国境内从事商业活动获利的情况下，依据所得来源地进行征税才具有合法性。当然，税收管辖权与权力有关。如果在一国境内的财产和活动产生所得，该国通常有权对该所得征税。

所得本身不具有任何地理位置属性，它是一个数量。该数量根据某些会计规则，通过与其他数量之间的加和减计算得出。然而，根据长期存在的国际公约，由于产生所得的财产和活动总是位于某个地点，所得也被认为具有地理位置属性。当所有的财产和活动都位于同一国时，该国便被视为明确的所得来源地。

7.1.2 Source-based Taxation

Taxation systems based on a sufficient connection between the relevant country and the taxable income apply the principle of "source-based taxation". Countries applying such a principle tax income derived from sources in their territory, regardless of the residence of the person deriving the income.

Under this principle, a country's claim to tax income is based on the country's relationship to that income. For example, a country would invoke the source principle to tax income derived from the extraction of mineral deposits located within its territorial boundaries. Source-based taxation is generally justified on the ground that the country has contributed to the creation of the economic opportunities that allow the taxpayer to derive income generated within the territorial borders of the country. Of course, jurisdiction to tax is also about power, and a country generally has the power to tax income if the assets and activities that generated it are located within its borders.

Income itself does not have a geographical location. It is a quantity, calculated by adding and subtracting various other quantities in accordance with certain accounting rules. By long standing convention, however, income is assigned a geographical location by reference to the location of the assets and activities that are used to generate the income. When all of those assets and activities are located in one country, that country may be considered to be the unambiguous source of the income.

1. 营业所得

来源国对营业所得的征税千差万别。然而，仍有两种常见模式。最常见的模式是，除某些特例外，营业所得只有在可以归属于位于一国的常设机构情况下，该国方可对其征税。在这些税制下，常设机构规则不仅是作为征税的前提条件，还是辨别应税所得的方法。只有所得可以归属于常设机构的情况下方可被征税。多数欧洲国家采取此种模式。

另一种常见模式是将常设机构规则(或其他同等功效的规则)作为对非居民进行征税的条件，而具体征税的程度则用更明确的来源地规则来确定。在采取此种模式的国家中，美国是最显著的例子。

2. 投资所得

除某些特例外，来源国对非居民取得的投资所得，例如股息、利息和特许权使用费征收预提税。对资本收益一般不征预提税。有关投资所得的来源地，一般是通过明确的来源地规则判定。除某些技术性特例外，多数国家都已采用下述来源地规则。

(1) 利息所得和股息所得的来源地为支付人的所在地。

---

1. Business Income

The taxation of business income by source countries varies considerably. Two general patterns, however, can be noted. The most common pattern is that business income is taxable by a country, with some exceptions, only if the income is attributable to a Permanent Establishment (PE) in the country. In these systems, the PE rules serve not only as a prerequisite to taxation but also as the means for identifying the income subject to tax. To be taxable, income must be "attributable" to the PE. Most European countries follow this pattern.

The other pattern is that the PE rules (or other equivalent rules) are used as a threshold requirement for taxation of nonresidents but explicit source rules are used for defining the extent of source taxation.The United States is the most prominent exemplar of the source rule approach.

2. Investment Income

With some exceptions, investment income derived by nonresidents, such as dividends, interest, and royalties, is taxable through a withholding tax imposed by the source country. Capital gains typically are not subject to withholding tax. The source of investment income is usually determined under explicit source rules. With some technical exceptions, the following source rules have been adopted by most countries.

(1) Interest income and dividend income have their source in the country of residence of the payer.

(2) 因无形资产而取得的特许权使用费来源地为特许权使用费产生的国家，它们一般是对无形资产提供法律保护的国家。某些类型的特许权使用费所得，例如播放影片的特许权使用费和计算机软件的特许权使用费，按某些国家法律可被分类至营业所得。

(3) 出租动产给他人使用而取得的租金，除经营租赁业务取得的所得外，来源地为动产使用国。经营租赁业务取得的租金收入一般适用营业所得规则缴税。

(4) 资本收益的来源地为销售方所在地，除非收益产生于营业资产或不动产的销售。不动产销售的收益来源于不动产所在国。营业资产的销售收益来源于使用营业资产的常设机构所在国。

3. 受雇人员和个人劳务所得

一般来讲，在多数国家，雇员、独立承包商或者专业人士提供个人劳务取得的所得，其来源地为劳务提供地。

---

(2) Royalty income paid with respect to intangible property has its source in the country where the royalties arise—typically the country that provides legal protection for the intangible property. Some types of royalty income, such as royalties paid for the showing of motion pictures and royalties on computer software, may be classified as business income under the laws of some countries.

(3) Rent derived from the use of movable property, other than income derived from the operation of a rental business, has its source in the country where the property is used. Rental income derived from the operation of a business is typically taxable under the rules applicable to business income.

(4) Capital gains are sourced in the country of residence of the seller unless the gains arise from the sale of business property or immovable property. Gains from the sale of immovable property are sourced in the country where the property is located. Gains from the sale of business property are sourced in the country where the PE using the property is located.

3. Income from Employment and Personal Services

The general rule in most countries is that income derived from personal services performed by an employee, an independent contractor, or a professional has its source in the country where the services are performed.

大多数国家兼采居民税收管辖权原则和所得来源地管辖权原则。因此，根据"无限纳税责任"，居民纳税人(有时包括即使居住在他国的本国国民)有义务对其在世界范围内的所得缴税。同时，根据"有限纳税责任"，非居民纳税人有义务对来源于或被视为来源于一国境内的所得缴税。

第二节　国际双重征税

大多数国家根据纳税人居民身份和所得来源确立征税权。如果没有相应的消除双重征税的方法，一国居民的外国来源所得可能被居民国和所得来源国同时征税。

一、国际双重征税的类型

导致国际双重征税的因素很多。不同的税收管辖权冲突将导致以下三种类型的双重征税。

Most countries apply a combination of residence-based and source-based taxation. Therefore, residents (and sometimes nationals, whether or not residents) are taxable on their worldwide income under what is generally referred to as an "unlimited tax liability". In contrast, non-residents are taxable only on income derived or deemed to be derived from sources within the territory, under what is generally referred to as a "limited tax liability".

7.2　International Double Taxation

Most countries tax on the basis of both the residence status of the taxpayer and the source of income. Consequently, foreign-source income earned by a resident of a country may be taxed by both the country of source and the country of residence, absent relief provisions designed to prevent double taxation.

7.2.1　Types of International Double Taxation

International double taxation can arise from a variety of causes. The following three types of double taxation arise from conflicts over tax jurisdiction.

1. 居民税收管辖权之间冲突

两个或两个以上国家都认为同一纳税人是本国的居民，从而对其同一笔所得行使征税权。一个纳税人同时被两个国家认定为居民，通常被称为"双重居民纳税人"。例如，A国可能将一公司视为其居民，因为该公司位于其境内，而B国则因该公司在B国内有管理机构而将其视为居民。再如，A国可依其国内税法将某个人作为纳税年度的居民，因为该个人本年度在国内驻留满183天。同一人也可被B国依其国内税法视为该国居民，因为该个人在B国居住多年且与B国保持着密切的经济与社会关系。与公司有关的居民税收管辖权冲突频繁发生，除非该公司故意使其自身成为双重居民以便在不同国家获得隐秘收益。

1. Residence-Residence Conflict

Two or more countries assert the right to tax the same income of a taxpayer because they claim the taxpayer is a resident of their country. A taxpayer that is a resident of two countries is commonly referred to as a "dual-resident taxpayer". For example, a corporation may be treated by Country A as its resident because it is incorporated therein, whereas Country B may treat that corporation as its resident because it is managed therein. As another example, Country A may treat an individual as its resident for a taxable year under its domestic tax rules because that individual was present in the country for 183 days during that year. That same individual may be treated as a resident of Country B under its domestic laws because the individual has lived in that country for many years and maintains close financial and social ties to that country. Residence-residence conflicts can occur rather frequently with respect to corporations, unless a corporation has intentionally made itself a dual resident to obtain the benefit of a loss in more than one country.

2. 所得来源地税收管辖权之间冲突

两个或两个以上国家都认为同一纳税人的同一所得来源于本国而同时行使征税权。比如，A 国的国内税法可能规定，如果销售行为是通过位于该国的办公场所实施的，则该非居民公司在该国的销售所得应在本国缴税。同时，如果待售货物的所有权转移发生在 B 国，则依 B 国的税法可对该非居民公司的销售所得行使征税权。考虑到 A 国与 B 国税收规则存在冲突，将 A 国办公场所的销售所得转移至 B 国会同时被 A、B 两国征税。

3. 居民税收管辖权与所得来源地税收管辖权之间冲突

居民国根据纳税人是本国居民而对其外国来源所得征税，同时，所得来源国根据所得来源于本国而对该纳税人的同一笔所得征税，从而形成双重征税。例如，A 国居民公司可在 B 国从事大量活动而获得所得。A 国可就该居民在世界范围内的所得征税，当然也包括在 B 国获得的所得。B 国就该居民公司来源于其境内的所得征税。双边税收协定的主要目的就是避免居民税收管辖权与来源地税收管辖权之间的冲突。典型的做法是，要求居民国放弃征税权或者服从所得来源地国家的征税要求。

2. Source-Source Conflict

Two or more countries assert the right to tax the same income of a taxpayer because they all claim the income is sourced in their country. For example, the domestic tax laws of Country A may provide that sales income of a non-resident corporation is taxable in that country if the sale was made through an office located in that country. In contrast, the tax laws of Country B may tax income derived from sales by a non-resident corporation if the transfer of possession of the goods sold took place within that country. Given this conflict in the tax rules of Country A and Country B, income derived from a sale made through an office located in Country A for delivery in Country B would be taxed in both countries.

3. Residence-Source Conflict

One country asserts the right to tax foreign-source income of a taxpayer because the taxpayer is a resident of that country, and another country asserts the right to tax the same income because the source of the income is in that country. For example, Company A, a resident of Country A, may earn income in Country B from extensive activities therein. Country A would tax Company A on its worldwide income, which would include the income earned in Country B. Country B would tax the income arising from the activities conducted within its territorial boundaries. A major objective of bilateral tax treaties is to provide for relief from such residence-source double taxation, typically by requiring the residence country either to give up its claim to tax or to make its claim subordinate to the claim of the source country.

二、避免国际双重征税

国际上对于采用何种方法避免国际双重征税尚未达成共识，但通常有以下三种方法。一国可选择其一使用，也可同时使用。

1. 扣除法

采用扣除法的国家对本国居民的全球范围所得征税，但在计算本国应税所得额时允许扣除在外国的已纳税额。实际上是将已缴纳的外国所得税和其他税收视作纳税人在外国从事经营并取得所得的当期费用予以扣除。扣除法是最不彻底的避免国际双重征税的方法。

许多国家在初建所得税制时采用扣除法。那时，各国税率较低，扣除法还可以接受。然而第二次世界大战后各国所得税税率相继提高，多数国家采用了免税法或抵免法作为避免双重征税的基本方法。

7.2.2　Relief from International Double Taxation

No international consensus has been reached on the appropriate method for granting relief from international double taxation. The following three methods are in common use. A country may use only one of these methods, or it may use some combination of methods.

1. Deduction Method

Countries using the deduction method tax their residents on their worldwide income and allow these taxpayers to take a deduction for foreign taxes paid in the computation of their taxable income. In effect, foreign taxes—income taxes and other types of taxes—are treated as current expenses of doing business or earning income in the foreign jurisdiction. The deduction method is the least generous method of granting relief from international double taxation.

The deduction method was used by a number of countries in the formative years of their tax systems. When worldwide tax rates were lower, it was an acceptable approach. As tax rates increased in the post-World War II period, however, most countries have adopted either the exemption method or the credit method as the basic method for relieving international double taxation.

2. 免税法

按照免税法，居民国只对本国居民来源于本国的所得征税，对于来源于外国的所得不再征税。也就是说，所得来源国拥有唯一征税权。由于只有所得来源国征税，免税法可以完全消除因居民税收管辖权和所得来源地税收管辖权之间冲突引起的国际双重征税。

只有个别国家对本国居民取得的所有来源于外国的所得予以免税。这些国家实际上只对来源于本国的所得征税。相对于全球征税原则，这种征税原则通常被称为"属地征税原则"。大多数采用免税法的国家只对有限的几种外国来源所得免税，如最普遍的经营所得和从外国关联公司取得的股息所得。而且，免税法也往往局限于外国已纳税所得或者至少在外国按某种最低税率已纳过税的所得。

---

2. Exemption Method

Under the exemption method, the country of residence taxes its residents on their domestic-source income and exempts them from domestic tax on their foreign-source income. In effect, jurisdiction to tax rests exclusively with the country of source. The exemption method completely eliminates residence-source international double taxation because only one jurisdiction, the source country, is imposing tax.

Very few countries have adopted the exemption method with respect to all foreign-source income earned by their residents. In effect, these countries tax only income from domestic sources. For this reason, they are often said to tax on a territorial basis rather than worldwide basis. For most countries using the exemption method, however, the exemption of foreign-source income is limited to certain types of income, most commonly business income and dividends from foreign affiliates. Furthermore, the exemption method is often restricted to income that has been subject to tax or subject to a minimum rate of tax by the foreign country.

3. 抵免法

根据抵免法，居民纳税人就外国来源的所得缴纳的外国税额可以冲抵本国应纳税额。抵免法可以完全消除居民国与所得来源国之间的国际双重征税。在运用抵免法时，当外国税率低于本国税率时，居民需要就外国来源所得缴纳本国税，本国税额等于国内外税率差乘以外国来源所得额。实际上，本国税收是在承认外国已纳税额基础上的补征，补征后使得外国来源所得适用的国内外平均税率恰好等于本国税率。

如果纳税人缴纳的外国税收的实际税率高于本国实际税率，实行抵免法的国家不会将外国税收高于本国税收的部分退还纳税人，也不会允许纳税人将这部分高出的税收用于冲抵本国来源所得的其他应纳税额。也就是说，外国税收的抵免额一般仅限于外国来源所得按照本国税法计算的应纳税额。许多抵免限额规定，在执行中有时较为复杂，却能防止外国税收抵免的滥用。由于有了抵免限额规定，当外国实际税率高于本国税率时，外国来源所得只按照外国税率征税。

3. Credit Method

Under the credit method, foreign taxes paid by a resident taxpayer on foreign-source income generally reduce domestic taxes payable by the amount of the foreign tax. The credit method completely eliminates international double taxation of the residence-source type. Under the credit method, foreign-source income is subject to domestic tax whenever the foreign tax rate is less than the domestic tax rate. The net domestic tax in such circumstances is an amount equal to the difference between the two tax rates multiplied by the foreign-source income. In effect, the foreign taxes are "made up" by domestic taxes so that the combined domestic and foreign tax rate on the foreign-source income is equal to the domestic tax rate.

Credit countries invariably do not pay tax re-funds when their taxpayers pay a foreign income tax at an effective rate that is higher than the domestic effective tax rate. Nor do they allow the excess foreign tax to offset taxes imposed on domestic income. In other words, the credit for foreign taxes paid is usually limited to the amount of the domestic tax payable on the foreign-source income. Various limitation rules, sometimes quite complex in application, are used to prevent what are perceived to be inappropriate uses of foreign tax credits. As a result of such limitations on the credit, foreign income is typically taxed at the foreign effective tax rate whenever the foreign rate is higher than the domestic rate.

4. 税收饶让抵免

税收饶让抵免是指居民国对于根据所得来源国一般税法本应缴纳但并未实际缴纳的税收给予抵免。之所以没有实际缴纳税收，通常原因是所得来源国为了吸引外资而对外国投资者提供了免税期或其他税收优惠措施。如果没有税收饶让，所得来源国税收优惠的真正受益者是居民国而不是投资者。因为投资者在来源国税收的减少将会导致居民国税收的增加。

税收饶让抵免是发达国家与发展中国家之间所签订税收协定的一个主要特征。许多发达国家将给予发展中国家税收饶让抵免作为税收协定的常规条款。有些发达国家为了鼓励向发展中国家投资，自愿在税收协定中给予发展中国家税收饶让抵免。其他发达国家只是勉强给予发展中国家税收饶让抵免。传统上，一些发展中国家将获得税收饶让抵免，作为与发达国家签署税收协定的条件。

---

4. Tax Sparing Credit

A tax sparing credit is a credit granted by the residence country for foreign taxes that for some reason were not actually paid to the source country but that would have been paid under the country's normal tax rules. The usual reason for the tax not being paid is that the source country has provided a tax holiday or other tax incentive to foreign investors as an encouragement to invest or conduct business in the country. In the absence of tax sparing, the actual beneficiary of a tax incentive provided by a source country to attract foreign investment may be the residence country rather than the foreign investor. This result occurs whenever the reduction in source-country tax is replaced by an increase in residence-country tax.

A tax sparing credit is primarily a feature of tax treaties between developed and developing countries. Many developed countries extend some form of tax sparing credits to developing countries by way of treaty as a matter of course. Some developed countries have voluntarily granted tax sparing credits in their treaties with developing countries as a way of encouraging investment in those countries. Other developed countries have granted the tax sparing credits only reluctantly. Some developing countries traditionally have refused to enter into a tax treaty with a developed country unless they obtain a tax sparing credit.

三、避免双重征税的协定范本

为减少或消除双重征税，国家间通常签订避免双重征税的协定。税收协定的历史可追溯到国际联盟。第一次世界大战期间，所得税越来越重要，国际联盟必须处理双重征税带来的问题，其制定了大量可供使用的双边税收协定范本。进入现代社会以来，《经济合作与发展组织关于对所得和财产避免双重征税的协定范本》(简称《经合组织范本》)是上述范本的主要传承者，并历经多次修改。而发展中国家和转型期国家特别感兴趣的则是 1980 年的《联合国关于发达国家与发展中国家间避免双重征税的协定范本》(简称《联合国范本》)。《联合国范本》以 1977 年的《经合组织范本》为基础，同时也体现了发展中国家的特殊利益。

1.《经合组织范本》

经济合作与发展组织(简称"经合组织")的起源可以追溯到 1960 年。当时，有 18 个欧洲国家与美国和加拿大共同组建了一个致力于经济发展的组织。目前，经合组织在全球有 35 个成员，涉及范围横跨北美、南美、欧洲和亚太地区。它们中既包括许多世界上最先进的国家，也包括墨西哥、智利和土耳其等新兴国家。

7.2.3　Model Convention on the Avoidance of Double Taxation

Tax treaty is an established way for countries to reduce or eliminate the risk of double taxation at the international level. The history of tax treaties can be traced to the League of Nations, which was pressed to deal with the problem of double taxation after income taxes became important during the First World War and which developed a number of models for use in negotiation of bilateral tax treaties. The major modern successor to these models is *the OECD Model Tax Convention on Income and on Capital* (*the OECD Model*), which itself has gone through various versions. Of especial interest to developing and transition countries is the 1980 *UN Model Double Taxation Convention between Developed and Developing Countries (the UN Model)*, which was based on the 1977 *OECD Model* but designed to take into account the special interests of developing countries.

1. The OECD Model

The origin of Organization for Economic Cooperation and Development(OECD) dates back to 1960, when 18 European countries plus the United States and Canada joined forces to create an organization dedicated to economic development. Currently, the OECD has 35 Member countries span the globe, from North and South America to Europe and Asia-Pacific. They include many of the world's most advanced countries but also emerging countries like Mexico, Chile and Turkey.

　　《经合组织范本》草案在 1963 年首次公布，1977 年和 1992 年先后进行了两次修订。之后，决定将其改装为活页形式，以方便随时增删修改。后来，每隔一段时间进行修订。由各成员资深税务专家组成的财政事务委员会主要负责协定范本的修订和其他有关国际税收合作的事项。该委员会通过常设秘书处和几个工作小组展开工作。负责处理税务问题的常设秘书处官员现在已成为税收政策和管理中心的一部分。该中心是于 2001 年建立的。工作小组由各成员国的代表组成，第一工作小组负责税收协定范本，并随时对与协定有关的事项加以密切关注。

　　对于资本输出国和资本输入国来说，《经合组织范本》更有利于前者。根据该范本，消除或减轻双重征税的方式，经常是要求所得来源国对缔约国另一方居民的所得免征部分或全部税收。如果两国在投资和贸易方面的往来大致相当，并且居民国对所得来源国减免的任何税收都予以征税，那么《经合组织范本》的这个特点还是颇为适宜的。但对于资本净输入国来说，以牺牲所得来源地税收管辖权来换取居民税收管辖权则是非常不利的。

The OECD Model was first published, in draft form, in 1963. It was revised in 1977 and again in 1992, at which time it was converted to a loose leaf format in order to facilitate more frequent revisions. Revisions were made at intervals. The Committee on Fiscal Affairs, which consists of senior tax officials from the member countries, has responsibility for the Model Treaty as well as other aspects of international tax cooperation. The Committee on Fiscal Affairs operates through the permanent secretariat and several working parties. The staff of the permanent secretariat dealing with matters of taxation are now part of the Centre for Tax Policy and Administration, which was created in early 2001. The working parties consist of delegates from the member countries. Working party No. 1 is responsible for the Model Treaty, and it examines issues related to the treaty on an ongoing basis.

The OECD Model favors capital exporting countries over capital importing countries. Often it eliminates or mitigates double taxation by requiring the source country to give up some or all of its tax on certain categories of income earned by residents of the other treaty country. This feature of *the OECD Model* is appropriate if the flow of trade and investment between the two countries is reasonably equal and the residence country taxes any income exempted by the source country. But for a country that is a net importer of capital, a tradeoff of source jurisdiction for residence jurisdiction is likely to be unfavourable under *the OECD Model*.

2. 《联合国范本》

相较于投资者的居民国，《联合国范本》总体上更偏向所得来源国或投资东道国的征税权。虽然这也是一些发达国家在双边协定中寻求的立场，但发展中国家长期以来更视其具有特殊的重要意义。

《联合国范本》体现了所得来源国税收管辖权原则与居民税收管辖权原则之间的妥协，尽管如上所述，它比《经合组织范本》更强调所得来源国税收管辖权。《联合国范本》无意具有规范性，而是让各国决策者知晓有关信息，了解不同情况下采取不同方法产生的后果。《联合国范本》的条文本身是不可执行的，不具有约束力，也不应被视为联合国的正式提议。相反，《联合国范本》旨在促进双边税收协定有关条款的谈判、解释和实际应用。

2. The UN Model

The UN Model generally favors retention of greater so called "source country" taxing rights under a tax treaty—the taxation rights of the host country of investment—as compared to those of the "residence country" of the investor. This has long been regarded as an issue of special significance to developing countries, although it is a position that some developed countries also seek in their bilateral treaties.

The UN Model represents a compromise between the source principle and the residence principle, although as noted above, it gives more weight to the source principle than *the OECD Model* does. *The UN Model* is not intended to be prescriptive, but to equip decision-makers in countries with the information they need to understand the consequences of these differing approaches for their country's specific situation. The provisions of *the UN Model* are not themselves enforceable. Its provisions are not binding and should not be construed as formal recommendations of the United Nations. Rather, *the UN Model* is intended to facilitate the negotiation, interpretation and practical application of bilateral tax treaties based upon its provisions.

《联合国范本》在具体做法上力求取得平衡。作为所得来源地税收管辖原则的必然结果，《联合国范本》的条文建立在所得来源国的共识基础之上：①对外国财产所得课税应当考虑该所得产生的费用，对扣除相关费用后的所得净值征税；②税收不宜过高，否则会阻碍投资；③应该考虑到与资本输出国分享所得的适当性。此外，《联合国范本》还体现了这样一种观念，即居民国适宜采取抵免法或免税法以避免双重征税。这一点与《经合组织范本》相同。

第三节　国际逃税与避税

经济全球化的多重特征使得越来越多的个人和公司得以逃税或避税。这些特征包括便利和快捷的交流，人员和财产流动的障碍逐渐消除，国际经济关系的范围逐渐扩大，各国税收制度存在差异并因此而导致不同国家间的税收负担差异，以及纳税人及其顾问越来越善于和精于使用各种不断发展的合法和非法手段规避各国税收制度。

The UN Model seeks to be balanced in its approach. As a corollary to the principle of taxation at source, the articles of *the UN Model* are based on a recognition by the source country that (a) taxation of income from foreign capital should take into account expenses allocable to the earnings of the income so that such income is taxed on a net basis, that (b) taxation should not be so high as to discourage investment and that (c) it should take into account the appropriateness of the sharing of revenue with the country providing the capital. In addition, *the UN Model* embodies the idea that it would be appropriate for the residence country to extend a measure of relief from double taxation through either a foreign tax credit or an exemption, as is also the case with *the OECD Model*.

7.3　International Tax Evasion and Tax Avoidance

Various features of the globalized economy have enabled an increasing number of individuals and companies to resort to tax evasion or tax avoidance. These features include the ease and rapidity of communications, the progressive elimination of obstacles to the movement of persons and property, the expansion of international economic relations, the differences in national tax systems and hence in the tax burden from country to country, and the growing sophistication and aggressiveness of taxpayers and their advisers in developing legal and illegal techniques for taking advantage of weaknesses in national tax systems.

一、逃税、避税、税收遵从和税收筹划

避税必须与逃税区分开来，后者是非法的，常涉及偷税或故意隐瞒收入不报。避税是指纳税人为了在合法的范围内最大限度地减少应税所得而作出的交易或安排。但是，对于一些过分的税收筹划，就很难划清避税和逃税的界线，并且各国政府界定的标准也各不相同。

1. 逃税

逃税通常与刑事犯罪有关，由故意违反税收管辖权规定的行为组成，包括蓄意向税收当局隐瞒事实。其性质是纳税人以欺诈或其他非法手段逃避法律义务。它源于非法活动导致的所得税逃避，如走私、贩毒和洗钱等。从更广泛的意义上来说，即使没有故意隐瞒所得或相关信息，逃税也可能包括因为粗心或疏忽未能依法缴纳应纳税款的情形。对于无意逃税行为，通常在补缴税款外还需另付利息和罚金。

7.3.1 Tax Evasion, Tax Avoidance, Tax Compliance and Tax Planning

Tax avoidance must be distinguished from tax evasion, which is illegal and usually involves either fraud or the intentional nondisclosure of income. Tax avoidance means transactions or arrangements entered into by a taxpayer in order to minimize the amount of tax payable in a lawful fashion. With some types of aggressive tax planning, the dividing line between avoidance and evasion is unclear, and the line may be drawn differently by different governments.

1. Tax Evasion

Tax evasion is usually associated with the commission of a criminal offense. It can be considered to consist of willful and conscious non-compliance with the laws of a taxing jurisdiction which can include a deliberate concealment of facts from revenue authorities. It is an action by which a taxpayer tries to escape legal obligations by fraudulent or other illegal means. It may result from the evasion of tax on income that arises from illegal activities, such as smuggling, drug trafficking, and money-laundering. In a broader sense, tax evasion may also encompass a reckless or negligent failure to pay taxes legally due, even if there is no deliberate concealment of income or relevant information. Notwithstanding unintended evasion normally leads to only a tax payment with interest and penalties.

一些常见的逃税行为如下所述。

(1) 纳税人在一国正在进行应纳税活动而未通知该国税务机关。

(2) 未能报告全部所得金额。

(3) 对虚假费用进行抵扣。

(4) 错误地要求对应纳税额进行不适当的减免。

(5) 未能正常缴纳到期税款。

(6) 故意在不缴纳到期税款的情况下离开该国。

(7) 违反法律义务或者不按税务机关要求，拒绝报告应税所得、利润或收益的相关信息。

Some common examples of tax evasion include the following acts.

(1) The failure to notify the taxing authorities of one's presence in the country if he or she is carrying on taxable activities.

(2) The failure to report the full amount of income.

(3) Deductions of claims for false expenses.

(4) Falsely claiming relief that is not due.

(5) The failure to pay over the proper amount of tax due.

(6) Departing from a country without paying a tax due with no intention of paying them.

(7) The failure to report items or sources of taxable income, profits or gains where there is an obligation to provide such information or if the taxing authorities have made a request for such information.

2. 避税

避税不是逃税。相比之下，避税则试图通过采取合法手段减少应纳税款的金额。当人们利用税法的漏洞或歧义安排事务时，避税便产生了。尽管使用的手段是合法的且不具有欺诈性，但其结果被认为是不正当的或是对法律的滥用。由于对避税行为的解释和法律适用存在主观性，在特定的情况下很难区分逃税与避税。一方面，各国的刑法有差异，使得根据一国法律属于犯罪的行为在另一国法律规定中可能不属于犯罪行为。另一方面，民法和刑法中有关税收欺诈的定义可能存在交叉，在特定的情况下是否追究其刑事责任尚需求助于行政自由裁量权。事实上，避税虽不是欺诈，但与反避税的司法或法律规定相冲突，其行为涉及从刑事诈骗到民事欺诈的违法范围，并不能有效减少应纳税额，而税收筹划在减税方面则具有合法性。

一些常见的避税行为如下所述。

(1) 纳税人可将住所迁移到低税或无税的国家。

(2) 纳税人可将国内来源所得转移给设立在避税港的受控外国实体(如信托或公司)。

2. Tax Avoidance

Tax avoidance is not tax evasion. Tax avoidance, in contrast, involves the attempt to reduce the amount of taxes otherwise owed by employing legal means. It occurs when persons arrange their affairs in such a way as to take advantage of weaknesses or ambiguities in the tax law. Although the means employed are legal and not fraudulent, the results are considered improper or abusive. Because of the subjectivity of the interpretation and application of tax avoidance, the borderline between evasion and avoidance in specific cases may be difficult to define. On the one hand, the criminal laws of countries differ, so that behaviour that is criminal under the laws of one country may not be criminal under the laws of another. On the other hand, the definitions of civil and criminal tax fraud may overlap, so that it is within administrative discretion whether or not to pursue a criminal fraud case in a specific instance.In reality, there is a continuum of behaviour, ranging from criminal fraud on one extreme, to civil fraud, to tax avoidance that is not fraudulent but which runs afoul of judicial or statutory anti-avoidance rules and therefore does not succeed in minimizing tax according to law, and finally to tax-planning behaviour which is successful in legal tax reduction.

Some common examples of tax avoidance include the following acts.

(1) A taxpayer can shift his or her residence from one country to another country that levies lower or no taxes.

(2) A taxpayer can divert domestic-source income to a controlled foreign entity, such as a trust or a corporation, established in a tax haven.

(3) 纳税人可在避税港设立子公司以取得外国来源所得，或者从设立在其他国家的子公司取得股息或其他分配。

(4) 如果有关国家间签有税收优惠协定，纳税人可通过设立在外国的子公司转移股息以降低对股息征收的预提税。

3. 税收遵从

税收遵从不同于避税和逃税。它被定义为依照税法的规定履行纳税义务，及时、准确地申报，按时、正确地缴纳应缴税款。避税与税收遵从的显著差异在于纳税人的意图。避税者试图少缴应纳税款，税收遵从者则希望所缴税款不少也不多。

4. 税收筹划

税收筹划是税收遵从的一部分，而不属于避税。税法反映了现代生活的复杂性以及所有纳税人合法安排自身事务的多重选择性。税法中的多重选项为纳税人提供了必要的选择机会以便他们准确地申报，这意味着确定他们想要纳税的准确金额必要时还需进行判断。

---

(3) A taxpayer can establish a tax haven subsidiary to earn foreign-source income or to receive dividends or other distributions from subsidiaries in other foreign countries.

(4) If advantageous treaties exist, a taxpayer can route dividends through subsidiaries established in foreign countries in order to reduce the withholding taxes on dividends.

3. Tax Compliance

Tax compliance is different from tax avoidance and tax evasion because it is defined as seeking to pay the right amount of tax (but no more) in the right place at the right time where right means that the economic substance of the transactions undertaken coincides with the place and form in which they are reported for taxation purposes. The significant difference between tax avoidance and tax compliance is the intent of the taxpayer. A tax avoider seeks to pay less than the tax due as required by the spirit of the law. A tax compliant taxpayer seeks to pay the tax due (but no more).

4. Tax Planning

Tax planning is a part of tax compliant behaviour, not tax avoidance. Tax law reflects the complexity of modern life and the multitude of choices and options available to all taxpayers when legitimately seeking to structure their affairs. This necessary offer of options within tax legislation creates the opportunity for choice on the part of the taxpayer and means that determining the right amount of tax (but no more) that they seek to pay does necessarily requires the exercise of judgement on occasion.

只要该判断意在使纳税人作出合法的选择，并且不会利用法律间的漏洞，那么纳税人选择如何安排自身事务的过程便是税收筹划的过程，属于合法、正当且为社会接受的行为。例如，纳税人依法选择在个人储蓄账户中存款，只要符合此类存款的各项条件，其选择行为便属于税收筹划。因此，不能指责他人使用个人储蓄账户存款的行为为避税行为。那些说此种行为属于避税的人毫无疑问是错误的。

二、逃税与避税的解决方法

全球化以及资本流动和外汇兑换的自由化，促进了经济可持续发展。然而，它们也使得避税和逃税的范围得以扩大，造成了大量的财政收入损失。国际避税与逃税引发了诸多问题。政府财政收入大量流失，如实履行纳税义务的诚实纳税人须承担额外的税负以填补税收缺口。税收遵从度高的国家将会因为贸易商品流向其他国家而走向衰落。

So long as the exercise of that judgement seeks to ensure that the taxpayer makes choices that exercise options clearly allowed by law and that they do not exploit unintended loopholes created between laws then that process of a taxpayer choosing how to structure their affairs is the process of tax planning, which is a legitimate, proper and socially acceptable act. For example, a taxpayer choosing to save in an ISA (Individual Savings Account) is exercising an option made available to them in law that is entirely tax planning so long as all the published conditions for saving in that way are met. As a consequence no one can accuse a person using an ISA of tax avoidance. Those who say they are tax avoiding can safely be said to be wrong.

7.3.2　Solutions to Tackling Tax Evasion and Tax Avoidance

Globalization and the removal of impediments to the free movement of capital and exchange controls have promoted sustainable economic development. However, they have also widened the scope for tax avoidance and tax evasion with consequential substantial loss of revenue. International tax avoidance and tax evasion cause many problems. Governments lose significant amounts of revenue and hence the honest taxpayers who do not escape their liability to pay tax must bear an additional burden to plug the gap. Countries where the tax compliance is the highest lose out, since the trade flows are diverted elsewhere.

1. 反逃税措施

1) 降低税率

高税率的盛行是逃税得以产生的首要和最主要原因。尽管逃税伴随着一定的风险，但仍然有巨大的利益。高税率会给纳税人进一步开展商业活动造成心理障碍，也会削弱纳税人进行储蓄和投资的能力与意愿。

2) 强化税务控告

政府应该全面调整，采取更积极的税务控告政策，对纳税人的内心形成威慑，使其尊重税法。此外，如果能够合理的定罪，必须追究逃税者的刑事责任。

3) 加强税收情报收集与涉税调查

为应对不断改进和日益复杂的逃税技术，政府有必要采取措施重新定位情报收集和涉税调查。政府掌控的情报调查机关也应彻底革新精简，以便妥善处理逃税威胁。

---

1. Anti-Evasion Measures

1) Reduction in Tax Rates

Prevalence of high tax rates is the first and the most reason for tax evasion, because this is what makes the evasion so profitable and attractive in spite of the attendant risks. The high rates of taxation create a psychological barrier to greater effort and undermine the capacity and the will to save and invest.

2) Vigorous Prosecution

The government should completely reorient itself to a more vigorous prosecution policy in order to instill fear and wholesome respect for the tax laws in the minds of the taxpayers. Further, where there is a reasonable chance of securing a conviction, the tax dodger should invariably be prosecuted.

3) Powerful Intelligence and Investigation

To cope with the increasing refinement and sophistication of the techniques of tax evasion, there is a need for complete re-orientation in the government's approach to its methods of intelligence and investigation. The machinery for intelligence and investigation at the command of the government should also be thoroughly overhauled and streamlined to tackle adequately the menace of tax evasion.

4) 强化账户管理与审计

法律可要求专业人员以及业务所得超过豁免限额的商人加强账户管理。如果有关商业或专业活动的销售额/营业额/所得超过豁免限额，可以制定法律要求被审计账户予以说明。

5) 加强税收稽查

为清点现金、核实库存和检查类似账户或文件，应税务官要求，并在可能的情况下，法律可授权税务官到访被评估人的任何处所。为了更好地评估涉税事项，税务官也可要求被评估人处所中的任何人提供任何额外信息和情况说明。

2. 反避税措施

1) 特别避税港条款

针对特别的滥用避税港行为，一些国家制定了具体规定。例如，德国对将住所迁移至避税港的人征收特别税。法国法律规定，如果纳税人无法说明交易的真实性，向避税港实体支付的有关利息和特许权使用费或者劳务费将不能进行抵扣。换句话说，纳税人对于抵扣的合理性负有举证责任。

4) Compulsory Accounts Maintenance and Audit

A statutory provision may be made requiring maintenance of accounts by all persons in profession, and by businessmen where the income from business is in excess of exempted limit. A provision may be introduced in the law making presentation of audited accounts mandatory in all cases of business or profession where the sales /turnovers /receipts exceed the exemption limit.

5) Powerful Survey

A statutory provision may enable the officer to visit any premises of an assessee for the purposes of counting cash, verifying stocks, and inspecting such accounts or documents, as he or she may require and which may be available there. He or she may also obtain any additional information and record statement of any person who is found at the premises, in respect of matters which would be relevant for making a proper assessment.

2. Anti-Avoidance Measures

1) Special Tax Haven Provisions

Some countries have specific provisions designed to deal with particular tax haven abuses. For example, Germany imposes a special tax on persons who move their domicile to a tax haven. Under French law, a French taxpayer cannot deduct interest and royalty payments or payments for services made to a tax haven entity unless the taxpayer establishes that the transactions are genuine. In other words, the onus of proof is placed on the taxpayer to justify such deductions.

2) 转让定价规则

许多国家制定了公司集团内或转让定价税制，以防止关联纳税人通过人为地抬高或降低关联交易价格向不同税收管辖区转移所得和费用。此类税制究竟是国际反避税规则还是一国基本税制的一部分，目前尚无定论。

3) 受控外国公司规则

一些国家制定了受控外国公司规则，以防止将消极收入和某些其他收入转移至并积累在位于避税港的受控公司。

4) 反税收协定滥用规则

为了防止滥用税收协定，一些国家坚持在税收协定中加入优惠条款的适用限制。滥用税收协定的典型表现为，非居民在一国设立法人实体以便享受该国所签署税收协定中的优惠待遇。

5) 资本弱化规则

一些国家采用了资本弱化规则，防止居民公司的非居民股东，以可抵扣的利息而非不可抵扣的股息形式，利用超额借贷资本获得公司的利润。

2) Transfer Pricing Rules

Most countries have inter-company or transfer pricing rules to prevent related taxpayers from carrying out transactions at artificially high or low prices in order to move income and expenses and various jurisdictions. It is arguable whether these rules are properly classified as international anti-avoidance rules or whether they are just part of a country's basic tax system.

3) Controlled Foreign Corporation Rules

Some countries adopt controlled foreign corporation rules to prevent the diversion of passive and certain other income to, and the accumulation of such income in, a controlled corporation established in a tax haven.

4) Anti-treaty Shopping Rules

Some countries insist on the inclusion of a limitation on benefits article in its tax treaties to prevent treaty shopping. Treaty shopping typically involves the establishment of a legal entity in a country by non-residents in order to get the benefits of the country's tax treaties.

5) Thin Capitalization Rules

Several countries have adopted thin capitalization rules to prevent nonresident shareholders of resident corporations from using excessive debt capital to extract corporate profits in the form of deductible interest rather than as nondeductible dividends.

第四节　主要的多边税收协定

大致来说，税收协定旨在消除商品和资本跨境流动的税收障碍，促进跨境贸易和投资的发展。这一总体目标是通过几个具体的操作性目标来实现的。

税收协定最重要的操作性目标就是消除双重征税。典型双边税收协定中的绝大部分实质性内容都以此为目的。历史上对消除双重征税这一目标的关注不应掩盖一个事实，即大多数税收协定还同样关注的另一个操作性目标——防止偷漏税。后者与前者并驾齐驱。尽管大多数税收协定都将防止偷漏税列为明确目标，但却很少有条款论及该目标实现的具体措施。甚至连"偷漏税"这一概念在典型的税收协定中也没有清晰的定义。

除了以上两个主要操作性目标之外，税收协定还有一些辅助性目标。一个是消除对外国国民和非居民的税收歧视；另一个是在缔约国之间进行情报交换。情报交换可以作为打击偷漏税的重要工具，也有利于国家向纳税人提供适当救济以避免双重征税。最后，大多数缔约国还在税收协定中制定了税收争端解决机制。

7.4　Main Multilateral Tax Treaties

The objective of tax treaties, broadly stated, is to facilitate cross-border trade and investment by eliminating the tax impediments to these cross-border flows. This broad objective is supplemented by several specific, operational objectives.

The most important operational objective of bilateral tax treaties is the elimination of double taxation. Most of the substantive provisions of the typical bilateral tax treaty are directed at the achievement of this goal. The historical emphasis on the elimination of double taxation should not obscure the fact that most tax treaties have another equally important operational objective—the prevention of fiscal evasion. This objective counterbalances the elimination of double taxation. Although the elimination of fiscal evasion is an explicit objective of most tax treaties, few provisions in those treaties are designed to achieve it. Even the meaning of the term "fiscal evasion" in the typical tax treaty is unclear.

In addition to the two principal operational objectives of tax treaties, there are several ancillary objectives. One ancillary objective is the elimination of discrimination against foreign nationals and nonresidents. A second ancillary objective is the exchange of information between the contracting states. The exchange of information can be an important tool in combating fiscal evasion and may allow countries to provide taxpayers with the appropriate relief from double taxation. Finally, most contracting states provide a mechanism in their treaties for resolving disputes arising from the interaction of their tax systems.

一、《多边税收征管互助公约》

　　《多边税收征管互助公约》是欧洲委员会根据经合组织财政事务委员会编写的第一份草案制定的。该公约于 1988 年 1 月 25 日向欧洲委员会和经合组织的成员国开放供签署。然而，直到 1995 年，公约才达到足够的签署国数量并生效。该公约于 2010 年通过议定书形式进行了修订。它为各国开展税收合作打击跨境逃税和避税提供了最全面的多边措施。修订后的公约于 2011 年 6 月 1 日向全球所有国家开放。2013 年，中国加入并签署了该公约。

7.4.1　*The Multilateral Convention on Mutual Administrative Assistance in Tax Matters*

The Multilateral Convention on Mutual Administrative Assistance in Tax Matters were developed within the Council of Europe, based on a first draft prepared by the OECD Committee on Fiscal Affairs. The Multilateral Convention was opened for signature on January 25, 1988 and is open to the Member States of the Council of Europe and the Member Countries of the OECD. A sufficient number of signatures has been obtained, however, to bring the Convention into force in 1995. The Multilateral Convention was amended by Protocol in 2010. It is the most comprehensive multilateral instrument available for all forms of tax cooperation to tackle tax evasion and tax avoidance for all countries. The amended convention was opened for signature on June 1, 2011. China joined and signed the Multilateral Convention on in 2013.

该公约通常要求每个缔约国向其他缔约国提供税收征管协助。考虑到税收的广泛性，公约提供了三种基本的税收征管协助形式：情报交换、税款追缴和文书送达。情报交换方面，各缔约国均须向其他国家提供其所掌握的一切可预见与其他国家的税务管理和征收工作有关的资料。即便不拥有，如应其他缔约国的请求，一缔约国也须利用一切可用的手段执行和实施其自身税法，以便获得与该其他缔约国在税收征管有可预见的相关性的各类税收情报。再者，由于各国程序性限制，公约要求每个缔约国应像对待自身税收主张一样，采取必要措施追索其他缔约国的税收主张。有关文书送达的规定，公约要求每个缔约国为此目的利用其国内法律，如同对待自身的税负一样。

二、《金融账户涉税信息自动交换多边主管当局间协议》

《金融账户涉税信息自动交换多边主管当局间协议》是一个多边框架协议，它提供了一个标准化的有效机制，以促进金融账户涉税信息自动交换，无须再行缔结其他双边协议。

The Multilateral Convention generally requires that each Contracting State provides administrative assistance in tax matters to each other Contracting State. The Convention provides for three basic categories of assistance, with regard to a wide range of taxes: exchange of information, assistance in the collection of taxes, and service of documents. With respect to the first category, each Contracting State is required to make available to the other States all information in its possession that is "foreseeably relevant" to the other States' tax administration and collection efforts. Each State must also utilize all means available to it in administering and enforcing its own tax laws to obtain foreseeably relevant information not in its possession if so requested by other States. Also, subject to various procedural limitations, the Convention requires each State to enforce tax claims of the other States as though the taxes were those of the enforcing State. The Convention's provisions on service of documents require each State to utilize its domestic laws for this purpose, as though the tax liability were owed to the serving State.

7.4.2 *The Multilateral Competent Authority Agreement on Automatic Exchange of Financial Account Information*

The Multilateral Competent Authority Agreement on Automatic Exchange of Financial Account Information (the MCAA) is a multilateral framework agreement that provides a standardized and efficient mechanism to facilitate the automatic exchange of information. It avoids the need for several bilateral agreements to be concluded.

该协议进一步规定了信息交换的范围与时间。根据协议第 7 条，辖区(即签署协议的某个国家或者地区)在签署本协议时应提交通知，随后的辖区间双边信息交换便开始生效。每个辖区所提交的通知内容包括：①确认该辖区存在必要的法律以实施统一报告标准，以及该辖区是否将以互惠或非互惠方式进行信息交换；②详细说明数据传输和加密的方法；③详细说明符合该辖区信息交换要求的数据保护措施；④确认该辖区具有适当的保密措施和数据保护措施；⑤列明协议项下有意愿与之进行信息交换的伙伴辖区名单。该协议项下，特定双边信息交换关系产生效力须具备三个条件：双方辖区批准生效《多边税收征管互助公约》、提交上述通知并互相列为伙伴辖区。

作为框架协议，该协议旨在确保每个签署国对其建立的信息交换关系进行完全、最终的控制，并确保每个签署国有关保密性和数据保护的自身标准始终得以适用。

该协议是在主管当局层面达成的，其法律依据是《多边税收征管互助公约》第 6 条。该条规定，只有在自身同意的情况下，缔约方才可相互自动交换信息。

The MCAA specifies the details of what information will be exchanged and when. Accordingly, the subsequent bilateral exchanges come into effect between those signatories that file the subsequent notifications under Section 7 of *the MCAA*. The notifications to be filed by each jurisdiction include (a)a confirmation that domestic Common Reporting Standard(CRS) legislation is in place and whether the jurisdiction will exchange on a reciprocal or non-reciprocal basis; (b)a specification of the transmission and encryption methods; (c)a specification of the data protection requirements to be met in relation to information exchanged by the jurisdiction; (d)a confirmation that the jurisdiction has appropriate confidentiality and data safeguards in place; (e)a list of its intended exchange partner jurisdictions under *the MCAA*. A particular bilateral relationship under *the MCAA* becomes effective only if both jurisdictions have the Convention in effect, have filed the above notifications and have listed each other.

Its design as a framework agreement means *the MCAA* always ensures each signatory has ultimate control over exactly which exchange relationships it enters into and that each signatory's standards on confidentiality and data protection always apply.

The legal basis for *the MCAA* (which is agreed at competent authority level) rests in Article 6 of *the Multilateral Convention on Mutual Administrative Assistance in Tax Matters (the Convention)* which provides for the automatic exchange of information between parties to the Convention, where two parties subsequently agree to do so.

三、《实施税收协定相关措施以防止税基侵蚀和利润转移的多边公约》

在 2015 年 2 月 G20 财长和央行行长会议的授权下，《实施税收协定相关措施以防止税基侵蚀和利润转移的多边公约》由 100 多个国家和辖区谈判达成，并于 2016 年 11 月 24 日获得通过。2017 年 6 月 7 日，70 多位部长和其他高级代表参加了该公约的签字仪式。签署方包括各大洲辖区以及不同发展水平辖区。

通过将经合组织/G20 税基侵蚀和利润转移项目成果转换为全球范围内的双边税收协定，该公约为减少政府间现有国际税收规则差异提供了解决之道。该公约修订了数千个旨在消除双重征税的双边税收协定的适用方式。在容许具体税收协定政策灵活实施的同时，该公约还实施各方均认可的最低标准，以防止税收条约滥用并改进争端解决机制。

7.4.3 *The Multilateral Convention to Implement Tax Treaty Related Measures to Prevent Base Erosion and Profit Shifting*

The Multilateral Convention to Implement Tax Treaty Related Measures to Prevent Base Erosion and Profit Shifting was developed through a negotiation involving more than 100 countries and jurisdictions and adopted on November 24, 2016, under a mandate delivered by G20 Finance Ministers and Central Bank Governors at their February 2015 meeting. On June 7, 2017, over 70 Ministers and other high-level representatives participated in the signing ceremony of the Multilateral Convention to Implement Tax Treaty Related Measures to Prevent Base Erosion and Profit Shifting. Signatories include jurisdictions from all continents and all levels of development.

The Multilateral Convention offers concrete solutions for governments to close the gaps in existing international tax rules by transposing results from the OECD/G20 Base Erosion and Profit Shifting Project into bilateral tax treaties worldwide. The Multilateral Convention modifies the application of thousands of bilateral tax treaties concluded to eliminate double taxation. It also implements agreed minimum standards to counter treaty abuse and to improve dispute resolution mechanisms while providing flexibility to accommodate specific tax treaty policies.

综 合 练 习

1. 什么是国际税收管辖权？

2. 居民税收管辖权与所得来源地税收管辖权之间的区别是什么？

3. 举例说明国际双重征税的类型。

4. 列出避免国际双重征税的措施。

5. 国际逃税和国际避税之间的区别是什么？

6. 列出国际逃税与国际避税的解决方法。

7. 简述主要的多边税收协定。

Comprehensive Exercises

1. What is jurisdiction to international tax?

2. What are the differences between residence-based taxation and source-based taxation?

3. Give an example of each type of international double taxation.

4. List measures to avoid international double taxation.

5. What are the differences between international tax evasion and tax avoidance?

6. List the solutions to international tax evasion and tax avoidance.

7. Give a briefing of main multilateral tax treaties.

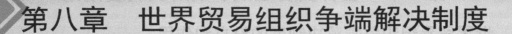

第八章 世界贸易组织争端解决制度

学习目标

了解世界贸易组织争端解决制度的背景知识。

了解世界贸易组织争端解决制度的作用、范围和主要原则。

掌握世界贸易组织争端解决制度的程序、功能以及专家组和上诉机构的职责。

Chapter 8   The WTO Dispute Settlement System

Learning Objectives

To know the background of the WTO dispute settlement system.

To know the role, coverage, main principles of the WTO dispute settlement system.

To grasp the WTO dispute settlement procedures, the function as well as the competence of the panel and the Appellate Body.

第一节　世界贸易组织争端解决制度概论

一、世界贸易组织争端解决制度的设立和作用

　　一体化的争端解决制度是世界贸易组织(WTO)所体现的多边贸易体制的重要部分。世界贸易组织争端解决制度建立在五十多年来不断演进的关税与贸易总协定(GATT)实践基础之上。不过这些实践主要源于在《1994 年关税与贸易总协定》第 22 条和 23 条基础上所做的一系列"非正式的"或"务实的"安排,对争端解决制度并没有起到实际的指导作用。《关于争端解决规则与程序的谅解》(DSU)共有 27 条和 4 个附件,进一步详细规定了争端解决的规则和程序,由世界贸易组织所有成员签署且适用于几乎所有的世界贸易组织协定。

8.1　Introduction to the WTO Dispute Settlement System

8.1.1　The Establishment and Role of the WTO Dispute Settlement System

　　The integrated dispute settlement system is an important part of the multilateral trading system embodied in the World Trade Organization (WTO). The WTO system of dispute settlement builds on the practices in the GATT as they have evolved over five decades. However, those practices had grown up largely in a series of informal or "pragmatic" arrangements based on Articles 22 and 23 of *the GATT 1994* that gave indeed little guidance. The rules and procedures of settlement of dispute are further elaborated in *the Understanding on Rules and Procedures Governing the Settlement of Disputes (DSU)*, with 27 articles and four appendices, subscribed to by all the WTO members and applicable to virtually all of the WTO agreements.

　　《关于争端解决规则与程序的谅解》(以下简称《争端解决谅解》)设立了世界贸易组织的争端解决机制，是提供多边贸易体制可靠性和预见性的核心。它旨在保护成员在世界贸易组织适用协议下享有的权利和义务，并根据国际公法解释的习惯规则澄清这些协议的现有条文。世界贸易组织总理事会作为争端解决机构召开会议，处理世界贸易组织成员之间的争端。当一个成员政府认为另一个成员政府违反某项协议或其在世界贸易组织作出的承诺时，争端就会由此产生。争端解决机构(DSB)负责《争端解决谅解》的实施，有权建立争端解决专家组和常设的上诉机构，将争议事项提交仲裁，通过专家组决议，上诉机构和仲裁报告，监督这些报告中所载建议和裁决的执行，如果发现被告方没有或不能遵照这些建议和裁定，则可以授权中止减让或报复。除了解决贸易争端外，争端解决机构的另一个重要职责是澄清和解释有关协议的现有规则，以作为维护成员权利和义务以及解决争端的前提。专家组或上诉机构通过的争端解决报告虽然仅对贸易争端的当事方具有约束力且并不构成先例规则，但对未来世界贸易组织贸易争端的解决将产生持续的影响。

The DSU sets up the dispute settlement system of the WTO and is a central element in providing security and predictability to the multilateral trading system. It serves to preserve the rights and obligations of members under the WTO covered agreements, and to clarify the existing provisions of those agreements in accordance with customary rules of interpretation of the public international law. The General Council of WTO convenes as the Dispute Settlement Body to deal with disputes between the WTO members. Such disputes may arise when a member government believes another member government is violating an agreement or a commitment that it has made in the WTO. The DSB administers the DSU and has authority to establish dispute settlement panels and a standing Appellate Body, refer matters to arbitration, adopt the panel, Appellate Body and arbitration reports, maintain surveillance over the implementation of recommendations and rulings contained in such reports, and authorize suspension of concessions or retaliation if a respondent party is found to be out of the compliance with those recommendations and rulings. Apart from resolving trade disputes, another important duty and function of the DSB is to clarify and construe existing rules of the covered agreements, which works as the premise of preservation of the rights and obligations of members as well as resolution of disputes. The adopted dispute settlement report of a panel, or of the Appellate Body, although binding only on the parties to a particular trade dispute and constituting no principle of stare decisis, will have a continuing influence on future resolutions of disputes within the WTO.

二、适用范围

　　只有作为世界贸易组织成员的政府和单独关税区才能以争端当事方或第三方的身份直接参与到解决争端中来。《争端解决谅解》适用于《建立世界贸易组织协定》《多边货物贸易协定》《服务贸易总协议》《与贸易有关的知识产权协定》《争端解决谅解》自身和诸边贸易协定下产生的争端。一些协议中也规定了争端解决条款，增添或变更了《争端解决谅解》的规定，但仅适用于就该特定协议引起的争端，也就是说，若《争端解决谅解》的规则和程序与上述协议的特殊或额外规则和程序之间存在差异，应以特殊或额外的规则和程序为准。

8.1.2　Coverage

Only governments and separate customs territories that are members of the WTO can participate directly in dispute settlement as parties to the case or as third parties. *The DSU* applies to disputes under *the Agreement Establishing the World Trade Organization (WTO Agreement)*, *Multilateral Agreements on Trade in Goods*, *General Agreement On Trade in Services(GATS)*, *Trade-Related Aspects of Intellectual Property Rights(TRIPS)*, *DSU* and *Plurilateral Trade Agreements*. Some of agreements above have dispute settlement provisions that apply only to disputes arising under that specific agreement that add to or change the rules of *the DSU*, that is, if there is a difference between the rules and procedures of *the DSU* and the special or additional rules and procedures set forth in the agreements above, the special or additional rules and procedures shall prevail.

以保障措施为例，按照《争端解决谅解》第 22 条的规定，如有关成员未能纠正被裁定违反世界贸易组织协议的行为，或未能在合理期限里符合建议和裁决，则该成员如收到请求，应在不迟于合理期限满前，与援引争端解决程序的任何一方进行谈判，以期形成双方可接受的补偿。如在合理期限结束期满之日起 20 日内未能议定令人满意的补偿，则援引争端解决程序的任何一方可向争端解决机构请求授权，中止对有关成员实施适用协定项下的减让或其他义务，也就是说，请求授权实施报复。但是根据《保障措施协议》第 8 条，若磋商未能在 30 日内达成协议，则受影响的出口方可在不迟于保障措施实施后的 90 日内，且在从货物贸易理事会收到关于中止的书面通知 30 日期满时，对实施保障措施成员方的贸易自行中止所适用的实质性相等的减让或其他义务。相比之下，《保障措施协议》对实施报复措施设置的限制更少。

Take the disputes with respect to the safeguard measures as an instance, pursuant to Article 22 of *the DSU*, if the member concerned fails to bring the measure found to be inconsistent with a covered agreement into compliance therewith or otherwise comply with the recommendations and rulings within the reasonable period of time, such member shall, if so requested, and no later than the expiry of the reasonable period of time, enter into negotiations with any party having invoked the dispute settlement procedures, with a view to developing mutually acceptable compensation, and if no satisfactory compensation has been agreed within 20 days after the date of expiry of the reasonable period of time, any party having invoked the dispute settlement procedures may request authorization from the DSB to suspend the application to the member concerned of concessions or other obligations under the covered agreements, that is, request authorization to retaliate. However, pursuant to Article 8 of *the Agreement on Safeguards*, if no agreement is reached within 30 days in the consultations, the affected exporting members shall be free, not later than 90 days after the measure is applied, to suspend, upon the expiration of 30 days from the day on which written notice of such suspension is received by the Council for Trade in Goods, the application of substantially equivalent concessions or other obligations to the trade of the member applying the safeguard measure. In comparison, *the Agreement on Safeguards* imposes fewer restraints on the implementation of retaliatory measures.

特定协议中特殊或额外的争端解决规则和程序如下(见表 8-1)。

表 8-1　特殊或额外的争端解决规则和程序一览

协议名称	特殊或额外的争端解决条款
《反倾销协议》	17.4 至 17.7
《海关估价协议》	19.3 至 19.5，附件 2，2(f)，3，9，21
《服务贸易总协议》	22.3, 23.3
《服务贸易总协议航空运输服务的附件》	4
《服务贸易总协议金融服务附件》	4
《对服务贸易总协议某些争端解决程序的决定》	1 至 5
《补贴与反补贴措施协议》	4.2 至 4.12，6.6，7.2 至 7.10，8.5，脚注 35，24.4，27.7，附件 5
《实施卫生与植物卫生措施协议》	11.2
《技术贸易壁垒协议》	14.2 至 14.4，附件 2

Special or additional rules and procedures of dispute settlement under specific agreements are as follows(see Table 8-1).

Table 8-1　List of Special or Additional Rules and Procedures of Dispute Settlement

Agreement	Special or Additional Dispute Settlement Clauses
Anti-dumping Agreement	17.4 through 17.7
Rules on Customs Valuation	19.3 through 19.5, Annex 2, 2(f), 3,9,21
GATS	22.3, 23.3
GATS Annex on Air Transport Services	4
GATS Annex on Financial Services	4
Decisions on Certain Dispute Settlement Procedures for the GATS	1 through 5
Agreement on Subsidies and Countervailing Measures (SCM Agreement)	4.2 through 4.12, 6.6, 7.2 through 7.10, 8.5, Footnote 35, 24.4, 27.7, Annex 5
Agreement on the Application of Sanitary and Phytosanitary Measures (SPS Agreement)	11.2
Agreement on Technical Barriers to Trade (TBT Agreement)	14.2 through 14.4, Annex 2

三、争端解决的程序

《1947 年关税与贸易总协定》中规定了解决争端的程序，但它没有固定的时间表，导致裁决很容易被拖延，许多案件拖延了很长时间却毫无结果。世界贸易组织争端解决机制引进的争端解决过程更具结构化，程序中的各个阶段规定得更为明晰，强调及时解决争端对于世界贸易组织有效运作的重要性。此外，它包含两项主要的创新，即规定上诉机构对专家组决定进行上诉审查，以及规定如果发现一个败诉方未遵守专家组或上诉机构报告的建议和裁决，没有撤销或改正其遭异议的做法，如何作出补偿或授权报复。

1. 磋商

世界贸易组织争端解决制度意在首先通过磋商解决争端，而非裁决。因此第一阶段被称为"磋商请求"，相关成员方首先尽量通过磋商来解决争端，即使案件进展到其他阶段，仍然可以进行磋商和调解。

8.1.3　Procedures for Dispute Settlement

A procedure for settling disputes did exist under *the GATT of 1947*, but it had no fixed timetables, rulings were easier to be put off, and many cases dragged on for a long time inconclusively. The WTO system of dispute settlement introduces a more structured process with more clearly defined stages in the procedure and emphasizes that prompt settlement is essential if the WTO is to function effectively. Moreover, it contains two major innovations, that is, one provision for appellate review of panel decisions by an Appellate Body, and the other provision for compensation or retaliation if a losing party found to be incompliance with recommendations and rulings of the report of the panel, or of the Appellate Body does not repeal or modify its objectionable practice.

1. Consultation

The WTO dispute settlement system is not designed to pass judgment, its priority is to settle disputes through consultation. The first stage is therefore known as a "request for consultations" as the members concerned will initially try to resolve the dispute by consulting with one another, and even when the case has progressed to other stages, consultation and mediation are still always possible.

如果一成员认为另一成员采取的措施剥夺了前者根据关税与贸易总协定或其他有关协定可获得的利益，则可要求与后者磋商。收到磋商请求的成员应当自收到请求之日起 10 日内作出回复，并应在收到磋商请求之日起 30 日内进行磋商，否则申诉方可以直接请求成立专家组。如果在收到磋商请求之日起 60 日内磋商未能解决争端，申诉方可以要求设立专家组，或者，如果两方一致认为磋商不能解决争端，那么两方可以联合请求成立专家组。在紧急情况下，包括涉及易腐货物的，成员应在收到请求之日起 10 日内进行磋商。如果在收到请求之日起 20 日内磋商未能解决纠纷，申诉方可以请求设立专家组。

2. 专家组

1）成立专家组

如果申诉方以书面形式提出请求，专家组应最迟在该项请求首次列入议程的会议之后的争端解决机构会议上设立，除非在此次会议上争端解决机构一致同意不设立专家组。因此，即使被诉方有能力控制其他大部分成员，也不可能阻止或延迟组建专家组。

If a member considers that a measure adopted by another member has deprived it of a benefit accruing to it under the GATT or under one of the other covered agreements, it may call for consultations with the other member. The member to which the consultation request is made by the complaining party shall reply to the request within 10 days after the date of its receipt and shall enter into consultations within 30 days after the date of receipt of the request, otherwise the complaining party may proceed directly to request the establishment of a panel. If the consultations fail to settle a dispute within 60 days after the date of receipt of the request for consultations, the complaining party may request the establishment of a panel. Alternatively, the two parties may make a joint request that a panel should be established if they consider that consultations will not resolve the disputes. In cases of urgency, including those which concern perishable goods, members shall enter into consultations within 10 days after the date of receipt of the request. If the consultations have failed to settle the dispute within 20 days after the date of receipt of the request, the complaining party may request the establishment of a panel.

2. Panel

1) Establishment of Panel

If a complaining party so requests in writing, an ad hoc panel shall be established at the latest at the meeting of the DSB following the meeting where the request is first placed on the agenda, unless the DSB decides by consensus not to establish a panel at that meeting. Thus, it is not possible for the respondent member party to prevent or delay the establishment of a panel, even if its position could command a majority of other members.

2) 专家组程序

(1) 首次听证(第一次实质性会议)之前。

专家组通常由秘书处任命的三至五名专家组成，负责接收各方的书面和口头陈述，在此基础上作出事实认定和结论提交给争端解决机构。专家组会议是封闭的，争端各方和利益相关方只有在专家组邀请时才可出席会议。

在专家组第一次实质性会议之前，争端各方应向专家组转交案件事实及其意见的书面材料。一般来说，申诉方首先提交书面材料，被诉方随后提交其书面材料。

(2) 第一次实质性会议。

在第一次实质性会议上，专家组将要求申诉方介绍案情，被诉方陈述其观点。专家组应当以书面方式邀请所有已通知争端解决机构其在争端中有利害关系的第三方，在专家组第一次实质性会议期间专门安排的会议上书面阐明其意见。

(3) 第二次实质性会议。

各方应在专家组第二次实质性会议之前向专家组提交书面辩驳意见，然后在该次会议上进行正式抗辩并口头辩论。被诉方有权首先陈述其观点，然后是申诉方。专家组可随时向各方提出问题，并要求他们在各方出席的会议上进行解释或另行作出书面解释。

---

2) Panel procedures

(1) Before the first hearing (the first substantive meeting).

The panel, normally consisting of three or five individuals appointed by the Secretariat, sits to receive written and oral submissions of the parties, on the basis of which it is expected to make findings and conclusions for presentation to the DSB. The panel shall meet in closed session. The parties to the dispute, and interested parties, shall be present at the meetings only when invited by the panel to appear before it.

Before the first substantive meeting of the panel, the parties to the dispute shall transmit the written submissions in which they present the facts of the case and their arguments to the panel. Generally the complaining party will make the first written submission, the respondent party will make the second written submission.

(2) The first substantive meeting.

At its first substantive meeting, the panel will ask the complaining party to present its case and the respondent party to present its point of view. All third parties who have notified their interest in the dispute to the DSB shall be invited in writing to present their views during a session of the first substantive meeting of the panel set aside for that purpose.

(3) A second substantive meeting.

The parties shall submit, prior to a second substantive meeting of the panel, written rebuttals to the panel, and then make formal rebuttals and present oral arguments at that meeting. The respondent party shall have the right to present its positions first to be followed by the complaining party. The panel may at any time put questions to the parties and ask them for explanations either in the course of a meeting with the parties or in writing.

(4) 报告的说明部分。

在审议反驳意见和口头辩论后，专家组将其报告的说明(即事实和争议点)部分发给当事方供其评论，其中载有相关事实，各方的观点总结，但不包括调查结果和结论。这一做法是为了发现一些可以纠正的错误，因为一旦出现错误，将会削弱最终报告的价值。

(5) 临时报告。

专家组收到各方对报告陈述部分的意见后 2 至 4 周内，将以临时版本的形式发布完整的报告，包括陈述部分和专家组的调查结果和结论，以供各方审查评议。

(6) 最终报告。

在专家组规定的期限内，各方可书面要求专家组在将最终报告分发给世界贸易组织各成员之前对临时报告的细节问题进行审议。应争端方要求，专家组将同争端方举行新的会议，讨论其收到的书面评论中所阐述的问题。如果在评议期内没有收到争端方的任何评论，临时报告即视为最终专家组报告，并立即分发给所有世界贸易组织成员。

---

(4) Descriptive sections of the report.

Following the consideration of the rebuttal submissions and oral arguments, the panel will issue the descriptive (factual and argument) sections of its report, containing the relevant facts, a summary of the positions of the parties to the dispute, and not including findings and conclusions, for their comments. The idea of this practice is to avoid mistakes that could have been corrected, and that should not be permitted later on to undermine the value of the final report.

(5) Interim report.

Within 2-4 weeks of receipt by the panel of comments on the descriptive part, the panel is to issue its complete report—first in an interim version, including both the descriptive sections and the panel's findings and conclusions, for review by the parties.

(6) Final report.

Within a period set by the panel, a party may submit a written request for the panel to review precise aspects of the interim report prior to circulation of the final report to all the members of the WTO. At the request of a party, the panel shall hold a further meeting with the parties on the issues identified in the received written comments. If no comments are received from any party within the comment period, the interim report shall be considered the final panel report and circulated promptly to all the WTO members.

一般而言，专家组的审理裁决期限，从专家组成立及其权限范围确定之日起到向争端各方分发最终报告为止，一般不超过 6 个月，紧急情况下不超过 3 个月。如果专家组认为不能在 6 个月内发布报告，可以请求争端解决机构延期，但不得超过 9 个月。实际上，给予专家组 9 个月的审理裁决期限已经相当普遍。

以下附上专家组工作时间表(见表 8-2)。

The period in which the panel shall conduct its examination, from the date that the composition and terms of reference of the panel have been agreed upon until the date the final report is issued to the parties to the dispute, shall, as a general rule, not exceed 6 months, or be within 3 months in case of urgency. If the panel considers that it cannot issue its report within 6 months, it may seek an extension from the DSB, but in no case should the period exceed 9 months. In practice, the nine-month period for the panel has become common.

Proposed timetable for the panel work is as follows(see Table 8-2).

表 8-2　专家组工作时间表

步　　骤	期　　限
1. 收到争端方第一份书面意见	申诉方：3-6 周 应诉方：2-3 周
2. 争端方及第三方参与的专家组首次实质性会议的日期、时间及地点	1-2 周
3. 收到争端方的书面辩驳	2-3 周
4. 争端方参与的第二次实质性会议的日期、时间及地点	1-2 周
5. 向各方分发报告的说明部分	2-4 周
6. 收取各方对报告说明部分的意见	2 周
7. 向各方分发临时报告(包括调查结果和结论)	2-4 周
8. 各方要求对报告部分内容进行审议的期限	1 周
9. 专家组审议期限，包括可能与各方再次召开的会议	2 周
10. 向争端方发出最终报告	2 周
11. 向其他成员分发最终报告	3 周

Table 8-2　Proposed Timetable for Panel Work

Steps	Time limits
1. Receipt of the first written submission of the disputing party	Complaining Party: 3-6 weeks Party complained against: 2-3 weeks
2. Date, time and place of the first substantive meeting with the parties or a third party	1-2 weeks
3. Receipt of the written rebuttals of the parties	2-3 weeks
4. Date, time and place of a second substantive meeting with the parties	1-2 weeks
5. Issuance of the descriptive part of the report to the parties	2-4 weeks
6. Receipt of comments by the parties on the descriptive part of the report	2 weeks
7. Issuance of the interim report, including the findings and conclusions, to the parties	2-4 weeks
8. Deadline for the parties to request review of part(s) of the report	1 week
9. Period of review by the panel, including possible additional meeting with the parties	2 weeks
10. Issuance of the final report to the parties to the dispute	2 weeks
11. Circulation of the final report to the members	3 weeks

3) 通过专家组报告

如果一成员方对专家组报告有反对意见，应至少在审议该报告的争端解决机构会议召开前 10 天以书面形式提出异议以及理由。争端方有权全面参与争端解决机构对专家组报告的审议，他们的意见也会完整记录在案。在专家组报告分发给各成员之日起 60 天内，该报告在争端解决机构会议上通过，除非一争端方正式通知争端解决机构其上诉决定，或争端解决机构经协商一致决定不通过该报告。实践中，争端方和其他成员均可就专家组报告提出意见，但除提出上诉外，即使争端解决机构中反对者占大部分，也无法阻止报告的通过。

3. 上诉审查

1) 上诉机构审查程序

争端解决机构设立了一个常设上诉机构，负责审理争端方对专家组案件的上诉。值得强调的是，只有争端方才可以就专家组报告提出上诉，第三方无此权利。上诉机构由七名权威人士组成，他们在法律、国际贸易方面和对有关协定项下的问题上有明显的专长，并且不隶属于任何政府机关。

---

3) Adoption of the Panel Report

Members having objections to a panel report shall give written reasons to explain their objections for circulation at least 10 days prior to the DSB meeting at which the panel report will be considered. The parties to a dispute shall have the right to participate fully in the consideration of the panel report by the DSB, and their views shall be fully recorded. Within 60 days after the date of circulation of a panel report to the Members, the report shall be adopted at a DSB meeting unless a party to the dispute formally notifies the DSB of its decision to appeal or the DSB decides by consensus not to adopt the report. In practice, the parties to a dispute and other members may give their views on the report, but, apart from appeal, they cannot block its adoption, even if the opponents command a majority of the DSB.

3. Appellate Review

1) Appellate Body Review Procedure

A standing Appellate Body is established by the DSB for hearing appeals from the panel cases by the parties. What should be stressed here is that only the parties to the dispute, not the third parties, may appeal a panel report. The Appellate Body is composed of seven persons with recognized authority and with demonstrated expertise in law, international trade and the subject matter of the covered agreements generally and unaffiliated with any government.

上诉只限于专家组报告所涉及的法律问题和专家组所作的法律解释。上诉机构将收取各方的书面和口头陈述，并可维持、修改或撤销专家组的法律裁决和结论。上诉机构被视为是必要的安全阀，以防止错误的专家组决定在争端解决机构自动通过。《争端解决谅解》的起草人同样也谨慎地注意到，上诉不能成为拖延的工具，并在《争端解决谅解》中规定，从争端一方通知其上诉决定起，到上诉机构分发其报告之日止，上诉审查程序一般不得超过 60 天。在任何情况下，该程序都不得超过 90 天。

2) 通过上诉机构报告

成员方可以就上诉机构的报告表达意见，但不能阻挠该报告通过。上诉机构报告应由争端解决机构通过，争端各方应无条件地予以接受，除非在上诉机构报告分发到各成员 30 天内，争端解决机构经协商一致不予通过。

An appeal shall be limited to issues of law covered in the panel report and legal interpretations developed by the panel. The Appellate Body will receive the written and oral submissions of the parties, and it may uphold, modify, or reverse the legal findings and conclusions of the panel. The institution of the Appellate Body is seen as a necessary safety valve to prevent erroneous panel decisions from being automatically adopted by the DSB. The drafters of *the DSU* were also careful to see to it that appeals not serve as an instrument of delay, and wrote into *the DSU* that the appellate review proceedings shall not exceed 60 days in general from the date a party to the dispute notifies its decision to the date the Appellate Body circulates its report. In no case shall the proceedings exceed 90 days.

2) Adoption of the Appellate Body Report

Members may express their positions on the report of the Appellate Body, but they cannot derail it. An Appellate Body report shall be adopted by the DSB and unconditionally accepted by the parties to the dispute unless the DSB decides by consensus not to adopt the Appellate Body report within 30 days following its circulation to all the WTO members.

4. 争端解决机构作出最终建议或裁决

《争端解决谅解》第 20 条概括了整个争端解决程序：除争端方另有约定外，自争端解决机构设立专家组之日起至争端解决机构审议通过专家组报告或上诉机构报告之日止的期限，在未对专家组报告提出上诉的情况下一般不得超过 9 个月；在提出上诉的情况下通常不得超过 12 个月。如果专家组或上诉机构延长提交相应报告的时间，则上述期限也相应地延长。

5. 争端解决机构建议和裁决的执行

争端解决的首要选择是实施争端解决机构的建议和裁决，其次才适用补偿和中止减让或其他义务等临时措施。《争端解决谅解》对遵守和报复问题的强调前所未有地严格和彻底，指出为了所有成员的利益而确保有效的争端解决，迅速遵守争端解决机构的建议或裁决是必要的。

《争端解决谅解》第 21 条规定了遵守程序的完整顺序和行为准则。

1）遵守的意向

在通过专家组或上诉机构报告之日起 30 日内举行的争端解决机构会议上，有关成员应向争端解决机构通报其执行建议和裁决的相关意向。

---

4. Final Recommendations or Findings of the DSB

Article 20 of *the DSU* summarizes the whole dispute procedures: Unless otherwise agreed to by the parties to the dispute, the period from the date of establishment of the panel by the DSB until the date the DSB considers the panel or appellate report for adoption shall as a general rule not exceed nine months where the panel report is not appealed or 12 months where the report is appealed. Where either the panel or the Appellate Body has acted to extend the time for providing its report, the additional time taken shall be added to the above periods.

5. Implementation of the DSB's Recommendations and Findings

The primary alternative for dispute settlement is the implementation of DSB's recommendations and rulings, otherwise compensation and the suspension of concessions or other obligations will be available as temporary measures. *The DSU* addresses the issue of compliance and retaliation in unprecedented strictness and thoroughness, stating that prompt compliance with recommendations or rulings of the DSB is essential in order to ensure effective resolution of disputes to the benefit of all the WTO members.

Article 21 of *the DSU* set forth a complete sequence to impose discipline on the process of compliance.

1) The Intent to Comply

At a DSB meeting held within 30 days after the date of adoption of the panel or Appellate Body report, the member concerned shall inform the DSB of its intentions in respect of implementation of the recommendations and rulings of the DSB.

2) 遵守的期限

如果成员认为立即遵守建议和裁决不可行，例如，如果需要通过立法来执行建议和裁决，该成员应确定一个合理的执行期限。依照《争端解决谅解》第 21 条第 3 款的规定，该合理期限应当如下所述。

有关成员提议的期限，只要该期限获争端解决机构批准；如未获批准，则为在通过建议和裁决之日起 45 日内争端双方同意的期限；若双方未能就执行的合理期限达成一致，则为在通过建议和裁决之日起 90 天内通过有约束力的仲裁确定的期限，依照一般原则，该仲裁确定的期限通常不得超过通过专家组或上诉机构报告之日起 15 个月。仲裁员由争端方协商指定，但如果在 10 天内未能达成协议，世界贸易组织总干事将在咨询各方后 10 天内任命仲裁员。

3) 判断是否遵守

如果在是否存在为遵守建议和裁决所采取的措施或此类措施是否与适用协定相一致的问题上存在分歧，此争端应由专家组决定，如有可能，应为原审理争端的专家组。专家组应在事项提交后的 90 天内发布报告，但不得对其决定提出上诉。

---

2) Time for Compliance

If the member explains that it is impracticable to comply immediately with the recommendations and rulings, for instance, if compliance requires action of legislature, the member shall have a reasonable period of time in which to comply. In accordance with Article 21 (3) of *the DSU*, the reasonable period of time shall be:

The period proposed by the WTO member concerned, if the DSB approves; or, if the DSB does not approve, a period mutually agreed by the parties to the dispute within 45 days after the date of adoption of the recommendations and rulings; or if no agreement is reached about the reasonable period for compliance, a period determined through binding arbitration within 90 days after the date of adoption of the recommendations and rulings subject to a guideline that the period should not exceed 15 months from the date of adoption of a panel or Appellate Body report. The arbitrator is to be appointed by agreement of the parties, but if they cannot do so in 10 days, the Director-General is to appoint the arbitrator within another 10 days after consulting the parties.

3) Judging Compliance

Where there is disagreement as to the existence or consistency with a covered agreement of measures taken to comply with the recommendations and rulings, such dispute shall be decided by a panel, if possible by the same panel that heard the original dispute. The panel shall circulate its report within 90 days after the date of referral of the matter to it but without the possibility of appeal from its decision.

4) 监督

即使被诉方声称已经遵守了报告中的建议或裁决，甚至申诉方和专家组都接受了这一主张，争端解决机构也应该对被通过的建议或裁决的执行情况进行监督。在建议或裁决通过后，任何成员可随时在争端解决机构提出有关执行的问题。除非争端解决机构另有决定，否则执行建议或裁决的问题在确定合理期限之日起 6 个月后，应列入争端解决机构会议的议程，并应保留在争端解决机构的议程上，直到该问题解决。在争端解决机构每一次会议召开前至少 10 天，被诉方应向争端解决机构提交一份关于执行建议或裁决进展的书面情况报告。

---

4) Surveillance

The DSB shall keep under surveillance the implementation of adopted recommendations or rulings even if the respondent party asserts that it has complied with the recommendation in a report, and even if the complaining party or the panel accepts that assertion. The issue of implementation of the recommendations or rulings may be raised at the DSB by any member at any time following their adoption. Unless the DSB decides otherwise, the issue of implementation of the recommendations or rulings shall be placed on the agenda of the DSB meeting after six months following the date of establishment of the reasonable period of time and shall remain on the DSB's agenda until the issue is resolved. At least 10 days prior to each such DSB meeting, the respondent party shall provide the DSB with a status report in writing of its progress in the implementation of the recommendations or rulings.

6. 补偿与报复

1) 补偿

如果被诉方未能使被认定与一适用协定不一致的措施符合该协定，或未能在合理期限内符合建议和裁决，如收到请求，应至迟于合理期限期满前，与申诉方进行谈判，以期形成双方均可接受的补偿。补偿范围并未明确，但应该包括被诉方对申诉方在产品或服务贸易利益方面给予减让。虽然没有明确的声明，但显而易见，此种情况下所作出的补偿必须符合最惠国待遇原则，即任何向被诉方供应产品的供应商都可以以相同的削减税率向被诉方出口产品。

2) 报复

如果在合理期限届满后 20 天内没有达成令人满意的补偿，胜诉方可以请求行使贸易报复权，即向争端解决机构请求授权中止对有关成员实施适用协定项下的减让或其他义务。《争端解决谅解》第 22 条第 3 款和第 4 款详细规定了报复的原则和程序。

(1) 中止减让或其他义务的程度应与利益丧失或减损的程度相当。

---

6. Compensation and Retaliation

1) Compensation

If the respondent party fails to bring the measure found to be inconsistent with a covered agreement into compliance therewith or otherwise comply with the recommendations and rulings within a reasonable period, it may, if so requested, and no later than the expiry of the reasonable period, negotiate with the complaining party for mutually acceptable compensation. Compensation is not defined, but may be expected to consist of the grant of a concession given by the respondent party on a product or service of interest to the complaining party. Though there is no explicit statement, it seems clear that the compensation in this context must be on an MFN basis, i.e. so that any supplier of product to the respondent party can bring the product into the respondent party at the same reduced rate.

2) Retaliation

If no satisfactory compensation has been agreed within 20 days after the date of expiry of the reasonable period, the prevailing party may request to apply the rights of trade retaliation, i.e. to request authorization from the DSB to suspend the application to the member concerned of concessions or other obligations under the covered agreements. Article 22(3) and (4) of *the DSU* set forth in detail the principles and procedures for retaliation:

(1) The level of suspension of concessions or other obligations shall be equivalent to the level of nullification or impairment.

(2) 首先寻求对与专家组或上诉机构认定有违反义务或其他造成利益丧失或减损情形的部门相同的部门中止减让或其他义务，称作平行报复；若申诉方认为不可行，可对相同协议下的其他部门寻求中止减让或其他义务，比如货物对应货物，服务对应服务，知识产权对应知识产权，即为跨部门报复；如果仍不可行，则寻求中止另一协定项下的减让或其他义务，即为跨协议报复。"香蕉案"就是跨协议报复的一个例子，厄瓜多尔获授权通过中止《与贸易有关的知识产权协定》下的义务，对欧盟限制其香蕉出口进行报复。

---

(2) Suspension of concessions or other obligations shall be in the same sector as the measure condemned by a panel or Appellate Body report, which is referred to as the parallel retaliation; if the complaining party considers that it is not practicable, then the suspension shall be in other sector governed by the same agreement, i.e. goods for goods, service for service, intellectual property for intellectual property, which is referred to as the cross-sector retaliation; and only if that is not too practicable, may there be retaliation by suspension of concessions or other obligations under another agreement, which is referred to as the cross-agreement retaliation. An example of cross-agreement retaliation occurred in the *Bananas Case,* when Ecuador received authorization to retaliate against the European Community's restriction on its banana exports by suspending obligations under the TRIPS Agreement.

在这种情况下中止减让的授权是半自动的，这意味着一经请求，争端解决机构应在合理期限结束后 30 天内，给予中止减让或其他义务的授权，除非争端解决机构经协商一致决定拒绝该请求。但是，如果被诉方对中止减让的水平提出异议，或声称申诉方请求中止减让时未遵循前述授权报复的原则和程序，则应提交仲裁。如原专家组成员仍可请到，则此类仲裁应由原专家组作出，或由经总干事任命的仲裁员作出，并应在合理期限结束之日起 60 天内完成仲裁。仲裁员的裁决视作最终裁决，当事各方不得再次寻求仲裁。依照《争端解决谅解》，仲裁员的裁决应立即通知争端解决机构，如授权中止减让的请求与仲裁员的仲裁一致，即给予授权，除非争端解决机构经协商一致决定拒绝该请求。

中止减让或其他义务是暂时的。一旦被诉方被认定与适用协定不一致的措施已经取消，则减让或其他义务的中止也应取消。无论申诉方是否采取了报复措施，争端解决机构应继续对已通过的建议或裁定的执行情况进行监督。

上述世界贸易组织(WTO)争端解决程序，如图 8-1 所示。

The authorization to suspend concessions in this context is semi-automatic, which means that the DSB, upon request, shall grant authorization to suspend concessions within 30 days of the expiry of the reasonable period unless the DSB decides by consensus to reject the request. However, if the respondent party objects to the level of suspension proposed or claims that the principles and procedures set forth above have not been followed when a complaining party has requested authorization to suspend concessions, the matter shall be referred to arbitration. Such arbitration shall be carried out by the original panel, if its members are available, or by an arbitrator appointed by the Director-General and shall be completed within 60 days after the date of expiry of the reasonable period. The arbitrator's decision is accepted as final one and the parties concerned shall not seek a second arbitration. *The DSU* requests the decision of the arbitrator to be informed promptly of the DSB and to grant authorization to suspend concessions if the request is in consistent with the decision of the arbitrator unless the DSB decides by consensus to reject the request.

The suspension of concessions or other obligations shall be temporary. As soon as the measure found to be inconsistent with a covered agreement has been removed by the respondent party, the suspension of concessions or other obligations shall be removed as well. Whether or not the complaining party has taken a measure of retaliation, the DSB shall continue to keep under surveillance the implementation of adopted recommendations or rulings.

The WTO dispute settlement process is as shown in Figure 8-1.

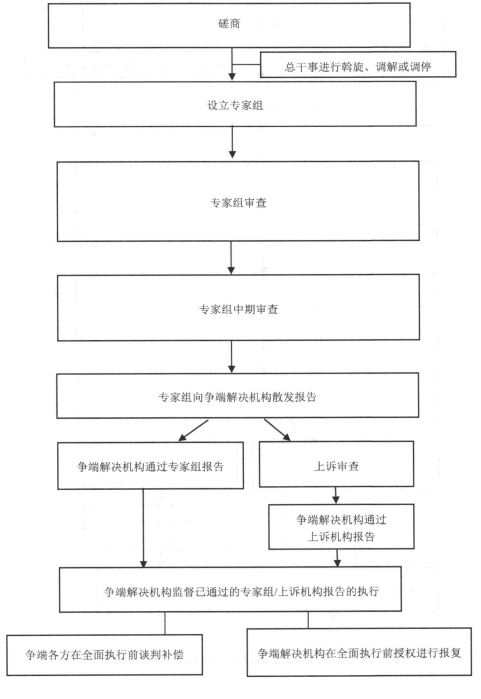

图 8-1　世界贸易组织(WTO)争端解决程序流程图

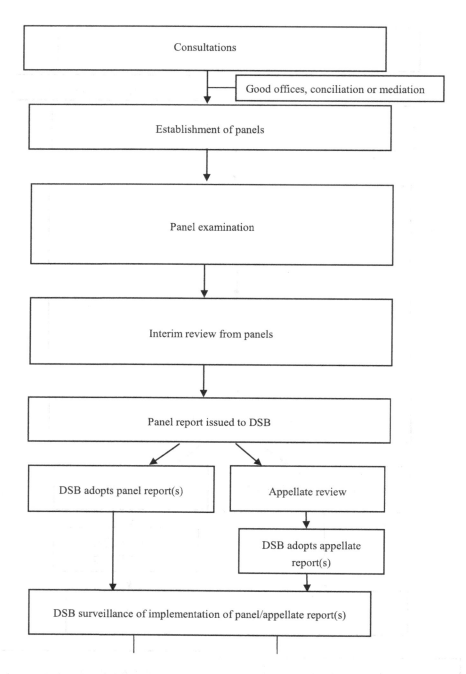

Figure 8-1　Flow Chart of the WTO Dispute Settlement Process

四、世界贸易组织争端解决的主要原则

1. 在多边体制中解决贸易争端

根据争端解决制度的规定，世界贸易组织成员同意将其争端提交世界贸易组织解决，而不是在一成员认为另一成员违反了世界贸易组织规则的情况下，单方面采取行动。世界贸易组织争端解决制度是提供多边贸易体制可靠和可预测性的核心，其鼓励并要求世贸组织成员通过多边争端解决机制解决贸易争端。《争端解决谅解》第 23 条规定，当成员寻求纠正违反义务情形或寻求纠正其他造成适用协定项下利益丧失或减损的情形，他们应当援用且遵守《争端解决谅解》的规则和程序；即除非依照《争端解决谅解》的规则和程序诉诸争端解决机制，各成员不得单方面作出效果上等同于认定已经发生违反《争端解决谅解》的情形，或利益已丧失或减损，或实现适用协定的目标受到阻碍的决定。

8.1.4　Main Principles of WTO Dispute Settlement

1. Resolving Trade Disputes with Recourse to Multilateral System

Under the rules of the dispute settlement system, the WTO members have agreed to bring their disputes to the WTO rather than take action unilaterally in cases where they believe that another member is violating WTO rules. The dispute settlement system of the WTO, serving as a central element in providing security and predictability to the multilateral trading system, encourages and requests the WTO members to resolve trade disputes through the multilateral dispute settlement system. Article 23 of *the DSU* states that, when members seek the redress of a violation of obligations or other nullification or impairment of benefits under the covered agreements, they shall have recourse to, and abide by, the rules and procedures of this Understanding; in such cases, they shall not unilaterally make a determination to the effect that a violation has occurred, that benefits have been nullified or impaired or that the attainment of any objective of the covered agreements has been impeded, except through recourse to dispute settlement in accordance with the rules and procedures of this Understanding.

毫无疑问,《美国贸易法》第 301 条规定,若美国贸易代表确定美国在任何贸易协定下的权利被拒绝,可获得授权采取报复行为,而世界贸易组织成员只能通过诉诸争端解决制度来采取贸易救济。多边争端解决制度的目标是避免可能破坏和扰乱国际贸易,导致各国在贸易政策方面不一致的单方行动。关键在于,世界贸易组织争端解决的司法化和遵守争端解决机构的建议和裁决的要求不仅要有利于申诉成员,也要有利于被诉成员。

2. 有效、迅速解决争端

世界贸易组织争端解决制度鼓励以友好的方式而不是胜诉来解决争议。除了强调诉讼程序、遵守和执行期限外,《争端解决谅解》还规定了不那么具有强制性的争端解决方法,斡旋、调解和调停。选择上述路径不妨碍诉诸专家组程序,如果双方同意,在请求成立专家到专家组成立之间的间隔内,甚至在专家组程序进行过程中也可以同时进行斡旋、调解和调停程序。实际上,超过一半的向世界贸易组织提起的争端已经得到友好解决,没有诉诸专家组程序。

Doubtless with an eye on section 301 of *the United States Trade Act*, which authorizes retaliatory action inter alia if the United States Trade Representative determines that the rights of the United States under any trade agreement are being denied, the WTO members shall not adopt trade remedies without recourse to the WTO dispute settlement system. The objective of the multilateral dispute settlement system is to avoid unilateral actions that could destabilize and disrupt international trade, and could lead to inconsistency among nations in terms of trade policy. The point is that the judicialization of dispute settlement of the WTO and the requirement of compliance with the recommendations and rulings of the DSB operates not only if a decision is rendered in favor of the complaining member but if the decision favors the respondent member.

2. Quick and Effective Settlement of Disputes

The WTO dispute settlement system encourages amicable settlement rather than the winning of cases. In addition to the emphasis on litigation procedure, compliance and enforcement deadlines, *the DSU* makes provisions for less coercive techniques of dispute as well, good offices, conciliation, and mediation. The option for one of these paths is without prejudice to resort to the panel procedure, and indeed may be used, if both parties agree, in the interval between a request for a panel and establishment of the panel, and even while the panel process proceeds. In practice, more than half of all disputes lodged with the WTO have been settled amicably without the need for a dispute panel.

　　除此之外，在提起申诉之前，《争端解决谅解》规定各成员应对按照这些程序采取的行动是否富有成效作出判断。一旦产生争端，世界贸易组织争端解决机制的目的就是确保就争端提供积极的解决方案。《争端解决谅解》规定的可选择的争端解决方案依次为：①提出争端各方都能接受且符合有关适用协定的解决方案；②若无法达成双方同意的解决方案，确保撤销与适用协定不一致的措施；③如果立即撤销措施不切实际，采用补偿作为临时措施，直至撤销不一致的措施；④暂停适用相关协定下的减让或其他义务。

　　世界贸易组织争端解决制度强调，迅速解决争端对世界贸易组织有效运转具有重要意义。为了迅速解决争端，《争端解决谅解》详细列出了解决纠纷时应遵循的程序和时间表。此外，《争端解决谅解》使被诉方无法在请求成立专家组、通过专家组或上诉机构的报告以及授权报复等关键环节行使其否决权来阻止争端解决进程，除非以协商一致方式拒绝通过专家组或上诉机构的报告，否则报告即自动生效。

Moreover, *the DSU* requires that, before bringing a case, members shall exercise their judgment as to whether action under these procedures would be fruitful. If a dispute arises, the aim of the WTO dispute settlement mechanism is designed to secure a positive solution to a dispute. The alternative schemes *the DSU* provides for dispute settlement are as follows in turn: (a)raising a solution mutually acceptable to the parties to a dispute and consistent with the covered agreements; (b)in the absence of above mutually agreed solution, securing the withdrawal of the measures found to be inconsistent with covered agreements; (c)if the immediate withdrawal of the measure is impracticable, resorting to the provision of compensation as a temporary measure until the withdrawal of the inconsistent measure; (d)suspending the application of concessions or other obligations under the covered agreements.

The WTO dispute settlement system emphasizes that prompt settlement is essential if the WTO is to function effectively. To secure quick settlement of disputes, *the DSU* sets out in detail the procedures and the timetable to be followed in resolving disputes. Moreover, *the DSU* makes it impossible for the respondent member to block the process of dispute resolving by using its veto at some crucial points, request for the establishment of a panel, adoption of the report of the panel or of the Appellate Body and authorization of retaliation, i.e. the report will take effect automatically by the DSB unless rejected by consensus.

第二节　专家组程序

　　争端解决专家组的职能是通过评估事实和信息，对案件适用世界贸易组织相关协定来评估向其提交的事项，并提出可协助争端解决机构解决问题的建议。在设计世界贸易组织争端解决机制时，设计者必须在一个常设机构和一个临时选定决策者的机构间作出选择。考虑到世界贸易组织法律文本数量众多而且时常模糊不清，选择决策者就显得尤为重要。目前的解决方案是选择临时专家组作为初审机构，而由常设的上诉机构进行复审。

8.2　Panel Procedures

　　The function of the dispute settlement panel is to assist the DSB by assessing the matter referred to it by evaluating the facts and information, applying the appropriate WTO agreements to the case and making a recommendation that will help the DSB resolve the case. When designing the WTO dispute settlement mechanism, its designers had to choose a standing body and a system for ad hoc selection of decision makers. Given that the often ambiguous texts and the vast volume of the WTO law, the selection of the decision makers is of much importance. The current solution designed is to choose ad hoc panels as the first instance body but with review by a standing Appellate Body.

一、专家组成员的选择

1. 专家组成员的资格

专家组由三名成员组成，在争端各方同意的情况下也可由五名成员组成。在大多数国际商事仲裁中，当事方一般各自选择一名仲裁员，共同选择或共同委托仲裁机构官员指定首席仲裁员，与之不同的是，世界贸易组织争端解决制度下的专家组成员全部由秘书处选定，在可能的情况下，专家组成员人选也应为争端方所接受。争端双方不得提名专家组成员；可以对被提名的专家提出反对意见，但须基于无法控制的原因。如果在专家组成立之日后 20 天内没有就专家组成员达成协议，总干事可应任何一方的请求并且在收到该请求之日起 10 日内，经与争端解决机构主席和有关委员会或理事会主席磋商，并在与争端各方磋商后，决定专家组的成员。

8.2.1 Selection of Panelists

1. Qualification for Panelists

The panels shall be composed of three panelists unless the parties to the dispute agree to a panel composed of five panelists. Unlike most international commercial arbitration in which each party typically chooses one arbitrator and either the two parties choose or an appointing authority selects the presiding arbitrator, panelists under the WTO dispute settlement system are all to be chosen by the Secretariat, if possible with agreement of the parties. The contesting parties do not nominate panelists; they can raise objection to a proposed panel member, but only for compelling reasons. If there is no agreement on the panelists within 20 days after the date of the establishment of a panel, at the request of either party, the Director-General, in consultation with the Chairman of the DSB and the Chairman of the relevant Council or Committee, shall appoint the members of the panel, after consulting with the contesting parties, within 10 days after receipt of a request by either party to do so.

关税与贸易总协定的传统是从政府官员中提名和选举专家组成员，通常是来自驻日内瓦的关税与贸易总协定代表。虽然这样做节省费用，而且比起从国外安排专家个人来，安排会议方面更为方便，但是随着争端解决制度规则导向性的发展，这种继续维系俱乐部般氛围的做法受到越来越多的批评。此外，吸收政府官员作为专家组成员，即使其以个人身份任职，不受其政府的指示，也往往会强调向专家组提交的争端的政治性问题，而非法律性问题。后来关税与贸易总协定改变了这一传统做法，改变了专家组候选名单，使其包括学术专家、退休法官和前政府官员。《争端解决谅解》要求专家组成员的选择能够确保成员的独立性，充分多样的背景和丰富的经验，他们应由资深的政府和非政府个人组成，包括曾在专家组任职或曾向专家组陈述案件的人员、曾任一成员方代表或《1947 年关税与贸易总协定》一缔约方代表或任何适用协定或其先前协定的理事会或委员会的代表人员、秘书处人员、曾讲授或出版国际贸易法或政策著作的人员，以及曾任一成员方高级贸易政策官员的人员。《争端解决谅解》还要求特定争端方或第三方的公民不得在与该争端有关的专家组任职，除非争端方另有约定。但在发展中国家是争端的一方的情况下，若该发展中国家提出要求，专家组应至少有一名成员应来自另外的发展中国家。

The tradition in GATT had been to nominate and choose panelists from government officials, often from the GATT representatives stationed in Geneva. While that saved in expenses and made scheduling of meetings easier than arranging for individuals to come from abroad, it tended to perpetuate the club-like atmosphere that has been increasingly criticized as the system became more rule-oriented. Moreover, having government officials on panels, even when serving in their individual capacities and without instructions from their governments, tended to emphasize the political, rather than a legal aspect of the disputes presented to panels. Later the GATT changed the tradition and modified the roster of panel members, including the academic experts, retired judges, and ex-governmental officials. *The DSU* requires that the panel members be selected with a view to ensuring the independence of the members, a sufficiently diverse background and a wide spectrum of experience, and composed of both governmental and non-governmental individuals if they are well-qualified, including persons who have served on or presented a case to a panel, served as a representative of a WTO member party or of a contracting party to *GATT 1947* or as a representative to the Council or Committee of any covered agreement or its predecessor agreement, or served in the Secretariat, taught or published on the international trade law or policy, or served as a senior trade policy official of a member party. *The DSU* continues to require that citizens of the parties to a specific dispute or of the third parties shall not serve on a panel concerned with that dispute, unless the parties to the dispute agree otherwise. But if a developing country is a party to a dispute, at least one member of the panel shall, if the developing country so requests, come from another developing country.

2. 利益冲突的问题

当一人被选为专家组成员时，就会出现利益冲突的问题。因此，《争端解决谅解》拒绝了争端各方指定专家组成员的想法，也不允许在没有无法控制的理由的情形下对被提名的专家组成员提出异议。无法控制的理由包括被提名人与企业或行业之间的财务关系，例如顾问、客户或重要股东，其可能会因案件的结果而获得收益或遭受损失。如果对被提名人提出异议，是因为其过去的著述或者曾在处理类似问题的专家组任职，则会产生更为困难的问题。此类信息属于应当披露的信息，并且争端解决机构发布其"行为准则"，要求所有在专家组、上诉机构任职的人员或仲裁员公开任何可能影响或对其独立性或公正性产生合理怀疑的信息，并附有需披露信息的说明性清单。被提名的专家组成员、仲裁员或专家应配合披露信息，例如，应当列明其著述的相关出版物或在各组织中的成员身份。

2. The Question of Interests Conflicts

When a persons is selected to serve as a panelist, the question of conflict of interest arises. For this reason, *the DSU* rejects the idea of appointing panelists by the parties to disputes and also rejects of challenges to nominations of panelists without compelling reasons. A compelling reason would include a financial connection, such as the counsel and client or significant shareholder, between a potential nominee and a firm or industry that would stand to gain or lose from the outcome of a case. A more difficult question would arise if a challenge were brought on the basis of a potential panelist's past writing, or past service on a panel that dealt with a similar question. Such information should be disclosed, and the DSB issued its Rules of Conduct calling for self-disclosure by all persons requested to serve on a panel, the Appellate Body, or as an arbitrator of any information that is likely to affect or give rise to justifiable doubts as to their independence or impartiality, accompanied by an illustrative list of information to be disclosed. A potential panelist, arbitrator, or expert should be forthcoming at the level of disclosure, listing, for instance, his or her relevant publications or membership in organizations.

　　然而，专家组成员的遴选标准——强调国际贸易法或政策方面的经验和专门知识——可能使得一些在著述、文章或在先前裁决中对可能提交争端解决专家组审理的争议事项作出评述的人得以提名。例如，申诉方因被诉方对其特定产品征收不当的反倾销税向争端解决机构提起诉讼，秘书处建议由某第三国的倾销问题专家担任专家组成员，其在著作中曾对通过反倾销法适用实施变相贸易保护主义的做法提出警示，被诉方是否因此有充分的理由反对任命该专家为专家组成员呢？披露不等同于取消资格，回答前述问题，应考虑保持专家组成员的专业素养高度，并且不能将偏见与经验和观点相混淆。事实上，对于专家组的任命问题早就存在申诉和反对意见，在近一半的案件中，总干事获授权指定了专家组。

However, the criteria for selection of panelists, which emphasizes experience and expertise in the international trade law or policy, is likely to lead to the nomination of persons who have gone on record in books, articles, prior decisions on issues that may come before the WTO dispute panels. For instance, a complaining party brought a case to the DSB against the respondent party for its improper imposition of an anti-dumping duty on a given product, the Secretariat suggests a panelist from a third country who is an expert on dumping, and who, in his or her writings, has warned against the use of anti-dumping laws as disguised protectionism. Does the respondent party have a compelling reason to challenge to appointment of this expert to the panel? The disclosure is not equated with disqualification, and the question such as the suggested above is answered in such a way as to maintain a high standard of expertise on panels, and not to confuse experience and points of view with bias. In fact, there have been complaints and objections of the appointment of experts, the Director-General appointed the panel in close to half the cases as authorized.

二、向专家组提供的信息

1. 成员提供信息的义务

一些司法和仲裁庭的程序中，原则上所获得的信息以争端方选择提供的为限，为寻求解决争端的积极方案，《争端解决谅解》采取相反的立场，其第 13 条"寻求信息的权利"规定每个专家组都有权从其认为适当的任何个人或机构寻求信息和技术建议。第 13 条进一步要求世界贸易组织的任何成员，无论是否是特定争端的一方，均应迅速和全面地答复专家组提出的关于提供其认为必要和适当信息的任何请求。一方面，成员方不得以所要求提供的信息可能是机密为由而拒绝提供给专家组；另一方面，该专家组需要维护信息的机密性，且"行为准则"规定每名专家组成员和上诉机构成员均须遵守这一要求。

8.2.2 Information Provided to the Panel

1. Members' Obligation to Provide Information

Unlike some judicial and arbitral tribunals which proceeding on the principle that they are limited by what the contesting parties choose to submit to them, *the DSU*, for finding a positive solution to disputes, takes an opposite position. Article 13 of *the DSU*, entitled "Right to Seek Information", states that each panel shall have the right to seek information and technical advice from any individual or body which it deems appropriate. Article 13 further requires that any Member of WTO, whether or not a party to a specific dispute, should respond promptly and fully to any request by a panel for such information as the panel considers necessary and appropriate. On the one hand, the fact that the information requested may be confidential is not the ground for not providing it to the panel; on the other hand, the panel is required to maintain the confidentiality of any information provided on a confidential basis, and the Rules of Conduct obligate each panelist and member of the Appellate Body to uphold this requirement.

2. 对专家的使用

专家组成员不熟悉科学问题等已成为争端各方阻挠争端解决进程的程序性手段。欧共体与美国之间就牛饲料中使用生长激素是否对牛肉消费者构成健康威胁产生的争端就是一例,欧共体认为存在健康威胁,而美国认为不存在。《争端解决谅解》规定,专家组可以从任何相关来源寻求信息,并可以就争议事项的某些方面咨询专家意见。关于一方提出的有关科学或技术方面的事实问题,专家组可以要求"专家审议小组"提供咨询报告。《争端解决谅解》的附录规定了此等专家小组的组成规则,包括避免任用争端当事方的公民。专家审议小组也可以从他们认为适当的任何来源寻求信息和技术建议。专家审议小组的报告属于咨询意见,在以最终形式提交给专家组前应提交给争端各方征求意见。

2. The Use of Experts

Some issues such as scientific questions that the panel members are unfamiliar with have become the procedural tactics of the parties to disputes to block the process of dispute settlement. An example is the dispute between the European Community and the United States about whether use of growth hormones in animal feed for cattle sets a health threat to beef consumers, as the European Community concluded, or sets no such a threat as the United States argued. *The DSU* provides that a panel may seek information from any relevant source and may consult experts to obtain their opinion on certain aspects of the matter. In respect of a factual issue concerning a scientific or technical matter raised by a party, a panel may request an advisory report from an 'expert review group'; an appendix to *the DSU* sets out rules for composition of such groups, including the avoidance of citizens of parties to the dispute. The expert review groups in turn may consult and seek information and technical advice from any source they deem appropriate. The report of an expert review group is advisory only, but it is to be submitted to the parties for their comments before being submitted in final form to the panel.

三、专家组的权限

应具体争端当事一方要求或双方的共同要求，专家组通过评估事实和信息，适用适当的世界贸易组织协定来对其审议的事项作出客观评估，从而作出裁定帮助争端解决机构提出建议或作出裁决，这即为"专家组的权限"，《争端解决谅解》第 7 条将其分为三类：①标准权限，是"按照×××协定(争端各方引用的适用协定名称)的有关规定，审查×××(争端方名称)在××文件中提交争端解决机构的事项，并作出有助于争端解决机构提出或作出裁决的裁定"；②争端各方可以在专家组建立后 20 天内就专家组权限另行约定，这称为商定的权限；③在设立专家组时，争端解决机构可以授权其主席与争端各方磋商设定专家组的权限，但须遵守有关上述标准权限范围和 20 天内另行约定等规定的约束。如果达成了标准权限之外的权限，任何成员可以向争端解决机构提出与此有关的任何问题。

8.2.3　Terms of Reference of the Panel

The panel, upon the request of one party or joint request of parties to a specific dispute, is to assess the matter referred to it by evaluating the facts and information, applying the appropriate WTO agreements to the case and to make a recommendation that will help *the DSB* resolve the case. This is known as the "terms of reference" of a panel, which falls into 3 categories as Article 7 of *the DSU* states: (a) The standard terms of reference is "to examine, in the light of the relevant provisions in (name of the covered agreement(s) cited by the parties to the dispute), the matter referred to the DSB by (name of party) in document ... and to make such findings as will assist the DSB in making the recommendations or in giving the rulings provided for in that/those agreement(s)"; (b) The parties to a dispute may agree otherwise within 20 days from the establishment of the panel, which is known as the agreed terms of reference; (c) In establishing a panel, the DSB may authorize its Chairman to draw up the terms of reference of the panel in consultation with the parties to the dispute, subject to the provisions concerning the standard terms of reference and above agreement otherwise within 20 days. If others than standard terms of reference are agreed upon, any Member may raise any point relating thereto in the DSB.

应该指出的是，无论对权限如何约定，专家组应处理任何适用协议或争端方引用的协定中的有关规定。实践中，准确的权限范围应在申诉方设立专家组的基础上确定，该要求需要指明被诉方采取的为申诉方认为与特定适用协定不符的贸易措施；如果未能指明，将被排除在小组的审议范围之外。专家组权限的重要之处在于，通过向争端方和第三方提供充分的信息并允许被诉方和利害关系方作出回应，实现了正当程序的原则，通过指明具体措施来确定专家组的权限范围。

第三节　上诉机构程序

对常设上诉机构作出的规定是《争端解决谅解》最具创意的方面之一。上诉机构是对专家组报告在实践中自动通过程序的必要补充，也是为解释特定的协定和世界贸易组织所涉协定提供连续性和一致性。特定争端方将专家组报告上诉至上诉机构的权利不受任何情形的限制。

What should be noted is that the panel shall address the relevant provisions in any covered agreement or agreements cited by the parties to the dispute regardless of the terms of reference. In practice, the exact scope of terms of reference shall be decided on the basis of the request of the complaining party for a panel which shall identify the specific measures by the respondent party that the complaining party deems inconsistent with specific covered agreement; measures not specifically identified will be excluded from consideration by the panel. The imperative of the terms of reference lies in that it satisfies the principle of due course by providing the parties to a dispute and the third parties with adequate information and then allowing the respondent party and other parties concerned to respond, and that determines the scope of a panel's terms of reference by identifying specific measures at issue.

8.3　The Appellate Body Procedures

The provision for a standing Appellate Body is one of the most innovative aspects of *the DSU*. The Appellate Body is a necessary complement to a process whereby reports of panels are automatically adopted in practice, and also is to provide continuity and consistency not only for interpretation of a given agreement but also for all the WTO covered agreements. The right of a party to a specific dispute to appeal a panel report to the Appellate Body is guaranteed not subject to any conditions.

一、上诉机构的成员资格

《争端解决谅解》规定，上诉机构由争端解决机构任命的七名人员组成，任期四年，每人可以重新任命一次。但是，对于世界贸易组织协定生效后即被任命的七人，其中三人的任期将在两年之后终止，以批次确定，从而不会有成员的完全更替。

由于无法得知多少争端被诉至世界贸易组织争端解决机制，而且有多少争端被上诉，《争端解决谅解》规定上诉机构人员应随时待命，但只要不涉及利益冲突，不用放弃其他专业工作。由于实际诉至争端解决机构的案件数量多于预期，而且对专家组报告提出上诉同样很多，所以在上诉机构的工作已经接近全职。

《争端解决谅解》第 17 条第 3 款规定，上诉机构应由在法律、国际贸易和各适用协议所涉主题方面具有公认专业知识的人员组成；上诉机构的成员不隶属于任何政府，不得参与审议任何可产生直接或间接利益冲突的争端；上诉机构的成员资格应广泛代表世界贸易组织的成员资格，这一点使上诉机构成员的选择比预期更复杂。

8.3.1　The Membership of the Appellate Body

The DSU provides that an Appellate Body shall be composed of seven persons appointed by the DSB for four-year terms and each person may be reappointed once. However, the terms of three of the first seven persons appointed immediately after the entry into force of the WTO Agreement shall expire at the end of two years, to be determined by lot, so that there will never be a complete turnover of the membership.

As there was no way to tell how many disputes would be brought under the dispute settlement system, and how many of these would be appealed, *the DSU* provides that the persons serving on the Appellate Body shall be available at all times and on short notice, but they needn't give up other professional employment, so long as no conflict of interests is involved. As more cases have been filed than could have been expected, and more final decisions have been appealed, service on the Appellate Body has become close to a full-time job.

Article 17 (3) of *the DSU* requires that the Appellate Body shall comprise persons of members of the Appellate Body, with demonstrated expertise in law, international trade and the subject matter of the covered agreements generally; the members of the Appellate Body shall be unaffiliated with any government and not participate in the consideration of any disputes that would create a direct or indirect conflict of interest; the Appellate Body membership shall be broadly representative of membership in the WTO, which makes selection of members of the Appellate Body a more complicated task than anticipated.

上诉机构的成员应 "在法律、国际贸易和所适用协议的事务方面具有公认的专业知识"，但是其中一些人在被选作上诉机构成员以前并不都是贸易专家；强调 "成员资格应广泛代表世界贸易组织的成员资格"，应理解为在地理位置、经济发展水平、对世界经济的重要性以及法律传统方面的代表性。在选择上诉机构的初始成员时，由总干事领导的委员会，包括四个世界贸易组织理事会主席以及争端解决机构，在二十三个国家的三十二名候选人中选出了七人。上诉机构目前的六名成员(空缺一人)，分别来自印度、美国、墨西哥、毛里求斯、比利时和中国，几乎代表了每一个洲，其中四人曾经研究过法律，一名曾是政府的高级官员和联合国办事处的代表；一些是海外投资以及多边贸易问题的专家，一些是争端解决程序的参与者，在大量争端解决案件中代表自己的政府作为上诉方和应诉方；来自发展中国家的有四人，来自发达国家的有两人。

As for the members of the Appellate Body shall have "demonstrated expertise in law, international trade and the subject matter of the covered agreements", some, but not all the members of the Appellate Body were trade experts before they were selected; the "membership shall be broadly representative of membership in the WTO" is also emphasized, which is understood to comprehend geography, levels of economic development, importance in the world economy and legal traditions. When selecting the initial members of the Appellate Body, a committee headed by the Director-General and including the chairmen of four of the WTO councils plus the DSB selected seven persons out of 32 candidates from 23 countries. The current six members of the Appellate Body (one vacancy), coming respectively from India, the United States, Mexico, Mauritius, Belgium, and China, represent almost every continent, of these, four have studied law and one has ever been a senior official of a government and the representative to the United Nations Office; some are experts of investments overseas as well as multilateral trade issues, some were participants in the dispute settlement process, representing their own governments in a number of dispute settlement cases both as a complainant and respondent; four are from developing countries and two are from developed countries.

二、上诉机构的职能

上诉机构中的三名成员组成一个上诉庭审理每一个上诉案件，每个上诉庭从中选择一名成员主持审理。选择上诉庭成员的过程应当确保所有成员的随机性及不可预测性，并且不论国籍都给予同样的机会，这意味着不存在审理人员总是重复的上诉庭，或专门审理特定类型案件的上诉庭。《争端解决谅解》要求上诉机构的成员不得隶属于政府，"不得参与审理任何可产生直接或间接利益冲突的争端"，但未规定如果成员是上诉方或被上诉方的公民，是否应被取消审理上诉案件的资格。当上诉机构发布《上诉审查工作程序》时，明确表示不会将国籍考虑在内，但是规定了针对上诉机构成员的其他利益冲突规则，这些规则也适用于专家组成员。《上诉审查工作程序》还规定，无论是否被选定进入上诉庭审理上诉，每一位上诉机构成员都应接收上诉中提交的所有文件，审理上诉的上诉庭在完成上诉机构报告前应与其他四名上诉机构成员交流意见。

8.3.2　Functioning of the Appellate Body

A division of three members of the Appellate Body is selected to hear each appeal; each division elects a presiding member. The process for the selection of divisions is designed to ensure randomness, unpredictability and opportunity for all the members to serve regardless of their national origin, which means that there are no permanent chambers that would put the same members together repeatedly or that would specialize in any specific kind of cases. *The DSU* requires that the members of the Appellate Body "shall be unaffiliated with any government" and "shall not participate in the consideration of any disputes that would create a direct or indirect conflict of interest", however, does not provides whether or not a member should be disqualified from hearing an appeal if the member is the citizen of both appellant party or appellee party of an appeal. When the Appellate Body issued its *Working Procedures for Appellate Review*, it made it clear that nationality would not be taken into consideration but elaborate other rules of conflict of interests for the member of the Appellate Body, which are the same as for panelists. *The Working Procedures* also provides that each member, whether or not selected to hear each appeal on a division, shall receive all the documents filed in the appeal, and that the division hearing the appeal shall exchange views with the other four Appellate Body members before the division finalizes the report of the Appellate Body.

三、上诉程序和审查范围

一般规定，诉讼程序自一个争端方正式通知其上诉决定之日起至上诉机构散发其报告之日止通常不得超过 60 天。上诉方应在提交上诉通知后 10 日内提交书面材料，被上诉方应在其后的 15 天内提交书面答复。《上诉审查工作程序》规定，一般应在提出上诉通知之日后 30 日内，换句话说，在收到被上诉人的书面答复后 5 天内举行听证会。上诉庭可在听证会上要求任何参与方提供额外报告。

8.3.3 The Appeal Process and the Scope of Review

As a general rule, the appeal proceedings shall not exceed 60 days from the date a party to the dispute formally notifies its decision to appeal to the date the Appellate Body circulates its report. The appellant is required to make its written submissions within 10 days after the notice of appeal, and the appellee shall submit its written response within 15 days thereafter. *The Working Procedures* provides that an oral hearing shall be held, as a general rule, within 30 days after the date of filing the notice of appeal, in other words, within 5 days after receipt of the appellee's written response. The division may request additional memoranda from any participant at the oral hearing.

《争端解决谅解》第 17 条第 6 款中规定，上诉应限于专家组报告涉及的法律问题和专家组作出的法律解释，并可维持、变更或撤销专家组的法律裁决和结论，即上诉机构不得审查专家组就事实问题作出的裁决。然而，何为不可审查的事实问题裁决，何为可审查的法律问题裁决，二者之间很难存在明确的界限。例如，假设 X 国(被诉方)要求某产品销售应符合一定标准，该国国内生产者比国外生产者更容易满足该标准。Y 国(申诉国)将 X 国诉至争端解决机构，声称 X 国的歧视性法规违反了《关税与贸易总协定》第 3 条第 4 款的国民待遇要求，将 Y 国的生产者排除在 X 国市场以外。X 国辩称其规定是为了保护人类健康，符合第 20 条(b)项，因此构成国民待遇要求的例外。Y 国认为 X 国的抗辩不成立，因为采取替代的非歧视性措施也可取得同样的结果；而 X 国认为替代措施是不可行的。专家组就第 20 条(b)项的抗辩作出裁决，败诉国，X 国，也可能是 Y 国，向上诉机构提出上诉。

The DSU states in Article 17(6) that an appeal shall be limited to issues of law covered in the panel report and legal interpretations developed by the panel and may uphold, modify, or reverse the panel's legal findings and conclusions, i.e. the Appellate Body shall review no panel's findings of fact. However, it may prove impossible to draw a sharp line between the unreviewable findings of fact and the reviewable findings of law. Suppose, for instance, Country X (respondent party) imposes a requirement for sale of a product under certain standards which are met more easily by domestic producers than by foreign producers. Country Y (complaining party) initiates a complaint against Country X before the DSB, asserting that its producers have been shut out of the market of Country X by Country X's discriminatory regulations in noncompliance with the national treatment requirement of Article 3(4). Country X defends that its regulation is necessary to protect human health under Article 20(b), and thus constitute an exception to the national treatment requirement. Country Y argues that the defense must fail because alternative non-discriminatory measures are available to achieve the same result; Country X contends that the alternative measures are infeasible. The panel issues a ruling on Article 20(b) defense, and the losing party, either Country X or Country Y, appeals the case to the Appellate Body.

那么该上诉提起的是法律问题还是事实问题呢？换句话说，该问题——此争议规定是否为保护人类健康所必需——是事实问题还是法律问题？要对前述第 17 条第 6 款的规定作出清楚阐释是非常困难的。需要关注的首要原则是，如果没有第二次审查，专家组的调查裁决和结论不会自动生效。前例所述的事实和法律相混合的问题应被视为法律解释，上诉机构应对此进行审查。进一步探讨前例，上诉机构不会就替代性环境法规的成本接收新的证据。但是，如上所述，对争议法规的必要性这一事实问题所做的结论，上诉机构应进行审查。对于包含法律和事实要素以及对争端裁决至关重要的类似裁决，例如"损害"和"相同产品"，应以同样的方式处理，这意味着上诉机构应当审查专家组的结论和据以得出结论的事实依据的充分性。

Does the appeal raise a legal question, or a factual question? In other words, is the question whether or not the challenged regulation is necessary to protect human health a factual question or a legal one? It is difficult to elaborate on the provision of Article 17(6) above. The prime principle shall be the concern that findings and conclusions of the panels shall not become automatically effective without a second review. It would follow that the kinds of questions mixed with facts and law illustrated in the above example should be regarded as legal interpretations, and the Appellate Body should make the competence-based review. To pursue the above example further, the Appellate Body should not take new evidence on the costs of an alternative environmental regulation. But the conclusion from the pure facts, as mentioned, on the necessity of the challenged regulation, should be reviewed by the Appellate Body. Similar findings containing elements of law and fact and often critical in determinations of trade disputes, such as injury and like product, should be treated in the same way, which means that the conclusion and the sufficiency of the factual data on which the panel based its findings should be reviewable by the Appellate Body.

　　此外，上诉机构已经注意到其肩负有指导任务，因此很少说"因为事项 Y 足以对案件作出裁断，所以不必审查事项 X"。今后可能会再次出现事项 X，上诉机构的指导将对未来争端各方和专家组都有用。相应地，即使一方在专家组程序中胜诉，该方仍可对某些裁决或法律推理提出上诉，上诉机构将对该上诉进行裁决。例如，在与《保障措施协议》有关的阿根廷鞋类案件中，欧共体对阿根廷对进口鞋类产品征收紧急关税提出申诉，在专家组程序获胜。但是，专家组裁决认为符合《保障措施协议》的措施也符合《关税与贸易总协定》第 19 条的规定，与欧共体的观点不相符，欧共体对这项裁决提起上诉，上诉机构在基本维持专家组裁决的同时，扭转了《保障措施协议》与第 19 条的关系问题，并就该问题作出了裁决，这可能对以后各国的实践和《争端解决谅解》的争端案件产生重要影响。

Moreover, the Appellate Body has seen its mission as a teaching and guiding one, thus rarely has said "issue X need not be decided because issue Y is sufficient to decide the case". Issue X may well come up again in the future, and the Appellate Body's guidance now will be useful to the parties and to future panels. Correspondingly, even if a party has prevailed before the panel, it may appeal certain rulings or legal reasoning, and the Appellate Body will rule on that appeal. For instance, in the Argentine Footwear case discussed in connection with *the Agreement on Safeguards*, the European Community had prevailed before the panel in its challenge to the imposition by Argentina of an emergency duty on certain footwear. But the panel had ruled, contrary to the position of the Community, that a measure that satisfied *the Agreement on Safeguards* satisfied the requirements of Article 19 of *GATT*. The Community appealed that ruling, and the Appellate Body, while upholding the "bottom line" ruling of the panel, reversed on the issue of the relation of the *Agreement on Safeguards* to Article 19, and gave a ruling on that issue that may be important in future practice of states and future cases under *the DSU*.

上诉时间表见表 8-3。

表 8-3　上诉时间表

	一般上诉	禁止性补贴上诉
	天数	天数
上诉通知	0	0
上诉人提交材料	0	0
其他上诉通知	5	2
其他上诉人提交材料	5	2
被上诉人提交材料	18	9
第三参与人提交材料	21	10
第三参与人参与的通知	21	10
听证会	30-45	15-23
散发上诉机构报告	60-90	30-60
争端解决机构会议通过上诉机构报告	90-120	50-80

Timetable for appeals see Table 8-3.

Table 8-3　Timetable for Appeals

	General Appeals	Prohibited Subsidies Appeals
	Day	Day
Notice of Appeal	0	0
Appellant's Submission	0	0
Notice of Other Appeal	5	2
Other Appellant(s) Submission(s)	5	2
Appellee(s) Submission(s)	18	9
Third Participant(s) Submission(s)	21	10
Third Participant(s) Notification(s)	21	10
Oral Hearing	30-45	15-23
Circulation of Appellate Report	60-90	30-60
DSB Meeting for Adoption	90-120	50-80

第四节　关于引起争议的行为：反诉和第三方的参与

一、反诉

在以往关税与贸易总协定争端解决的实践中，反诉曾是扩大争端和阻挠争端解决程序的一种方式。《争端解决谅解》第 3 条第 10 款规定，如果发生争端，所有成员都将真诚地参与争端解决程序以努力解决争端，关于不同事项的起诉和反诉不应联系在一起。然而，对于何为"不同"，《争端解决谅解》并没有作出明确界定，而且并不拒绝合并单一的争端。

8.4　About Contentious Acts: Counterclaims and Participation of Third Parties

8.4.1　Counterclaims

In the experience of dispute settlement in the GATT, counterclaims (or counter-complaints) had ever been used as a way to extend controversies and to frustrate the dispute settlement process. Article 3 (10) of *the DSU* states that, if a dispute arises, all members will engage in the dispute settlement procedures in good faith in an effort to resolve the dispute and that the complaints and counter-complaints in regard to distinct matters should not be linked. However, *the DSU* does not define the word "distinct", and the consolidation of a single controversy should not be rejected.

例如，X 国对从 Y 国进口的产品 B 征收反补贴税，理由是 Y 国对产品 B 的生产或出口提供了非法或"可诉性"补贴。因此，Y 国将 X 国诉至世界贸易组织专家组，对 X 国征收反补贴税提出异议，认为 Y 国提供的补贴符合《补贴与反补贴措施协议》第 8 条第 2 款的豁免规定，属于不可诉补贴。X 国应当被准许在同一专家组提起反诉，要求裁定 Y 国的补贴不满足适用环境例外的条件或超过了第 8.2 条允许的补贴额度。可见，合并审理的优势，包括避免产生不一致结果的可能性，它比因为允许反诉而导致审理拖延更重要。但是，假设 Y 国就 X 国对前例中产品 B 征收反补贴税的行为另行向专家组起诉，现在，X 国在同一专家组抗辩，称 Y 国在类似情形下也对来自 X 国的产品 C 征收反补贴税，那么 Y 国的行为不过是五十步笑百步而已。在这种情况下，X 国的起诉应另案处理。第二个案件涉及不同的事实情况，不能以 Y 国征收了类似的反补贴税，甚至"大家都这样做"来作为对 Y 国起诉 X 国征收反补贴税的抗辩理由。

For instance, suppose Country X imposes a countervailing duty on product B imported from Country Y, on the basis that Country Y has provided an illegal or "actionable" subsidy on the production or export of product B. Country Y thus brings a complaint before a WTO panel challenging the imposition of that countervailing duty by Country X, contending that the subsidy is not actionable, because it qualifies for the exemption stated in Article 8.2 of *the Agreement on Subsidies and Countervailing Measures*. Country X should be permitted to bring a counter-complaint before the same panel seeking a declaration that Country Y's subsidy for product B does not qualify for the environmental exception or exceeds the amount immunized by Article 8.2. So the advantages of consolidation, including avoidance of the possibility of inconsistent outcomes, outweigh the dangers of delay that may be caused by permitting counter-complaints. However, suppose Country Y brings a complaint before a panel challenging imposition of a countervailing duty on product B by Country X as in the case above, Country X now wants to put before the same panel the assertion that Country Y has imposed a countervailing duty on product C from Country X under similar circumstances, contending that the pot should not be permitted to call the kettle black. In this case, Country X's complaint should be required to stand on its own. The second case involves different factual situations, and it should be no defense to Country Y's complaint that Country Y has adopted a similar measure or even that "everybody does it".

二、第三方参与

《争端解决谅解》将第三方定义为对专家组审议的事项有实质利益并向争端解决机构通知其利益的任何成员。作为第三方，Z 国可能在 X 国和 Y 国间交由争端解决机构处理的某项争端中有利益。假设 X 国采取一项限制措施，在受到 Y 国异议同时，也可能损害 Z 国制造商在 X 国市场的竞争机会。若 Z 国现在就同一限制措施起诉，则其申诉可与 Y 国的申诉合并审理。《争端解决谅解》第 9 条规定，若一个以上成员就同一事项请求设立专家组，在可行的情况下，应设立单一专家组审查此类起诉。在 1995 年美国和委内瑞拉之间的改良汽油案中，委内瑞拉认为美国对改良汽油的法规存在歧视性，巴西 3 个月后提起了类似的诉讼，争端解决机构经双方同意将两项起诉合并。两个起诉的合并和巴西提交材料导致专家组散发最终报告拖延了大约 3 个月，但是好在并没有使诉讼过度复杂化。

8.4.2　Participation by Third Parties

The DSU defines a third party as any member having a substantial interest in a matter before a panel and having notified its interest to the DSB. A third party, Country Z, may have interests as follows in a dispute brought before the DSB between Country X and Country Y. Suppose a restriction imposed by Country X and challenged by Country Y may also impair the opportunity of Country Z's producers to compete in the Country X's market. If Country Z now files a complaint to challenge the same restriction, its complaint may be consolidated to the Country Y's complaint in a single proceeding. Article 9 of *the DSU* states that, where more than one member requests the establishment of a panel related to the same matter, a single panel should be established to examine such complaints whenever feasible. In the Reformulated Gasoline case between the U.S. and Venezuela of 1995, Venezuela challenged as discriminatory a United States regulation on reformulated gasoline, Brazil brought a similar complaint three months later, and the two complaints were consolidated by the DSB with the agreement of the parties. The consolidation of the two complaints and separate submissions on behalf of Brazil led to a delay of some three months in the issuance of the final report of the panel, but otherwise did not unduly complicate the proceeding.

当 Z 国对 Y 国起诉 X 国的案件中就某个事项有利益，但和诉讼的主体事项没有重大的贸易利益时，就会出现不同的情况。Z 国可能想就 X 国某项被诉的措施表达其立场和论点，或者 Z 国可能有法规在效果上与被诉的法规类似，可能希望对这些申诉提出自己的抗辩，或者公开表明其法规与被诉措施是不同的。《争端解决谅解》规定，在专家组第一次实质性会议期间，专家组应给予第三方表达意见并提出书面陈述的机会。第三方不会参加随后的书面材料交换或听证会，但专家组将充分考虑他们的利益。第三方不能上诉，但如果他们作为第三方参加专家组程序，他们可以向上诉机构提交书面意见，并有机会表明立场。

A different situation is presented when Country Z has an interest in an issue presented in a case brought by Country Y against Country X, but does not have a major trade interest in the subject of the complaint. Country Z may want to add its positions and arguments to the challenge to the measures being implemented by Country X. Alternatively, Country Z may have legislation or regulations in effect similar to those being challenged, and may wish either to present its own defense to the challenge or to put on record why its regulations or legislation is distinguishable from the measures being challenged. *The DSU* provides that a third party shall have an opportunity to be heard by the panel and to make written submissions at the first substantive meeting of the panel. Third parties will not participate in subsequent exchanges of written submissions or hearings, but their interests will be fully taken into account during the panel process. Third parties cannot make an appeal, but if they participated as third parties in the panel proceeding, they may make written submissions to the Appellate Body and be given opportunity to present their positions.

综 合 练 习

1. 与《1994 年关税与贸易总协定》中争端解决的规定相比，《争端解决谅解》有哪些创新之处?

2. 简述世界贸易组织争端解决制度的主要原则。

3. 专家组权限和上诉机构权限的区别有哪些?

4. 简述世界贸易组织争端解决的可选择方案的顺序。

5. 简述报复的原则和程序。

Comprehensive Exercises

1. In comparison with provisions of the dispute settlement of *GATT 1994*, what are the major innovations of *the DSU*?

2. Give a briefing of the main principles of the WTO dispute settlement system.

3. What are the differences between the panel's terms of reference and that of the Appellate Body?

4. Give a briefing of the sequence of alternative schemes the WTO provides for dispute settlement.

5. Give a briefing of the principles and procedures for retaliation.

参 考 文 献

[1] 陈晶莹，邓旭. 国际商法[M]. 北京：中国人民大学出版社，2010.

[2] 王粉萍. 国际贸易实务[M]. 北京：北京理工大学出版社，2010.

[3] 沈四宝，王军. 国际商法[M]. 北京：对外经贸大学出版社，2008.

[4] 屈广清，徐红菊. 国际技术贸易法[M]. 大连：大连海事大学出版社，2011.

[5] 李强，杨帆. 国际技术贸易法[M]. 北京：中国人民公安大学出版社，2003.

[6] 李正华. 知识产权法学(中英双语)[M]. 北京：知识产权出版社，2012.

[7] 韩永红. 国际贸易法[M]. 北京：对外经贸大学出版社，2008.

[8] 姜作利. 国际商法[M]. 北京：法律出版社，2007.

[9] 孙法柏. WTO 与国际经济法[M]. 北京：对外经贸大学出版社，2008.

[10] (美)Brian J. Arnold，(美)Michael J. McIntyre. 国际税收基础[M]. 张志勇等译. 北京：中国税务出版社，2005.

[11] Ray August. *International Business Law: Text, Cases and Readings (Fourth Edition)*. Pearson Education International LTD, 2004.

[12] Pascal Lamy. The General Agreement on Trade in Services: An Introduction. [2016-03-29] http://search.wto.org.

[13] Bernard Hoekman. The General Agreement on Trade in Services. (A paper presented to an OECD Workshop on The New World Trading System, edited by G. Raby, Paris: OECD, 1994).

[14] Harry G. Broadman. International Trade and Investment in Services: A Comparative Analysis of the NAFTA, International Lawyer, vol.27, 1993.

[15] Carsten Fink and Martin Molinuevo. East Asian Free Trade Agreements in Services: Roaring Tigers or Timid Pandas?

[16] Pierre Sauve and Anirudh Shingal. Reflections on the Preferential Liberalization of Services Trade, NCCR Working Paper No. 2011/05. [2011-06-12].

[17] Martin Roy. Endowments, Power, and Democracy: Political Economy of Multilateral Commitments on Trade in Services (WTO Working Papers), 2010.

[18] John Cross, Landers, Mireles and Yu. Global Issues in Intellectual Property Law. West Academic, 2010.

[19] James Bonomo. Monitoring and Controlling the International Transfer of Technology. 1998.

[20] Prabuddha Sanyal. Modes of International Technology Transfers: Role of R&D Intensity, Spillovers and Intellectual Property Rights, VDM Verlag, 2008.

[21] S.P.Subedi. *International Economic Law*. University of London Press. 2007.

[22] Joel P. Trachtman. The International Economic Law Revolution, University of Pennsylvania Journal of International Economic Law, 1996.

[23] Committee of Experts on International Cooperation in Tax Matters, Introduction to international double taxation and tax evasion and avoidance, https://www.un.org/esa/ffd/wp-content/uploads/2014/10/7STM_CRP11_Introduction_2011.pdf

[24] UNCTAD, Taxation, https://unctad.org/en/docs/iteiit16_en.pdf

[25] United Nations Model Double Taxation Convention, https://www.un.org/esa/ffd/wp-content/uploads/2014/09/UN_Model_2011_Update.pdf

[26] Model Tax Convention on Income and on Capital 2010 (Full Version), https://doi.org/10.1787/mtc_cond-2010-en